Andrew Sardanis was born in colonial
to Northern Rhodesia in 1950. He pai̇   ̣pendence
movement and played a major role in   ̣̇̇̇̇̇̇ustration of the country.
After a business career that took him to almost all the sub-Saharan countries
he now takes care of Chaminuka Nature Reserve near Lusaka, Zambia. He
is the author of *Africa: Another Side of the Coin* and *A Venture in Africa* (both
published by I.B.Tauris).

ZAMBIA

THE FIRST 50 YEARS

Reflections of an Eyewitness

ANDREW SARDANIS

I.B. TAURIS

LONDON · NEW YORK

Published in 2014 by I.B.Tauris & Co Ltd
6 Salem Road, London W2 4BU
175 Fifth Avenue, New York NY 10010
www.ibtauris.com

Distributed in the United States and Canada Exclusively by Palgrave Macmillan
175 Fifth Avenue, New York NY 10010

ISBN: 978 1 78076 821 2 (HB)
        978 1 78076 822 9 (PB)
eISBN: 978 0 85773 698 7

A full CIP record for this book is available from the British Library
A full CIP record is available from the Library of Congress

Library of Congress Catalog Card Number: available

Typeset in Sabon by Free Range Book Design & Production Limited

Printed and bound in Great Britain by T.J. International, Padstow, Cornwall

Contents

List of Illustrations

Plate Section: Zambia and its People as seen by its Artists

All images are from The Chaminuka Art Collection
Photographs by Leonard Musabula

Selected Images:
A. *Afternoon Bath* by Adam Mwansa
B. *Akalela Dance* by Petson Lombe
C. *Amalila* (Meal Time) by Godfrey Setti
D. *Kimanyukunyuku* (Colonial Pioneers) by Stephen Kapata
E. *Business As Usual* by Mulenga Chafilwa
F. *Icishiba* (Water Hole) by Shadreck Simukanga
G. *Inkalata* (The Letter) by Stary Mwaba
H. *Kakachema* (Herd Boy) by Adam Mwansa
I. *Mandevu Market* by H. Mulenga
J. *Nganakula* (When I Grow Up) by Mapopa M'tonga
K. *Ovina Vimbuza* (Dancer) by Henry Tayali
L. *The Struggle Continues* by Henry Tayali
M. *Ukusombola* (The Harvest) by Flinto Chandia

Presidents (by Geoffrey Phiri):

N. *Iminwe ya Gold* (Hands of Gold) Frederick Chiluba 1991–2001

O. *Oyela Kumalo Opatulika* (Saint Patrick's Retreat) Levy Mwanawasa 2001–8

P. *Ifimalayo Fimofinefye* (Same Promises Again and Again) Rupiah Banda 2008–11

Q. *Ntungulu* (Ululation) Kenneth Kaunda in Retirement 2013

ACKNOWLEDGEMENTS

My thanks first go to my wife, Danae and Evaristo Mudenda who were bombarded with the draft of every chapter hot off the press and gave me frank opinions and valuable suggestions; and to Bob Lilien for suggesting the title. Also, to my two researchers: Chela Mutale and Timothy Theo. They roamed Lusaka, the Copperbelt, and the internet for information and spent hours on the phone trying to get me appointments, often with little success. (Not their fault; the nature of the subject made many people reluctant to talk.) Last, but not least, to Sam Tafuma, who drove me to the corners of Zambia in the course of my research.

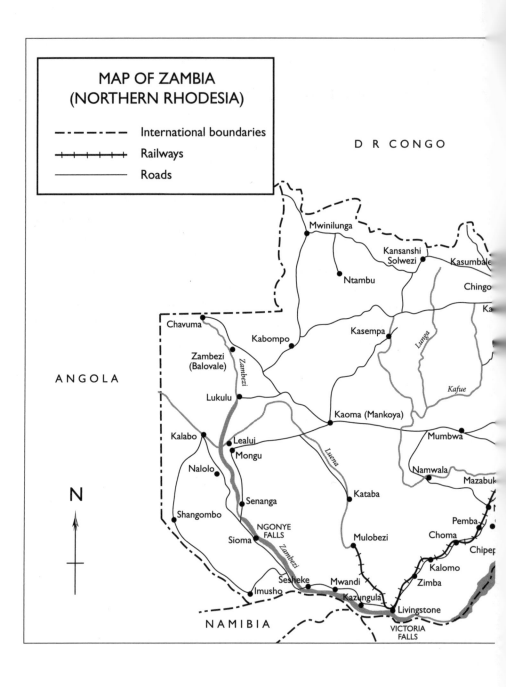

MAP OF ZAMBIA
(NORTHERN RHODESIA)

- – · – · – International boundaries
- +++++++ Railways
- ——— Roads

D R CONGO

ANGOLA

NAMIBIA

N

Mwinilunga
Kansanshi
Solwezi
Kasumbale
Ntambu
Chingo
Ka
Chavuma
Kabompo
Kasempa
Lunga
Zambezi
(Balovale)
Zambezi
Kafue
Lukulu
Kaoma (Mankoya)
Mumbwa
Kalabo
Lealui
Mongu
Nalolo
Namwala
Mazabuk
Luena
Senanga
Kataba
Shangombo
Pemba
NGONYE
FALLS
Mulobezi
Choma
Sioma
Chipep
Zambezi
Kalomo
Sesheke
Mwandi
Zimba
Imusho
Kazungula
Livingstone
VICTORIA
FALLS

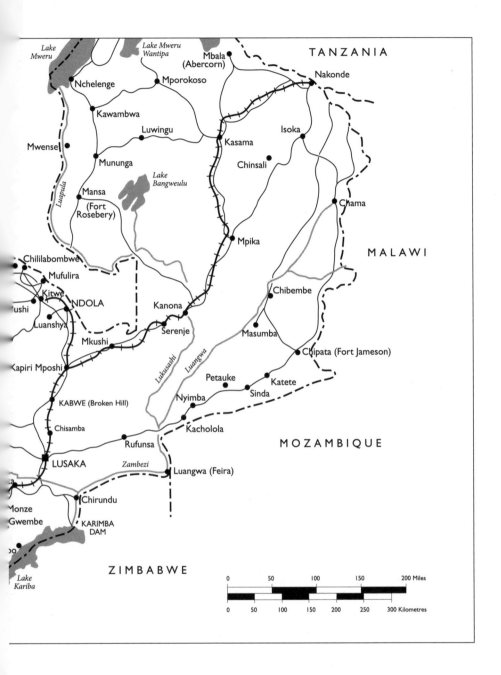

To the people of Zambia, present and future

Συμβούλευε μὴ τὰ ἥδιστα, ἀλλὰ τὰ βέλτιστα.
(Counsel not what is most pleasant but what is best)
Solon, the Athenian Lawmaker

INTRODUCTION

I arrived in Zambia (from Cyprus) when it was still called Northern Rhodesia, in October 1950 at the age of 19, with no particular plan in mind, and I have been here ever since. In August 1951, I started a peripatetic kind of existence in the North Western Province, with the task of buying produce in the districts of Balovale (now Zambezi), Kabombo and Mwinilunga, in order to secure return loads for my sister's husband's trucks that were delivering government goods to the province. In my book *Africa: Another Side of the Coin* (published in 2003 by I.B.Tauris & Co Ltd), I described my life: 'I was a nomad with a truck. I slept wherever I happened to be when darkness fell. In the truck, in government rest-houses, in shops, on people's verandas, in village huts and in the open air by the campfire; on a camp bed or on the ground – after a bout of tick fever, always on a camp bed. I washed in the nearest stream ...'

It was the best thing that could have happened to me. In the process I got to know and appreciate the people. I became a Zambian instead of a Rhodesian, which was the fate of most whites who came to the country before independence. My Zambian assimilation was completed after 1957, when I got my own house in Chingola and connected with the urban black intelligentsia, most prominent amongst them Valentine Musakanya and Sikota Wina and, later, Henry Shikopa and his Munali schoolmates.

Valentine was the head clerk at the District Commissioner's Office, the highest civil service rank a black man (only a handful of women had the educational background for those jobs at the time) could aspire to. (In those days, black government employees were not referred to as civil servants; they were called 'Boma clerks'.) He was studying for an external degree in Philosophy and Social Science with the University of South Africa and as his course included some Greek papers, I started helping him out. Apart from discussing his university papers, we talked about almost every subject under the sun – not least about colonialism, racism, white domination, the nationalist movement, and independence.

Sikota was a journalist working for *Nchanga Drum*, the mine newspaper for blacks. (There was also *Nchanga News* for the whites.) He had joined the

Drum after he had been expelled from South Africa's Fort Hare University for taking part in anti-government demonstrations. He later left Chingola and the *Drum* and became the editor of *African Life*, a monthly society magazine that he turned into a political and highly nationalistic publication. Inevitably he became one of the leaders of the Zambia Africa National Congress (ZANC) and was rusticated by Governor Benson together with Kenneth Kaunda and the other ZANC leaders, finally becoming the publicity chief of the United National Independence Party (UNIP), which succeeded ZANC. He and I worked closely together on UNIP's publicity during the campaign for the 1962 election, which ushered in the first African government in Northern Rhodesia.

Henry, from the first crop of Form VI Munalians, an elite corps in those days, joined Mwaiseni Stores in 1959 and brought with him a complement of Munali graduates, which expanded my circle of friends and acquaintances around the country and gave me a more universal appreciation of the political picture, which until then covered mainly Chingola and the North Western Province.

Both Valentine and Sikota would play crucial roles in post-independence Zambia with Valentine starting as the first black secretary to the Zambian cabinet and Sikota, somewhat incongruously, as Minister of Health. Henry went on to a prominent Zambian and international business career after independence.

My work and political activities notwithstanding, in 1962 I made time to go to Cyprus and marry Danae, the girl I had met the year before when I was there on holiday. We returned to Chingola in April and I soon found myself roped into the 1962 elections as UNIP candidate for the Kabombo constituency, one of those convoluted colonial arrangements that, supposedly, aimed at 'getting the two races to learn to work together'. The Kabombo National Constituency (and 13 others) had two candidates each (one black and one white), who, in order to get elected, had to attract at least 20 per cent of the vote of one of the races and 10 per cent of the other, voting separately. The results proved that the two races were not prepared to work together: I received 92.1 per cent of the African votes and 3.2 per cent of the white votes, while Willie Nkanza, my fellow candidate from Chitokoloki, received 93.3 and 2.3 per cent respectively. None of us was elected and 12 of the 14 national seats remained vacant. (I covered the twilight years of colonialism, the liberation struggle, and the early history of Zambia in great detail in my book *Africa: Another Side of the Coin*.)

After independence, Kenneth Kaunda, the first president of Zambia, appointed me Chairman and CEO of the Industrial Development Corporation (INDECO), with the mandate to promote Zambian participation in business. We planned the Mulungushi reforms together in 1968, in order to give a fillip to Zambian business, and after their announcement he gave me the additional job of Permanent Secretary (Director General) to the Ministry of Commerce and Industry, in order to facilitate their implementation. A few months later the ministry was expanded to include the mines and changed its name to Trade Industry and Mines. After the Matero reforms, which gave the government 51 per cent controlling interest in the Zambian mines, I became Permanent Secretary to the new Ministry of State Participation and a few weeks later Permanent Secretary to the Ministry of Finance at the same time. I left the government on 31 January 1971. Some of these events get a mention in the pages that follow, but they are covered in greater detail in *Africa: Another Side of the Coin*.

After government, I set up together with Henry and some old colleagues from INDECO, an African multinational business group which, over the years, spread into 31 African countries. I covered my business career in a book titled *A Venture in Africa* (published in 2007 by I.B.Tauris & Co Ltd). Apart from covering our business activities, the book gives a glimpse of the conditions and politics prevailing in many of the countries we operated in. But the political and economic developments in Zambia have always been uppermost in my mind and were covered in great detail. They are, of course, further discussed and analysed in this book.

What follows is a detailed examination of most major events in our history since independence and their effect on our development and progress, based on my in-depth knowledge of the country and its people, and the inner workings of its government.

PROLOGUE

'If we had persevered under colonialism a little longer we would have been better trained to handle our affairs after independence', a group of young Zambians once told me. I hope that they will read this book. They will then realize that if we had not gained our independence they would never have had the opportunity of making such a comment.

Ruminating on our history I went through a whole range of emotions. There was the proud beginning with the hoisting of our national flag to the tune of our national anthem and the exhilaration with the delirious celebrations of the crowds, which followed; and many happy and sometimes awkward moments, as we embarked upon project after project in the process of creating a new nation. One stands out in my mind: the opening of UNZA, the first ever university in Zambia. Kenneth Kaunda introducing Julius Nyerere, the first president of Tanzania and keynote speaker, described the neglect of education by the colonial government and broke down reminiscing that, after his father's death, the Lubwa School refused to enrol him because his mother did not have the two shillings and sixpence fee. It took some 20 minutes before he composed himself to finish his speech, a period that felt like eternity. Nyerere, who followed, broke the ice with his easy charm when he started with: 'Ken, you do not know what problems you are bringing upon your head, opening this school. University students are uncontrollable, they go on strikes and on protest marches; they will be descending on State House shouting and making demands, and telling you how to run the country,' before he proceeded to extol the virtues of university education.

And there were the anxious moments, when after the declaration of UDI we did not know where our supplies would come from and worried that everything would come to a grinding halt; and the distressing moments when the various political factions within UNIP started fighting each other; and the heroic and tense moments, when Kaunda wholeheartedly immersed himself and the country in the liberation wars of Southern Africa and the Rhodesians and the Portuguese and the South Africans were attacking our villages and various strategic targets, some of them in the centre of Lusaka.

And the painful moments, when UNIP introduced the 'One Party State' and declared itself 'the sole custodian of the people's interests' (the phrase appals even now, as I write it 40 years after the event); and the nation lost direction and was going around in circles, verging on the brink of bankruptcy and causing untold hardship and misery to its people for a decade and a half.

And there were the pleasant surprises when the people of Zambia told UNIP 'enough is enough' and Kenneth Kaunda, unlike some other African leaders, got the message and reintroduced multiparty democracy and bowed out. And the disappointment when the hoped for renaissance did not materialize because many of the politicians who followed turned out to be worse than their predecessors, and the nation started floundering again. But one thing remained firm: the people's commitment to democracy. When Chiluba who had succeeded Kaunda attempted to stand for a third term the people cried a deafening 'No' and showed him the door.

Such has been our political history since independence: a purposeful beginning followed by many blunders; confusion, at times bordering on chaos, interspersed with flashes of sensible action and good work. Yet, we made real progress; so much so that people of my generation can look back with some satisfaction at what has been achieved. This was mainly due to the Zambian genius that is not cowed by adversity and carries on regardless, improvising short-term solutions and taking advantage of opportunities, whenever they come along. And the people's inexhaustible patience to hold tight until the right time comes to act, that produced the amazing stability of Zambia.

But I do not measure our performance by the political developments only. Many achievements stand out. We started off as second class citizens in our new nation that was dominated by foreign business and a foreign middle class. We now dominate not only politically, but socially and economically too, with many successful Zambian businessmen and women, and many professionals, lawyers and judges and doctors and engineers and lecturers and professors and senior government officers and other highly trained and educated people. And we have a thriving diaspora too, holding its own in the international market place and adding to the collective national sophistication, albeit from a distance. My major disappointment with all these highly successful young people, whom I otherwise admire and approve of, is that they do not seem to take any interest in politics, so much so that at the presidential elections of 2011, the main contestants turned out to be two septuagenarians.

This book is a detailed account of the many twists and turns of our history. Inevitably the early part has echoes of my first book *Africa: Another Side of the Coin* even though at times it reaches different conclusions. I hope that the reader will recognize this as the result of deep reflection and more mature thinking. In writing this book I had uppermost in my mind, Solon's aphorism 'Counsel not what is most pleasant but what is best'. I did not sweep any of our many mistakes under the carpet and I did not exaggerate our many successes either. I particularly highlighted the mistakes in the hope that future leaders will take note and avoid them and I urge friends to see my criticisms in this light.

Fifty years is a short period in any nation's history. The future is endless and I commend it to the future generations. I am confident that they will do better than their forefathers. I am sure that they will make this country great and a jewel in the crown of Africa.

Part I

A Nation in the Making

1. ZAMBIA, PROUD AND FREE

The Union Jack came down at 11:56 p.m. on 23 October, and the Zambian flag was hoisted at 00:01 a.m. on 24 October, 1964. Zambia was born. Northern Rhodesia was no more.

The ceremony took place at the Lusaka Independence Stadium, specially built for the occasion. At midnight the huge crowd went wild at the sight of their young president, Kenneth Kaunda (he was only 40 years old at the time), hoisting their own national flag for the first time, to the tune of their national anthem, played by the Zambian Army Band, also for the first time. The Union Jack had been lowered by Sir Evelyn Hone, the last governor of Northern Rhodesia, who was accompanied by The Princess Royal representing the British Queen.

The long ceremony that preceded the event in order to keep the waiting crowds entertained until midnight was more like a lament for the departing empire than a celebration for the birth of the new nation. Naturally enough. The ceremony had been put together by departing British civil servants and army officers. It was billed as a 'military tattoo', defined in the Oxford English Dictionary as a 'military entertainment consisting of an elaboration of the tattoo (a drumbeat or bugle call) by extra music and military exercises usually at night and by torch or other artificial light'. 'Beating the retreat' might have been an equally appropriate definition of the proceedings, which the upmarket whites of Lusaka (and some recently promoted Zambian senior civil servants) who occupied the stalls followed in prissy colonial solemnity. The whites could hardly be expected to rejoice, I guess.

The real Zambian celebrations were improvised after midnight by the huge crowd spread over the hill on the opposite side. They were spontaneous, unruly, deafening, and catching. But, at least one highbrow British wife was not moved. At the Independence Ball the following evening, to which Danae and I had been invited, she asked: 'Did you see the enthusiasm of the crowd when the fireworks went up? Fireworks appeal to simple minds, of course,' she declared.

How did all this come about, and in such a short time? When I arrived in the white dominated British Protectorate of Northern Rhodesia in October 1950,

11

filled with Cypriot revolutionary fervour against colonialism, I could not in my wildest dreams imagine that in exactly 14 years Northern Rhodesia would give way to a new African ruled country named Zambia. The irony is that British colonialism created Zambia, maybe, without intending to. It thought that it was creating Northern Rhodesia, as a white man's country, which it would rule for centuries. And that the faceless natives who inhabited the area before the white man came along would be happy to serve him for ever.

And who were the Zambians? There is very little information about the early history of Northern Rhodesia, but we must remember that, at the end of the nineteenth century, the area that now falls within the borders of Zambia was not a defined single country. It was a huge, very sparsely populated area, inhabited by a collection of people, who knew very little about each other. They had diverse ethnic backgrounds and spoke different languages; and there would have been very little interaction between them, except at the edges of their respective areas. For a start, travelling far would have been rare because of the hazards involved: on foot, on paths through thick forests with abundant and dangerous wildlife. And it would have been pointless too, because all the people of the area engaged in the same kind of activity: subsistence agriculture. They all produced the same crops and they had little need to trade except, perhaps, food in periods of drought. So people would have been reluctant to venture far from their own areas, with the exception of those who lived along rivers and could travel in canoes. As a result people would have known very little about each other; and the people who lived far apart like, for example, those who lived around present day Kasama and Chipata or Choma would have known even less.

The history before the second half of the nineteenth century is even more obscure, as the Colonial Office report on the territory for the year 1929 explains:

> From the very early days when the hordes of migratory Bantu swept southward from Central and Northern Africa, Northern Rhodesia has been subject to constant invasion from stronger tribes on its borders, so much so, that the vast majority of the present native population, though of Bantu origin, is descended from men who themselves invaded this country not earlier than 1700 A.D. One or two tribes, numbering now only a very few thousand, such as the Masubia of the Zambezi, are all that remain of the inhabitants of Northern Rhodesia prior to that date. Though the story of these invasions has passed into oblivion, their traces remain in the extraordinary number and diversity of races and of languages in the country.
>
> At the present time statistics are available of seventy different tribes resident in the territory, of which the most important are the Awemba (108,665),

Achewa (75,058), Angoni (51,004), Awisa (49,030) in the Eastern Districts; the Barotse (65,250), Batonga (94,546), Balenje (37,662), Balala (40,880), Balovale (32,672), Bakaonde (35,397), Baila (21,486) in the Western Districts; and the Asenga (62,294) and Alunda (60,761) members of which are resident in both Eastern and Western Districts. There are said to be 30 distinct native languages in use, of which Chiwemba and Chinyanja have been adopted for educational purposes in the Eastern Districts and Chitonga (closely allied to Chila) and Sikololo in the Western. In addition to these, Chinyanja is in use as the official language of the police, and is probably the language most generally spoken by Europeans; it is, in reality, a Nyasaland language – the word means 'Language of the Lake' – but it is also spoken to some extent round Fort Jameson.

(I attach the history part of the report as Appendix I in order to highlight the level of ethnic fragmentation, but also, more importantly, the lack of cohesion amongst the people who inhabited the area that has, since the onset of colonization, formed Northern Rhodesia and now Zambia.)

As I indicated above, the conclusion must be that colonialism created Zambia and the Zambians, even though in the process it arbitrarily cut across villages and chiefdoms. As a result people living near borders still have family living in Angola, the Congo, Tanzania, Malawi, Zimbabwe and Namibia. The various people described in the Colonial Office report only got close to each other in the various compounds of the Northern Rhodesian towns where they came to work for the white settlers. Over the years, they bonded: they lived together, they worked together, they socialized, they intermarried, they struggled against the exploitation of the settlers, and they created a common conscience. They fought for their independence and they emerged as Zambians.

The settlement of whites was slow. Very few trickled into Northern Rhodesia in the latter part of the nineteenth century, after David Livingstone's 'discovery' of the Victoria Falls and the British South Africa Company's (BSAC) push northwards. They were mainly missionaries (some came into the western and northwestern parts from Portuguese West Africa, now Angola), a few farmers and traders and BSAC agents and administrators. But their numbers remained small, totalling less than a couple of thousand during the First World War and rising to about 4,000 at the time of Northern Rhodesia's declaration as a British Protectorate in 1924. The local population at that time was very small too: around one million. When I arrived in the country in 1950, the local population was just over 1.7 million and the whites numbered some 35,000. At independence, the Zambian population numbered 3.5 million and the whites 74,000, a large part of which were British civil servants and their families who left immediately afterwards. There were also some 9,000 Indians and 2,300 people of mixed descent (referred to locally as coloured).

Development started with the discovery of copper early in the twentieth century. Just before the end of the nineteenth, Cecil Rhodes' BSAC had 'obtained' (I use quotes because the legitimacy of the acquisition must be in doubt as the Paramount Chief of Barotseland had no jurisdiction over most of the areas he ceded) the mineral rights over the entire country west of the Kafue River which formed the boundary between what was then known as North Western and North Eastern Rhodesia. As was customary at the time, it needed a concession from the chief of the area for this purpose. BSAC secured one from Lewanika I, the Paramount Chief of Barotseland for whom it arranged British Protectorate status in June 1890 under the Lochner Concession (named after Cecil Rhodes' agent Frank Elliot Lochner who made the arrangements). The Paramount Chief's territory did not stretch that far. The Colonial Office report for 1929, copied in Appendix I, defined it as follows:

> The Barotse under Lewanika enlarged their kingdom by conquering one or two of the surrounding tribes, such as the Bankoya and the Balovale. Beyond these limits their authority was both nebulous and ephemeral. In the year 1890 Lewanika asked for British protection and on the 27th June the Barotse Concession was signed, by which Lewanika recognized the Protectorate of Queen Victoria and gave to the Chartered Company certain mining and commercial rights over the whole of his dominion. Lewanika, on his side, received a yearly subsidy of £2,000.

When all this was happening there were no defined borders of the chief's domain, so they could be improvised on the say-so of the chief, or that of the odd traveller, or, more to the point, according to the interests of the concessionaire. BSAC was looking for copper deposits which at the time were believed to be along the Kafue River. Having obtained mining and commercial rights 'present and future' from Lewanika, Rhodes needed to ensure that the chief's territory stretched to the Kafue. For the task, he commissioned François Coillard, a missionary of the Paris Evangelical Society who had been living in Lealui, the Litunga's capital, since 1885. Coillard obliged: he set the eastern boundary on the Kafue River, which was obviously his main brief, the southern on the Zambezi River to the Chobe junction, followed by the Linyanti River up to a longitude of 20 degrees east, which he set as the western boundary. He set the northern boundary on the watershed of the Congo and the Zambezi rivers. To achieve all that he must have used a combination of sources: Lewanika's own word and folklore on the extent of the Lewanika 'empire' and 'spheres of influence'. Not everybody agreed with him, though, least of all the Portuguese. They declared a dispute for the sections of the purported 'Lewanika Empire' that usurped their territory. The issue was adjudicated by King Vittorio Emmanuelle of Italy in 1905 and the western boundary was changed to what it is at present: at East 22 degrees longitude. The northern boundary was never accepted by the Lunda and Luvale people, who kept making protests to the Northern Rhodesia Government and on 25 September 1938, the then governor, J. A. Maybin, appointed a Commission of Inquiry under Sir Philip J. MacDonnell with the mandate:

> To examine and report upon the whole question of the past and present relations of the Paramount Chief of the Barotse nation and the Chiefs resident in the Balovale [now Zambezi] District both east and west of the Zambezi River, with special reference to the ownership of land and the methods by which the tribes have been governed, and to make recommendations for the future.

The commission's recommendation was to 'give to these tribes the right to govern themselves and the freedom from alien [sic] rule, which to every other tribe of Northern Rhodesia is given as a matter of course'. (It appears that Sir Philip did not consider the British rule as alien.) The decision spelled the end of the Lozi hegemony over the Luvale and the Lunda and shifted Barotseland's northern border to the south of the Zambezi and Kabombo districts. Narrowly defined, the Lewanika chiefdom is currently confined within the borders of what is now Barotseland or Western Province, as it was renamed in 1968. Like the Luvale and the Lunda none of the many tribes inhabiting the huge area between the Barotse borders and the Kafue River (Kaonde, Lamba, Ila, Tonga, Toka, Leya, Mbunda and many smaller ones) would ever accept that the Barotse Chief had jurisdiction over them. And many Nkoya still don't, even though their area lies within the present borders of Barotseland.

After 1924, when Northern Rhodesia was established and was itself declared a British Protectorate, Barotseland was administered as a province of Northern Rhodesia. But the British South Africa Company kept paying mineral rights to the Paramount Chief for copper mined in Lamba country (over which he had no jurisdiction) right up to the eve of independence.

Copper and iron were first mined by the local people and there are 'national monuments' of early mining in parts of the country and old copper and iron artefacts in museums. But mining that started in the first decade of the twentieth century accelerated in the mid- to late twenties as a result of international demand for copper from the electricity and automotive industries in the United States and Europe. By the end of the twenties the Bwana

Mkubwa, Luanshya, Mufulira, Nkana and Nchanga mines were in operation, owned by the Anglo American Corporation, a part-British and part-South African group, and the Rhodesian Selection Trust, an American and British group. During the economic depression of the early 1930s, the mines had to curtail operations and lay off large numbers of staff, both whites and local. The impending Second World War resuscitated the industry and by the end of the thirties the mines were booming again. As copper was a strategic material and its supply became vital for the Allies during the war, mining development intensified and large numbers of white miners were recruited, mainly from South Africa. For the unskilled jobs local labour was recruited from various parts of the country. During the war years, the white miners realized that their services were indispensable and grabbed the opportunity to secure not only high salaries but a closed shop agreement with the mine owners.

The effect of all this was the creation, within the country, of a master society of whites, completely unrelated to the local people and living apart. The whites who had the skills and were in charge of all economic and social activity mainly lived in attractive towns. The blacks carried on their traditional existence in the rural areas living in small villages sprinkled all over the countryside and surviving mainly on subsistence farming. Those who were recruited to serve the whites and perform manual unskilled jobs in the towns and in the mines lived in high density compounds with only the barest of facilities and a pittance for wages. (When I arrived in Zambia the average black worker was earning 17 shillings and sixpence for a 30-day ticket plus a bonus of two shillings and sixpence for uninterrupted work. In other words he was getting £1 ($3 in those days) over a 35-day period. In addition he received some 400 g of mealie meal for every day he worked. The miners, the elite corps of the workforce, earned £3 per month.)

The two races did not interact, except at work, as masters and servants. But the body of the indigenous people, though disparate (multi-tribal, multilingual and from different parts of a very sparsely populated large country – some 290,000 square miles or 750,000 square kilometres in extent – with very few roads and, with the exception of canoes on large rivers, no other type of communication infrastructure) learned to co-exist, even though they started off as complete strangers. As time went by, they integrated and developed a common identity, under the colonial administration. As I pointed out already, urbanization, intermarriage and the independence movement strengthened the Zambian identity, which now prevails over the tribal. Tribal antagonisms were no more pronounced then than they are now, and they have never escalated to serious inter-tribal hostility then or now. People know that they need each other and present day antagonisms revolve around competition for jobs and positions, securing contracts and business advantages, and mutual teasing about each other's customs and shortcomings, real or invented.

The final outcome was that after the Second World War, Northern Rhodesia unlike the British colonies in West Africa was a typical Southern African British Territory, where South African and Rhodesian white settlers had the upper hand and were openly antagonistic towards the Colonial Office, as the reader will see later in this chapter from the comments Roy Welensky, their leader, made at a Victoria Falls conference in 1949. The British were in control of the administration, under the direction of the Colonial Office in London. But British and South African companies and the Southern African white settlers were in control of everything else: of the copper mining industry, business, communications, farming, schools, churches, and so on, generally every economic and social activity. The local people referred to as 'natives' officially, but commonly called 'boys' and 'girls' (and sometimes 'munts' and 'kaffirs') regardless of age and status by the white 'masters' or 'bwanas', had a separate existence in the service of the settlers. A substantial number of Indians, descendants of workers brought in the early part of the twentieth century to build the railways, were mainly shopkeepers.

There was complete separation of the races. The towns were divided into European areas, African areas and Indian areas; they had separate housing, shopping, schools, churches, clubs, sports teams, playing fields and all other social activities. The existence in Kamwala of a Hindu temple and a mosque, standing side by side, separated only by a garden wall is a monument to Northern Rhodesia's racial segregation and the authorities' high handedness. Kamwala was the Indian township of Lusaka and some British official must have decreed the two plots to be situated next to each other, a forced neighbourliness that probably does not exist anywhere else in the world and neither religion would normally have been happy with. Chilenje, Kabwata and Matero were the black townships. The main town (Fairview, Rhodes Park, Villa Elizabetta, Northmead, Thorn Park, Woodlands) was for whites only. A similar pattern existed in all urban centres.

Education was geared entirely for the benefit of whites: first class school buildings, separate for kindergarten, elementary and secondary, small classes, plenty of teachers. For Africans, who outnumbered the whites 50:1, elementary schools ending at standard VI (grade 7) existed only in urban areas. In rural areas schools ended at standard IV or standard II (grades 5 or 2) depending on their remoteness. In the entire North Western Province (where I spent most of the fifties) an area of some 50,000 square miles divided into five large districts with a population of some 150,000 at the time, there were only three standard VI schools, all set up by missionaries, of which only two accepted black boys (girls were not going to school in those days). The government did not consider it necessary to build at least one full elementary school in the capital of each district.

The Northern Rhodesian Government obviously did not consider that blacks deserved high school education. (The white settlers were definitely against it.) For a total population of two million that Northern Rhodesia had in the mid-fifties, it built only one, the Munali boys' high school in Lusaka, where it trained clerks for the administration. Together with two other high schools, again built by missionaries (Saint Canisius by the Jesuits for boys and Chipembi by the Methodists for girls) they made the total of three for the black population of the entire country. African education was not a Northern Rhodesia Government priority or, more accurately, was deliberately suppressed, of which more later.

And it was not only education that was suppressed. Artisan training fared worse. Under an agreement between the mining companies and the European Mineworkers Union all forms of training for skilled jobs were exclusive to white miners' children. The few Africans in that sector did not have any formal qualifications, having picked up their skills working as 'spanner boys' or 'hands' assisting white artisans. Blacks were essentially destined for manual labour and low level clerical jobs. All shop assistants were white. Blacks were not allowed into European residential areas except as domestic servants during daytime, or when residing in one roomed houses at the end of the 'master's' garden. European shops, banks and other establishments in white areas were out of bounds. Their staff with the exception of messengers and cleaners was entirely white. Blacks were not allowed to enter, even as customers; they could get service on the sidewalk, through a hatch, if they needed to and could stomach it. (In the late fifties, when consternation over the African conditions started building into the national struggle for independence, Robinson Puta, a prominent Chingola businessman and firebrand wanted to buy a bed and was directed to the usual hatch where he paid for it. He was then invited inside to collect it but he refused to enter the shop. He wanted it delivered to him through the hatch where he paid, he told the assistant, much to the amusement and approbation of other black customers, waiting for their turn at the hatch.)

Of course, Africans did not have political rights either. Their 'interests' were represented in the Northern Rhodesia Legislative Council by a couple of whites specially appointed by the governor of Northern Rhodesia for that purpose. The situation was bad enough but worse was to come in the form of the Federation of Rhodesia and Nyasaland. Unbelievably, in the decade when decolonization started in earnest everywhere else, the Federation of Rhodesia and Nyasaland, which brought together the colony of Southern Rhodesia and the Protectorates of Northern Rhodesia and Nyasaland, came into being. The British could no longer resist the pressures of the whites of Southern and Northern Rhodesia for amalgamation and agreed to the establishment of the Federation instead. In the package they included Nyasaland, which they wanted to get rid of, because they did not consider it a viable economic unit and it was costing them too much money to support.

The Federation was heralded as the embodiment of racial partnership. It would set an example to white South Africa whose racial segregation policies were looked down upon by the British, even though, at the time, a similar situation obtained in their own territories in the region. It would force the whites and the blacks to live together in racial harmony, they said. And the answer to the black protests against it was that the economic development that would follow the Federation would make the Africans of Northern Rhodesia and Nyasaland accept it, even if in the meantime they did not like it.

The aspirations of the local whites were rather different. They were not thinking of racial partnership. They were aiming at taking over. They were confident that as time went by they would wrest control from the Colonial Office, which they distrusted, and remove the small safeguards provided in the Federal constitution in order to placate the Africans. Roy Welensky, the leader of the white settlers of Northern Rhodesia was quite blunt about it. At a conference of settlers organized at the Victoria Falls in 1949, he said: 'As far as the Colonial Office is concerned, you realise, and I am certain that everyone must, that we detest the Colonial Office Government ...' (Robert Rotberg, *The Rise of Nationalism in Central Africa*).

The Africans of Northern Rhodesia did not buy the Federal concept either. They distrusted any association with Southern Rhodesia, where the settlers had been in control of the government since 1923. They were afraid that the Land Apportionment Act, which appropriated 50 per cent of the land of Southern Rhodesia for the benefit of a handful of whites, would spread to Northern Rhodesia with the Federation. And they were afraid that the mining wealth of Northern Rhodesia would be used for the benefit of the settlers, which is exactly what the revenue from the mines was used for. The people of Northern Rhodesia protested as loudly as they could through the few African organizations that existed during that period: the African Urban Council, the African Mineworkers Union and the African Trade Union Congress and the African National Congress. And together with the Africans of Nyasaland (now Malawi) they also protested in London. Dr Kamuzu Banda, who at the time had a medical practice in London but would later become the first president of Malawi, and Harry Nkumbula, who at the same time was studying at the London School of Economics and would on his return home become the leader of the African National Congress of Northern Rhodesia, sent a jointly signed memorandum to the Colonial Office rebutting the arguments in favour of the Federation. They pointed out that:

> of all the Europeans of Central Africa, those of Southern Rhodesia have the worse antipathy towards Africans ... They look upon Africans as inferior beings with no right to a dignified and refined existence and fit only as hewers of wood and drawers of water for Europeans ... They do not even pretend that they are in Africa to help the Africans, but blatantly declare that they are in Africa to live and to rule. In all their dealings with the Africans they always assume the attitude of conquerors ... [And] it is these Europeans ... who will rule and govern the Federation ... but under the government provided by Southern Rhodesia the relationship between us and the authorities will be one of slaves and masters and the cardinal principle ... domination.
>
> (*The Rise of Nationalism in Central Africa*)

But all African protests were ignored. The Federation was imposed in October 1953 and its constitution and governance turned out to be exactly the opposite of racial partnership. The Federal government was the government for the Europeans: Immigration, Finance, Defence, Commerce and Industry, Transport, Works and Power became Federal responsibilities. And three unashamedly racial ministries were established: European Education, European Agriculture and European Health, all generously funded. The equivalent Northern Rhodesian Departments (later called Ministries) of African Education, Health and Agriculture remained chronically underfunded.

Yet, the imposition of the Federation had an unanticipated beneficial consequence: it opened the eyes of the nationalist movements to the imminent danger of European domination and galvanized their resolve to fight for independence. (Those interested will find the history of the national struggle in great detail in my book, *Africa: Another Side of the Coin.*) They were successful: the Federation which ended officially in October 1963, though the administrative arrangements continued up to the end of the year, turned out to have been a short ten-year parenthesis in the history of the region.

One year later, Zambia was independent.

2.   UNPREPARED AND UNREADY BUT DETERMINED AND ENTHUSIASTIC

We woke up the morning of 24 October 1964, masters of our own destiny in our new nation of Zambia. We had our own government, our own president, our own cabinet, our own flag, our own national anthem, our own coat of arms with the national motto 'One Zambia, One Nation'. We had only one black engineer, three black doctors and three black lawyers and some 90 other black university graduates, working mainly as teachers and senior civil servants. We had 884 men and just 77 women qualified at School Certificate level, some 4,000 at Form II level, mainly working in the civil service, and a few thousand junior teachers, junior clerks and policemen and semi-skilled workers with just elementary school education (standard IV or VI).

To paraphrase Porgy's song (from Gershwin's musical *Porgy and Bess*) 'we had plenty of nothing, but nothing was plenty for us'. We had gained our independence. We were free, determined and very enthusiastic, and blissfully ignorant of the pitfalls that lay ahead. There was no problem we could not handle, we thought. The problems turned out to be many and immediate. Wealth and the economy were in foreign hands. And so were the skills. We had no experience in government but, worse, we had no idea how most things functioned. And many services started coming apart.

When the British civil servants started departing as their contracts with the Colonial Office expired we discovered that we did not have enough operators for the manual telephone exchanges of the time. The operators had been mainly wives of British civil servants and they were going away with their husbands. The job was simple enough and Zambians were trained in a few months, but in the meantime using the telephone became a nightmare. One needed to dial a dozen times for a connection. A similar problem arose with junior officers and secretaries in the government ministries, again jobs performed mainly by British wives. They were more difficult to replace. Zambian men easily filled the junior clerical jobs but we only had a total of 77 Zambian women with high school education never mind trained secretaries. 'Sunshine girls', as we named them, from England, Ireland and the Caribbean had to be recruited in a hurry on two-year contracts that were later extended, which gave time to train Zambians, locally and abroad. Mercifully, not all British civil servants departed immediately. Some decided to stay on under new contracts with the Zambian government that provided them with housing and local salaries, while Britain paid a supplement in sterling. This arrangement lasted for a couple of years only, but it gave us breathing space.

Immigration and Customs had been a Federal government responsibility, and did not employ many Zambians even at clerical levels. Youngsters had to be recruited in a hurry; they had little knowledge of the outside world but they were very conscientious and very serious about their duties. Passing through Immigration and Customs became a hit-or-miss exercise. One Sunday morning I received a message that an Irish consultant we were expecting from London for Chilanga Cement had been detained on arrival by Immigration and was being sent back on the same plane, because 'he did not have a visa'. I rushed to the airport – the City Airport which was serving as the Lusaka International Airport until a new one was built. The young officer who was handling the case was adamant that visitors from Ireland needed a visa. When I insisted that we check the list together, he realized that the country he was looking at was Iceland! And a customs officer once scolded me for not declaring some seashells he found in my briefcase. I explained that I picked them up on the beach in Dar es Salaam for my children and that they had no value. He would have none of it until his supervisor confirmed it to him.

The only television station in the country had been established in Kitwe during the Federal years. It covered the Copperbelt, which had a large white population, the only yardstick for any development during the Federation, and had no capacity to transmit to the rest of the country. Miraculously, within two months, it was transplanted to Lusaka in time for Kenneth Kaunda to broadcast his New Year's message to the country. But the broadcasters did not follow. They decided to return to Southern Rhodesia instead. New ones had to be hastily recruited and some senior civil servants volunteered as newscasters to fill the gap. Their English was not always the best. I remember one officer reading the evening news and repeatedly pronouncing the Philippines as Philippeins. Someone must have corrected him, because a couple of days later Palestine turned into Palestinn. The most amusing were the weather reports. They were read after the main news by officers of the meteorological department. Newly recruited, they were all very young and terribly nervous. I remember one young man reciting the day's precipitation at the various towns in alphabetical order. When he came to Lusaka he hesitated. 'Lusaka – nil' he whispered. Then he stopped, scratched his head and murmured: 'Argh! But it rained.' After that he shrugged his shoulders and murmuring 'maybe it did not rain near the gauges' he proceeded to finish the bulletin.

Everybody was learning on the job but the pressures were legion: new ministries and government departments needed offices and furniture and equipment and vehicles. Zambian civil servants had to be brought into Lusaka and the other major towns from outlying districts in order to plug holes created by the various departures. They needed housing. Most major countries from West and East and the newly independent Africa wanted to open diplomatic missions. The mining companies that after the end of the Federation transferred their head offices from Salisbury (now Harare) to Kitwe also wanted to open in Lusaka. There was a huge demand for offices and houses, but very few were available – mainly houses belonging to departing British civil servants – and they were snapped up as soon as they came on the market. All this created an economic boom, with the construction industry benefiting the most. Demand for labour increased, but unemployment increased too, because many more people flooded into the towns in search of jobs than jobs became available – a problem that persists to this day. Shanty towns sprang up on the periphery of Lusaka. The municipal services became stretched to the limit. Water had to be rationed because the Lusaka water supply depended on boreholes that proved inadequate for the increased demand. The Kafue water pipeline that now supplies Lusaka did not start operating until 1970.

***

Despite the many problems it encountered at independence, the first government was performing well. The governing party, the United National Independence Party (UNIP) was still a mass movement and functioned more like a coalition of the major tribal groupings of Zambia, with Kenneth Kaunda in charge holding it together and trying to inject cohesion like he knew he had to do with everything and everybody in the country when he coined the national motto: 'One Zambia, One Nation'. There were four major factions each with very strong leadership: Simon Kapwepwe, Justin Chimba, Robert Makasa, Leo Changufu, Clement Mwananshiku and Alex Shapi were leading the North (the Northern and Luapula Provinces and the Copperbelt that had produced more firebrands for the national struggle than anywhere else); Reuben Kamanga, Grey Zulu, Dingiswayo Banda and Wesley Nyirenda the East; Arthur and Sikota Wina, Nalumino Mundia and Munu Sipalo the West. Mainza Chona and Elijah Mudenda were more like stand-ins for the South, which was overwhelmingly loyal to Harry Nkumbula, the veteran freedom fighter and leader of the African National Congress (ANC). Peter Matoka, Samuel Mbilishi and Humphrey Mulemba from the North Western Province and Solomon Kalulu from the Central were less influential. The ANC, the original independence movement, formed the opposition in parliament. The UNIP leaders had broken away from it in 1958. They initially established ZANC, the Zambia African National Congress, and later UNIP after Governor Benson banned ZANC. They all hailed from rural areas and were attuned to the way people lived in the villages as well as in the towns. They had differences but they shared bonds forged during the struggle for freedom. The experiences of sharing prison cells or internal exile made it easy to reach compromises. Together with their leader, President Kaunda, they were fiercely nationalistic and were united in their determination to move the country forward and make up for the many decades of colonial neglect.

The permanent secretaries, as the civil service heads of the various ministries are called, were a different bunch. Except for a handful of college educated young men with little or no civil service experience, the majority had been selected by the departing provincial administration. Their education was limited, but they had many years of service as head clerks in rural stations. They were familiar with administrative routine but many were also steeped in the thinking of their British bosses, who regarded the freedom fighters as hooligans. Along with their departing former bosses they also viewed their ministers with disdain. They sneered at them, they mimicked their undereducated English and tried to make them look naive and ignorant. Their former British bosses, who at independence reversed roles and became their principal assistants and trainers, continued the indoctrination: 'Our political masters,' they scornfully repeated referring to the new ministers, 'are mainly poorly educated, inexperienced men who knew how to throw stones but have no idea what it takes to run the country. If we leave it to them they will ruin it. We are the ones who can keep it going.' By the 'we' they meant themselves, of course, although they knew they were on their way out. In the meantime they were prepared to put up with their former clerks occupying exalted positions. (As CEO of INDECO and later as Permanent Secretary, I observed this behaviour first-hand. But as I had freedom fighting roots, the departing British officers treated me with caution and some hostility which shielded me from direct indoctrination. But Mick Wagner, the then undersecretary of the Ministry of Commerce and Industry, who thought of himself as my boss, INDECO being an organ of the ministry, could not resist trying a number of times. The contempt in his voice whenever he referred to 'our political masters' still rings in my ears.)

During the 1962 election, which brought about the first African government in Northern Rhodesia, the rallying cry of the whites was the need to 'maintain standards'. That phrase was never amplified. They never bothered to define the standards they were looking for. They never said that they were concerned about the future of the standards of justice, morality, efficiency and so on. A cynic might rightly have concluded that the word 'standards' was a metaphor for their own privileges: essentially, that was what they wanted to preserve. Now that independence had come about they added two new imperatives: independence for the civil service and no political interference, again metaphors for maintaining the status quo. And some Zambian senior civil servants readily accepted that their remit included the task of ensuring that the politicians kept their paws out of running the government. They considered political interference a cardinal sin and cried foul at new initiatives or appointments that might undermine their control. They labelled them as political interference and resisted them fiercely. It did not seem to occur to them that the ministers had fought for independence precisely because they wanted to change the status quo and were unlikely to hand over that task to a group of acolytes of the British administration. (My own appointment as chairman of INDECO was delayed by one month, because it was labelled political and fought against by Dick Hallett, my predecessor who was on secondment from the Bank of England as Governor of the Bank of Zambia. And the entire 'all-white' staff of INDECO resigned en masse the first day I set foot in the office. More details in my book *Africa: Another Side of the Coin*.) The UNIP youth wing labelled such civil servants as 'colonial souls', an epithet which they resented but equally and perversely wore like a badge of honour. Amazingly, for the first three or four years, the ministers were quite sanguine about this state of affairs. They put up with the sneers and the rearguard action while, nonetheless, they introduced many new government programmes and sweeping reforms.

The ministers' agenda was clear: the black people of Zambia had been the labourers in Northern Rhodesia working for white bosses – settlers or itinerants. The Zambians had to evolve, as fast as possible, to the levels needed to run a modern society. Independence would only become meaningful when the nation became capable of taking care of all its needs with nationals in control. And the society needed to amalgamate into 'One Zambia' instead of remaining split in three distinct racial groups: the affluent white and Indian middle classes and the impoverished black workers, of Northern Rhodesia. But, more importantly, the Zambian national identity should supplant the tribal.

In other words, the fathers of the nation set out to develop the Zambian society along the lines the Northern Rhodesian whites had set up, perhaps colonialism's greatest unintended but inevitable contribution to the independent nation. The whites had not embraced the local people and effectively had banned them from experiencing the way whites lived. But the local people observed and absorbed the colonial way of life and they determined to make it their own. They knew that the target was ambitious and that they were setting themselves a mammoth task but they intended to achieve it, not by hurting the whites, but by raising their own standards, through education, training and hard work.

They were in a hurry to get started when a bolt struck from the south.

3. UDI: A New Landscape in Africa

On 11 November 1965, one year and a few days after Zambia's independence, Ian Smith, the white prime minister of the colony of Southern Rhodesia, unilaterally declared independence (UDI) from Britain, effectively staging a coup d'état against the British Crown. He renamed the country Rhodesia, dropping the 'Southern' component of the name. A new white ruled 'independent' country was thus planted in the southern region of Africa, alongside South Africa and the two Portuguese colonies of Mozambique and Portuguese West Africa (PWA, now Angola), breaking the pattern of African liberation that started with Ghana's independence in 1957.

The expectation had been that after the demise of the Federation and the independence of Zambia and Malawi, Britain would negotiate some kind of gradual progression towards African rule in Zimbabwe along the lines of a complex constitution devised in 1961 by the then Prime Minister of Southern Rhodesia, Sir Edgar Whitehead. Originally, that constitution had been rejected by Joshua Nkomo, the leader of ZAPU (Zimbabwe African People's Union), the only African party of any significance at the time, for conceding too little and by the whites for opening the way for black domination, but that was the period of decolonization and everybody was expecting that some compromise would in the end be worked out. Instead, the Whitehead Constitution led to the creation of the Rhodesian Front, a new hard line white settler political party and the emergence of an even more hard line leader, Ian Douglas Smith, whose philosophy was: 'the white man is the master of Rhodesia; he built it and intends to keep it' (Robert Good, 'U.D.I.'). The whites rallied around him and in the May 1965 elections Ian Smith's Rhodesian Front won all the white seats in parliament. Harold Wilson, the then British prime minister, urged them back to the negotiating table naively declaring at the same time that Britain did not want to have to fight its 'kith and kin' in Rhodesia. Ian Smith, whose slogan was 'no black rule during my lifetime' took Wilson's statement as a licence to go ahead. He plunged Rhodesia into a 15-year civil war that he inevitably lost. He tore his country apart and destabilized the whole region in the process. And 'his people', the Rhodesians, as in effect the overwhelming majority of the white Zimbabweans still think of themselves, are continuing to suffer the repercussions of their defeat to this day.

The UDI turned out to be a major blow to Zambia because it had been tied to the Southern African trading system since the beginning of the twentieth century. Its external trade depended on the Rhodesia Railways and was routed through South Africa and Mozambique: copper was exported through the ports of Durban, Port Elizabeth and Beira and imports were mainly sourced in South Africa, until the establishment of the Federation, when the Southern Rhodesian industry developed and became the main supplier of the Zambian market. But products not available in South Africa and Rhodesia continued to transit through the ports of South Africa and Mozambique. Yet, six weeks after UDI, Zambia's access to these routes was cut off. Just before Christmas 1965 Harold Wilson together with Lyndon Johnson, the American president, declared economic sanctions against Rhodesia, which hurt Zambia's economy more than they hurt Rhodesia's, as the latter was buttressed by white ruled South Africa. The sanctions included an embargo on the supply of fuel enforced by the British Navy, which intercepted fuel tankers destined for the Rhodesian pipeline at Beira. Wilson and Johnson naively thought that without oil for the pipeline the Smith regime would collapse 'within weeks'.

Not so we told Cledwyn Hughes, the Secretary for the Commonwealth in Harold Wilson's government who came to inform us of the impending measures and assure us that Britain, together with the United States and Canada, would ensure that we did not run out of fuel. We pointed out that the intended measures would be useless because South Africa would supply fuel to Rhodesia, in order to keep it as a buffer zone against black Africa. We emphasized that 'collapse within a few weeks was a pipe dream'. Prophetically, as it turned out, we guessed that the Smith regime would last 15 years. We explained that all storage facilities had been built in Bulawayo and Salisbury (Harare) during the Federal days and as a result Zambia's internal stocks were extremely low. All we had in hand was 12 days' supply of petrol and 22 days' of diesel. And we emphasized that we had no alternative import routes. The Benguela Railway line from Elizabethville (Lubumbashi) to Lobito Bay (now Benguela) on the Atlantic coast had only limited capacity and as it passed through Portuguese West Africa it would not be a reliable alternative because of Portugal's close relations with South Africa and its declared 'neutrality' towards the Rhodesian regime. The British minister departed assuring us that Britain would meet the additional costs we might incur in diverting our supply routes.

We spent our Christmas holidays organizing a fuel rationing system. All we could afford was four gallons of petrol per vehicle per month – a mean New Year's present to the motorists of Zambia from their new government. An airlift for fuel started immediately but the only international airport that could take the big jets of the day (Boeing 707 and DC8) was in Ndola. Lusaka was still using the City Airport, which apart from the British Overseas Airways VC10, could only take smaller turbo prop planes. Fuel started trickling in but only in minute quantities. We needed a land-based solution passing through reliable friendly countries.

We spent the ensuing five years trying to divert our imports and exports from the Southern African ports mainly to the port of Dar es Salaam. It was a heartbreaking slog and often demoralizing but we had no alternative. We persevered. The Great North Road was atrocious, particularly during the rainy season, and the journey from Lusaka to Dar, a distance of some 1,100 miles, lasted ten days or longer. The conditions were so bad that the route was named 'the hell run'. Nevertheless it became the lifeline of Zambia for the period. Everybody who had a truck and wanted to participate was engaged but as more imports and exports were routed through Dar bottlenecks started to appear. The most serious was the port itself, which did not have the capacity to handle the volumes of cargo we were putting through it. Another problem was the availability of 45-gallon galvanized drums to carry the fuel. There were only two sources of supply, India and South Africa and when we exhausted the supply from India we had to resort to South Africa. As we could not transit through Rhodesia, we had to route them by sea to Dar. But Tanzanian regulations did not allow the importation of South African goods and every time we needed a new consignment President Kaunda had to appeal to President Nyerere for special dispensation. As time went by, we spread to other routes, none of them satisfactory: Benguela Railway to Lobito Bay on the Atlantic Ocean, Nampula in Mozambique by road through Malawi, Mombasa in Kenya by road through Tanzania, and we still had to use the Rhodesia Railways, for bulk cargo like wheat and other grain to and from Beira.

We were paying for these costs, as well as the construction of the supporting infrastructure, relying on the promised reimbursements from Britain, but when the time for reconciliation came, a couple of years later, the British only paid £14 million. One of their excuses for the meanness was that our economy was doing much better than theirs, as Judith Hart, the British Minister for Overseas Development, told us during one of the negotiating sessions. And, later, Britain devalued the pound and we lost UK£20 million from our national reserves, which, at the time, were still managed by the crown agents in London because the colonial arrangements had remained in force.

Within a couple of years we absorbed the entire spare capacity of the port of Dar es Salaam, hauling some 20,000 tons of fuel and other supplies per month. It was costing the earth. Even though the American government paid for the reconstruction of the worst parts of the Dar–Lusaka road in southern Tanzania we needed additional and cheaper routes. We needed a railway line to Dar and more immediately a fuel pipeline. Kenneth Kaunda wrote to the British prime minister asking him to assist. According to his experts, the prime minister replied, the pipeline would cost at least UK£45 million and take three years to build. The railway would cost many hundreds of million and the survey alone would take three years. 'The Smith regime would not last that long,' he concluded in a letter that left us dumbfounded. We built a pipeline in 16 months at a cost of UK£16 million and the Chinese built for us a first class railway within three years. They did not bother with advance surveys. They laid the line as they went along, and after it started operating they went back and reinforced weak points – a sensible method, bearing in mind the distance and the terrain. More importantly they financed the entire foreign cost, including the cost of Chinese labour, through a 30-year loan at 1 per cent per annum interest.

We spent time and energy sorting out trade routes, but we did not neglect development. Government revenues were high. Thanks to the Vietnam War the price of copper was ever rising, reaching levels above UK£600 per ton, meteoric in those times. Arthur Wina, the then Minister of Finance, did not let the opportunity pass. Unlike his successors in the early years of the twenty-first century who dithered over a similar windfall after the privatization of the mining industry, he negotiated with the mining companies a sharing formula in the form of export levy that gave the government 50 per cent of all revenue above £300 per ton. And as the prospects for copper looked promising the mining companies started opening new deposits. Optimism was spreading and even the settlers started feeling that maybe independence was not so bad for them, after all. Their bullying mode returned. 'Independence may be yours but the money is still ours,' they taunted.

The government could afford to spend in order to bridge the development gap created by the colonial neglect and it did. Education needed the most immediate attention. In the very late fifties the Northern Rhodesia Government had built a few more high schools in some of the major towns and in each provincial capital. And at independence the school buildings that had been reserved for the whites became available to all and black children obtained access to the former 'whites-only' schools, but these covered only urban centres. The numbers were not nearly enough and the rural areas remained neglected. To remedy the situation, the government decided to establish one high school in each district capital, and it called for tenders for some 40 new school buildings. As the construction industry was already overstretched the tenders came in very high, way above the Public Works Department's estimates. The whites, who viewed every action of the new government with a jaundiced eye, sneered. Why build so many schools in one go? A few schools every couple of years would have been within the capacity of the construction industry. A true enough observation if the consideration was just the cost of the school buildings. But that was not the issue. The ever growing young population could no longer be contained in the subsistence economy of the rural areas. They were trekking to the towns in search of work, but without education and skills they could not find any. The schools were necessary in order to provide the foundation for their further training: for technical schools, colleges and other schools for higher learning as well as the University of Zambia. None of these institutions existed at the time but plans were well advanced for their establishment. The country could not wait for another decade to make a start. And, in any case, the increased demand for construction capacity started attracting new companies, foreign and local, after which rates became competitive again.

Capacity-building takes time and in the meantime we had to break the job colour-bar that carried over from the colonial days. I never expected the whites to put up so much resistance to change. Appeals and exhortations for the training and promotion of Zambians fell on deaf ears. Zambianization was anathema to them even though it was never rejected out of hand. Promises would be made and immediately forgotten – or worse. There was much bigoted thinking in most settlers' and foreigners' minds: blacks were lazy; they could not be trusted; a black man could not accept another black as a boss; no black could do a European man's job, and so on. The latter was developed to a fine art by the mining companies and resulted in the gross overmanning of the industry. Although the companies professed fervent support for Zambianization, together with the European Mineworkers Union they used every trick in the book to sabotage that effort. They imported personnel experts from South Africa, ostensibly to assist. They invented delaying tactics. They tabulated the jobs performed by Europeans and they prepared long-term profound-looking plans with annual targets. The basis of these, dreamed up together with the European Mineworkers Union, no doubt, was job fragmentation, which meant that jobs performed by whites needed to be split between two or sometimes three Zambians. Many years later, when the mining industry was being privatized after three decades under government control the root cause of the overmanning had been forgotten and it was attributed to political patronage. To be fair, political patronage was also rampant but was more pronounced at the higher echelons of the industry.

We had to swallow all these plans and discuss them seriously and be polite and thank them for their efforts when we knew all along that the basic jobs had been performed by Zambians over many years, under the supervision of

Zambians. Except that black supervisors were not called supervisors or foremen, but 'gang leaders' or 'capitaos' and, of course, they always had an unnecessary token boss, who was white.

It would take three or four years before we cracked the Zambianization problem and we would employ an entirely different and much more radical method: a radical reorientation of the economy towards greater Zambian participation and control. In the meantime, the government had to tackle many other immediate and more urgent issues.

4. HARD WORK AND FANTASIES

Agriculture was the preserve of the whites in colonial times, and more so during the Federation. The white farmers formed the main constituency of the United Federal Party (UFP), the governing party in the Federal and the Southern Rhodesia governments, which also held most of the elected seats in the Legislative Councils of Northern Rhodesia until 1962 and Nyasaland until 1961. They were pampered with easy loans from the Land and Agricultural Bank for purchasing and clearing land, vehicles, equipment, and most crucially pre-planting finance. More scandalously the Grain Marketing Board paid higher prices for their produce than it did for the black farmers'. Not surprisingly, therefore, agricultural production emanated almost entirely from white farmers and, after independence, when some of them started drifting back to Rhodesia and South Africa and a couple of years of drought followed, shortages began to occur. Again the settlers taunted: '200 white farmers were feeding Northern Rhodesia but Zambia cannot feed itself.'

The reality was that at independence, there were no Zambian farmers except at subsistence level and there was no commercial farming tradition amongst Zambians, except for a very small number in the Southern Province where they had interacted with white farmers for some decades. The peasants elsewhere were never encouraged or incentivized to produce for sale. They were subsistence farmers although they did produce small surpluses, which they sold for cash to local traders who on-sold to the Grain Marketing Board. In a few areas, they also produced crops for sale, like ground nuts, sorghum and millet. As far as beef was concerned, the Southern and Western Provinces had huge numbers of cattle (estimated at two million at the time), but very few appeared on the market, because peasants used to count their wealth in heads of cattle and only sold when they needed cash, and the cash needs of subsistence level families were very small.

The Ministry of Agriculture embarked on a number of schemes to remedy the situation. None produced results. At the beginning they perceived that the traders were parasitic to the market and decided to replace them with the Rural Marketing Board (RMB), which was given the monopoly to buy the entire rural crop and deliver it to the National Agricultural Marketing Board (NAMBOARD). The thinking was that the traders exploited the peasants by paying very low prices. And the hope was that because of its monopoly RMB would have lower costs and therefore pay higher prices to the producer. The scheme proved a disaster because of inefficient collection, erratic payments to the farmers and a wasteful transportation system that depended on hired vehicles from towns travelling empty to destinations sometimes three or four hundred miles distant in order to collect the produce. In reality, the traders had been paying better prices than the Rural Marketing Board because they transported the produce as a return load on the trucks that brought their supplies from the Copperbelt and the towns along the line of rail. In calculating what to pay the producer, traders did not include any cost for transport of the produce to the line of rail because they loaded that cost on the goods they brought for their shops. Because of this they could afford to pay high prices for the produce, in the knowledge that the money they paid out would return to them through increased shop sales.

Alongside the Rural Marketing Board the Ministry of Agriculture established the Credit Organization of Zambia (COZ) in order to finance the farmers' needs for implements, tools, seed and fertilizers. COZ never got properly organized and drowned in a sea of bad debts within a few years. It took many years of experimentation to strike the right solution and that was government subsidized inputs (seed and fertilizer) distributed on credit through NAMBOARD, which had succeeded the old Grain Marketing Board after independence. NAMBOARD was repaid by deduction from the value of grain delivered at the end of the season. This scheme proved successful, so much so that by the early eighties even the Northern Province, never famous for its agricultural competence, was producing three to four million bags of maize a year.

The industrial sector proved more successful. Through the Industrial Development Corporation of Zambia (INDECO), the government embarked upon a number of projects to ease the import and export bottlenecks that resulted from UDI and the Rhodesian sanctions; to kick-start local manufacturing which the Federation had steered towards Southern Rhodesia; to generate local production using local inputs, in order to substitute imported products; and generally to promote Zambian participation in business. INDECO was quite successful. Within three months of UDI it managed to put on the road between Dar and Zambia 200 30-ton trucks with 50 additional trucks every subsequent month to a total of 500. On 12 May 1966, exactly six months after the declaration of UDI, these were consolidated into the Zambia Tanzania Road Services, a company owned jointly by the governments of Zambia and

Tanzania and Intersomer, a subsidiary of Mediobanca, a major Italian merchant bank that provided the finance. And by September 1968, Presidents Nyerere and Kaunda officiated at the opening of the Dar-Ndola pipeline, owned 65 per cent and 35 per cent respectively by the governments of Zambia and Tanzania. It was built in 16 months, against Harold Wilson's estimate of 45 (in his letter to Kenneth Kaunda (KK) responding to his request for British help). The most significant trade route redirection project, TAZARA, the Dar-Kapiri Mposhi Railway, was built by China after direct negotiations with the governments of Zambia and Tanzania.

Amongst the early projects INDECO embarked upon were the two Intercontinental hotels in Lusaka and Livingstone, which opened in June and September 1968. It proved easier to build the hotels than to man them. The Intercontinental in Lusaka needed some 300 employees, but no trained staff were available in such numbers in Lusaka, which until then had only one small hotel of international standards, the Ridgeway, and no training facilities of any kind. The head office of the Intercontinental Hotels Company in New York sent some trainers a couple of months before the opening. They remained for some time after the opening together with staff seconded from their Ethiopian operations to supervise and refine the skills of the new Zambian staff. Naturally it takes time for people to get into the finer points of a new job. As the chairman of the hotel, one day I was called to State House and was presented with a plate of somewhat overcooked pancakes, which Archie Levine, one of Kaunda's many retainers from Britain thought fit to present to KK when he met him that morning. We shrugged our shoulders and laughed. We had bigger problems to worry about than a plate of burned pancakes that had been immediately replaced anyway and Archie did not go hungry to State House. Did we feel guilty for the inefficiency? The answer is no; we were rather pleased with ourselves for achieving as much as we did in such a short time. But the whites around us, local and itinerant, were trying to make us feel that we were useless, and would never be able to match their Western standards – some still do to this day.

On many occasions we were browbeaten or energized and got lost in cul-de-sacs pursuing impossible projects dreamed up by all sorts of fantasists who were attracted to our freshness – like *inswa* (flying ants) to the lights – and were bombarding us with countless ideas on how to race into a new ideal society of their own imagination. The biggest victim of these new 'missionaries' was Kaunda himself who, perhaps because of his passionate ambition to make a success out of Zambia, was more gullible than the rest of us. The problem was that he was in charge and therefore attracted more such zealots than anybody else and at the same time he had the authority to disseminate their ideas through the many 'pink memos' from his office that required immediate attention. I had been the target of many memos, like the following, which was addressed to the Ministers of Labour, Commerce and Industry and me in INDECO:

> I discussed with you the possibility of co-management, i.e. between the employers and the employees. With Chilanga more or less controlled by INDECO I wonder whether we could not experiment with the Bonn method.

And another addressed to me:

> Traditionally and culturally our society is based on cooperation thereby giving us a continuing basis, or at least an opportunity of not developing a selfish angle based on individualism ... Give loans only to cooperatives.

Many of these fantasists were itinerants, and some managed to attach themselves to KK for varying periods of time but others had regular appointments in various ministries. The maddest ideas came from Professor Mars, an Austrian who was attached to the Ministry of Mines by the Economic Commission for Africa. He conceived the idea of establishing in Lusaka the 'Lusaka Virgin Metal Exchange' in order to compete with the London Metal Exchange (LME). And he did not stop there. He wanted us to embark on a campaign to persuade the central banks of all major countries to hold some of their currency reserves in copper. John Mwanakatwe, the then Minister of Mines, swallowed the idea hook, line and sinker despite the advice of Dominic Mulaisho, the permanent secretary and the other senior officers of the ministry. Naturally the idea came to nothing but it generated a lot of debate and wasted a lot of government time.

After copper, the most glamorous subject in government, those days, was UDI and our transport routes. They naturally attracted the attention of the professor. He came to see me: 'Did you ever consider Mtwara as the main port for Zambia?' he asked. Mtwara is the southernmost port of Tanzania near the Mozambique border. I explained the difficulties: the port was undeveloped; it was more than 1,200 miles away, over mountainous terrain sometimes rising to 10,000 feet; it had a bush track for a road. He lost his temper. He had been on that road and he knew all about it. But his plan was different: a straight road from Mtwara to Mbamba Bay on Lake Malawi, across the lake by ferry and on to Lusaka and the Copperbelt by road. I was incredulous: 'two transhipments, two countries to cross, a brand new port at Mtwara, and two ferry ports and a number of new ferries on Lake Malawi, a brand new road, through mountainous terrain, buying ferries and assembling them on Lake Malawi! Did you consider the cost and the time it will take?' I asked the professor; 'And would the volume of traffic justify it?' I asked. Now the professor became really angry. He reminded me that, during the Second World War, the Burma highway was built in a few weeks. 'When there is a will there is a way,' he shouted and stormed out of my office threatening to report me to the President. I again shrugged my shoulders. And I heard nothing from the President.

Robert Oakeshott in INDECO had a more socially friendly solution to our route to the Indian Ocean: a timber-fired railway; timber plantations on the way, employing thousands of workers to grow the trees and chop the wood and load it on the trains. Unlike the professor, Robert was a likeable person, with a great sense of humour and nostalgia for the 'good old days'. When we declared petrol rationing he was ecstatic. Zambia does not need private cars, he opined. Bicycles are the answer, and as far as he was concerned, the horse. He started coming to the office on horseback. It was the rainy season and sometimes he arrived dripping wet, but full of smiles and very pleased with himself.

But normal life was productive. Another successful INDECO project was Kafue Textiles, a 1,000-loom textile mill that came into production in 1968. As was usual in those days, the white community declared it a folly. Zambia did not produce enough cotton and the government would have to import it at high costs to keep the textile mill in production, they sneered. Yet as soon as Kafue Textiles started buying cotton, production increased. A second mill of 3,000 looms built by the Chinese in Kabwe a couple of years later was also able to procure its requirements locally. And cotton, produced mainly by peasant farmers, became a major non-traditional Zambian export as a result. But both mills, as well as the entire clothing industry they generated, were not able to survive the onslaught of 'salaula' (second-hand clothes) that flooded the country during the Chiluba administration and those that followed. Luckily cotton production is still thriving in the rural areas, particularly in the Eastern Province and the western districts of the Central Province, bar occasional hitches emanating from the gyrations of the value of the Kwacha, as I shall explain later. In 2010 Zambia produced 121,908 tons of cotton.

The biggest industry INDECO established was Nitrogen Chemicals of Zambia (NCZ), which produced ammonium nitrate for fertilizers and mining explosives. INDECO also acquired a minority stake in NCZ's biggest customer, Kafironda Explosives, the only producer of explosives for the mining industry in the country. Taking a minority share in order to encourage promotion of a new industry or expansion of an existing one became a pattern. Thus INDECO took a 12 per cent interest in Zambia Sugar in order to encourage the development of Nakambala Sugar Estate in Mazabuka by the British company Tate & Lyle and 45 per cent in Chilanga Cement partly owned, at the time, by the Commonwealth Development Corporation of the UK, in order to facilitate the construction of a second cement plant on the Copperbelt. And INDECO did not just confine its activities to the urban areas. As rural production of maize increased INDECO established milling companies in major rural centres in order to stop the unnecessary transportation of maize to towns for milling and return. It also promoted rural hotels, either directly such as the 'Lyambai' in Mongu or by financing local businessmen such as the 'Kwacha Relax' in Kasama, and rehabilitated others like the Crested Crane in Mpika, that had been built by the Imperial Airways in the 1930s as a stopover for its flights between London and Johannesburg, which in those days used to take a week.

The government paid special attention to housing with the introduction of site and service schemes around Lusaka and other major urban centres. It had realized early on that the colonial system of building townships for black workers was unsustainable. The nation simply did not have the resources to build houses for the hundreds of thousands of rural migrants trekking to Lusaka, the Copperbelt and the other urban centres in search of work. And it could not stop them by regulation like the colonial authorities used to do. In their later years, the colonial authorities and the mining industry had in fact built tolerable high density housing for the African town dwellers. But its purpose was as much to control their movements as to house them. The African Residential Areas on the periphery of all major towns were strictly regulated and were administered by a 'Location Superintendent' whose powers were draconian.

'Private Property – Trespassers will be Prosecuted' signs were prominent at the entrance of all the segregated African residential areas, called locations, compounds, or euphemistically, townships. The legal position was that only registered residents were allowed to live there. Visitors needed permission from the Location Superintendent, so residents had to rush to the Location Office to get a permit whenever a visitor called, regardless of whether he was a parent, a grown-up child, or a friend. The visit would then be limited to a specific number of days, preferably very few. A visitor without a permit was an 'illegal resident' and could be arrested. The location police were entitled to search for illegal residents any time they pleased and they usually chose four o'clock in the morning. They would then arrest all the 'illegals' and march them to the police station at first light. This early morning parade was a regular occurrence. There are no statistics about how many of those 'illegals' were criminal. They were, predominantly, innocent people staying with relatives who may have arrived late, or whose permit may have expired, being harassed by the bloody-minded 'Location Police'.

A democratic government could not impose control on the movement of its people and would never muster adequate resources to build houses for the unstoppable stream of rural people flooding the urban centres in search of work. It decided instead to allocate serviced plots for people to build their own. The municipalities allocated and subdivided the land, laid down basic services such as roads, water and electricity and sold the plots. This is how Mutendere, Kaunda Square in Lusaka and many similar ones in other major towns were born. People initially built one or two rooms and later on expanded as their income improved. As time went by, some extremely good houses developed in those areas, which have now become thriving (but highly congested) suburbs. And as time went by property developers also emerged, building houses for rent in those suburbs, some of whose quality is, unfortunately, questionable at times.

The star achievement of the government of the new nation, however, was in education. The neglect of education during the colonial period was legendary and is illustrated in the following table published in the UN/ECA/FAO economic survey in 1964 titled: '1963 Stock of educated Africans in Zambia by Highest Examination passed'.

	Males	Females	Total
Standard IV	86,900	23,300	110,200
Standard VI	28,200	4,200	32,400
Form II	3,940	480	4,420
School Certificate	884	77	961

The survey rightly concludes: 'The Zambian population, on the eve of Independence, is in terms of education one of the least prepared populations in the whole of Africa' (M. J. Kelly, *The Origins and Development of Education in Zambia from Pre-colonial Times to 1996*).

Somehow, the government of Northern Rhodesia did not want to get involved, so education remained mainly in the hands of missionary societies until the mid-forties. In 1945, out of a total of 1,112 schools in the country 1,062 were run by missionaries, 28 by the government and 23 by native authorities. Two annual reports of education administrators in 1934 and 1936 sum up the government's thinking on black education as follows: 'The policy of the government has always been to build a sound foundation of village education to improve and develop the primary school and diffuse education as widely as possible among the people rather than concentrate attention and expenditure on the higher education of a select few' (Peter Snelson, *Educational Development in Northern Rhodesia 1883–1945*). In other words: we have to be fair (the ever-present colonial 'firm but fair') and treat all blacks, rural or urban equally. Or perhaps more truthfully: 'We do not really want educated blacks around, especially in the towns, and we do not care about the rest. But we do recognize we need to be seen to be doing something so let the missionaries in the bush educate some people to standard II.' And they subcontracted that type of primary education to them. This attitude of the Northern Rhodesia Government (NRG) was no different from that of the Nationalist Government of South Africa, which was articulated more bluntly by Hendrik Verwoerd, South Africa's notorious Minister of Native Affairs, some 20 years later when in 1953 he declared: 'there is no place for the Bantu in the European community above the level of certain forms of labour' (Susan Williams, *Colour Bar, The Triumph of Seretse Khama and his Nation*).

In the urban areas the Northern Rhodesian Government (NRG) only cared about education for the whites, as is evident from the fact that 'in 1938 the education budget for the 1,200 European school children was higher than that of the 120,000 African children at school'. T. A. Coombe in his *The Origins of Secondary Education in Zambia; Part I: Policy making in the Thirties* says the following: 'advanced education for Africans was regarded by some whites with hostility, by others with suspicion and by few (if any) with enthusiasm … Any form of education which was likely to prepare Africans to compete with local Europeans for employment raised an outcry; this invariably threw the government onto the defensive and reinforced their cautious attitude towards the educational advancement of Africans' (M. J. Kelly, *The Origins and Development of Education in Zambia*).

In 1933, the colonial government must have felt that it had to do something more for the advancement of blacks so it established, in Lusaka, the Central Trades School (later renamed Hodgson and, after independence, David Kaunda) offering four-year courses in woodwork and building, with leather work and thatching added later. A more important development in black higher education, however, occurred in 1938 when the Native Training Centre (later named Munali) was established in Lusaka. Its mission was to train African clerks for government departments and for the private sector; it initially included a teacher training section, which was later transferred to Chalimbana (*Educational Development in Northern Rhodesia*). As I said earlier, Munali remained the only government-sponsored secondary school for black boys in Northern Rhodesia till the very late fifties, which together with the Catholic St Canisius and the Presbyterian Chipembi completed the trio that educated black children at secondary level until just five years before independence.

At independence, the government of Zambia was painfully aware of the wilful disregard for African education by the colonial and Federal systems and was determined to catch up as soon as possible. It made tremendous strides. By 1968, primary school enrolment was twice as high as that of 1964, while the secondary school enrolment was three times as high. And in March 1966 the University of Zambia (UNZA) opened its Ridgeway Campus followed by the opening of the Great East Road Campus in March 1968. So, Arthur Wina, the then Minister of Education, had every right to brag in parliament on 8 October 1968:

> Let me say, Mr. Speaker, in a general summary of the measures so far announced that some of them represent the Government's determination to ensure that no matter what happens, no matter whether the four fat years in which we have enjoyed expansive prosperity in spite of the buffetings, strictures and setbacks of UDI are followed by four or even seven lean years, the educational system of this country shall not run on flat tyres.
>
> (*The Origins and Development of Education in Zambia*)

It was an altogether extraordinary achievement. Despite the dislocation caused by UDI, the UNIP government was making spectacular progress in transforming the country from a neglected colony with a first world component in the form of the mining industry owned and manned mainly by whites, to a well-rounded African country.

But the unity of UNIP had already started to crumble.

5.   Political Turbulence and Rhodesian Spies

Kaunda's tribal balancing in the cabinet, the civil service and other prominent national appointments was mocked repeatedly by the Zambian civil service elite. Yet, like the national motto, 'One Zambia, One Nation', tribal balancing was the result of his innate knowledge of the country and its people. And it was successful right through his administration, though not as effective in calming tribal antagonisms in later years. The system sacrificed some efficiency, of course, but it gave the provinces the feeling that they all had an equal say in the administration and the smaller tribes did not run the risk of being steamrolled by the bigger ones. The UNIP constitution tied his hands over the appointment of his vice president (he had to appoint the UNIP Vice President in that position) so he had to appoint an Easterner, Reuben Kamanga, who was the Vice President of UNIP when he formed his first government, even though the Bemba speaking people of the Northern and Luapula Provinces, apart from being more numerous, had made a greater contribution to the freedom movement and their leader Simon Kapwepwe had greater gravitas and a bigger claim to the position. He had already placated Kapwepwe with the argument that the rest of the country would have difficulty in accepting two Bemba speaking childhood friends to the two topmost positions in the nation, when he appointed Kamanga.

Both Kaunda and Kapwepwe hailed from Chinsali but Kaunda was not of the Bemba tribe. His parents, David and Helen, had settled there in 1904, when his father chose Lubwa as the place to establish a Church of Scotland Mission amongst the Bemba people. He had been sent by the Livingstonia Mission of Nyasaland (now Malawi) to do the search. David Kaunda settled in Lubwa and lived there with his family until his death in 1932. Kenneth, his youngest child and the future President of Zambia was born in Lubwa in 1924. By the time David died, 28 years after his arrival, the family must have got completely localized and out of touch with Nyasaland. So his mother stayed on in Lubwa and Kenneth and his siblings grew up and had their early education in the area. Kaunda spoke only Bemba and no doubt he never thought of himself as different from the other children. Yet, 32 years after independence his Zambian bona fides would be challenged in order to prevent him from re-contesting the presidency. But I'll cover that issue later.

Kapwepwe was appointed Minister of Foreign Affairs, a much more substantial job than the nebulous position of the vice president. He performed well and seemed happy in the position, which, particularly after the declaration of UDI that made Zambia a frontline state, acquired great significance. But his inner circle was aggrieved and as time went by persuaded him that his exclusion from the vice presidency was an affront to the Bemba people, which he had the duty to remedy. Inevitably in the end Kapwepwe succumbed to his tribesmen's pressures and at the UNIP General Conference in August 1967 he challenged Reuben Kamanga for the position of the UNIP Vice President and won. He automatically became the vice president of the country, according to the requirement of the UNIP constitution. But he won the election without any support from other national heavyweights. His support came from peripheral elements of the Central Committee and by making an alliance with the two Tonga members, Mainza Chona and Elijah Mudenda, whose political credentials were insignificant. They both were highly educated, with Chona being the first black lawyer in the country and Mudenda having a degree in plant pathology from Cambridge. They had also been long serving senior members of the Central Committee but they did not have a political constituency in their own province, which was solidly behind Harry Nkumbula, the opposition leader and President of the ANC. Yet under Kapwepwe's patronage, Chona and Mudenda displaced two Lozi heavyweights, Munu Sipalo and Arthur Wina, as UNIP National Secretary and National Treasurer. And a little-known lady from the Northern Province replaced Mukwae Nakatindi, another prominent Lozi, as Director of the Women's Brigade.

The most serious repercussion of Kapwepwe's bid was the elimination of the two most prominent Lozi politicians: Arthur Wina, one of the best Ministers of Finance Zambia had and Munu Sipalo, a populist heavyweight and an extremely effective Minister of Agriculture at the time. They, together with Arthur's brother Sikota and Mukwae Nakatindi, represented the enlightened Lozi leadership that had secured UNIP's Barotse triumph when it swept all ten parliamentary seats in the 1964 election, much to the chagrin of the Litunga and the Barotse royal establishment. Kapwepwe should have taken this into consideration and sought a broader alliance. But the top man was Kaunda and he cannot be absolved of all blame for the debacle and its long-term effects. He was the president and Kapwepwe was his childhood friend. When he saw that the vice presidency was coveted by the Bemba and other major tribes and all the senior politicians, he should have devised a scheme along the lines of 'tribal balancing' in the cabinet and the upper echelons of the civil service and apply it to the vice presidency as well. A rotating vice presidency would have bought unity for a few more years, and kept UNIP focused on its national reconstruction task, even though it was inevitable that eventually some of the factions would have drifted out.

After his successful election, Kapwepwe and his supporters monopolized most senior positions in the new Central Committee, which upset the other provinces particularly the East. And Kaunda, wounded by what he must have considered as a Bemba rebuke, overcompensated by including the Ministry of Finance in Kapwepwe's vice-presidential portfolio, an unnecessary generosity that relegated Arthur Wina to the Ministry of Education and enhanced Kapwepwe's prominence in the cabinet, upsetting the other provinces even more. The result was that the delicate balance of 'give and take' that ensured democracy and good governance in UNIP and the nation as a whole, was lost. Tribal interests became supreme and acrimony reigned. So much so, that a few months later, in February 1968, Kenneth Kaunda walked out of an unruly UNIP National Council meeting and resigned as president declaring that he was not prepared to preside over a federation of tribes. He withdrew his resignation the following morning after he was besieged by delegation after delegation during the night, begging him to stay on.

In terms of national politics, the near-term damage from all this was that Arthur Wina and Sipalo went on to lose their parliamentary seats in the 1968 general elections, and UNIP was annihilated in Barotseland losing all but one of the Barotse parliamentary seats to the United Party, a newly formed Lozi political group. Without Arthur Wina and Sipalo the Lozi retreated to their laager and Kapwepwe, unwittingly perhaps, had sown the seed for the Barotse discontent that would later culminate in demands for secession from Zambia. Other factors would later contribute to the Barotse discontent, not least of which was its renaming as Western Province, which I shall discuss later.

And the long-term damage would be the eventual breakup of the democratic UNIP and the declaration of the 'One Party' State. Apart from Barotseland UNIP would lose support in the Northern and Luapula Provinces and the Copperbelt, which it would not be able to evaluate or even notice because of the creation of the 'One Party' system. After its introduction, election results became unrepresentative of political support, because seats were contested by two candidates, pre-approved by the UNIP Central Committee. They also became irrelevant because UNIP had the monopoly of political power anyway. I shall return to these issues later.

The turmoil within UNIP spread to the civil service. Despite the strains between the senior civil servants and the politicians, Valentine Musakanya, the secretary to the cabinet and head of the civil service since independence, had managed to keep the service away from direct political control. But Kapwepwe did not like it and in this he found many eager supporters in the cabinet and a couple of senior permanent secretaries, who ganged up against Valentine. Amazingly, Kapwepwe fell in with the two permanent secretaries despite the fact that they emanated from Barotseland and the Southern Province, while Valentine hailed from Kasama, the heart of Bemba-land. The position of the secretary to the cabinet was abolished and replaced by that of secretary to the government. Even though the cabinet secretary's position would later be reinstated, the civil service remained under direct political control, with presidents appointing all senior civil servants ever since. Valentine was offered the position of Minister of State for Finance but he refused to accept it because he did not want to serve under Kapwepwe. He accepted instead the position of Minister of State for Technical Education in which he excelled.

Another major casualty of UNIP's turmoil was the chief justice, James Skinner, Irish by birth but a dedicated Zambian nationalist and founding member of UNIP. The Angolan and Mozambique liberation wars were in full swing at the time and large numbers of Portuguese forces were stationed along the Angolan and Mozambique borders with Zambia. They were constantly harassing the Zambian villages along the borders, accusing the people of harbouring guerrillas. They were making frequent incursions destroying crops and granaries. They even bombed villages from the air and blew up the Luangwa Bridge, which cut communications with the Eastern Province and the port of Nampula in Mozambique, which we were accessing through Malawi at the time.

In June 1969, Zambian policemen captured two Portuguese soldiers inside Zambia at Chavuma, in the North Western Province, near the border with Angola. They were tried by the Lusaka Resident Magistrate, a Ghanaian, and sentenced to a fine of K2,000 ($2,400), or two years' jail in lieu each. Their government did not bother to pay their fine and they were sent to jail. The whites in Zambia were up in arms: the Portuguese soldiers were white and their sentence was racially motivated, they said. They concocted all sorts of myths about their presence in Zambia: the soldiers came into Zambia because they wanted to defect; they were invited to Zambia by the immigration officers at the Chavuma border; and in any case their sentence was unreasonably harsh according to the whites of Zambia: a total $4,800 fine for the two, which their government did not bother to pay.

A High Court white judge who arbitrarily decided to review the case quashed the conviction and ordered the release of the two Portuguese soldiers. Kaunda had been out of the country and when he returned he publicly demanded an explanation from the Chief Justice asking: 'Are the judges defending the interests of the people or foreign interests?' Having to respond publicly Skinner, under pressure from the other judges, all of them white at the time, chose the self-righteous route and emphasized the independence of the judiciary, even though, as his friend, I know that his views of the white judges were no different to Kaunda's, and that he was trying to ease some of the biggest racists out. All hell broke loose as a result of Skinner's response and after a couple of days of public demonstrations against him he had to leave the country in a hurry much to the regret of a remorseful Kenneth Kaunda. Kaunda's furious public reaction was uncharacteristic and was due to the political tensions caused by Kapwepwe's 'takeover' of UNIP's Central Committee. Most of the demonstrations against Skinner were spearheaded by senior Bemba politicians who, paradoxically, had been Skinner's comrades for years. The most prominent of the placards carried by the demonstrators read: 'THE ONLY GOOD WHITE MAN IS THE DEAD ONE'. Another anti-white placard read: 'A WHITE MAN WILL NEVER BE A ZAMBIAN'. They were both captured in a picture published on the front page of the *Times of Zambia* with Justin Chimba, my minister at the time and a personal friend of both myself and Skinner, standing next to them. I was furious and pointed out to Justin the next day that, like James, I am also a white Zambian. Chimba's smiling response was 'come on Andrew, those banners do not mean anything. They were just for the demonstration' – a comment typical of the lateral thinking of many people from the North. Indeed the banners did not mean a thing as I well knew and the passage of time has proved. But this does not mean that it was easy to bear.

1. President Kaunda – *Namukhonto* (The Warrior) by Remmie Sichalwe

Kapwepwe's tenure as vice president was not a happy one. Some would say that he alienated too many people and very few trusted him; his friends might say that everybody ganged up on him and both statements would have a grain of truth. In August 1969, he resigned from UNIP and consequently as vice president of the country, declaring that some of his colleagues never recognized his position and were abusive towards him. Incredibly he also claimed that because of his position the Bemba people came under persecution.

Kaunda took the opportunity to reorganize UNIP. He resigned as party president and took the position of secretary general of the party, announcing at the same time that as president of the country he would no longer be bound by the composition of UNIP's Central Committee in appointing his cabinet. He dismissed the entire Central Committee and appointed an interim one consisting of 11 members, including Kapwepwe who agreed to withdraw his resignation for a period of 12 months. The customary tribal balancing was relaxed and four Bemba were appointed to the new Central Committee, against three from the East with the other major provinces getting two or none. Kaunda's actions were intended to show that he still had the upper hand, but Kapwepwe's shadow was constantly looming in the background and Kaunda's behaviour became erratic and inconsistent, leaving the impression that he was acting under duress. The political tensions within UNIP inevitably spread to the country at large and brought to the surface grievances against the whites that had remained suppressed.

In the meantime, the whites lived in their own cocoon. As they did before independence, they never cared about how the blacks were doing or what they or their government thought. As far as they were concerned, business was good, they were doing very well and their attention was more focused towards Rhodesia and Ian Smith, whom most of them admired and some of them spied for.

The most prominent espionage incident involved the pilot of the Anglo American Corporation's HS125 jet plane and four other senior employees of the corporation, including Anglo's Industrial Relations officer at Rhokana Mine, who had just retired as Lieutenant-Colonel of the Zambian army. They had installed a tape recorder near the seat that Kaunda used on his frequent charter flights within the region. The incident was examined by a tribunal headed by Mr Justice Pickett, another High Court prominent racist judge who nevertheless confirmed that the group had been spying for the Rhodesian Intelligence. One of the more well-known foreign journalists who lived in Zambia at the time was Antony Martin, a stringer for the London *Financial Times* who later published the magazine *Central African Economist*. Below, I quote his take on the attitudes of the whites, as published in his book *Minding Their Own Business*:

> Most of the white business community stopped short, no doubt, of actual espionage for Rhodesia. But I can remember how much more shock and outrage was in expatriate circles at the detention of the men [the Anglo employees] than at the subsequent revelation of their activities. That in itself gives a good

idea of the underlying expatriate attitudes. Another variation of the same theme was the constant disparagement of Zambia's efforts to develop new transport routes. The deals with the Italians were attributed to corruption; it was freely predicted (against all reason) that the pipeline would turn out an expensive flop; while the formation of the Zam-Tan Road Services, the new company responsible for haulage on the Great North Road was greeted with endless jokes and bitter complaints … But the trouble was that expatriate businessmen, in general, knew little and cared less about what the government was thinking – one reason, no doubt, why the Mulungushi reforms caused so much surprise and dismay when they came.

(Antony Martin, *Minding Their Own Business,
Zambia's Struggle Against Western Control*)

The government's patience with the whites was completely exhausted and Kaunda decided to take action. In a speech to the UNIP National Council at the Mulungushi rock near Kabwe, where the Zambia African National Congress was founded in 1958 Kaunda delivered his famous Mulungushi reforms speech which left no doubt in anybody's mind as to who the country belonged to and who was in charge.

6. Fast Track for Zambian Business?

Kaunda opened his Mulungushi speech as follows:

First I want to talk about the Resident Expatriate Enterprise. Economic activity in Zambia is dominated by the European and Asian business communities whose members have been in the country for many years. Since Independence, my Ministers and I have been making repeated appeals to the members of these communities calling on them to identify with the nation and urging them to Zambianise their businesses as soon as possible. I am very pleased to say that many have responded to our pleas and have identified themselves with the country by taking up Zambian nationality and making sincere efforts to train Zambians to skilled and executive positions. There is, however, an appreciably large number of others who have chosen to remain outside the national family. They have kept only one foot in Zambia in order to take advantage of the economic boom created by the Transitional and First National Development Plans. The other foot they have kept outside Zambia, in South Africa, Britain, Europe, India, or wherever they come from, ready to jump when they have made enough money, or when they think that the country no longer suits them. I am afraid the period of grace is over. These people must now make a final choice. We do not want to keep them here against their will. We are a proud Nation. At the same time it is not fair that we should allow them to make off with the jam and the butter and leave crumbs of dry bread for our people.

He then proceeded to announce a number of economic measures intended to give a fillip to Zambian enterprise. He confined expatriate trading to major towns only, reserving the rest of the country for Zambian citizens. He also reserved for Zambians only all permits for the extraction of building minerals, such as sand, stone and clay for quarrying and brickmaking. Road transport permits for the operation of buses, taxis, and internal freight services were also reserved for Zambians or companies where Zambians owned 75 per cent of the shares. He extended the provisions of the exchange control regulations applicable to foreign investors to include local expatriates while he gave complete exemption

51

from the regulations to companies owned 51 per cent by Zambians in order to encourage settlers to take on Zambian partners. He set 1 January 1969 as the date of implementation of the reforms giving affected parties eight months to make alternative arrangements, which he emphasized, included obtaining Zambian citizenship by those eligible. (Amazingly, until then, nearly four years after independence, only some 600 whites and Indians had acquired Zambian passports.) He also decreed that all contracts for public works below K100,000 ($120,000) should be awarded to Zambian companies only and in hopeful anticipation of rapid Zambian business development he asked the Minister of Finance to investigate the establishment of a stock exchange, which never materialized during his administration.

The main thrust of the measures was to give space to African businessmen to develop away from competition from better financed and more experienced foreign-owned enterprises. The inspiration originated from the economy and social structure of the rural areas. One of the unintended advantages of the colonial administration was that it was not interested in the rural areas that had nothing to offer the colonizers. So it did not disturb their traditional way of life and as all politicians of that era had their roots in the rural areas, they knew that all the activities mentioned above were common in every village and rural town.

Though I had been born in Cyprus and only arrived in Northern Rhodesia in 1950, I was as familiar with the rural way of life as most of my friends because I had the good fortune to spend my early years, almost the entire decade of the 1950s, in the North Western Province of Zambia specifically with the Lunda and the Luvale people. They were a shining example of self-sufficiency and initiative even under the near primitive conditions of those days. They lived at subsistence level, though they did produce some cash crops such as ground nuts, and gathered honey and beeswax from the forest and fish from the Zambezi River and its many tributaries. They grew their own food: cassava, millet, rice, sorghum, bananas and other fruit, and raised pigs, sheep and goats. They kept what they needed for themselves and sold the surplus to the surrounding areas, using the Zambezi River for transportation. They exported cassava in dugout canoes to Barotseland, where they bought cattle for slaughter because due to the prevalence of tsetse fly they could not keep them for long in the districts. They exported the cash crops by road to the Copperbelt, some 400 miles away.

This trade contributed to the evolution of the necessary services within the various communities, the most important being trading and transport, albeit at basic levels: dugout canoes for river transport, second-hand army trucks that frequently broke down for the Copperbelt run, and small shops that stocked clothing and blankets, but also roofing sheets and glass panes and bolts and nuts and nails and a few pockets of cement from time to time. They faced competition from superior operations run by settlers but as the latter concentrated around the Bomas and the larger groups of villages the local entrepreneurs held their own. (A Boma was the capital of a district where the district commissioner and a handful of white officers lived surrounded by numerous African clerks, district messengers and other attendants.) I want to emphasize that, though mostly illiterate and with meagre resources, the rural people were able to take care of their own needs and their society generated and maintained the services it required. Making bricks to build a house (housing standards were very high for those years: Kimberley bricks and perfectly thatched roofs, some of the old houses are still serviceable) was usually a mutual assistance effort with family and friends lending a hand, but, in the larger villages, small contractors emerged. Bricklayers and carpenters who acquired their skills after serving in the Public Works Department or the various missions developed into small contractors capable of building schools and teachers' houses and shops and clinics. And from those small beginnings, some of them developed into larger transport and building contractors and shop owners. We felt that if that much had been achieved in the villages, a similar effort in the urban areas where people had better education and markets were bigger would achieve greater success, so we used it as a model for opening up the urban business sector to Zambians.

After announcing these measures Kaunda proceeded to castigate the exorbitant building costs in the country. By that time the construction industry had grown and there was adequate competition so he attributed the high prices to profiteering by the builders' hardware manufacturers and merchants and demanded that they sell 51 per cent of their shares to INDECO, so that the government would be able to exercise some control over their profit margins. (His comments were justified. The Intercontinental Hotel in Lusaka was under construction at the time and was supervised by the American company Bechtel that I had employed through INDECO as engineer managers. When they received the tenders for the aluminium windows and doors they advised that they could import them at half the price from the United States. I gave them the OK much to the disgust of the local white manufacturer and the expatriate community who accused me of not caring for the local industry, which I had been appointed to develop.) Kaunda also ordered control of some retail shop chains, the biggest of which was owned by the British group Bookers Ltd, which was quoted on the London Stock Exchange. Bookers, whose chairman at the time had been the leader of the British Liberal Party, must have decided to disengage from Africa and the third world. It had already sold its chain of shops in Guyana to the government and after Zambia it also sold its shops in

Malawi to the governing Malawi Congress Party. It was their offer that made Kaunda include retail chains in the Mulungushi reforms, expecting them to prop up the emerging Zambian traders.

The measures relating to the 51 per cent control of what in fact was an extremely small number of companies were immediately declared Marxist, but as I was personally involved in their inception and implementation I can vouch that at that time they were motivated by nothing else but a desire to kick-start Zambian participation in business, as the new licensing regulations which formed the bulk of the measures testify. With this in mind I have always classified them as economic nationalism and in that sense they proved quite successful despite the rearguard action against them and their exploitation by the politicians in later years.

INDECO negotiated the various 51 per cent acquisitions and paid in full out of self-generated profits without them becoming a burden on the national budget. My biggest concern was the lack of Zambian management resources in INDECO and the country at large, and we made sure in the agreements that we would not lose the management expertise of the businesses we acquired until we trained Zambians, a task which, I knew, could not be realized for some years. Being the majority shareholders we took control of the company boards and appointed the chairmen, but we left it to the minority to recommend suitable candidates for managing directors who we vetted thoroughly before appointing. The formula worked well and we received many praises in international business circles and publications, particularly the London *Financial Times*.

The whites who lived in wilful ignorance of what was going on in the African community and had no inkling of the tensions within UNIP and the government greeted the Mulungushi reforms with a mixture of resignation and 'I told you so'. They either did not read Kaunda's speech or ignored the main thrust of the measures, which, as I said, was to open a fast lane for the development of Zambian business. And as in Southern Africa nationalism had always been synonymous with communism they focused on the 51 per cent acquisitions, which they declared as the Marxism they had always anticipated.

There was no justification for this conclusion, as Antony Martin explains:

> The best way of looking at the Mulungushi 'revolution' we are now in a position to conclude is to see it as a marriage of convenience between the philosophical and political thinking of Kenneth Kaunda on the one hand and the business sense of the best of his advisers on the other. Regarded in the abstract as a socialist blueprint it can easily be criticised as too mild and too eclectic ... Mulungushi was then the product of a mixture of influences: Kaunda's political thinking, itself moulded by events like UDI and the reappraisal of relations with the

West and the role of Expatriate business, which it induced; a growing awareness that it would be futile for Zambia to rely primarily on foreign investment for its development; the realization that the internal political situation with its mutually reinforcing syndrome of tribalism and frustrated expectations, needed a striking new Presidential initiative. If set beside Arusha [Tanzania's socialist reforms announced by President Nyerere the previous year] it can be seen more as a reaction to a complicated and tense situation, much less as a product of coherent thinking in pursuit of a well-defined goal.

(Minding Their Own Business)

I don't think that the basis for the Mulungushi reforms should be considered in the context of any political ideology. And their success or failure should be viewed in terms of the long-term transformation of the economy they engendered. As Martin rightly perceived, the reforms were dictated by the circumstances of the time: political independence versus the continuing foreign domination of the economy and the hard line approach of foreign and settler business, which held tight to its advantages and showed no inclination of opening up to local advancement, while at the same time it openly idolized Ian Smith and his regime in Rhodesia.

Similar circumstances prevailed in most African countries at the time, without the UDI ingredient of course, from the Congo to Nigeria, to Ghana, to Liberia, to Sierra Leone and nearer home, Tanzania, Kenya and Uganda. Most newly independent countries took measures to open their business sector to greater local participation. Individual reforms were naturally tailored around local thinking and customs but they all had a common aim: greater local participation in business. President Nyerere's reforms, for example, were based on Ujumaa, the spirit of cooperation that prevailed within villages or extended families, which was not dissimilar to the self-help and cooperation that prevailed in Zambian villages. As Nigerians already had a substantial presence in the business sector, and a Nigerian Stock Exchange was functioning efficiently, the Nigerian reforms were geared towards greater involvement of Nigerian nationals in management, as opposed to controlling State interest in existing businesses. In countries where the local business was still at an embryonic state, like in Zambia, the parastatal sector provided support and augmented indigenization.

The most important element of the reforms was the unambiguous message they conveyed: that the colonial style dominance of the business sector was coming to an end. Despite their initial hostile reaction the entrenched settler and foreign-owned business recognized that it had to come to terms with the new reality. And over the years the business sector gradually changed to the substantial Zambian participation that prevails now, with the change having been achieved without fuss, or violence.

As we shall see in between we had many ups and downs, for example: economic problems experienced as a result of the Rhodesian civil war and the tightening of the sanctions against Rhodesia and South Africa; the collapse of the world commodity markets resulting from the oil price explosion and the consequent collapse of the price of copper; the mindless self-serving policies of UNIP after its mutation into the One Party dictatorship, which brought about the paralysis and stagnation of the 1980s; Chiluba's blind assault on all Kaunda's achievements without regard to their usefulness to the nation. But, the above notwithstanding, we can boast that the transition was achieved painlessly and without major dislocations to the economy, in contrast to what happened later in Zimbabwe. There, Mugabe was hailed by the Rhodesians and the West as a wise leader, because he followed the Lancaster House agreements to the letter, so much so that he even allowed the Rhodesians to have their own election in 1985, voting on a 'whites only' voters' roll five years after independence (and they all voted for Ian Smith). The unfortunate result of Mugabe's early tolerance was the violent nature of the change when it inevitably came about.

Naturally, not everybody agrees with this point of view. In a chapter titled '"The Devil you Know": The impact of the Mulungushi reforms on the retail trade in rural Zambia, with special reference to Susman Brothers and Wulfsohn, 1968–80', contained in a recently published book *One Zambia, Many Histories* the author, Hugh Macmillan, comes to the conclusion that the 'Mulungushi Economic Reforms had disastrous results for most Zambians – especially those in rural areas.'

This, of course, was and probably still is the Rhodesian settler point of view, though the subject of the Mulungushi reforms hardly ever comes up these days as the country has moved on in the towns and in the villages. The author was obviously influenced in his assessment by his own background, but more so by two books he had written: *Zion in Africa: The Jews of Zambia* and *An African Trading Empire: The Story of Susman Brothers and Wulfsohn 1901–2005*, particularly the latter. The Susman Brothers and Wulfsohn (SBW) were very early settlers and their 'Empire' and their clans that followed became very strong supporters of the Federation and its Prime Minster Roy Welensky. Maurice Rabb, SBW Zambian CEO for many years, served as a United Federal Party Member of the Northern Rhodesia Legislative Council. Their preferred solution, like that of most whites, was that independence should never have come about and the Federation should have continued. (Maurice Gersh, a close associate of SBW and mayor of Kitwe, was another ardent supporter of the United Federal

Party and became an enthusiastic proponent of a 'New Federation' scheme that would consist of Southern Rhodesia, Barotseland, the Copperbelt and Katanga in exchange for the independence of the rest of Northern Rhodesia and Nyasaland; I explain Roy Welensky's attempts to promote this scheme later, in Chapter 23.) And, once independence came, such people believed that African leaders should 'have the sense' not to interfere with the status quo, particularly the business sector, hence the title of Macmillan's paper: 'The devil you know.'

After the Mulungushi reforms Susman Brothers and Wulfsohn offered INDECO a 51 per cent share in their chain of retail shops in rural areas, including those in Barotseland and the North Western Province even though they were not obliged to do so. They obviously considered this as the better option in their long-term interest. They could have taken a different course if they wanted to, such as selling individual shops or groups of shops to their Zambian managers and helping them with their operations until they got repaid, or having members of their clan born in Zambia acquire Zambian citizenship, which they were entitled to do. They did not want to do the latter and as far as I know most members of the SBW clans emigrated to South Africa and England.

Macmillan exaggerates the dislocation of trade in the rural areas, obviously influenced by the views of SBW. (In fact the major dislocation, which was inevitable, in view of the radical changes in the trade licensing system that the Mulungushi reforms brought about, lasted for only a couple of years, much shorter than we had anticipated.) And in support of his argument he gives as an example an encounter he had in 1984 (sixteen years after the reforms) in Mutomena in Barotseland, with 'a man with an ox drawn sledge (scotch cart?) who, he says, was making a six-day trek to Sioma in the hope of buying maize meal'. (He was probably a local shopkeeper who was doing a regular trip to Sioma to buy supplies for his shop; he would have only needed a bicycle if he just intended to buy mealie meal for the family.) But Macmillan also refers to government-owned empty shops, a common phenomenon in the mid-eighties, in rural areas as well as towns. Many factors were responsible for that condition: the oil price, the collapse of the price of copper, the sanctions against South Africa, after many years of sanctions against Rhodesia and last but not least, the paralysis and stagnation the 'One Party' system had brought about. But in typical settler fashion Macmillan laments the good old days through the mouth of an old teacher as follows:

An old and wise teacher at Sipuma on the Angolan border road assured me that things had not always been as bad as this. In a mini-lecture on post-colonial economic decline and rural underdevelopment he recalled the days of the Witwatersrand Native Labour Association, which had made the road to facilitate the recruitment of labour for the South African gold mines and of Susman Brothers and Wulfsohn which had run well stocked stores in remote places … I had myself encountered a part of the Susman Brothers & Wulfsohn trading network when as a seventeen-year old youth, I visited Balovale, now Zambezi, in the North Western Province in 1962–3. I was then impressed, as other visitors were by A.F. Serrano's remarkably well-stocked shop.

The comment 'Post-colonial economic decline and rural underdevelopment' was of course the received wisdom for a couple of decades after independence, not only in relation to Zambia, but in relation to all African countries. But, as years went by, most people stopped talking about the mythical development of blacks during the Federation of Rhodesia and Nyasaland, recognizing at last that such development was not part of the Federal agenda. And as a person who spent the best part of the fifties in the North Western Province and experienced first-hand the total economic neglect and complete absence of rural development I can vouch that at independence we did not inherit rural development to undermine. The reader will have seen in these pages and will see later in this book (or in much greater detail in my book *Africa: Another Side of the Coin*) that in the 1950s the North Western Province, an area of 50,000 square miles and some 150,000 inhabitants, had no secondary schools and only two standard VI (elementary) schools, both run by missionaries: one at Chitokoloki Mission near Balovale in the west of the province, and one at Mutanda Mission near Solwezi in the east, some 350 miles apart. It did have a third one at Sakeji in Mwinilunga district (some 200 miles north-west of Mutanda) but that was for white missionary children only. There were standard IV schools in the capital of each of the five districts and a few standard II schools in some major villages. By contrast 'the post-colonial underdevelopment' that Macmillan is so contemptuous of has brought about, according to the 2010 Educational Statistical Bulletin, 748 schools of which 58 are secondary. There was only one government hospital in the province at Balovale; there were three others, at Chitokoloki near Balovale, Mukinge Hill in Kasempa, and Kallene Hill north of Mwinilunga all run by missionaries. And for trunk roads there were only bush tracks and, as a result, only three-ton trucks were allowed in the province. And the economy was subsistence agriculture as it had been for generations, augmented by occasional remittances from miners and other town dwellers.

But Macmillan also sings the praises of the Witwatersrand Native Labour Association (WENELA), which according to his old and wise informant 'had made roads to facilitate the recruitment of labour for the South African gold mines'. (It had to; the provincial administration never seemed to have funds for district roads. Even the main roads were barely passable in the rainy season, maintained by gangs of workers using hoes, and shovels.) But we should not feel nostalgic of WENELA. It did not contribute to the development of the areas it recruited in. It denuded the villages of Barotseland and the North Western Province of their men and dislocated village societies and reduced food production, sending unsuspecting peasants to distant South African mines to work for a pittance and live in the notorious mine hostels. Yet Macmillan could not resist lamenting 'the post-colonial economic decline and rural underdevelopment' through the mouth of the old Zambian, who was probably passing on received wisdom that he knew whites liked to hear, while deep down he did not believe a word of it, a common practice during colonial times.

As regards Antonio Serrano's 'remarkably well stocked shop' I can tell him that he was in fact 'impressed' with the SBW 'European' shop in Balovale, where blacks were not allowed. They could be served in the other five shops down the road: three belonging to SBW, one to Norton & Co and one to North Western Trading later named Mwaiseni, which I had built. The shop that impressed him catered for the members of the provincial administration and other colonial officers of Balovale and the white missionaries in the district, as well as Portuguese customers from the Angolan side of the border (it was also used by the provincial administration for special, 'whites only', events: I attended a black tie party there, on the occasion of the 1958 Balovale Agricultural show).

Macmillan goes on to criticize an INDECO instruction that rural shops with sales of less than £5,000 per month should be disposed of or close down. He attributes the decision to INDECO's inability to run small shops profitably, arguing that SBW were able to do so and coming to the conclusion that it was the incompetence of the other INDECO shop-chains that influenced the decision. Nobody would dispute SBW's superior competence in this field – it had been running rural shops in those areas for half a century before independence – but the instruction had nothing to do with their profitability. INDECO concluded that shops with small turnovers operated in small villages where local people could emerge to provide service, which was in line with the spirit of the reforms.

And one general comment about the book *One Zambia, Many Histories: Towards a History of Post-colonial Zambia* (Gewald, Hinfelaar and Macola (eds)). It contains twelve papers on politics, religion, the economy, the labour movement, the women's lobby, and the civil society, written by eight foreign and four Zambian academics. The Zambian academics have a clear understanding and convey an unadulterated picture of what they are writing about, while most of the foreigners, like Macmillan, stretch facts to suit their arguments in order to prove their predetermined conclusions.

***

Kaunda did not mention the Mining Companies in the Mulungushi speech, except to express his disappointment at the lack of mining development and highlight that their dividends amounted to as much as 80 per cent of their profits. But I am sure the two mining companies, the Anglo American Corporation and the Rhodesian, conveniently converted to Roan Selection Trust after independence, did not sleep easy after the Mulungushi announcements. They would find out what was in store for them soon enough.

7. CONTROL OF THE MINES

The mineral royalties had been a bone of contention in Zambia ever since I remember. Under the Lochner agreement the British South Africa Company had acquired those rights in perpetuity, but even Roy Welensky considered it unacceptable and managed to clinch a deal under which they would terminate at the end of 1986. The first African government of Northern Rhodesia, after it came to power in 1962, made a number of attempts to buy the mineral rights from the British South Africa Company. The first attempt was made in 1963 and the company demanded £35 million but would not accept Northern Rhodesia government bonds, without the guarantee of the British government, which luckily the British government refused to give. A second attempt to buy the mineral rights was made in September 1964. Arthur Wina, by that time Minister of Finance, flew to London and held meetings with the company and the British government. This time the British South Africa Company dropped its demand to £18 million. Arthur offered £2 million, and asked the British government to make up the balance. But Sir Alec Douglas-Home, the British prime minister of the time, refused and again the talks ended in deadlock. The matter was eventually resolved in Lusaka, a few hours before independence. By then Britain had a new government under the Labour Party. Antony Martin describes the event:

> The scene was thus set for a tense little backstage drama played out in Northern Rhodesia's dying hours. The participants included Zambian ministers and officials, the new British Commonwealth Secretary, Mr. Arthur Bottomley, the outgoing Governor of Northern Rhodesia, Sir Evelyn Hone, the elderly President of the British South African Company, Mr. Paul Emrys-Evans, and the chairman of Anglo American, Mr. Harry Oppenheimer, who was also a director of the B.S.A. Company of which Anglo was the biggest single shareholder. Presented, at a garden party at Government House on Northern Rhodesia's last day, with a final take-it-or-leave-it offer of £2 million from Zambia plus another two from Britain, Emrys-Evans was reduced to the humiliating position of having to beg for a guarantee that the whole amount

61

would be free of tax. None was forthcoming. Left to himself, Emrys-Evans gave in and accepted the terms behind a tea tent.

(Minding Their Own Business)

After independence, the two mining companies made a big fuss over the royalties. They declared that they were an obstacle to further mining development because they were levied on the value of copper produced, which added to production costs and made the Zambian copper uncompetitive. The government countered with the simple logical argument that the formula was the same as that used by the British South Africa Company, which they paid for many decades without demur. But the mines did not mind paying the mineral royalties to the British South Africa Company, because most of the money they paid would go back to their pockets as a result of the interlocking shareholdings between them. As at independence the BSA mineral royalties were ceded to the government of Zambia, that benefit was lost and the royalties became a real cost.

As I said earlier, in his Mulungushi speech Kaunda made no hint that he was contemplating any action towards the mining companies, even though the government was fed up with them and their attachment to the European Mineworkers Union, a very determined opponent of its Zambianization and training initiatives. By that time the Ministries of Trade and Industry and the Ministry of Mines were amalgamated into the Ministry of Trade, Industry and Mines and I was appointed permanent secretary with a mandate to prepare new legislation in order to attract new mining investment and also find a solution to the 'mineral royalties' problem. And as a 'just in case' measure the government proceeded with a referendum to remove Clause 18 of the Independence Constitution, which provided that any amendments should be approved by a referendum where at least 51 per cent of the total number of voters on the roll (as distinct from votes cast) voted in favour. The referendum was held on 17 June 1969 and the country (with the notable exception of Barotseland) dutifully voted for its removal – no mean achievement bearing in mind the '51 per cent of the roll' hurdle. Its removal gave parliament the right to change the constitution by a two-thirds majority, a privilege which, unfortunately, has been abused, repeatedly, since. And its significance was that the government could from then on change the mineral rights arrangements through an act of parliament.

We had finished drafting the new Mining Development Act, which was intended to become the centrepiece of Kaunda's speech to the UNIP National Council on 9 August 1969 (a Monday) at Matero. On the subject of royalties, I had settled on a new mineral tax of 51 per cent of profits, to replace both the royalties and the export tax I mentioned earlier. It changed the old formula from a percentage of the value of copper produced to a profit-related formula that the mining companies had been crying for. And I thought it would sound like the 51 per cent acquisitions of Mulungushi, which by then had become Kaunda's signature tune. But two days before the expected announcement, on Saturday afternoon, Kaunda called me to State House. 'You know, Andrew, we have to take 51 per cent of the mines,' he said. He argued that as the new Act included a provision that gave the government an option to subscribe up to 51 per cent of the capital of every new project, we could not avoid doing the same for the existing mines. The argument was logical, but we were both aware that such a measure could enrage the two major international companies, which owned the Zambian mines. We spent some time weighing the pros and cons, particularly the reaction of the Anglo American Corporation, one of the world's biggest mining companies at the time and a South African one at that. Could we pull it off? In the end we decided to risk it. And it worked. As with the Mulungushi acquisitions, INDECO was mandated to handle the takeover. For the negotiations Kaunda appointed a committee of three under my chairmanship, the other two being the Attorney General, Pat Chuula and the Permanent Secretary of the Ministry of Finance, Emmanuel Kasonde.

Kaunda's speech covered every aspect of government activity and lasted some four hours. It was jubilantly received by the delegates, who were happy to go home after it finished without presenting the censure motion against Kapwepwe that had been agreed by most delegates from seven of the eight provinces of the country. But this, as I said earlier, did not stop Kapwepwe's slide towards the exit.

The London market took the Zambian measures in its stride. The two companies' shares lost some 25 per cent of their value but the *Financial Times* editorial the next day (10 August 1969) was very sanguine and amazingly well informed. It said:

President Kaunda's announcement that the Zambian Government is to take 51 per cent interest in the copper companies has some resemblance to the devaluation of the franc: it is not the event itself that has taken everyone by surprise, but its timing. The timing may very well have been influenced by the President's wish to outmanoeuvre the extremists in his own party; his recent brush with the judiciary suggested that he is acting at present under heavy political pressure. But it has been expected since independence that in Zambia, as in other African countries, the Government would eventually wish to take control of the country's main economic resources. The copper companies, which account for 95 per cent of its export income and 56 per cent of the government's revenue, were plainly high up on the list and their share prices have long discounted the probable future.

Our early meetings with the mining groups were very tough and we worried that the predictions of the white community that 'we had bitten off more than we could chew' might prove right after all. The price tags bandied about were exorbitant and the threats that the white miners were ready to resign en masse worrisome. I decided to probe the latter and, together with Emmanuel Kasonde, we set up meetings with the white miners in each Copperbelt town. The atmosphere in those meetings was no different to what I had experienced during the 1962 election campaign, when I was a UNIP candidate for the Kabombo constituency that included Chingola and Bancroft (now Chililabombwe). The white miners' rhetoric was still the same: the country was no longer suitable for bringing up their children whose career prospects were now limited because they lost the automatic right to apprenticeship on the mines; they were worried about their own safety underground because of the now inevitable promotion of black miners to positions for which they were unqualified as well as the safety of their families when they were on shift. One miner complained that he felt unwanted in the country and gave as example the treatment he was receiving at the post office and banks. He stopped short of asking that blacks should not enter banking halls, or that he should have the right to jump the queue like the good old days; Emmanuel and I grinned in despair.

When they realized that we were not intimidated by their antics, the two mining groups, Anglo American Corporation and American Metal Climax, settled down to sensible businesslike negotiations and unbelievably we had a deal by 18 October 1969. The white miners did not resign en masse, and the safety of the mines was not compromised by our Zambianization policies. The safety record of the mining industry remained exemplary, except for the Mufulira disaster, which was due not to mistakes by the miners but to bad mining methods employed by the previous owners who many years before had decided to cut corners in order to increase profitability.

The deal was approved by cabinet before the end of October and we were able to announce it officially. The press release said:

H.E. the President announced today that the Cabinet has ratified the agreements reached between the Government negotiating team and representatives of the mining companies. The agreements will come into effect on the 1 January 1970.

H.E. disclosed that the combined book value of the mining assets of RST and Anglo American Corporation will be calculated as at 31 December 1969 and is expected to be approximately 410 million Kwacha. The government's share of 51 per cent will therefore be approximately 209 million, representing 84 million for RST and 125 million for AAC and will be held through INDECO.

INDECO will issue Bonds guaranteed by the government and bearing interest at 6 per cent. These will be repaid in semi-annual installments over eight years in the case of RST and twelve years in the case of AAC. The payment each year to RST will be approximately 13.5 million Kwacha and 14.5 million for AAC. The agreements include a special provision whereby payments can be accelerated by paying two thirds of the dividends received from each group if this sum exceeds the fixed annual payments. If prices of copper remain as high as they have been during the last three years, payments should be achieved much earlier.

H.E. disclosed that the mining groups will be reorganized so that Nchanga, Rhokana and Bancroft mines, together with the Rhokana refinery will form one unit to be named Nchanga Consolidated Copper Mines Ltd. while Mufulira, Luanshya, Chibuluma, Chambishi and Kalengwa mines together with the Ndola Copper Refinery will form a second unit to be named Roan Consolidated Copper Mines Ltd.

The existing mining groups have been given management and sales contracts at a fee of 1.5 per cent of the gross turnover plus 2 per cent of the profits. H.E. reiterated the assurances given in his speech at Matero that exchange control regulations permitting remittance of only 50 per cent of the profits will now fall away for the mining companies. He also gave an assurance that taxation of the mining industry in Zambia will not exceed the 73 per cent which will arise out of a combination of the proposed mineral tax and present income tax. The Zambian taxes are already high and any increase would discourage further mining development.

H.E. expressed thanks to the negotiating teams and said he was pleased with the terms of the agreement. He said it was a favourable deal for Zambia, yet one that was fair to the mining groups. He said: 'We have succeeded in retaining the exclusive services of two of the leading mining groups in the world and I am confident that as a result the Zambian mines will remain as always in the forefront of world mining.'

On the question of labour relations the President reaffirmed that the takeover in no way meant that the expatriate workers were any less welcome or needed. He reiterated the assurances he gave in September that the pension fund would be externalized and that he would issue instructions for this to be quickly completed. He reminded Zambian workers that the Nation's share of the profits of the mining industry is 87 Kwacha for every 100 Kwacha profit and appealed to them to work hard and increase production in the interest of the Nation.

(More extensive details of the deal can be found in the full cabinet memorandum in Appendix II.)

The deal was over and the agreements were now in the hands of the lawyers who would take another six months to complete them. INDECO had the task of preparing to monitor the year end takeover accounts of the mines and we had to augment our accounting staff in a hurry. And it was not just accountants we needed. We needed a completely new structure in order to supervise the mining investment that was worth many times more than the industrial side of INDECO.

8.   THE POLITICIANS TAKE OVER

Not unlike Valentine Musakanya over the civil service I, naively, thought that I could insulate government enterprise from direct political control. After the takeover of the mines I could feel many avaricious eyes focusing on the enterprise and the possibilities it offered for political advancement and personal enrichment. I decided therefore to create a structure that would accommodate overall but indirect political control of the parastatal group and a forum where politicians, trade unionists, Zambian businessmen, and academics would receive frequent reports on operations and progress, and give guidance without direct involvement in the management of the individual businesses. The President would select such people to sit on the board of a holding company named the Zambian Industrial and Mining Corporation (ZIMCO). Below ZIMCO there would be its two subsidiaries: INDECO holding the industrial investments and MINDECO the mining ones. (The establishment of MINDECO gave rise to a new joke in the white community: the only thing left now is for Kaunda to take control of the shebeens and the bars and put them under a new affiliate to be named SINDECO.) The President would be chairman of the board of ZIMCO and its managing director would be a businessman (initially me) guiding the operations as chairman of its two subsidiaries. As the first managing directors of INDECO and MINDECO, I had chosen two prominent civil servants: Andrew Kashita and Dominic Mulaisho who, I thought, apart from being highly educated were sophisticated and cosmopolitan.

We were ready to settle down as a team and begin setting up the detailed structure to run this colossal and complex organization when, in January 1970, I was shunted by the new secretary general in charge of the civil service, to the Ministry of Finance, as permanent secretary. My new appointment was in addition to my ZIMCO responsibilities. The Ministry of Finance is the citadel of the civil service but I was primarily a businessman who had agreed to serve in the government in order to promote Zambian enterprise; I did not want anybody to get the idea that I had now settled for a career in the civil service and could be sent from pillar to post at anybody's whim. I nevertheless accepted the appointment and coped with all my responsibilities. I had to work a 70-hour week and the only time I managed to spare for the family was Sunday afternoons.

In the meantime the political climate started turning ugly. The Kapwepwe issue remained unresolved causing a great deal of uncertainty and instability. Because of the open rift between him and Kaunda, servility and sycophancy started creeping in, everybody displaying excessive loyalty to the chief, lest he be accused of supporting his rival. Everybody would rush to the airport to see him off whenever he set off on one of his frequent trips and receive him when he came back. But with all my responsibilities I had little time to spare and resented the practice. It was not just the hundreds of man hours lost that annoyed me. The bluff camaraderie, the backslapping, the hugging and the 'cordial' handshakes of people who were ready to plunge daggers in each other's back sickened me. Besides, Kaunda and I started developing major philosophical differences on the interpretation of the economic reforms. In order to draw to his side the trade unions, then a notoriously Bemba dominated body, Kaunda started making statements along the lines of the 'ZIMCO group was a passing phase of state capitalism that will lead to workers' participation'. I was furious and I sent him a long letter on the subject, the salient points of which read:

> To refer to the present situation as State Capitalism implies to my mind, and I am sure to that of many others, that greater worker participation will bring greater economic rewards. It encourages workers to think of themselves as an exploited group and though you have stated that you expect the transition to last a long time, I am afraid that its mere mention will generate forces that will accelerate it … In Zambia the workers, far from being oppressed, are already an elite and to increase their power and hence their economic rewards is to make them more of an elite. In addition, they are few while the peasants form the greatest part of our society and in comparison to the workers they are very poorly rewarded … In Zambia, urban workers can raise wages and yet resist paying more for their food. This is done not because they are consumers but because they are voters. There is a limit to the extent that the State can redress the balance since urban workers, as well as being strong economically, are strong politically. For these reasons we must be very careful about introducing any system which might enhance the power of the urban workers …
>
> In my view the only substantial abuse of trust by the State at the present time is the extensive patronage system in Zambia. Attached is a cutting from a recent *Zambia Mail* which attempts to put a veneer of respectability over the recent appointment of five UNIP members to jobs in INDECO … The

most distasteful part of my work consists of finding jobs and loans for people, not necessarily because they have any special claim, but because they are Party faithful ... During your absence I have been besieged as much as ever by men with letters of introduction from various people. Attached are copies of letters from the Vice President. They are all introducing people from the Northern Province and they are merely examples of what I received from him and other ministers. To give a man a loan from government or INDECO funds on the basis of his party or tribal affiliation, regardless of whether there is a possibility that it will be repaid, is a form of exploitation, which merits the name 'State Capitalism'.

In composing the above letter, I came to realize that the successful implementation of the reforms had unleashed forces for control of the state enterprise that I would not be able to handle and I did not want to be part of. So I became absolutely firm in my conviction that it was time to move on. I did not want to depart in acrimony like Valentine Musakanya and others of my Zambian friends. Worse still I did not want a James Skinner experience. For me Zambia was more than UNIP, its government or any of its politicians. It was the land, and its people with whom I had become an inseparable part. I delivered the letter to him personally along with my letter of resignation. It was also dated 1 June 1970, exactly five years after I joined. I asked to be released at any time that suited him before 1 December 1970. I explained that I had no plans for an alternative career; that I would probably set up as a consultant and would be glad to take ad hoc assignments from him. He did try to make me change my mind, to the extent that he sent me and Danae on a ZIMCO-paid holiday, but that did not change me. In the event, I left on 31 January, 1971.

And the assault on state enterprise began in earnest. Within six months of my departure Ackson Soko, the Minister of Commerce, became chairman of INDECO and Humphrey Mulemba, the more ambitious Minister of Mines took a complete stranglehold over the mining industry, becoming not only chairman of MINDECO but also chairman of each of its two mining subsidiaries, Nchanga and Roan. I could not resist a last attempt to put things right and I wrote to Kaunda stressing the dangers of ministers involved in both policy formulation and company operations. He should separate the two and make his ministers concentrate on policy and allow the companies freedom to organize their operations in a businesslike manner, I said. I received no reply. I realized that I was completely out of touch, but I did not suspect at the time the underhand plan being hatched by Tiny Rowland, the wheeling and dealing CEO of Lonrho (London Rhodesia Mining Company), a London quoted

African conglomerate, the Chairman of UNIP's Committee for the Economy and Finance, who was at the same time Minister of Mines and supremo of the mining industry and some other senior government functionaries, to make a killing out of the ZIMCO bonds. I'll cover this later. In the meantime the political pot was boiling.

9.   Sir Arthur Benson's Ghost

After a long period of political uncertainty, during which senior ministers traded accusations of tribalism, embezzlement and even rape, Kapwepwe was ready to walk into the abyss and deliver himself to his enemies. And Kaunda did not lift a finger to prevent it. Kapwepwe resigned from UNIP on 22 August 1971 and formed the United Progressive Party (UPP). At his press conference, where he announced UPP's formation, he said:

> Most of us leaders have turned into opportunists and we have lost the love of the people and political direction. We have fallen victims of flattery to the imperialists South of us and to the West. We no longer mind what happens to the people of Zambia or to their children's future. We have lost our national objectives, we have lost the revolution, we have killed the party UNIP. It may be there in name but it has no spirit, it has no democratic principles, it stands empty and stagnant.

Many senior Bemba ministers and MPs followed Kapwepwe to the UPP and Kaunda was swift in resorting to the Public Security Regulations, a remnant of the colonial legislation that gave the governor of Northern Rhodesia draconian powers. Within a week he detained three prominent members of UPP including the only two from the Eastern Province, who gave it a national, as opposed to a Bemba, character. And on 30 September 1971 he detained 115 others including Justin Chimba, my former minister. In the by-elections that followed on 23 November (under the Zambian Constitution when an MP crosses the floor he has to re-contest his seat) all UPP candidates, with the exception of Kapwepwe, lost. Kapwepwe won his Mufulira West seat, but he was nevertheless arrested when Kaunda resorted to the Public Security Regulations for the third time on 12 February 1972. In addition to Kapwepwe he arrested 122 others bringing the total UPP detainees to 238. Sadly, Kaunda's reasons for those arrests did not contain anything more concrete against Kapwepwe than Sir Arthur Benson's did when he arrested Kaunda, Kapwepwe and the other Zambia African National Congress (ZANC) leaders on 12 March 1959. I quote below from both addresses to the country for the reader to judge:

Governor Benson, 12 March 1959:

> Twice within the last fortnight Government statements have warned everybody in the country that any interference whatsoever with the rights of the voters will not be tolerated. In spite of this certain leaders of the Zambia organisation [Benson's name for ZANC – the country was still Northern Rhodesia] have deliberately continued their plan, by spreading uncertainty and fear, to prevent African voters from exercising their newly won right. This they have done openly in public; but worse – far worse – is what they have done privately in the villages and in the towns, at night. There they have instituted a reign of terror. They have placed men in fear of their lives; they have threatened death and mutilation to their wives and children. They have invoked witchcraft and other unmentionable cursing in order to deter their fellow Africans from voting. And because these things take place in private and at night, with no witnesses, they are desperately difficult to deal with in law. This is on all fours with what happened to millions of law abiding Americans when the comparatively few Chicago racketeers established their protection rackets, corrupted local governments, ruled by the gun, the sap, the knuckle duster, the bicycle chain and went on to establish the organization of killers which is known as 'Murder Incorporated'.

Kenneth Kaunda, 4 February 1972:

> What we have witnessed are the most outrageous actions aimed at the destruction of life and property without regard to the sufferings of innocent and law-abiding citizens. The record of the United Progressive Party since its birth has been a catalogue of misguided wild statements and actions typical of hooligans and people without sense of direction. They have engaged in bombing houses and buildings; they have beaten innocent people, stoned cars and threatened people's lives, particularly national leaders and any others who have openly disagreed with them. Loyal supporters of the ruling Party have been attacked. Leaders of UPP have sought, in a very dangerous manner but in vain, to isolate one section of our community in the Northern Province from the rest of the society … In their frustration, the UPP elements have time and again mounted the most vicious campaign of slander and other forms of black propaganda to malign government and individual leaders in society, to undermine the confidence of the masses in their government and hence cause disaffection amongst them. They have engaged in the most shameless manufacture of big lies reminiscent of Hitler.

Sir Arthur Benson, the godfather of the Public Security Regulations, bragged that he designed them in order to 'nip in the bud, any plan or conspiracy, which if left to develop might endanger the public peace …' And when could he impose them? According to Sir Arthur: 'if the Governor is satisfied that any action has been taken or is immediately threatened, which, if continued, would empower him to declare a state of emergency; or which, in his view, will probably lead to such a situation …' In other words: capriciously, on a hunch, or for political expediency, regardless of whether he had compelling reasons or not. And as the governor or the Zambian presidents who followed him never had convincing evidence to present to the country in order to justify their actions, they resorted to absurd generalities and analogies, like: 'They have engaged in bombing houses and buildings; they have beaten innocent people, stoned cars and threatened people's lives' and 'mounted the most vicious campaign of slander and other forms of black propaganda' and 'Hitler' (Kaunda) or 'They have placed men in fear of their lives; they have threatened death and mutilation to their wives and children. They have invoked witchcraft and other unmentionable cursing' and 'Murder Incorporated' (Benson).

These regulations had horrified me when Governor Benson first used them in 1959. And I brought this matter up with Kaunda on 15 December 1962, the day the first African government was sworn in, when I was driving him from Ndola to Kitwe for his first live appearance on television, the very day he was appointed Minister of Local Government and Leader of the 'Unofficials' (as distinct from British civil servants appointed by the governor by virtue of their position) in the Northern Rhodesia Legislative Council. I urged him to announce his intention of an early repeal of the Public Security Regulations. To my astonishment he responded: 'No Andrew, if these regulations are good enough for the British they are good enough for us.' Unfortunately he left them on the statute book and used them repeatedly during his administration. And, decades later, in 1998, his successor Chiluba would use them to incarcerate him for six months.

And 50 years later on 6 December 2012 Michael Sata, the fifth president, made a statement that the act which he thought was a bad law when in opposition is in fact good. 'When you are in government that is when you realise that there will be no government when there is no sanity in society. There will be no government when there is no order in society. And you have to assist the weaker people …' This incensed the civil society and the Law Association of Zambia, which set out to declare the Act unconstitutional, a subject that I shall cover later.

With the formation of the UPP, Kapwepwe, unwittingly, played straight into the hands of his enemies to the detriment of the nation. In UNIP he was a powerful and influential figure, held in awe because of his history in the independence movement, and his grass root support amongst the Bemba people. Out of UNIP, as head of the UPP he would inevitably end up as the leader of a regional grouping, not unlike Harry Nkumbula of the ANC who ended up as just the leader of the Tonga-Ila people in the Southern Province. But Kaunda was hurt and overreacted, resorting to unseemly and demeaning persecution. If he had kept his cool, and let Kapwepwe find his own way, he would have retained the moral high ground and earned appreciation and respect from many people in the Northern Province, and the Bemba middle class; and reconciliation would have been easier. But the persecution made the Bemba close ranks and Kaunda's support amongst them plummeted. The UNIP grandees from other parts of Zambia with constituencies on the Copperbelt, and other urban areas with large numbers of Bemba voters panicked because they feared that they would lose their positions and their often undeserved prominence. They did not want to risk their parliamentary seats in urban centres with large Bemba populations and they persuaded Kaunda to proceed with the establishment of a 'One Party State'. Kaunda would later say that he accepted the suggestion as a means of uniting the country and giving himself free time to devote greater attention to the struggle for the liberation of Southern Africa which was intensifying at the time. Cynics might say that like his colleagues he got cold feet, if not about his own early chances of re-election, which were undeniable at the time, but about the uncertainty of elections and the need to measure up to future unknown competitors. So he decided to play it safe through the 'One Party' arrangement. After the 'One Party' was imposed, the elections became a farce: two UNIP candidates contesting parliamentary seats against each other. The seat would go to UNIP, but the result did not indicate whether UNIP had a following in the constituency. Many people held the view that after the declaration of the One Party State, UNIP's support remained solid in the Eastern Province, but it became very patchy in the North, and the rest of the country. In Barotseland, as I said earlier, it disappeared completely.

In 1964 Kaunda had assured parliament that UNIP would never impose a 'One Party State'. If it ever came about it would come through the ballot box, he promised. Yet, on 15 March 1972, he appointed a commission to write a 'One Party' constitution and 'ascertain the wishes of the people', not by referendum, or through a general election, but by consultation. He appointed 16 mostly convenient commissioners, representing UNIP, the Zambia Congress of Trade Unions, the Defence Forces, the University of Zambia, the Church, the Civil Service, the House of Chiefs, the Attorney General, the National Council for Commerce and Industry, and unbelievably, the Chairman of the Anglo American Corporation's Zambian subsidiary, and Harry Nkumbula and

Nalumino Mundia, Leader and Deputy Leader of the opposition party, the African National Congress. Not surprisingly, the last two refused to accept. As chairman of the commission, Kaunda appointed Mainza Chona, Zambia's first lawyer and also UNIP's first president (while Kaunda was in detention). His deputy was Humphrey Mulemba, until then a minor politician from Solwezi, who would thrive under the One Party regime reaching the position of party secretary general and thus, for a while, ranking number two to Kaunda. (Under the One Party constitution the position of the vice president was abolished with the Secretary General of UNIP ranking as number two to the head of state.) The commission reported on 13 December 1972 'the unanimous support' of the people of Zambia for the establishment of what Kaunda called with a straight face 'One Party Participatory Democracy'. He would later lament that he did not call it 'The Party of National Unity', a feat he in fact accomplished some time later by astutely persuading Harry Nkumbula to surrender the ANC. Harry obligingly signed the 'Choma Declaration' in July 1973, merging the ANC with UNIP 'in the interest of national unity'. Most senior ANC leaders were appointed to ministerial or other important government positions, with the exception of Harry who chose to remain a private farmer, as Kapwepwe had done after December 1972, when he was released from jail.

With the 'One Party Participatory Democracy', UNIP's behaviour became bizarre and irrational, different leaders pursuing different agendas, for their own political ends and often for their personal enrichment. To achieve their goals they needed Kaunda's support and he in turn sided with whichever group pursued an agenda that would give him maximum political mileage. His first target was MINDECO and the mining industry.

10. The $100 Million Con

At a press conference, at 7:30 in the morning on 31 August 1973, a fuming Kenneth Kaunda announced the immediate abrogation of the mining agreements, the cancellation of the management contracts with the Anglo American Corporation and RST and the government's intention to acquire unfettered control of the mining industry. And, folly of follies, the repayment of the ZIMCO bonds at par!

A few months earlier, in May 1973, friends in the metals business phoned to tell me that they had noticed unusual market activity in ZIMCO bonds. As the reader will remember from Chapter 6, the acquisition of 51 per cent of the mining companies was paid for by ZIMCO issuing government-guaranteed bonds to a total value of K209 million (some $300 million at the time), bearing interest at 6 per cent per annum: bonds totalling K84 million were issued to RST for the purchase of the Roan group of mines, and K125 million to ZCI, an Anglo American Corporation subsidiary in Bermuda, for the purchase of the Nchanga group of mines. The bonds had a face value of one Kwacha (roughly US$1.50 in 1973) each, and were repayable semi-annually out of dividends over a period of eight years for RST and twelve years for Anglo. The companies had floated them on the market and at the time they were trading at 48 American cents, i.e. approximately a third of their face value (see detailed calculation later). I suspected that perhaps the Ministry of Finance was the buyer taking advantage of the huge discount, but when I returned to Zambia and sniffed around I came to the conclusion that it was not. I mentioned the activity to Kaunda but he did not react and I decided that he may not have taken it in; after all I did not expect him to be familiar with how stock markets worked. As events turned out he must have been fully aware of what was happening but he chose not to discuss it.

I would find out later in a chance conversation with an executive of stockbrokers Loeb Rhoades, who had acted for him, that the buyer of the bonds was Tiny Rowland. He obviously hatched a scheme to persuade the Zambian government to redeem the ZIMCO bonds early – and therefore pay full value – while he bought on the market at a third of the price. His principal collaborator must have been the Minister of Mines of the period, who was at the same time the chairman of the UNIP Economics and Finance Committee. He was known to be very friendly with Tiny Rowland and a frequent guest at Hedsor Wharf, his country home near Cliveden, in England. And the ostensible reason was easy to concoct: the agreements were too favourable to the two mining groups and they were, as the President angrily declared in his press conference, constricting government in its 'task of completing the program started at Mulungushi on 19 April 1968 in order that the people of Zambia may have effective control of their economy'.

I was away from Zambia at the time and did not see Kaunda's performance but, as a friend intimated to me later, Kaunda was visibly angry when he opened the press conference at 7:30 in the morning and fumed right through his press statement. He frequently departed from his text in order to utter threats against the capitalists, foreign and local, who were exploiting Zambia.

The litany of reasons the President gave to the press to justify his action paid no regard to either facts or common sense. Kaunda's rhetoric and performance and the follow-up measures reeked of an elaborate attempt to make the public believe that the government had to step in and save the nation from the exploitation of Anglo and RST regardless of the expense involved.

For those interested in a closer study, I set out Kaunda's full statement to the press and my letter to him dated 19 September 1973 rebutting his arguments in Appendix III. In summary Kaunda's arguments and my rebuttal were as follows:

(KK) In the last three and a half years the working relations with our partners in the mining industry have been good. However, certain provisions in the agreements have proved detrimental to our national interests. I would like to refer to some of these:

1, Effective control. The effective control of the industry was vested firmly in the minority shareholders.

(AS) Not true. Under the articles of association of the two companies, Nchanga and Roan, the government had majority on the boards and appointed the chairman. The minority shareholders had the right to recommend the managing director. However the majority of the board, i.e. the government-appointed directors could refuse to appoint or if it had appointed it could remove a managing director who did not comply with the wishes of the majority. In that case the minority shareholders would have to find a replacement who should ideally be a strictly professional mining man whose interest lay in the technical efficiency of the operation. In other words the government had all the powers it needed to impose its will. And as the

Chairman of the Mindeco board was none other than his Minister of Mines, he could have used the powers granted to him by the Articles of Association of each mining company to achieve what he considered to be in the best interest of the nation.

(KK) 2. Power of veto by minority shareholders. The minority shareholders have power of veto in respect of a wide range of actions and decisions. These include the winding up of operating companies and disposing of assets or granting of any of its concessions, mining or other substantial rights to others, enlarging the companies' activities, making any financial commitment, borrowing of money, appropriation in respect of capital expenditure or expenditure for exploration or prospecting, etc.

(AS) This was aimed at ensuring that the companies remained essentially mining companies and did not diversify into other areas which might prove against the interest of the minority shareholders, which is exactly what the government would do later, through the infamous Mulungushi Investments, a major factor in the eventual destruction of ZCCM. Similarly, that the majority shareholder did not arbitrarily use surplus funds to further his own interests to the detriment of the minority which, again, is exactly what the government did after taking over absolute control and which contributed to the eventual collapse of ZCCM. As regards the limit of the borrowing powers of the directors, this was set at twice the amount of the share capital. The paid up capital of NCCM was K253 million and RCM K121 million, therefore the borrowing powers of the directors extended to K506 million and K242 million respectively. Adding the reserves that each company could capitalize, the borrowing powers of the directors could in fact extend to K730 million for NCCM and K394 for RCM (a total of $1.5 billion, in those days). Those figures were so large that they were unlikely ever to be needed and if utilized to the full, the companies would have overextended themselves and their future would be in jeopardy. Such provisions are sensible and standard in all private companies where there is a substantial minority. Their removal and the arbitrary redirection of ZCCM into unrelated fields in the interest of the ruling party but not the nation led to the eventual decline and collapse of ZCCM.

(KK) 3. Formula for redemption of Bonds. The agreement provides for a fixed minimum amount to be paid each year of ZIMCO bonds, irrespective of profitability of the companies. They also provide for acceleration of the redemption of bonds when profits are high. But there is no provision for extending the period of bond redemption during lean years when there is a sharp decline in the profits due to decline in the price of copper or natural disasters like in the cave-in at Mufulira mine in 1970.

(AS) So, in order to avoid the possibility of ZIMCO having to cope with acceleration at some uncertain and unknown date in the future, the government burdens the nation with a huge payment of $231 million in cash and redeems them! Amazingly Kaunda did not see the absurdity of his argument. But while there was an acceleration clause in the agreements, the interesting fact was that conditions had never reached the point where it could be invoked. The reason was that during the negotiations the acceleration clause was used as a carrot to obtain the concession from the minority shareholders to pay only a small proportion of the dividends for bond redemption in the first year of operations. As the negotiating committee we had calculated that in view of the buoyant conditions of the copper market, whose duration was uncertain, it was more advantageous for ZIMCO to retain the first dividend in its entirety. Events proved that the decision was correct. For subsequent years, it was in the hands of the government directors to ensure that the board paid minimum dividends. Clause 118 (B) of the Articles of Association defined dividends payable each financial year as being the 'aggregate amount equal to the consolidated net profits of the company and its subsidiaries for each financial year as shown in the audited accounts of the company in respect thereof after deduction therefrom of: appropriations in respect of capital expenditure and expenditure for exploration and prospecting and of reserves for necessary working capital, having regard to market conditions and short term liquidity requirements of the company, as may in each case be approved by the directors' Clause 118 (B) (iii). In view of the above the Minister of Mines, as the supremo of the mining industry could instruct the government directors to reduce the dividends to any amount, or pay nothing at all. All they needed to do was to insist that the entire capital expenditure be appropriated out of profits and that adequate provisions in respect of exploration, prospecting, working capital and liquidity be made. To the best of my knowledge the minister and the board had failed to make recourse to this clause.

(KK) 4, Financial disadvantages. Exchange control. The minority shareholders enjoy preferential treatment in respect of exchange control regulations, which permit automatic externalization of profits, dividends, management, and sales fees.

(AS) The exchange control regulations allowed foreign companies to declare dividends equal to 30 per cent of the capital or 50 per cent of the profits. Despite the provisions that the above regulations should not become less favourable during the duration of the bond redemption it is interesting to note that in fact the companies' dividends were substantially below the '30 per cent of capital, 50 per cent of profit formula'.

(KK) 5. Taxation. The agreements provide that RCM and ZCCM will not be subjected to any increase in mineral taxes, export taxes, income taxes, royalty payments, withholding taxes, or any other revenue measures as long as any of the bonds are outstanding. The two companies are allowed to write off all their capital expenditure in full in the year in which they are incurred. Prior to these agreements capital expenditure incurred was spread over the life of the mine.

(AS) The taxation undertaking was given because the taxation was already so high that added to the government's shareholding of 51 per cent it brought the government's share of the profit to 87 per cent of the total. The allowance to write off the new capital expenditure in the year it is incurred was not part of the agreements. It was a provision to the Tax Act, which followed as a result of the new Mining Act that came into force in 1970; the old capital expenditure was still being written off over the life of the mines. Immediately after independence the write-off period for capital expenditure was set for five years. However, as this had not attracted new mining investment and as the new act provided for total taxation of 73 per cent of profits plus participation which raised the government's share to 87 per cent, it was decided that new capital expenditure should be written off in the year it was incurred in order to ensure that new investors recoup their investment before they start paying tax. It is important to emphasize that the write-off of the capital expenditure in the manner described is not tax relief but postponement of tax.

(KK) 6. Utilization of profits. The agreements provide that profits from the mines cannot be used for non-mining activities. In other words, the mining companies cannot be forced to use mining profits in the interest of the Zambian economy if the minority shareholders would prefer to use that money out of Zambia as dividends. Our experience in the last three and a half years has been that they have taken out of Zambia every ngwee [penny] that was due to them. A major part of the capital for expansion programs of both companies has been obtained from external borrowings and not from internal profits. You may be interested to know that right now my government is being asked to approve an external borrowing by the two companies of about K65 million!

(AS) The provision that mining resources should not be used in unrelated activities was absolutely right and sensible. By ignoring it, after the abrogation of the original agreements the government caused the destruction of ZCCM. The ZCCM resources were repeatedly raided to finance hare-brained schemes like the establishment of the notorious Mulungushi Investments, a conglomerate ready to undertake anything and everything from manufacture to construction, engineering, agriculture, tourism, and even dry-cleaners and a commuter train in Lusaka, none of which were relevant to the mining industry and never generated any returns. Why would Kaunda get upset that the mines wanted to borrow externally? Their 'reference to government' would have been the application to the Bank of Zambia for exchange control approval and the resulting loan would not have affected the government finances in any way. But a provision of the original agreements compelled RST and Anglo to an investment contribution of K15 million and K12 million respectively 'from funds not subject to exchange control' (i.e. their funds from outside the country) 'for the development of existing or new mining ventures in Zambia considered to be commercially viable by the board including the Baluba and Chambishi underground mining projects'.

(KK) 7, Sales and marketing. The agreements give the minority shareholders the sole and exclusive right to provide sales and marketing services for the metals and minerals at a very high fee.

8, Management and consultancy. The agreement also states that the minority shareholders will provide sales and marketing services for a large fee. Although most of this work is performed in Zambia the minority shareholders have entered into separate arrangements with non-resident companies for reasons best known to themselves, but not comprehensible to us.

(AS) Naturally part of the work was performed locally. But the local engineers needed access to the vast external resources of the Anglo American and RST, both highly experienced and internationally respected mining houses, which was the essence of the management agreements in the first place. If some of the fees were considered too generous in the light of experience the simplest solution should have been to renegotiate them. To sever ties with the expertise of the two international mining groups was foolhardy.

(KK) 9, Zambianization. There is of course the vital question of Zambianization in the mining industry. The agreements made no provision whatsoever on this vital issue. And of course related to this matter is that of recruitment, which was left entirely in the hands of the minority shareholders, again at a high fee to themselves.

(AS) This was an emotive issue before the Mulungushi reforms. But, after the 51 per cent acquisitions the government had control of the boards of all the operating subsidiaries. It had the absolute right to just order Zambianization of any department it considered lagging. Inclusion of Zambianization provisions in the original agreements would have weakened the government's position because it would have given the minority partners the opportunity to argue and negotiate afresh.

And the President went on with a straight face!

(KK) I mention all these to show some of the problems we have experienced with the agreements as presently constituted. Countrymen, we cannot allow this situation to continue. It has to be changed. But let me assure you and the rest of the world once again, that as a Party and Government we will always endeavour to find reasonable and honourable solutions to our problems in accordance with our philosophy of humanism.

However we still have the task of completing the program started at Mulungushi on 19th April 1968 in order that the people of Zambia may have effective control on the affairs of their economy. In accordance with the mandate given to me by the nation, I decided that with immediate effect:

- Outstanding bonds should be redeemed.
- Steps should be taken to ensure that RCM and NCCM revert to the old system of providing for themselves with all the management and technical services which are now being provided by the minority partner.
- A new copper marketing company wholly owned by the government should be established here in Zambia.
- The Minister responsible for mines shall be the chairman of RCM and NCCM.
- The government will appoint the managing directors of both RCM and NCCM.
- Mindeco shall cease to be the holding company for RCM and NCCM.
- The Minister responsible for Finance will hold shares in RCM and NCCM for and on behalf of the government.
- The rest of the mining operations which are not connected with RCM and NCCM will continue to be administered by Mindeco and the status of Mindeco therefore will be equal to that of RCM and NCCM.
- Normal taxation provisions and exchange control regulations will apply to RCM and NCCM and the Minister responsible for Finance and the Governor of the Bank of Zambia are instructed to take appropriate measures.

He then announced the appointment of an implementation committee under the chairmanship of the Minister of Mines, who was also Chairman of the Economics and Finance Committee of UNIP's Central Committee.

I was stunned. This was a classic case of 'cutting your nose to spite your face'. By that time I was completely out of the system and had no way of knowing who the author of that shameless speech was. But its creation reeked of Tiny Rowland. And its aim was to alarm and panic Kaunda into redeeming the bonds at full value so that Rowland and his accomplices would make a fortune. I did ascertain that the decision was made after a series of meetings at State House which were attended by the then Minister of Mines, the then

Minister of Finance and his permanent secretary, the Governor of the Bank of Zambia and the State House Economic Advisor to the President. Dominic Mulaisho, the CEO of MINDECO who had greater knowledge of the affairs of the two mining groups than anybody else, was conspicuously excluded from those meetings. And Rowland, the boss of Lonrho, who had easy access to State House was a frequent participant according to my information.

The President ought to at least have had some misgivings about the veracity of the statement that was prepared for him. He should have checked the facts before he made such an earth shattering decision, with untold repercussions on the economy of the country. If he chose not to discuss the issue with me, he knew where else to check them: the other members of the negotiating team, Pat Chuula and Emmanuel Kasonde, the lawyers who wrote the agreements and Dominic Mulaisho and the accounting department of MINDECO. I had raised concerns about the market activity in ZIMCO bonds directly with him. Surely that should have made alarm bells ring.

Who sold the scheme to the President? Obviously Rowland, but he would not have disclosed its potential for personal enrichment. I know Kaunda well. He committed many blunders for political reasons but he was not the type who would deliberately have gone ahead in order to make money for himself, or anybody else for that matter, at the expense of the nation. And I do not think that Rowland would have dared to suggest the scheme directly to him in the first place. The scheme must have been promoted through the Minister of Mines and some of the other influential government officials I mention above who then concocted the litany of grievances, on which Kaunda acted.

The above notwithstanding, I decided to remind the President of the facts. By mid-September, I managed to get a meeting with him. He was sitting on the fence. The following day, I sent him a memorandum, which I copy in full in Appendix III. In the process of writing it, I recognized the futility of the exercise. Kaunda was not interested in the facts and my letter was unlikely to change the government's course. I did not receive a reply and I suspect that he probably never even read it.

What were the repercussions? The financial report of the Bank of Zambia for the year 1973 reveals the cost of the bond redemption as K149.4 million, or $231.57 million at the Kwacha–Dollar rate of K1 = $1.55, that was quoted in the same BOZ report as prevailing at the time. This means Kaunda blithely paid out of the National Treasury $231 million in order to redeem the ZIMCO bonds: $93 million for the bonds issued to RST which had nearly six more years to run and $138 million for those issued to the Anglo American subsidiary ZCI with 8.5 years to run. And as the Treasury was short of funds his Minister of Finance and the Governor of the Bank of Zambia had to arrange in a hurry a short-term loan of $125 million at the exorbitant interest rate of 13 per cent per annum. He used the funds to pay the ZIMCO bonds that had an interest rate of 6 per cent per annum (less than half the 13 per cent interest on the new loan contracted for their repayment). Interest rate and tenor apart, the ZIMCO bonds had two other very significant advantages: they did not constitute a direct government obligation, and were being repaid out of dividends. And if the mines became unprofitable in the future they could be renegotiated.

But the most damning aspect of the government's folly was that it paid $231 million when it could have bought the bonds on the market for just $110.88 million, thus saving the country $120.12 million instead of making a present of it to Rowland and his friends, and possibly to some residual bondholders who had held on to the bonds they bought when they were placed on the market. (It was mentioned at the time that one of the major British universities was amongst those buyers.)

I calculated the residual value of the bonds as follows: as the total Kwacha value of the bonds issued in 1970 was K209 million and the cost of the redemption was K149.4 million, it follows that the government had already paid instalments totalling 59.6 million or 28.52 ngwee per bond leaving a balance of 71.48 ngwee as the full redemption value. This means that converted to American dollars at the rate of K1 = $1.55 reported by the Bank of Zambia as the rate of the period, the government paid $1.10 per bond outstanding while their market price was 48 American cents. In other words it could have bought the bonds at 48 American cents each but was bluffed by Rowland and paid $1.10! I have not been able to ascertain the number of bonds Rowland actually bought so I am unable to make an accurate calculation of the value of his loot but my guess would put it at around $100 million. What I cannot guess is how much he shared with his Zambian accomplices – I had a hint that they must have received a share, a couple of years later when one of them made me an offer of £10 million to buy the business I had set up in London. The offer was credible because it came through the accountants, Peat Marwick (now KPMG) and when I questioned the source of the money I was told that it was Arabian. Apparently a rich Arab had been so impressed by a book on Arab–African relations that the 'would-be buyer' had written that he gave him £10 million as a present. As I do not believe that Arabs, or anybody for that matter, would readily throw their money away in that fashion I assumed that the funds behind the offer were Rowland's attempt to gratify him and at the same time take over my business which was becoming very successful at the time. Needless to say I declined.

Kaunda, like most politicians, was always ready to make pronouncements and take actions entirely for political expediency. And, after the defection of Kapwepwe, he had become very jumpy and beholden to the higher echelons of

UNIP. And they turned into an agglomeration of rumour mongers reporting imaginary plots that Kapwepwe, supposedly assisted by Kaunda's internal enemies (their rivals in the party, really), was supposed to be hatching against him. He obviously thought that the abrogation of the agreements suited him politically, so he went ahead regardless of the fraudulent intent and the financial damage he caused the nation.

The combination of the heavy borrowing for the early repayment of the bonds, the abrogation of the mining agreements that resulted in unfettered UNIP control of the mining companies, the oil price explosion and the collapse of the commodity market, the expansion of ZCCM into mindless and unprofitable commercial activities through Mulungushi Investments, and the struggles for the liberation of Rhodesia, Namibia and South Africa, put the country on a slippery economic slope for the next three decades. As time went by, foreign exchange became scarce and the country developed foreign payment arrears running into many months. With no foreign exchange available, imports became erratic and food shortages developed. It was sad to enter a shop whose shelves were empty, or had exaggerated displays of the few items that shopkeepers managed to secure. Mealie meal shortages developed too and women had to get up in the middle of the night and line up for the small quantities that might come on the market and which were snapped up by 8:30 in the morning.

Paralysis and stagnation set in, but Kaunda did not seem to take notice. Instead of pausing for breath and trying to find solutions to the country's problems, he embarked on a new social initiative. This time it was the real thing: the socialist revolution and the complete regimentation of the society under the dictatorship of UNIP.

Part II

The UNIP Dictatorship

11. 'The Sole Custodians of the People's Interests'!

After tearing up the mining agreements and with the One Party regime firmly in place, Kenneth Kaunda plunged headlong into a 'socialist revolution'. His rhetoric changed. 'Humanism', his political slogan, was replaced by 'revolution' and the 'comrades' became 'militants'. The 'national struggle' changed from being a fight against 'poverty, hunger, ignorance and disease' to being a fight against 'capitalism and its off-shoots of imperialism, colonialism, neo-colonialism, fascism and racism'. He declared the 'United National Independence Party supreme and the sole custodian of the people's interests' and ordered the constitution changed to reflect the 'Supremacy of the Party over other institutions in the Land', including parliament and the cabinet. His goal became 'the establishment of a humanist state where there will be no private enterprise', thus ditching the Mulungushi reforms, whose purpose he had declared in 1968 to be the development of Zambian enterprise. He declared that 'land is a gift from God and cannot be sold and especially be made the subject of speculation by inhuman exploiters' and as a result he ordered that all real estate transactions should cease and real estate agencies should close down. He blamed the capitalists, Zambian and foreign, for all the country's ills and malpractices and promised regulations to stop them from practising their wicked ways and urged their relatives and their employees to report on them. (And to be on the safe side he also set up a very extensive State Security Department. It was ubiquitous and it was oppressive. In hotels, bars and restaurants, one would often notice a 'waiter' milling around one's table without doing anything in particular, except eavesdropping. And telephone conversations became coded and allegoric because it was always safest to assume that they were bugged.) He announced the nationalization of the cinemas so as to prevent them from corrupting the country's morals. He also 'streamlined' the media so that 'our young revolutionary workers in this field from now clearly reflect the official thinking of the Party and its Government'.

It is hard to say who the architects of this new departure were and who prepared the announcement. Luckily, either by default, or by design, Kaunda did not follow up with any legislation to put these outlandish pronouncements into effect. No legislation prohibiting private enterprise or the sale of land was promulgated and the real estate agents remained in business. But regulations were introduced entrenching the UNIP Central Committee as Zambia's highest authority, a privilege that was constantly abused politically and economically for the glorification and enrichment of its members but also for the perpetuation and expansion of its hegemony. But, again, the laws of Zambia were not amended to transfer the responsibility of the ministers under the laws of Zambia to the equivalent members of the Central Committee. So, the ministers maintained their executive authority, but the Central Committee was in theory capable of determining policy and instructing them what to do, a privilege they exercised and no minister ever had the courage to stand up to them because he would be thrown out.

All these constraints in the governance of the country also restricted Kaunda's ability for wider consultation and advice. He ended up having to run the country with just the Central Committee of the party, an incestuous body that effectively appointed itself. Its members were supposed to be elected by the Party General Conference. But the party functionaries, who comprised the National Council and had the task of organizing the Party Conference and usually manipulated its resolutions, were appointees of the Central Committee. So the members of the Central Committee remained in their posts for years using the National Council to ensure that they were elected by acclamation. (Kaunda would produce his own list of candidates, generally reappointing the existing members, and then challenge the delegates at the Party Conference to produce an alternative list if they disagreed; the apparatchiks in the National Council made sure they never did.) And as the Central Committee was the supreme governing body it kept inventing more and more powers for itself. It even vested itself with power to approve all candidates for parliamentary elections, thus emasculating the only concession to democracy left in the 'One Party' constitution, which in theory allowed party members to compete in parliamentary elections against each other.

And it used this power to veto the candidature of every intelligent candidate it thought might become a thorn in its flesh if elected to parliament. Disgracefully, one of its victims was Arthur Wina, who was vetoed from contesting a constituency in Livingstone. Arthur had been the UNIP representative in the United States, and had abandoned his Master's degree studies at UCLA (University of California Los Angeles) in order to stand as UNIP candidate in the 1962 election. He and his brother Sikota were instrumental for the most spectacular achievement of UNIP in that election: the delivery of Barotseland to the Nationalists, despite the Litunga's alliance with the UFP, the party of the settlers. But more importantly he was one of the most educated and capable politicians of his time. The result was that parliament and cabinet became rubber stamps to the whims of the Central Committee. Even so, and just in case the occasional principled MP would dare raise his voice, a powerful member of the Central Committee could bypass parliament and promote pet projects through the party, circumventing laws and procedures.

This was the route that Humphrey Mulemba, the Central Committee member for the Economy and Finance, chose for the development of the so-called TIKA Iron and Steel Mill near Solwezi, his home district. It was going to be developed jointly by UNIP and Energoprojekt, a Yugoslav contractor, hence the name TIKA, an acronym for Tito-Kaunda. The contract for this project was signed in 1973 but it got bogged down in the procurement of finance, as happened with most projects where Yugoslavs undertook to provide it: in the end the government of Zambia had to borrow internationally on its own name. It had been easy for Zambia to raise finance for the two hydroelectric schemes at Kafue and Itezhi-Tezhi that the Yugoslavs built. But nobody wanted to finance an iron and steel project in a landlocked country with an extremely small steel consumption, a couple of thousand miles from the coast. So UNIP and Energoprojekt resorted to 'export finance' from Germany and the United States where the American Export Import (EXIM) Bank and its German equivalent financed the manufacture of parts of the plant against guarantees from the Bank of Zambia (again a direct Zambian obligation probably by arrangement with the then governor and not properly authorized). As the Yugoslavs and UNIP were not able to raise any form of long-term funds for the construction of the project the various components of the plant ended up in warehouses in Germany and the United States costing a fortune in demurrage.

In 1979 the government realized that the project was a white elephant and decided to close it down. To do so it had to ask parliament to authorize a preliminary payment of K2 million to cover legal fees in order to ward off actions from some of the unpaid manufacturers and other creditors in the hope that it would eventually sell the plant and recover some of the money. Titus Mukupo, the MP for Kawambwa persuaded the House not to give its approval until the minister gave a full account of the affairs of TIKA. Titus was the veteran journalist and politician who had led the second revolt against Harry Nkumbula that resulted in the split of the African National Congress in 1959, and culminated in the creation of UNIP, with Mainza Chona as its first president, followed by Kaunda. Thanks to Mukupo, the whole sordid story of TIKA was revealed in parliament by the then Minister of Mines Mufaya Mumbuna. The various costs reported in the minister's statement as payments, outstanding claims, interest and storage charges added up to some $100 million, though at the time figures as high as $150 million were circulating. The minister's statement was long and complex, but I summarized it from the parliamentary records for my book *Africa: Another Side of the Coin* and I attach the summary as Appendix IV for those interested in the greater detail.

So in addition to the $231 million that the nation spent unnecessarily to redeem the ZIMCO bonds at a loss of $121 million, the nation poured another $100 million down the TIKA drain. Yet nobody was blamed and nobody was dismissed.

In the 'One Party State' the party was in charge; its officers did not have to account for their actions and, sadly, no one dared to question them too loudly, Mukupo's daring effort being a rare exception. The nation's self-appointed rulers had risen to Olympian heights of detachment and were not able to notice anything untoward, never mind lift a finger to do something to stop the decline and collapse of the country. As far as they were concerned they were the ultimate in patriotism and wisdom and would do what they liked. They persuaded themselves that the Zambian people loved them and only the 'capitalists' and the 'enemies of the people' complained. And they dealt with the 'enemies of the people', mercilessly.

But the great people of Zambia did not love them, as they would show a few years later when they forced the reintroduction of multiparty politics. For them life was becoming harder by the day. To be fair, life was becoming very hard right through Africa at that time as a result of the oil price explosion and the collapse of the commodity markets, but UNIP's mindless policies did not help, and the early redemption of the ZIMCO bonds and the drain of TIKA decimated the national reserves and increased the nation's debt burden unbearably.

Kaunda's infatuation with socialism did not last very long. Within a year or so, he handed over the country's socialist education to his deputy, Grey Zulu, who had the position of party secretary general and under the new order ranked second to the president in the national hierarchy. Zulu spent months on end travelling around the country spreading the Marxist gospel, though I don't think anybody other than the UNIP cadres paid much attention. Kaunda concentrated on entertaining visiting VIP comrades. Comrade Tito paid frequent visits in those days, but their purpose was to secure more contracts for the many Yugoslav companies that had set up in Zambia. The Kafue hydroelectric scheme, which had been bypassed during the Federation in favour of Kariba in order to ensure that the Kariba Power Station was located in Southern Rhodesia, as well as the Itezhi-Tezhi dam upstream, were built by Yugoslav contractors. The contracts were awarded on the basis of 'contractor finance'. But the Yugoslavs failed to secure the finance and in the end the

Zambian government had to raise the funds from international institutions directly. Comrade Ceausescu of Rumania was also a visitor, but his purpose was to sell ARO jeep type vehicles and tractors, to the police and the Ministry of Agriculture, which never lasted for more than six months on the road. I do not recollect visits from senior Soviet comrades.

The major focus of Kaunda's attention then turned to the liberation of Southern Africa. It was a cause he believed in and carried with dedication and sincerity, though at times he pursued very unorthodox lines that infuriated his fellow frontline presidents and the leaders of the various independence movements. Curiously Tiny Rowland, the boss of Lonrho and the perpetrator of the abrogation of the mining agreements was closely involved in most of Kaunda's more embarrassing initiatives.

12. Kaunda and Thatcher Tango: Rhodesia Vanishes

In 1973, at the behest of Rowland, Kaunda tried to arrange a meeting between Samora Machel and Jorge Jardim, an ex-Minister of Commerce and Industry of Salazar, the infamous Portuguese dictator. Jardim had emigrated to Mozambique in the early fifties and he had obviously been mandated to persuade Samora Machel to establish a 'moderate' FRELIMO wing inside Mozambique, which the Portuguese were obviously intending to use as a bargaining platform for a slow evolution of 'self-rule' leading to independence along the lines of the British decolonization process. Machel, who was winning the war, angrily rejected the idea and refused to meet them. But Jardim and Rowland persevered and amazingly Kaunda agreed to meet other Portuguese envoys including a delegation of officers of PIDE, the Portuguese secret police (David Martin and Phyllis Johnson, *The Struggle for Zimbabwe*). Rowland also used his connection with Kaunda to ferry messages from John Vorster, the then Prime Minister of South Africa whose dream was to create an economic community with 'moderate' African countries and who wanted to use Kaunda as a bridge. Somehow Kaunda did not see any contradiction between his support of the African National Congress and his contacts with Vorster. Instead, he allowed them to expand into a wider circle which included Rowland and an Afrikaner Lonrho South Africa director by the name of Marquard de Villiers, various officials of the South African government, such as Dr Eschel Rhoodie, Secretary for Information; General Hendrik van den Bergh, head of the Bureau of Public Security (BOSS); Hilgard Muller and Pik Botha, Ministers of Foreign Affairs at different times, and Mark Chona, his Foreign Affairs assistant; Vernon Mwaanga, Zambian Minister of Foreign Affairs after some years as Zambia's Permanent Representative to the United Nations; and various others.

In their book *The Struggle for Zimbabwe*, David Martin and Phyllis Johnson report some extraordinary messages conveyed to Vorster by the Lonrho team, designed to indicate that Kaunda was ready to follow policies that were contrary to those of the OAU or the relevant independence movements. In reference to

FRELIMO one such statement, reported to have been conveyed through Mark Chona, said: 'Nationalist movements such as FRELIMO should be recognized as an important political factor whose assistance in the formulation of future political framework cannot be ignored', a position at odds with Machel's refusal to consider any other solution but a complete FRELIMO victory, which was close at hand. With regard to Rhodesia, Rowland is reported quoting Mark Chona, Kaunda's go-between with Rowland and the South Africans, that Kaunda's view was: 'a white victory in Rhodesia was impossible; a black victory was possible but undesirable'. None of these messages accord with Kaunda's public pronouncements and, in my view, his real thinking; but the fact that he developed so much familiarity with Rowland and the South Africans that they were able to claim to be conveying his inner thinking is extraordinary.

To cap it all, as late as 1977, when Smith had realized that he was losing the war and started another round of delaying tactics in the form of an internal settlement with Muzorewa and Sithole, Rowland arranged for all of them to visit Lusaka for a meeting with Kaunda. They tried to keep the visit secret with the Lonrho jet that brought them landing at the City airport, which was rarely used and the meetings taking place at the State Lodge, outside Lusaka instead of State House. Somehow, Joshua Nkomo, the leader of the ZAPU wing of the Patriotic Front and Mugabe's co-leader, was also on board. Nkomo's presence was never explained, though it was well known at the time that Rowland was promoting him as the future President of Zimbabwe in preference to Mugabe, a naive notion bearing in mind the numerical strength of Mugabe's Shona (80 per cent of the population) to Nkomo's Ndebele (20 per cent). Nothing was actually achieved at that meeting except to infuriate Mugabe when it leaked. In fact Mugabe never trusted Kaunda, as this exchange with Robin White on the BBC World Service highlights:

> Mugabe: Well, I think President Kaunda has been the principal factor in slowing down our revolution. He has arrested our men, locked them up, and within his prisons and restriction areas there have been cases of poisoning and there have also been murders.
>
> White: By who?
>
> Mugabe: By his men, by Kaunda's army.
>
> White: You have proof of that, do you?
>
> Mugabe: Yes, thirteen of our people were shot dead cold bloodedly. And one cannot regard this as an act conforming to the principles of humanism.
>
> White: Those are very strong charges. I mean a lot of people would say that nobody's done more for Rhodesian Nationalists, than President Kaunda. He has suffered more and Zambia has suffered more than any other country.

Mugabe: True, no one denies that Kaunda has done quite a lot for us. But that's no reason for negating his past.

(*The Struggle for Zimbabwe*)

And Mugabe's trust in Kenneth Kaunda would not have improved when De Villiers, the South African Lonrho board director, who was also in Lusaka during the meeting with Smith, made the following comments about the private meeting between Kaunda and Smith:

They had half an hour of private audience and I spoke to President Kaunda after and he was most impressed with Ian Smith. He said it would be difficult to explain to other members of the OAU how impressed he was with Mr. Smith's honesty and integrity of purpose and he found him a very pleasant individual ... Ian Smith was equally impressed with President Kaunda. It was a meeting that was conducted with the greatest sense of endeavour to get together, and to stay together and to find a solution.

(*The Struggle for Zimbabwe*)

In my view, De Villiers's comments were either a racist's wishful thinking or another one of the many deliberate attempts to put out another myth of Smith's 'magic touch', which enabled him to mesmerize his supporters and made them believe that he would win the war. But I can't believe that Kaunda would buy it. He was not so naive as to see sincerity and honesty in Smith, one of the most devious operators of all time. In fact his own description was that Smith's tactics were the kicks of a dying horse. The question, though, still remains: why did he allow himself to become a pawn in Rowland's scheming in the region?

Rowland's scheme that caused the abrogation of the Zambian mining agreements was a Zambian issue of which Kaunda was in charge, and in the 'One-Party' State that Zambia was at the time he did not have to account to anybody about it. But the liberation of Southern Africa was an African issue and it concerned the OAU and the frontline states, as well as the Liberation movements and their leadership. Inevitably the Kaunda–Smith meeting in Lusaka leaked and the OAU was up in arms. Even Nyerere who was Kaunda's friend raised searching questions and Mugabe was furious. He made it clear that he did not believe Kaunda's version of the meeting with Smith (*The Struggle for Zimbabwe*).

Yet Mugabe would get another set of favours from Kaunda and a reason to be eternally grateful. The Commonwealth Prime Ministers' Conference of August 1979 took place in Lusaka after a great deal of hesitation by Margaret Thatcher, the British prime minister. She had never been to Africa before; she did not trust the African leaders and having the meeting next door to Rhodesia made her uncomfortable. According to Kaunda, she first tried to persuade the Queen that it would not be safe for her to fly to Lusaka to perform the official opening, in case of a possible terrorist attack. She did not succeed even though she tried to enlist the support of the Australian prime minister to her cause. As a result Thatcher eventually had to come to Lusaka herself, in order to attend the conference. Lord Carrington, her Minister of Foreign Affairs at the time describes in his book *Reflect on Things Past* how nervous she was. During the flight he noticed that Thatcher had on her table a pair of very large dark sunglasses. When he queried their purpose, bearing in mind that the flight would be arriving at night, she explained: 'I am absolutely certain that when we land in Lusaka they are going to throw acid in my face.'

Lord Carrington's description of their arrival:

> It was pitch dark and as we came to a halt we heard a great shouting outside. The doors were opened and Margaret descended first, into a sea of white eyes and white teeth which, like the shouting were impossible to distinguish as friendly or otherwise. Next day the Zambian Press reported, most inaccurately, that a trembling Margaret Thatcher had deliberately arrived in the dark to dodge the demonstrations. On the contrary (and we had little control over flight and arrival times: one never does), Margaret marched down the aircraft steps totally serene. No dark glasses. Kenneth Kaunda greeted her warmly, and they were all cheering her! Her apprehension had shown her inexperience and mistrust of Africa – soon rectified as she met the African leaders and with few exceptions found them most agreeable people.
>
> (Peter Alexander Rupert Carrington, *Reflect On Things Past,*
> *The Memoirs of Lord Carrington*)

And Kaunda carried on with the charm at the first banquet, asking Margaret Thatcher to dance, while his wife danced with her husband Denis. The outcome of the Commonwealth Prime Ministers' Conference was the decision to hold a conference at Lancaster House in order to resolve the Rhodesian problem. Lord Carrington's take:

> Thus we came to Lusaka and I have described how the Prime Minister's fears of personal animosity proved largely groundless and how she at once blossomed in the warmth of Kenneth Kaunda's friendly personality, dancing with him enthusiastically as she did at the first party. The Lancaster House Conference which followed was attributed by some to a 'Commonwealth initiative' in which Britain reluctantly concurred. That was nonsense. Margaret Thatcher and I arrived in Lusaka with perfectly clear intentions of what we intended to

achieve. We knew what we wanted and we got it. Margaret played the hand extremely well and bore with equanimity a certain amount of predictable abuse from some of her Commonwealth colleagues, delivered at banquets as well as meetings.

(*Reflect On Things Past*)

Kaunda's relations with British prime ministers were always uneasy, affected by the schizophrenic attitude they adopted about their kith and kin in Rhodesia and their support and the supply of arms to the South African apartheid regime. But it always remained civil with Wilson and Callaghan. The exception was Ted Heath. Heath was a prickly character and Kaunda considered him responsible for the demise of Milton Obote, the President of Uganda. According to Kaunda, Obote did not want to go to the Singapore Commonwealth Prime Ministers' Conference in 1971 because he had misgivings about the security situation in Uganda. He was prevailed upon to do so, by the so-called Mulungushi Club, comprising leaders of the frontline states (bordering with Rhodesia and the Portuguese colonies and South Africa). At issue was the perennial Rhodesian problem and Britain's increasing supply of arms to South Africa over which the frontline presidents, Kaunda, Nyerere, and Obote, had a private meeting with Heath. Apparently Heath was very annoyed and in the heat of the discussion, according to Kaunda, he blurted out: 'some of you, who are giving me trouble now, you will not be able to get back to your homes'. (It was commonly believed in Africa at the time that Lord Aldington who was the chairman of the Tory Party as well as the chairman of General Electric Company (GEC) was behind Idi Amin's coup; he was afraid that with Obote in charge GEC did not have a chance of winning the turbine contracts for a hydroelectric scheme under construction at the time.) Heath's comments rattled Obote who at the same time had received a telephone call from Uganda asking him to rush back because trouble was brewing. He attempted to get the first flight out of Singapore (by British Airways to Nairobi) but was told that it was fully booked. British Airways' refusal to take Obote, combined with Heath's comment about some of them not being able to reach home, confirmed the belief of the three frontline presidents that British Airways had instructions to prevent Obote from reaching East Africa in order to give Amin time to complete the coup. Apparently Amin had developed cold feet at the last minute. When Obote, eventually, did manage to get to Nairobi, Amin was fully ensconced. That the Amin coup had been organized by the British is now common knowledge and it is supported by the fact that Britain not only gave immediate recognition to his regime, but had Amin to London on an official visit staying at Buckingham Palace by July 1971 (the coup had taken place on

25 January 1971). But let me add Lord Carrington's take on Heath and his relations with African leaders:

> It is too easily forgotten that Heath was a tough Prime Minister and a pretty harsh opponent if he thought Britain was being unjustly criticized. I recall a Commonwealth Prime Ministers' Conference in Singapore, which we all enjoyed, when Heath turned on a number of colleagues who were attacking us over the question of arms for South Africa. He silenced his attackers. He called humbug by its proper name ... There was also the memorable occasion when Kenneth Kaunda of Zambia came to London in October 1970, again in order, he said, to explain how strongly he felt about Arms to South Africa. I attended a meeting at No. 10 where both sides explained their (familiar) positions with courtesy and moderation and then dispersed to change for a small dinner at No. 10. While changing for dinner Heath turned on the television news and learned that on arrival at London Airport Kaunda had told a news conference that he had come to Britain to appeal to the British people over the heads of their Government ... When we were reunited for dinner the mood was black. We sat down to dinner in silence ... We moved in silence to the drawing room, and I said, desperation in the voice, 'We've had a very interesting evening.' The Prime Minister spoke for the first time and with menace. He addressed Kaunda: 'Very interesting! And what I don't understand we take full account of your problems. We know you trade through Rhodesia with South Africa. You sell thousands of tons of copper to them. We understand it – you have to get power from Kariba Dam, and we make facilities for you to do so by intervention in the United Nations. What we do not understand is why you – while accepting all this from us – should totally ignore what we consider to be our own vital concerns.' Heath then relapsed into silence. The effect on Kaunda was electrifying. His eyes rolled, he clasped his arms, he swayed from side to side intoning, 'My God, my God, my God. Never did I think I would hear a British Prime Minister speak to me like that. My God, my God, my God.' His entourage took their cue ... The Zambian High Commissioner thought it was time to go home and the Prime Minister led his Party down the stairs, past the Cabinet room, to the door where they all passed through the night, no further word spoken. I don't think that Kaunda loved Ted Heath thereafter, but I know he respected him.
>
> (*Reflect On Things Past*)

Carrington was very wrong about Kaunda's respect for Heath. His comment about Kaunda 'not loving him but respecting him' was another colonial aphorism on how to treat the natives, along the lines of 'firm but fair'.

Back to the Rhodesian conference: Mugabe and Nkomo did not want to go to Lancaster House. They were 'forced' to do so, after tremendous pressure from Kaunda, Nyerere, and Machel. The conclusion must be that Kaunda's fraternization with Smith and Vorster and P. W. Botha, misguided though it was, in no way diminishes his contribution to the independence struggle in Southern Africa for which he made many personal and national sacrifices. Without his taking such a firm and unequivocal stand, without offering shelter to the independence movements of Zimbabwe, Namibia and South Africa and their guerrilla forces the complete liberation of Africa before the end of the twentieth century would not have been achieved.

But despite taking advantage of him time and again during the Rhodesian war, when it ended with the defeat of Ian Smith, and Zimbabwe was born under a black government the white South Africans who considered that their apartheid country remained the last bastion of the white civilization in Africa had no scruples about reminding Kaunda that they were serious about keeping South Africa in 'civilized' (read 'white') hands. They had already warned him, anyway, during their fraternization period when Vorster made it clear that while he was ready to talk about Rhodesia, Mozambique and even Namibia, South Africa had no intention of moving from its rigid policy of separate development. 'In white South Africa the whites will rule and let there be no mistake about it … And if there are any of you [black leaders] who nourish hope for one man one vote, in the white parliament then you are being misled because it will not happen,' he had declared (*The Struggle for Zimbabwe*).

13. A Maverick Troublemaker and a Gentlemen's Coup

I do not believe that the South Africans wanted to oust Kaunda. I do not think they could countenance the international outrage that such interference in the affairs of a long established, peaceful, and conflict-free African country would have provoked. They were sufficiently savvy to realize that their long-term interest in Africa would be better served by a policy of live and let live in the southern region. And even though there was near collapse of the Zambian economy, discontent amongst the masses had not reached a violent point. As events would unfold, it never would and in the end change came about through the ballot box.

Knowing Kaunda's unshakeable commitment to the total liberation of Africa, the South Africans simply wanted to put him on notice that they would not tolerate too much Zambian support for the African National Congress (ANC). By that time the ANC had its main office and many prominent ANC exiles had homes in Lusaka, but the South Africans would not have wanted to see guerrilla bases and training camps in Zambia (they were mainly confined to Angola and Tanzania at that stage). Their aim, therefore, was not to promote a successful coup, but to embarrass Kaunda and make him look to the South African might with some degree of fear and respect, along the lines they had achieved in their relationship with Botswana.

And I do not know who thought up the coup. The protagonist was Pierce Annfield, a ne'er-do-well Lusaka lawyer who had been drifting between Zambia and South Africa over the years. Annfield was born in Chingola and his father had been the general secretary of the European Mineworkers Union, a notoriously racist body that was constantly fighting for 'job reservation' for white mineworkers in order to prevent African advancement on the mines. One of its many successes had been to reserve artisan training exclusively for children of white miners, thus blocking the advancement of the next generation of Africans too. Annfield was educated in Rhodesia and South Africa and trained as a lawyer in Britain. I had met him in the early seventies and came to the conclusion that he was unburdened by any principles or firm convictions. In the mid-seventies he joined a legal practice and when the owner died of cancer at a young age, he seemed to have inherited both his widow and the practice, which had some of the most prominent Zambian dissidents, including Kapwepwe amongst its clients. So it could well be that the idea of a coup occurred to Annfield first who then sold it on to the South African intelligence that embraced it and financed it, money for the project being one of Annfield's paramount needs, no doubt. I cannot think where else the huge sums of money utilized could have come from. Definitely not from Annfield who did not have any, nor from Arabs or other mythical friends as some of the circulating versions would have us believe.

Kapwepwe was obviously his first and most important recruit. At the time Kapwepwe was at the height of his discontent. After many years in the wilderness, he swallowed his pride and rejoined UNIP in 1978. He made an attempt to stand as a candidate for party president against Kaunda, but instead of allowing him to stand and lose the election, the UNIP Central Committee, notoriously sycophantic towards Kaunda, clumsily rejected Kapwepwe's nomination on the grounds that he had not been a member of the party for a continuous period of five years, an arbitrary rule they drummed up for the occasion. This made him and his followers conclude that Kaunda treated him unfairly because he was afraid of him. Annfield ingratiated himself to Kapwepwe by suing UNIP and Kaunda for flouting the electoral rules during the UNIP convention of September 1978. Not surprisingly he lost the case; but he made a grateful and devoted friend.

Over the years there have been different versions of how the idea of a coup crystallized. It appears that the first aim was civil strife through strikes, riots, and protests. Kapwepwe and Annfield are supposed to have tried to persuade the Trade Union leaders to start the ball rolling with a general strike, but, when they refused to cooperate, they settled on a military coup as the alternative.

After Kapwepwe, Annfield's two most prominent Zambian recruits were Valentine Musakanya and Edward Shamwana. He met and befriended Valentine at the Lusaka Flying Club (they were both amateur pilots) and they jointly bought a Bonanza single engine plane. I am not surprised at the recruitment of Valentine. He was going through a period of uncertainty, having been excised out of government service and seen his plans for the future of the civil service frustrated. He did manage to get what everybody, except perhaps himself, would have considered an enviable job with IBM as the manager for its operations in the region, in which he excelled as is obvious from the offer of promotion as manager for the whole of Africa, which would have taken him to Paris. But in 1978, the government withdrew his passport on the specious grounds that he was speaking ill of the 'Party and its Government' while travelling abroad, one of the many nasty and cruel measures of the 'One Party' era, that destroyed people's livelihoods and made UNIP an object of hate. Valentine did not much like politicians in general, and though there was no love lost between him and Kapwepwe under whom he had refused to serve as Deputy Minister of Finance, his dislike of Kaunda, whom he held responsible for the deterioration of the civil service and the collapse of his own career, was greater. The surprise recruit was Edward Shamwana, one of only three Zambian lawyers at independence. He was an Ila amongst an almost entirely Bemba group, a commissioner of the High Court and tipped to be the next chief justice. He was also part of the State House golf group, playing regularly with Kaunda.

There are many versions of how events developed the latest being a book published in 2012, by one of the convicted conspirators (G. Y. Mumba, *'The 1980 Coup': Tribulations of the One Party State in Zambia*). The financing and recruitment of mercenaries are the murkiest parts of the story. Arab money is bandied about, a tradition now firmly established in Zambia to cover the provenance of funds of questionable origin. According to Mumba's *'The 1980 Coup'* he and Valentine Musakanya collected a cash contribution of $500,000 in Paris from an 'Arab friend' of one of the plotters and brought it to London where I am supposed to have converted it into Kwacha for them. In a spy-novel plot, the exchange is reported to have taken place in a restaurant. First of all I categorically deny that I was ever involved in such a transaction. I have never set eyes on the purported $500,000, nor did I collect it in a restaurant or anywhere else for that matter, or give Mumba the Kwacha equivalent. (I wonder how many briefcases are needed to carry such an amount.) But Mumba's scenario is naive beyond belief. For a start he does not explain how such a large amount of cash can be transported on a regular flight from Paris to London without being detected by officers of two different European Customs Authorities ever vigilant for narcotics cash. (Even though there were no body scanners at the time, briefcases were scanned and I know that dollars and British pounds always showed up on the screen, because I frequently carried cash for one or other of the group banks when I travelled: I had to show the documentation I was carrying in order to be allowed to take it through.) Neither does he explain why the exchange into Kwacha had to take place in a restaurant when at the time I had both an apartment and an office in London, places very familiar to Valentine who was a frequent visitor. And how could I, or anybody for that matter, have the Kwacha equivalent of such a huge amount of dollars in a current account in a bank in Zambia and a Kwacha chequebook in London handy in order to issue a cheque? But equally importantly, what would I have done with such a huge sum of cash dollars, which would have been illegal to hold and impossible to bank, transport and utilize? With regard to the Kwacha cheque, Mumba does not say if I issued it as a 'cash cheque' and on which bank in Zambia. (Needless to say he does not seem to have given any thought as to which bank would have cashed such an astronomic sum without asking any questions.) Alternatively, assuming the cheque was issued in favour of a specific individual, who was the beneficiary and how would a cheque of that size pass through the bank clearing system without the Bank of Zambia or the paying bank reporting the details to state security, which was pervasive at the time? But let me copy from Valentine's *Papers* his description of Mumba (both had been arrested and detained as coup conspirators):

> Many stories have been told about him during the few days he had remained at Central Prison. He was haughty, outspoken, and addressing the prisoners to the effect that their liberation had at last arrived ... Goodwin is a typical specimen of the Bemba aristocracy. The Bemba aristocracy always believe not only in their inherent aristocracy but also in the vocal aggression to make others believe so. Their aristocracy has no foundation in wealth or known education but essentially in being Bemba. Goodwin's belief in this is supported by an outstanding command of the Bemba language. Bemba, I must admit spoken by an arrogant expert has a mind-boggling and enslaving effect upon those to whom it is directed.

Yet funds did appear to have been flowing freely to the plotters: to purchase a farm to house and train the mercenaries, reported as costing $250,000, to feed and pay the mercenaries for many months, to pay for guns either stolen from the Zambian army or bought in South Africa by Annfield, who, Mumba reports, transported at least one load of them from South Africa hidden in a cargo of tiles consigned to his business. And the generous sponsors, in addition to the Arabs, appear to have been either Annfield himself who according to *'The 1980 Coup'* was making frequent trips to South Africa, or unnamed friends and associates of his, obviously all code names for the South African government. The meetings of the plotters seem to have been taking place mainly in Annfield's office or house, with Mundia Sikatana, his law partner and another 'patriotic coup plotter', mostly present, according to Mumba. Sikatana, according to rumours that circulated after the arrests, appears to have in fact been a double agent acting as a Zambian government mole in the plotting group and reporting the proceedings to a cousin who was a senior officer at State House.

The initial scheme entailed Kapwepwe's escape from Zambia in order to set up a government in exile: Zaire (now the Democratic Republic of the Congo) was considered as the seat of Kapwepwe's government, as well as South Africa and, incongruously, France. Zaire must have been discounted for fear that Mobutu would hand them over to Kaunda, and I discount South Africa because, deep down, Kapwepwe was a patriotic Zambian and cooperation with the then South African government would have been abhorrent to him. *The 1980 Coup* alleges that a jet had in fact arrived to take Kapwepwe to France on 19 January 1980. It appears that he was prevaricating and made the excuse that he wanted to say goodbye to his daughter Sampa, a medical doctor working in Kalulushi at the time. Waiting for Kapwepwe the pilots proceeded to Livingstone to see the Victoria Falls, but Kapwepwe died on arrival at Kalulushi (stroke induced by the pressures on him to do something that he found repugnant?), so the first plan aborted.

The second scheme was more outrageous than the first. The decision was to organize a coup under the leadership of Edward Shamwana. From the charges that followed, it appeared that Edward, Valentine and Annfield tried to recruit the President's pilot and persuade him to land Kaunda's plane at 'an unauthorized place so that the President would fall into the hands of an armed band who would force him at gun point to sign a declaration renouncing power' according to the charge sheet. The 'bandits' were (according to the charge sheet) 65 young men collected at Mwinilunga by a Congolese mercenary called Deogratias Symba who was recruited to train and lead them. I have no doubt that most of those youngsters went along because they thought that they were being offered jobs in town. (Some versions describe the 65 as being Katangese gendarmes.) The accused were also charged with attempting to buy uniforms and ammunition from army depots. This more or less gives a complete picture of the plot.

It was going to be a 'gentlemen's coup'. No bloodshed, irreproachable behaviour, and strict adherence to protocol! When I read the details in the charge sheet, I had visions of this group of polite Lunda youngsters, impeccably dressed in Zambian army fatigues emerging from the bush as KK's plane landed, clapping hands on bended knees, and exclaiming 'Kalombo Mwane', the Lunda traditional greeting for a chief. Valentine, at their head, would then present the 'Black Book' to Kaunda and ask him to sign governing authority to Shamwana. (When the President is about to leave the country, he has to sign an instrument passing governing authority to the Vice President during his absence. During the early years of independence, the instrument was presented to him in a black folder, just before the plane took off, by the secretary to the cabinet – Valentine – who was the custodian of the 'black book'.) The 'coup procedure' had its origin in Cabinet Office routine and obviously came straight out of Valentine's mind. (I wondered if he had planned to request the

Cabinet Office to lend him the 'black book' and State House stationery for the purpose.)

As the government knew their every secret, it was not surprising that when the plotters were about to strike, on 14 October 1980, the Zambian army attacked first. Some of the mercenaries managed to escape, but the senior conspirators were picked up over the next few days. Miraculously Annfield, cynically abandoning his comrades, fled to South Africa the day before in the Bonanza he owned jointly with Valentine Musakanya, warned perhaps by his partner, Sikatana, who must have been in the know. (Annfield returned to Zambia briefly after the change of government and tried to claim the farm he bought in order to house the mercenaries, but the farm had been confiscated by the government and he was not successful.) Sikatana was not arrested until many months later, obviously in order to belatedly cover his double agent identity and placate his erstwhile co-conspirators' families who became very indignant. He turned state witness and was released.

It took until August 1981 before treason charges were proffered against 13 accused, which included Valentine Musakanya and Edward Shamwana. Before they were officially charged, they were kept in the Lusaka remand prison and I would visit them whenever I returned to Lusaka. Most of the time, I found them in high spirits and quite unrealistic about their prospects. They thought that they were politically important and that Kaunda would not be able to sustain the outcry of the Bemba and Tonga-Ila people, their respective tribal groups, for very long and would have to come to a compromise. Every time I visited, one of them would dip his hand in my pocket and collect all the cash I carried. It helped their relations with the wardens, they explained. The method was devised by Edward: in this way, I could not be accused of giving money to a prisoner; it had been stolen from me, he explained.

I do not know who fanned their hopes, but I knew that in the country at large there was no outcry about their incarceration. Both Valentine and Edward were respected members of the society and held in awe, because of their education and achievements, but they had no political following and the country had come to the conclusion that they had indeed been preparing a coup. My own advice was to ask for Kaunda's forgiveness before the case went to court. That would have been the 'Zambian thing' to do; Kaunda always behaved as a magnanimous and forgiving Christian and I had no doubt that he would indeed have been lenient. Unfortunately, neither they nor Valentine's family (Edward's family lived in England at the time and I did not know their views) were prepared to swallow their pride. In the end they chose the 'heroic' route to jail, which cost Valentine five years' incarceration and Edward ten.

But there is nothing heroic about a coup. It is evil and usually leads to greater suffering than the one it is supposed to alleviate, often for decades to come. We have had many examples of coups in Africa and elsewhere and I cannot recollect one that can be described as beneficial; its consequences were never greater democracy and better governance but harsher dictatorship and chaos. And the perpetrators were never intelligent patriotic citizens, but mainly greedy and ambitious hare-brained men, mostly army junior ranks or disgruntled individuals. I loved Valentine like a brother and Edward was a very close friend. Both of them were intelligent, compassionate and wise, and neither falls within my definition of a likely coup plotter. And neither would have wished to become a puppet of the South African government. Over the years I puzzled to divine their motives and could come to only one conclusion: a period of instability and weakness that we all go though sometime in our lives. I do not know Edward's circumstances, but I do know that Valentine was going through a rough patch at the time having just experienced the vengeful treatment of the 'One Party State'. Annfield must have exploited his vulnerability and drafted him in, along with Edward. They both closed their eyes to the South African connection, bluffing themselves that Annfield was a true patriotic Zambian genuinely wanting to rid the country of the 'One Party State' and sweeping under the carpet the unpalatable source of his funds.

Like all major trials in African countries it took a few years for the court to hear the case and come to a verdict. All except one were convicted of treason and sentenced to death. They appealed and the verdict on the appeal was delivered by the Chief Justice on 2 April 1985. Valentine, whose defence had been diligently prepared by John Mwanakatwe (the first ever Zambian university graduate who had studied for his degree by correspondence and later qualified as a barrister while serving as Northern Rhodesia Assistant Commissioner, in London), was acquitted and released in 1985, but he never found a new niche. He died in 1994 at the age of 62. As there has been some controversy over the success of his appeal which some attributed to the Supreme Court rejecting a confession extracted from him under torture and which the trial court should not have admitted as evidence, I wish to set the record straight: I know that many detainees were tortured during the 'One Party' period. In my book *Africa: Another Side of the Coin* I report the details of another friend's (Michael Chileshe's) torture. But it did not happen to Valentine. The book *The Musakanya Papers* (2010), quotes Valentine's own narration of his arrest and interrogation (on pages 62–70); he does not mention that he was tortured. But the editor, Miles Larmer, added the following at the bottom of page 70:

It is unclear why Musakanya makes no specific mention of his torture at the hands of his interrogators. Subsequent evidence presented and accepted by the courts demonstrates conclusively that the statement on which his initial conviction rested was extracted by the use of torture and ruled inadmissible as a result.

I do not know where the editor came across the 'subsequent evidence' of torture, but I know there is none. Valentine's acquittal was not based on the inadmissibility of his confession because it had been obtained under torture but the inadmissibility of the notes taken by the police during his interrogation at Lilayi, which the trial court accepted as evidence, as John Mwanakatwe, his lawyer, in his autobiography explains:

> It was in the early days of his [Valentine's] detention at Lilayi that he was subjected to a prolonged interrogation. Eventually the police managed to get him to 'tell it all' to their satisfaction. The so called 'Interrogation Notes' were later perceived by the police as a convenient confession by Valentine Musakanya during the treason trial ... I wanted to know as much as possible from our own client about the police interrogation at Lilayi Police Station ... Within a few days Valentine Musakanya had felt at ease with the officers at Lilayi. They were friendly and courteous. He told them all that they wanted to know.
>
> (John Mwanakatwe, *John Mwanakatwe, Teacher, Politician Lawyer*)

In a different book, *One Zambia, Many Histories* (reprinted 2009) which also contains an essay by Larmer, under the title 'Enemies Within? Opposition to the Zambian One-Party State, 1972–1980', Mwanakatwe's above description of 'prolonged interrogation' is interpreted as a polite code for torture, which is simply not correct. Valentine, in his *Papers*, reported his interrogation as lasting from 3:30 in the afternoon to five the next morning; he also reported Edward's as lasting from two in the afternoon of 31 October 1980 till six the following morning; and he mentions no torture either for himself or Edward. With regard to Goodwin Mumba's interrogation which preceded his, Valentine says:

> I heard a lot about the tortures perpetrated by the Special Branch during interrogation and many in the cell who had undergone the treatment exhibited scars in various parts of their anatomy. It sent my blood cold. I consequently enquired whether Mumba had been tortured and was told that, though visibly roughed up and exhausted from long hours of interrogation, he did not appear to have been tortured – maybe afterwards.

It would have been strange for Valentine to have shown so much awareness of torture likely to have been meted out to others, and so much fear of it, to omit to mention his, if it had, in fact, taken place. But the very title of the book *One Zambia, Many Histories* says it all: the Lembani Trust editors appear to have set out to reinvent the history of Zambia. As I said earlier, some foreign academics' papers in the book stretch facts to suit their arguments in order to prove their predetermined theories.

But back to Mwanakatwe's book. Valentine's behaviour that Mwanakatwe describes above ('within a few days Valentine Musakanya had felt at ease with the officers at Lilayi. They were friendly and courteous. He told them all that they wanted to know') would have been typical. If he decided that his interrogators were 'nice' but 'misguided' people he would have proceeded to give them a lecture on how the UNIP policies had been harmful and how the country could be run better, and what the government should have been doing, and how they should perform their own duties, a quality born out of his desire to 'educate' people, in true Valentine style. The need for change would have naturally flowed through in the course of his 'sermon' and from it the inevitable 'confession'.

The interrogation notes are taken as a guide to the officers who will later obtain the 'warn and caution' statement, which the accused must sign. Astutely Mwanakatwe recognized that, on their own, they would not constitute evidence acceptable by the court. So he set up a strategy to ensure that Valentine did not subsequently say anything to incriminate himself. Apart from the interrogation notes, the only evidence connecting him with the coup would have been that of General Kabwe, the Zambia air force commander who had been tasked to divert the President's plane. But the general had been a co-conspirator turned state witness and his evidence needed corroboration in order to be admitted. Mwanakatwe avoided the risk of corroboration by ensuring that Valentine in his official 'warn and caution' statement remained silent so that he would not repeat what he had said at Lilayi. Having nothing else to corroborate Kabwe's testimony about Valentine's involvement, the prosecution tabled the 'interrogation notes' as exhibit 100 during the trial. Mwanakatwe was rightly expecting the judge to reject it as inadmissible. And he later ensured that he did not call Valentine to give evidence in his own defence in case the prosecution extracted the corroborating evidence it needed during cross-examination. Unfortunately, despite Mwanakatwe's assessment, the trial judge admitted the 'interrogation notes' and Valentine was convicted along with the others.

But, on appeal, the Supreme Court rejected the interrogation notes. According to Mwanakatwe's autobiography 'a number of passages in the judgment illustrate the Supreme Court's abhorrence of the State's effort to use the interrogation notes as a substitute for a confession'. The Supreme Court concluded:

Clearly the interrogation notes were, to all intents and purposes, admitted as evidence and used by the trial Court as if they were a substitute for a properly admitted confession. This was misdirection. The significance and purpose of interrogation is to aid police investigations, not to later turn it into evidence. It would be undesirable to promote the status of interrogation notes to the status or quasi status of confession since, for obvious reasons, the police would usually be tempted to prefer the former. In this case Appellant Valentine Musakanya made a statement to the police subsequent to the interrogation (the one he gave under Mwanakatwe's advice) but because it was apparently of no interest to them, they preferred to fall back to the interrogation notes, which had been made as an aide-memoire and not for the purpose of production in Court.

(*John Mwanakatwe*)

Mwanakatwe's strategy triumphed in the end. Valentine was acquitted but the death sentences of Edward and the others were confirmed. They were later commuted by the President to a term of 15 years' imprisonment. They were all granted amnesty in 1990, when Kaunda decided to scrap the 'One Party' constitution and reintroduced democracy in the country. At a press conference on his release Shamwana admitted his involvement in the coup and justified it on the grounds that there were no alternative options in those days for expressing opposition to the regime, a far-fetched excuse. The reality was that even though the 'One Party' regime was quite fierce and callous, some form of democratic protest never stopped, and was exercised frequently, against food shortages, high prices and so on. And when all is said and done, unlike Valentine, Edward was part of the establishment playing golf with Kaunda and negotiating with him to be appointed chief justice.

Later I discovered that the British MI6 had also been aware of the preparations for the coup. Valentine had flown to London and spoken to Daphne Park, his ex-boss at the British Consulate in Katanga and later head of station for MI6 in Lusaka under the guise of British Deputy High Commissioner. By that time Park, who had retired and lived in Oxford, had been publicly named as one of the MI6 directors in a number of articles in the London *Observer*. Valentine never revealed if he was encouraged or otherwise and I never found out what MI6 did with the information. Strictly speaking they should have reported it to Kaunda but, years later, Kaunda assured me that they never reported anything to him.

Conditions in the country were going from bad to worse. Despite the independence of Zimbabwe and the opening of the southern routes, shortages of essential commodities were getting worse, mealie meal queues were getting longer and the people were getting angrier.

14. DISARRAY

Even though he no longer had the excuse of the Rhodesian sanctions to soothe his conscience that what the country was going through was its contribution to the liberation of Zimbabwe, Kaunda remained amazingly sanguine about the continued hardships. By that time he had become hostage to the Central Committee of UNIP and the other retainers he kept around in the form of cabinet ministers, army commanders, police commissioners, intelligence officers, State House special assistants, and other senior functionaries. He kept shuffling the same people around from one portfolio to the next. And they took it for granted that theirs was a job for life as long as they kept UNIP in power. It was like a game of musical chairs and it had become a long established custom. I witnessed its genesis in the middle of 1970, and it made me get out of government in January 1971. Valentine Musakanya had recognized it too and tried to stop it, as is obvious from a memorandum he sent to Kaunda on 24 March 1971. Very perceptively, he said:

> Unfortunately, most of these reforms have not aimed at improving the quality of government or solving administrative problems but rather to accommodate political pressures or to fit some incompetent individuals from one ministry they have destroyed into another which, in some cases they equally succeed in destroying ... We have now reached a point where further reorganization or reshuffles are just going to produce a reversion to square 1 or square 2, or square 4 because we have been through all the squares of government organizations.

More than a decade later, the same people were occupying the UNIP musical chairs; by that time they had formed an iron curtain between Kaunda and the public and kept him out of touch with reality.

The unfettered government control of the mines had similar unfortunate repercussions. The quality of the management declined and the CEOs and most other head office executives who were appointed by the government performed more like senior clerks, instead of senior executives of the most important industry in the country. They displayed an amazing ability to grovel in front of their bosses, and bark at everybody else. They squandered the resources of ZCCM on hare-brained wasteful projects, a few of their own invention but mostly dictated by the politicians or their friends and, in the process, transformed ZCCM from a respectable mining house into a mindless conglomerate encompassing all sorts of irrelevant businesses.

As the original agreements with the International Mining Groups that would have prevented it had been thrown to the wind in 1973, ZCCM became the dustbin of sundry unrelated businesses divined by politicians and its inept and sycophantic management. If the public complained that the price of mealie meal was high, the politicians would decree that it was due to profiteering by the millers. ZCCM would then be instructed to buy the milling companies in order to save the general public from the millers' exploitation and ZCCM's management would oblige paying large sums of ZCCM money without protest. An example of how far this folly had spread was the 'Cleanwell' subsidiary. Somebody, or his wife, high up must have complained about the quality of dry-cleaners in Lusaka, so ZCCM management came up with the 'Cleanwell' group of dry-cleaning shops in most major towns. And that was not all. On the fallacious argument that because of instability in Zaire (now D. R. Congo), Zambia was vulnerable to attacks from the north (a far-fetched notion in the eighties when Zimbabwe, Mozambique and Angola were already free and the only 'hostile' country in the region was the remote South Africa), the government decided to nationalize all privately owned tourist resorts, fishing operations and even crocodile farms on Lake Tanganyika. ZCCM was again mandated to negotiate and finance these acquisitions. And it went one step further. It proceeded to buy a number of irrelevant farms owned by white settlers in the Northern Province, thus assisting them to realize their investments at high prices and depart.

While the international institutions and the donor countries were trying to put a stop to the expansion of the state-owned business sector, ZCCM became the vehicle for continued government business expansion regardless. It created a subsidiary under the name of Mulungushi Investments and embarked upon all sorts of ventures, in engineering and construction, mining, shaft sinking, transport, agriculture, tourist resorts (on Lake Tanganyika, Lower Zambezi and the two main Game Parks), photographic and hunting safaris, crocodile farms, a tractor assembly, dry-cleaners, anything the politicians or its management divined. These were only some of the outlandish projects that ZCCM sank money into. Huge sums were also invested in large agricultural projects such as the Munkumpu irrigated wheat scheme, way outside ZCCM's capabilities and expertise, which never made a profit. And in Njangi, a commuter train project in Lusaka, some 300 miles from the ZCCM operations. In fact none of the Mulungushi enterprises was viable in the real world of business, outside the patronage of ZCCM.

The most apt description of ZCCM, at that time, as 'a State within a State', came from London stockbrokers Kitcat Aitken & Co. At a time when the price of copper was low and ZCCM should be conserving all its resources to finance its operations, its Mulungushi Investments subsidiary became a bottomless pit, swallowing tens, perhaps hundreds of millions of dollars that should have been properly applied to new mining equipment and mine rehabilitation, in order to stem the ever increasing decline in copper production, year after year.

The rest of the parastatal sector was an even bigger disaster. The appointment of senior management was either political or nepotistic. Competence and expertise were irrelevant. And this pattern followed through the ranks. Most companies squandered their working capital and were not able to replace inventories or finance routine maintenance of their plant and equipment, which resulted in severe shortages right through the country. So the nation was sinking deeper and deeper into the morass of economic decline, but its government did not seem to care and did not bother to look for ways out of the vicious circle. It seemed to lack the collective determination to introduce the necessary measures and give them a chance to take effect. Instead of focusing on fundamentals, it was tinkering at trivialities.

In October 1985, it attempted to remedy the disparity between the market and the official value of the Kwacha. Instead of allowing the Kwacha to float in order to find its proper level, it allowed only a partial float: just for commercial transactions. It still maintained the official rate for all official transactions, thus penalizing all exporters, ZCCM most prominent amongst them, who had to surrender their export earnings to the Bank of Zambia at the official rate. The Kwacha immediately dropped from K2.17 to the dollar to K5.25 and by early 1987 it had dropped to K21, which meant that ZCCM and other exporters who were initially losing more than half of their income were later losing as much as 90 per cent. Unbelievably, the IMF gave its blessing to this policy. When the Kwacha was showing signs that it might stabilize at around K25 to the dollar, the government got cold feet and reversed course. It fixed the Kwacha to a parity of eight to the dollar, a revaluation of over 300 per cent! But tinkering with the parity of the Kwacha could not solve the country's real problem, which was the huge foreign payment arrears. The so-called 'foreign exchange pipeline' was three to four years long and extracting payments out of it had become the 'mother' of corruption, with the allocation of the scarce foreign exchange for imports or other payments ranking a close second. At the same time, the budget deficit had become unbridgeable and the revenues of ZCCM had to be raided time and again with the connivance of the IMF in order to reduce the gap to more presentable levels. The method used was a new mineral export tax, unbudgeted and hidden from the public, imposed on ZCCM retrospectively and adjusted to reduce or completely eliminate the budget deficit – an exercise repeated year after year with the connivance of the IMF.

I maintained periodic visits to Kaunda and every time I saw him I tried to persuade him that the problems of the country went to the heart of his government. The United National Independence Party had served its purpose, I told him. It had brought independence to the nation but that had been two decades earlier and UNIP had rested on that achievement long enough: moreover, it had exploited it to the hilt. Probably less than a million people out of a total population of seven million in the mid-eighties, remembered the colonial days and the independence struggle, or cared much about it. Their main concern was their everyday lives, how to get jobs, how to feed their families and educate their children. They were angry about the shortages of essential commodities that had become a way of life. The women did not want to get up at dawn and stand in line in order to buy mealie meal. There were solutions to these problems and he had a duty to find them. He could start with liberating the country through retiring some of the old 'freedom fighters' who were constricting it and holding a lid over the emergence of younger people, fresh thinking and new approach. I reminded him that the greatest achievement of his administration had been in education and people development. In the 20 or so years of independence the nation had developed plenty of young enlightened people with good educations, professional qualifications, and open minds that he could use. The UNIP Central Committee had become a millstone around his neck and that, for the sake of the country, he ought to break free of and get new blood into the government.

And I suggested some practical solutions: I pointed out that the sale of the state companies could generate substantial cash inflows for the government and at the same time act as catalyst to revive the economy. I argued that by then, government participation in business had achieved its purpose – it had brought about substantial Zambianization of the economy. The parastatal sector was very large but by the mid-eighties there was also a large number of Zambian-owned businesses, along with the large expatriate business sector, which having remained in the country so long after independence was more ready to conform. But, more importantly, there were now large numbers of Zambian executives, working locally or seeking opportunities in neighbouring countries. It was these Zambian executives, able to compete internationally, who were the shining success of the Mulungushi reforms and not the government companies many of which had squandered their capital and were in dire need of recapitalization.

116

I highlighted some of the many internationally marketable companies such as the breweries, the textile companies, the engineering companies, the international hotels, transport companies and trading companies. Most of them were not running well because they lacked resources to rehabilitate and renew their equipment. Others had eaten into their working capital because of incompetent management. But they would still make attractive acquisition targets and some of them would command premium prices. The income from their disposal would cover some of the many holes in the budget and reduce the government deficit. The foreign exchange pipeline could be reduced too by releasing pipeline funds to the queuing lenders for the purpose of purchasing government companies, or making any other kind of investment in Zambia. The release of pipeline funds would not in itself make a positive cash flow difference to the country. But it would reduce an international obligation and facilitate new investment. The economic advantage would come because the new investors would then have to introduce new capital for rehabilitation of the plant and equipment and revitalization of the businesses taken over. And the revitalized businesses would generate employment and tax revenues. Adopting this process would revive a large part of the industrial and commercial sector. As regards the smaller government companies, they could be sold to Zambian businessmen on easy terms, giving a new fillip to that sector.

Kaunda always displayed keen interest in these schemes. In April 1988, on the occasion of the 20th anniversary of the Mulungushi reforms, he even asked me to put the scheme down in speech form, which he intended to deliver to the UNIP National Council. I did but he never delivered it. He seemed to be suffering from complete paralysis of will. Maybe his associates assured him that everything was well in the country. But dissatisfaction was percolating and it came to the boil when a junior army officer attempted a coup that shook Kaunda out of his lethargy.

In July 1989, this coup, though unsuccessful, set off a series of protests directed at Kaunda himself followed by serious riots and looting in most major towns. The jolt made him review his position and accept that the One Party system was no longer working. He realized that he needed to reintroduce democracy in the country and even though his term of office had four more years to run, he did not try to cling on to power for the remainder of the period. He set the process for new elections as speedily as possible, much to the consternation of his inner circle. They did not want to risk losing their privileged status, which deep down they knew they did not deserve, and they fought a rearguard action for more than a year to delay progress. But the Zambian people and the Western countries were impatient for change.

The 'Movement of Multiparty Democracy' (MMD) was starting to take shape. It was promising to do away with the One Party rule, its corruption and incompetence, reintroduce democracy and free enterprise, liberate the economy from the shackles of excessive government controls, to cut down the size of government – all of them lofty goals, which gave it the edge. (It would do little on the government reform front and as far as corruption is concerned it would elevate it to levels never before experienced in Zambia.) And it had some very sincere and honest leaders in its ranks: people who had excelled in the early Kaunda administrations but did not fit into the 'One Party' atmosphere. They had either been thrown out of UNIP because they were a threat to the clique that dominated the Central Committee or left because they could not tolerate the stifling atmosphere that prevailed. There was also the usual collection of UNIP dropouts and fence sitters (ready to jump but only after they saw the UNIP ship actually going down), trade unionists and sundry hopefuls, not an untypical collection for a forming mass movement. Unfortunately when the MMD leadership election took place, the trade unionists grouped together and ensured that their chairman was elected as the leader of the new party. Frederick Titus Jacob Chiluba was an undereducated accounts clerk, working for a Swedish heavy equipment company, who had manipulated himself to the leadership of the Trade Union Congress and had held that position for many years. He and his MMD high command would produce a type of administration that the UNIP Central Committee would have approved. The MMD intelligentsia, defeated, licked its wounds and hoped that it would get the opportunity to make its contribution when the MMD formed the government. (They did but their contribution turned out to be short-lived because they were thrown out of the MMD like they had been thrown out of UNIP.)

Kaunda appointed a commission to produce a new constitution and after a year of consultations which included all civic organizations, the churches and the MMD itself, the new constitution was approved by parliament and elections were held on 31 October 1991. Inevitably, after the paralysis and stagnation of the 1980s and the excesses of the One Party system, Kaunda suffered a crushing defeat receiving only 24 per cent of the votes cast to Chiluba's 76 per cent. He graciously bowed out.

Part III

New Brooms?

15. THE LOVE AFFAIR: TRICKY FRED AND THE WEST

Frederick Chiluba, the new president elected on 2 November 1991, may have been, as I already said, an undereducated accounts clerk, but he was a gifted Machiavelli. And he proved his credentials from day one. Even before he was sworn in, he cheered the Western countries by dismissing the heads of major parastatal companies, in a highly theatrical fashion: the ZCCM chief executive, Francis Kaunda, was bundled out of the building by armed police the morning following Chiluba's election, before the new president was sworn in. The ZCCM London manager was subjected to similar treatment through a notorious London-based Zambian wheeler-dealer who arrived there in a chauffeur-driven Rolls Royce. Chiluba cheered the West with these antics, so when a couple of days later he produced a cabinet as large as Kaunda's, even though a small cabinet had been one of the cornerstones of his election campaign, nobody complained.

Chiluba's education was Form II (grade 9), the level of some of the older members of the first cabinet of Zambia. But the first Zambian cabinet ministers had been in the freedom movement for years, travelled internationally, attended conferences and courses, and acquired political sophistication. Moreover, they were inspired by nationalism and a vision to make up for the neglect of colonialism. Chiluba's international exposure had been the odd visit to the International Labour Organization Headquarters in Geneva and his vision was to bask in the glory of the presidency and use its power for personal enrichment. He did not have any understanding of what the country needed or the intellectual capacity to judge what had been achieved since independence, what was good and needed to be built on and what should be discarded; and he did not have a vision for the future. He had been infused with anti-Kaunda rhetoric in speech after speech written for him during the election campaign and he cunningly perceived that discarding the Kaunda legacy would endear him to the West and give him the freedom to pursue his personal agenda. And the West did love him because they realized that he had no principles, unlike Kaunda whose fierce and unwavering nationalism they detested and feared.

The above notwithstanding, I, naively, thought that I should try to educate the new president.

'Come on, Mr Sardanis, it was Marxism, pure and simple.' That was his response to my analysis of the thinking behind the Zambian economic reforms of the 1960s. I thought the new president needed some briefing on the evolution of business in Zambia, the economic nationalism that prompted the Mulungushi reforms and an assessment of the foreign direct investment possibilities and their consequences that he seemed to be banking on. I gave him a run-down of the economic reforms around Africa in the 1960s and explained to him that, regardless of their individual flavour, they all had a common motive, and that was economic nationalism. I tried to make him understand that if the governments of the 1960s had not taken the measures they did, business evolution in Africa would have remained in foreign hands blocking local progress. I pointed out that in Zambia government participation in business had achieved its purpose: it had brought about substantial Zambianization of the business sector, but more importantly, the development of Zambian business executives and managers. In view of this the parastatal sector could be privatized, provided that measures were taken to ensure maximum Zambian participation. Chiluba's later implementation of the privatization policy would turn out to be more like sharing the loot amongst MPs and other MMD grandees, keeping the more juicy bits for himself, and selling off only what was of no interest to him and his cronies – a subject that I shall cover in detail later.

On foreign direct investment (FDI) I cautioned him to lower his expectations because at that time, investment in Africa was not one of the priorities of foreign capital. I explained that foreign direct investment would certainly be attracted to petroleum and the mining of other primary commodities, hydroelectric and telecommunications projects, as well as large agricultural projects that would involve huge stretches of land. I cautioned that FDI would bargain hard and demand extremely generous concessions that would override the country's business and land distribution norms and tax legislation for years to come. But he held on to his electoral campaign momentum and the conversation was dominated by his electoral slogans, without much understanding of what they stood for: free enterprise, democracy, the evils of state enterprise, corruption; and Kaunda's Marxism, of course. For a man who had named his three sons Castro, Tito and Mikoyan, the metamorphosis was remarkable.

A couple of months later Chiluba attended his first OAU Heads of State meeting in Senegal where he stunned everybody with his sermon. It was brimming with evangelical fervour (he was a 'born again') warning his fellow Heads of State that the Day of Judgement was nigh and they must repent and change their ways. They should stop building monuments to themselves and start building silos instead. (Ironically after Chiluba's own demise, his half-finished 'monument' intended to house his grandly called 'Institute for Democracy and Labour Relations' went under the hammer because the new government refused to complete it.)

In the meantime, in Zambia, Chiluba set about persecuting his predecessor. Kaunda was accused of having stolen State House property (his books that he kept on the bookshelves of his study at State House). Front page pictures of KK standing amid packages and books strewn all over a warehouse floor, with policemen searching for government property may have gratified Chiluba but highlighted his meanness and revolted many Zambians. (Chiluba would get his just deserts in 2004 when, facing charges of plunder, his property received the same photo opportunity in another warehouse. Chiluba's 'loot' was not books, though. According to his claim the government confiscated 21 trunks and 11 suitcases containing 150 suits, 300 shirts, and 50 pairs of multi-coloured shoes on elevated platforms, possessions that would have made Imelda Marcos, the notoriously extravagant wife of the Philippine dictator jealous. Chiluba was indignant at the pictures of what he called 'his underpants' spread all over the front pages. It was his own clothing and it was after all his, he said, but the State's contention was that it had been procured from a Swiss outfitter at the cost of $1,100,000 and paid through a government account.)

And he set about destroying as many of the achievements of independence as he thought would impress his sponsors. Nothing remained untouched. Even the national logo, 'One Zambia, One Nation' was suppressed, though he did not dare remove it from the coat of arms. But the biggest victim was the economy. The IMF and the World Bank as well as the donor countries wanted privatization of the government companies without delay, a suggestion I had put to him during our meeting, along with the recommendation that he should try to secure maximum Zambian participation in the process. He had promised it to the international community, he had promised it to the country, and he knew he had to deliver. But he soon recognized the merits of ZCCM as a potential personal milch cow that would make him rich and he did not want to part with it in a hurry. For similar reasons he did not want to part with any of the major government companies such as Zambia State Insurance, Zambia National Commercial Bank, ZAMTEL and ZESCO (the telecommunications and electricity companies), Nitrogen Chemicals and Kafue Textiles. Some of those companies would be milked for his party, the MMD (paying for conferences, election campaigns, and so on), as well as his government, which never felt obliged to pay its electricity or telephone bills. But he had to show some progress on the privatization front. In 1992 he created the Zambian Privatisation Agency, which sold some 150 companies divided into 280 businesses. According to RAID (Rights and Accountability in Development):

> Privatization in Zambia has been described as 'a looting exercise' by the anti-corruption group Transparency International. Many of the provisions to ensure transparency in principle have been disregarded in practice. According to one commentator the program has stalled 'amid accusations of incompetence, graft, and asset-stripping' and has become 'a source of corruption.' Transparency International and Zambian journalists have accused a cabal of ministers and officials of buying smaller businesses at bargain prices while failing to close on the sale of major industries. A former Minister for Legal Affairs confirms that Ministers were party to information about the lowest acceptable bid prices. The ZPA does not have a clear-cut responsibility, let alone the capacity, for monitoring whether businessmen and politicians have bought shares through third party proxies, even though this is illegal under the Privatization Act. Furthermore, when remaining Government holdings in some of the larger businesses are publicly floated, the ZPA has no duty to gather information about how many shares individuals have purchased. The fact that most smaller companies have been sold direct to investors by-passes the more stringent disclosure requirements under the Securities and Investment Act.
>
> A copy of ZPA's consolidated list of political leaders, public officers, and individual citizens who have bought former state owned companies was obtained from ZPA in January 1998. The last transaction date given is January 1997 and hence the information requires updating. From the list it can be ascertained that eighteen businesses had been sold to politicians and public officers. Twelve shops and trading outlets in towns across the country were bought by ten MPs including among their number seven Ministers or Deputy Ministers. Hotels were bought by the Minister for Local Government and Housing and a former MMD Party MP. A dairy farm near Lusaka was sold to the Deputy Minister for Transport. A much larger farm of 10,000 hectares in Copperbelt Province was sold to RDS Investments Limited, which is owned by the immediate family of Ronald Penza, the then Finance Minister. Consolidated Tyre Services Limited was bought by Amon Kambole Sikazwe and Chibulu Jane Penza. The Penzas had also bid for the strategically important Mpulungu Harbour on Lake Tanganyika, but Ronald Penza was killed before the sale was awarded. The former Finance Minister's business interests had been subject to press scrutiny following his sacking by the President in a cabinet reshuffle in March 1998. Less than nine months later, in late November, Penza was shot dead at his home in an apparently bungled robbery. Those suspected of the crime were all shot in

extrajudicial killings by police. Some believe that Penza was assassinated and accuse the authorities of a cover-up … The investigation into Penza's murder and the killing of several of the suspects has been roundly condemned by human rights organizations.

(In addition to the Chiluba theory, I heard a number of different versions regarding the motives of this murder, ranging from Angolan diamond smugglers who had not received payment for diamonds they had delivered, to a businessman who had been advising him how to conceal his considerable offshore wealth, which according to the rumour his family was not able to access after his death.)

The RAID report continued:

> There are apparent anomalies in that politicians named in the press as owning newly privatized companies do not appear in the ZPA list. A former MMD Finance Minister completed the purchase of the General Pharmaceuticals Company based in Kabwe in May 1994 … It is alleged that, subsequent to the sale, the company was stripped of its assets, employee housing was sold to the Zambian military, the main plant was disposed of, and the workforce sacked without severance pay. This must represent a violation of the right to housing and the right to just and favorable conditions of work. The Parliamentary Committee on Public Investments has also expressed its concern over asset stripping by parastatal managers in companies prior to their privatization. The ZPA has itself noted that: 'Management of certain State Owned Enterprises (SOE) provided themselves extraordinary and excessive benefits in anticipation of privatization. This created difficulties in negotiations and had a negative impact.'

Many sales of state-owned companies were made on credit, against the better judgement of the Privatisation Agency and had to be repossessed some years later because the owners did not keep up with their instalments. But while Ministers and Deputy Ministers and MPs were getting the small businesses, Chiluba had an eye for the big ones.

Zambia Airways was established in 1967 and had been managed initially by Alitalia and later by Aer Lingus. Over the years it had a limited but, from a Zambian tourism point of view, extremely useful network of overseas destinations (Rome, Frankfurt, Amsterdam, Larnaca, London, West Africa, New York, Bombay). It was giving good and reliable service, had a good reputation amongst international agents, its overseas routes were profitable, but, more importantly, it had strategic sources for inward tourism. It had an extensive local schedule covering all tourist destinations within Zambia but also, for political reasons, a lot of rural towns where traffic was minimal rendering the entire internal services operation unprofitable. It was grossly overmanned and loss-making and needed reorganization. Instead, it was put into liquidation. The result was a major setback for Zambian tourism. After the demise of Zambia Airways, international visitors could only get to Lusaka by South African Airways via Johannesburg or by the British Airways' thrice weekly flight via Harare and had to travel internally by single or twin engine chartered planes, at exorbitant cost. As a result, Zimbabwean tourism blossomed and Zambian withered.

What Zambia Airways needed was efficient management: not liquidation. It owned its offices in London and New York, both valuable pieces of real estate that could have been sold to generate liquidity to put it back on its feet. But if rumours circulating at the time are to be believed, liquidation was not Chiluba's original intention. His plan was to close down Zambia Airways and replace it with a new one, operated by an Australian domestic airline, in which he would have a major share, but the Australians got cold feet at the last minute. He would try similar schemes a number of times during his administration.

While Chiluba was only tinkering with privatization, he dashed headlong into mindless economic policies that damaged irreparably the country's economic base, through an overzealous prolonged implementation of an IMF ordained 'structural adjustment programme', in 1993. The first target was the interest rates. The average base lending rate in Zambia rose from 60.6 per cent per annum at the beginning of the year to 214.4 per cent at the end of March and 241.7 at the end of June before it started falling to 239.9 at the end of September and 132.5 at the end of December (Bank of Zambia Report 1993 – Table 12.2, page 44). Even the World Bank was up in arms with this Zambian self-flagellation and during a visit to Washington senior officials asked me if I could do something about it.

I decided to go and visit Chiluba. I had not seen the man since our first encounter at the beginning of 1992. It was a memorable meeting; I described it in my book *A Venture in Africa* and I copy it below.

> Chiluba was sitting behind the desk in the presidential study at State House in Lusaka, where over many years in the past I had countless meetings with Kenneth Kaunda – familiar ground for me. The desk and the furniture were the same, arranged in the same order as they always had been: the desk opposite the entrance, with a large sofa to its right and an easy chair facing it, at right angle to the sofa. But there was a difference. Whereas Kaunda used to work mostly in a golf shirt, Chiluba was in suit and tie. He stood up to greet me and he did not go back to the desk. He showed me to the easy chair and he sat on the sofa. I explained to him the reason for my visit and my worries over the effect

of prolonged high interest rates on the economy. He immediately went into a sermon on the structural adjustment gospel. 'Mr. Sardanis, I sleep structural adjustment, I dream structural adjustment, I breathe structural adjustment ... We have to kill inflation.' He carried on with a chant on the effects of inflation on people's incomes, etc.

I do not mind arguing with presidents, but when reasoning gives way to slogans I switch off. I sat back observing his performance, my mind not even taking in what he was saying. He is an extremely small man, with unusually small eyes, set deep into his skull, and at that time he seemed 'possessed' by his sermon. But what struck me most was his attire. Light grey suit with darker pin stripes, grey shirt and a very colourful tie, with splashes of blue and yellow and green, over grey background, a similar handkerchief hanging down from his breast pocket. When his shoes came into focus (crocodile leather, coloured green, sitting on two-inch cork platforms), I decided I was wasting my time. The vanity displayed by his attire seemed to underline his empty head: his inability to think and put what he heard to logical test and make a judgement.

I concluded the meeting and left and never set eyes on the man again until six years later.

16. THE PLUNDER

Interest rates remained high for the whole of 1993, destroying the few industries that survived the foolish free market policies that had been decreed by the IMF, and that Chiluba implemented early in his administration and followed religiously ostensibly in the hope of competition and better prices for the consumers. He had to comply with the wishes of the international institutions and the donor countries on macroeconomic policy because he had no intention of making progress on the privatization of the mines, which he wanted to milk as long as possible. And being incapable of calculating the consequences he went over the top, as the enforcement of the high interest rates for a period three times as long as the IMF decreed highlights. In the process he destroyed the small industrial base of the country that had survived the stagnation of the 1980s.

The free market policy was imposed uncritically without regard to the origin and pricing of the imported products and their effects on local production. The farmers of Zambia were up in arms. South Africa was subsidizing the export of agricultural products to the extent of 17.5 per cent and they were flooding the Zambian market. They took the matter up with Chiluba's Minister of Agriculture at the time, the second white man that Chiluba had chosen for the position. (In fact all the ministers of agriculture in the early years of his administration were either whites, or Indians.) Tough luck he told them; and ignoring the South African export subsidies which he should have used to ban the import of the relevant products, he admonished the farmers to learn to live in the global market place.

But, before that, Chiluba had already destroyed peasant agriculture, by abolishing the marketing infrastructure that supported it without introducing an alternative. The National Agricultural Marketing Board (NAMBOARD) which had succeeded the Grain Marketing Board of the Northern Rhodesian and Federal periods had been in existence since the Second World War. In the Federal days it was used to support the white farmers by paying higher prices for their produce than it paid to Africans. But some years after independence, it became the mainstay of peasant agriculture and their only source of pre-planting finance. It distributed seed and fertilizers on credit to peasant farmers, getting reimbursed by deducting their cost from the value of the crop they delivered. NAMBOARD's abolition meant that, at a stroke, the peasant farmers lost their only source of pre-planting finance and the only body with established facilities to buy their produce. The result? The World Bank reported that 60–70 per cent of smallholders (i.e. all peasants except those living near the towns) have not benefited from government measures to stimulate agricultural production. In other words, the benefits went to the white farmers, naturally enough bearing in mind that his first Minister of Agriculture was a white farmer himself.

I suspect that when the IMF decreed the abolition of NAMBOARD, it expected the millers to fill the vacuum, but nobody had bothered to investigate if they had the financial capacity to do so. At that time the millers used to draw their maize from NAMBOARD as and when they needed, so they had neither the surplus funds nor the finance facilities necessary to cover a whole year's requirements, during the short harvest season. And they did not have the storage facilities either. Chiluba decided that the party faithful should come to the rescue and make some money in the process. He gave out generous loans to his cronies ostensibly in order to buy produce in the rural areas. But, as I said earlier, at the same time he pushed the interest rates to over 200 per cent per annum. It did not need a financial genius to calculate that one would be better off remaining in Lusaka and buying treasury bills with the money he received for buying maize instead of languishing in the rural areas – and that is what most would-be grain buyers did. So the produce was left to rot and the following season the peasant farmers did not have any money to buy seed and other agricultural inputs. Most of those loans to the party faithful were not repaid and were transferred to the Food Reserve Agency, which inevitably had to be created in order to succeed NAMBOARD. When food production dropped, Guy Scott, Chiluba's first Minister of Agriculture, offered incentives to the white commercial farmers to produce maize, thus reversing the Kaunda policy of producing the national requirements of maize through the peasants and steering the white farmers towards producing export crops.

In the previous chapter I described the beginning of the privatization process and the way many of the state companies were bought by MMD grandees and other senior functionaries. But did they ever pay and how much? RAID, in 1998, reports attempts to trace the receipt and disposal of the privatization proceeds but seems lost in the byzantine accounting methods of the Zambian Privatisation Agency (ZPA) and the government. Summarizing the period to June 1997 it states:

By adding up the cash generated from each and every sale, the total amount up until the end of June 1997 was in the region of 143 billion Kwacha. Some of this amount was on differed payment terms, but, by the same date, at the very least K100 billion should have gone into the Privatisation Revenue Account (PRA). Unofficial estimates put the actual amount passing into the account at less than half this figure. At the end of June 1997, the balance in the account was believed to be, approximately, thirty billion Kwacha ... At other times, although very large sums of cash were generated from the sale of valuable medium-sized operations or from the sell-off of the largest companies of all, no money was listed going into the PRA.

No real progress was made on the privatization of the mines until Chiluba's second term, despite increasing pressures from the multilateral institutions and the donor countries. The reasons were partly the same as those for the other big companies, but ZCCM had an additional attraction: Chiluba was able to give directions on metal sales and even before the end of his administration one major scam surfaced: he had granted exclusivity on all cobalt sales to an Israeli company, Metal Resources Group (MRG). An audit, initiated by the donor countries, that was carried out in 2001 revealed that MRG was buying the cobalt at a fraction of its international price and making huge profits. The audit, which was carried out by the Mauritian subsidiary of Anderson Worldwide, one of the major International Accounting Practices at the time, calculated 'discrepancies' on the MRG contracts amounting to $60.1 million.

The first official step towards the privatization of ZCCM came in the form of an announcement in the budget speech in January 1995. A mining privatization team was appointed within ZPA followed by the appointment of the London investment bank N M Rothschild & Sons and the legal firm Clifford Chance as consultants. Their report early in 1996, recommended the unbundling of ZCCM into 12 components to be sold separately, a recommendation similar to one that had been made a couple of years earlier by German consultants. Having managed to avoid progress for so long, Chiluba was under immense pressure to do something urgently, so much so that the World Bank refused to disburse funds under the Economic Recovery Promotion Programme until it saw real movement on the mine privatization front. But, again, he very skilfully managed to prolong the process by changing the privatization structure and bringing new players on board. In March 1997, he superimposed on the Zambian Privatisation Agency a new team named 'the GRZ/ZCCM Privatisation Negotiating Team' (PNT), under the chairmanship of Francis Kaunda (the erstwhile ZCCM chairman whom he had, unceremoniously, dismissed in 1991 before he even took the oath of office). The World Bank was taken in by this new trick and agreed to fund F. Kaunda's salary in the hope that he would accelerate the privatization process – a forlorn hope, as it turned out, because F. Kaunda's appointment was intended to achieve exactly the opposite. The appointment was in fact made contrary to the provisions of the Privatisation Act, a minor detail for Chiluba because as far he was concerned he was the law. And to make sure he personally had the final say he superimposed a Committee of Ministers (read: himself) as the final decision makers on the sale of the mines.

The first new investment in mining was outside the privatization scheme. First Quantum Minerals of Canada bought the Bwana Mkubwa disused mine and surface tailings for $26 million in 1997. As no mining costs were involved, Bwana Mkubwa turned out to be the lowest cost producer in the world at the time. First Quantum then turned its attention to the nearby Luanshya mine. It made a bid for Luanshya and was selected by ZPA and its consultants, the London Investment Bank N M Rothschild, as the winning bidder. While detailed negotiations were taking place in order to finalize the deal, F. Kaunda's PNT intervened and demanded revised bids, which resulted in the award of Luanshya to a new company named Roan Antelope Mining Corporation (RAMCOZ), owned by Gokul Binani, an Indian metal trader operating out of London who had no mining experience of any kind. First Quantum was furious with the award. In a strongly worded letter to F. Kaunda, its chairman wrote:

> To its extreme surprise on 17 June 1997 FQM was asked to submit a revised bid at only two days' notice. FQM duly complied with this request, despite the unreasonably short notice, even though a re-bidding exercise was clearly inconsistent with all discussions FQM was having with ZCCM, ZPA and NM Rothschild. FQM does not accept, after this effort and consistency of behaviour on its behalf that ZCCM had grounds to announce another party as the purchaser without first establishing that there were irreconcilable differences in negotiations with FQM. Of concern to us are reports that Binani appears to have received details of our bids and had knowledge of private correspondence between FQM and ZCCM and their advisers ... If what we are hearing about the bidding process is true then the board of FQM may be obliged to seek legal advice to establish what formal recourse it may take to protect its position and obtain legal remedies. We would emphasise that any perception that the privatisation process has not been conducted with transparency, consistency and correctness will be alarming to the international financial markets.
>
> (Francis Kaunda, *Selling the Family Silver: The Zambian Copper Mines Story*)

The details of Binani's winning bid with First Quantum's in brackets were: cash $35 ($34) million, new equity investment $21.7 ($20) million, commitment for new investment $69 ($70.4) million, contingent investment $103 ($26.3) million, ZCCM participation 15% (17.5%): a 'neck to neck' outcome (except for the nebulous $103 million 'contingent investment' that Binani stuck to the tail of his offer) which seems to justify First Quantum's contention that copies of its bid were passed to Binani. A combined report made by RAID and AFRONET (Inter-African Network for Human Rights and Development) dated January 2002, makes the following comments on the issue:

> Binani's last minute bid bettered First Quantum's offer by a precise margin, prompting First Quantum to allege that details of its own bid had been leaked. Binani had no copper mining experience, had not conducted full underground studies, and analysts question whether it had the necessary financial backing to fund its ambitious plans for the Luanshya operations. The fears have proved to be well founded. The deterioration of employment conditions, coupled with persecution of the local union leader, prompted unprecedented industrial unrest in Luanshya in November 1998. There have been negative repercussions for social provisions in the local community. Management of the mine has led to a series of financial crises culminating in the mine going into receivership in November 2000.

The liquidity problems at Luanshya mine had surfaced soon after the RAMCOZ takeover amid rumours that the copper proceeds were not being remitted to Luanshya regularly. But the government bent over backwards to keep it going, ordering the government-owned Zambian Electricity Corporation (ZESCO) to supply electricity despite huge unpaid bills, and ordering the then also government-owned Zambia National Commercial Bank (ZANACO) to grant additional facilities ignoring huge arrears. At one stage the government even contemplated diverting a World Bank facility intended for mineworkers' retrenchment to RAMCOZ. This is revealed by F. Kaunda in his own book *Selling the Family Silver*. He describes it thus:

> Mines Minister lent a sympathetic ear to RAMCOZ over their problems and tried to get the government to help by approaching his colleague at the Ministry of Finance to extend a World Bank facility on ZCCM retrenchment to Maamba Collieries and the Luanshya/Baluba Mine.

But the Finance Minister of the time wisely put a stop to it. (I wonder what the World Bank and the Mineworkers Union would have to say if such a scandalous attempt had succeeded.) The government's official justification for such extraordinarily generous gestures to Binani was the need to keep the mine operating and the workers employed. But the real reasons may have been completely different. The RAID report puts it as follows:

> This blatant, initial disregard for due process and accountability presaged the unrest and infringement of rights which occurred in Luanshya little more than a year after the sale was concluded. It must also be noted that the allegation has been made in public that President Chiluba had a vested interest in the award of sale to Binani and now owns shares in the enterprise. The accusation has been denied by the President, but calls for full disclosure of share ownership persist.

In November 2000, ZANACO was forced to pull the plug, Chiluba's entreaties notwithstanding. By that time it had been placed under the supervision of the Bank of Zambia because it was drowning in bad debts, having suffered a loss of K65 billion from just RAMCOZ and the Zambia National Oil Corporation (another Chiluba creation), and the many uncollectable debts owed by politicians and their businesses.

First Quantum went on to become one of the major mining companies in Zambia. In addition to the expansion at Bwana Mkubwa it partnered Glencore in purchasing Mufulira Mine (renamed Mopani) and in 2001 it finally purchased from Cyprus Amax its 80 per cent interest in the Kansanshi copper and gold deposit, which was expected to produce 145,000 tons of copper and some 80,000 ounces of gold per annum.

The involvement of Chiluba kept surfacing in deal after deal. The RAID report continues:

> Allegations have been made in a reputable business journal that public money has been siphoned-off into private offshore companies, many of them based in the British Virgin Islands where confidentiality laws are strong and disclosure requirements are minimal. The article repeats the accusation that the web of corruption includes the President who owns assets beyond the purchasing power of his salary including properties in Belgium, the Netherlands, South Africa, and Zambia as well as stakes in an emerald mine and a lime producer.
>
> The sale of Ndola Lime was handled by Francis Kaunda's negotiating team and not by ZPA. Two leading players in the industry, Chilanga Cement and Portland Cement, tabled bids. Yet the sale was awarded in September 1998 to Socomer SA, a small Belgium firm with neither the relevant background in cement production nor apparent access to the necessary large-scale finance required to invest. Sources within the Ministry of Finance were quoted in the

Zambian press raising serious questions about the merits and transparency of the deal. Attention was drawn to Chiluba's close contacts with Socomer, including his friendship with the majority shareholder in the company. Both Socomer, through a statement from its lawyers, and the ZCCM negotiating team rejected the allegation of any links between the company and the President or the Democratic Republic of the Congo. There is presently some doubt as to whether Socomer has the finance to complete its purchase of Ndola Lime and whether other bidders are to be invited to reconsider their original tenders. However, conflicting reports suggest that Socomer is itself seeking to reduce its bid for the company to below 10 million dollars [it in fact offered 5.6 million] because of the prospect of Anglo American insisting on a five year fixed price for lime for use by Chilanga Cement while it refurbishes former ZCCM facilities.

In *Selling the Family Silver*, F. Kaunda, who at the same time was negotiating with Anglo's ZCI the purchase of Konkola, reports that as a result of the exclusion of the Ndola Lime Company from the Konkola deal, ZCI reduced its deferred cash consideration from $75 million to $56.25 million, thus valuing Ndola Lime at $18.75 million. What was amazing was that he was ready to sell Ndola Lime to Socomer for $5.6 million when the nation could have made $12.9 million more if he had kept Ndola Lime in the Konkola deal. Instead, he steadfastly supported Socomer to the bitter end, despite the better judgement of ZPA and its chairman, Luke Mbewe, who put up a gallant fight. Eventually, the Socomer sale collapsed and Ndola Lime remained with ZCCM-IH, the entity that succeeded the original ZCCM.

Another scandal involving another of the so-called ZCCM non-core assets, which properly should have also been handled by ZPA, was the sale of Kagem, a very profitable emerald mine, with an excellent international reputation for its high quality emeralds. The RAID report contends that the high quality gems were sold clandestinely to the detriment of the country and the other shareholders. It reports:

Kagem Mining, an emerald producer, was due to be sold in late 1999 under the fourth tranche of privatization. While the Government has a majority stake, forty-five per cent of the shares are owned by an Israeli gem company, Hagura which is running existing operations. The MUZ has expressed its dissatisfaction with returns from the company under private management: good quality stones mined in Zambia are apparently resold for much higher prices in the Far East. It has been alleged that President Chiluba has an interest in Hagura. Allegations have also been voiced in the

Zambian press that the President and a former Finance Minister have shared in the privatization proceeds and even sanctioned company liquidations for personal gain.

The report continues to express worries that it had not been possible to verify where proceeds of known substantial sales had been deposited:

> At other times, although very large sums of cash were generated from the sale of valuable medium-sized operations or from the sell-off of the largest companies of all, no money was listed as going into the PRA. Nor was it revealed where this money went. The list of unaccounted for revenue includes: Zambia Sugar Company – $14.8 million; Munkumpu/Nchanga Farms – $7.2 million; and Mpongwe Development – $507,000. The complete list is unquestionably much longer and is almost certain to include other significant sales. This diversion of funds was confirmed by the Committee on Public Investment in December 1997. In its report on privatization, it notes instances when the GRZ/ZCCM Privatization Negotiating Team has sold ZCCM assets such as schools without the prior authorization of the ZPA board.

And the RAID/AFRONET report highlights another questionable method used in the disposal of ZCCM's non-core assets:

> His [The Attorney General's] office had queried the disposal of certain assets by 'deed of gift' in a way not provided for under the law, but to no avail. The Parliamentary Committee despite extensive questioning of key parties declared itself unable to obtain a full and true list of all ZCCM non-core assets and could not verify what was owned, what had been sold to whom, at what price, or on what payment terms. It confirmed that the proceeds of such sales had not been remitted to PRA and that, contrary to the law, neither the ZPA Board, nor the Attorney General or the Minister of Finance and Economic Planning had signed/approved the sale of a number of non-core assets, which had therefore been sold illegally by the GRZ/ZCCM PNT.

In other words, through the Privatisation Negotiating Team Chiluba was doing whatever he liked, legal, or illegal. And he was not just giving assets away as gifts. The report reveals a much bigger problem – the fate of the proceeds from some of the largest sales:

> Proceeds from all ZCCM completed sales to the end of 1999 – Konkola North, Chibuluma, Kansanshi, Power, Luanshya/Baluba, Chambishi, Ndola Precious

Metals Plant, and Chambishi Cobalt and Acid Plants – should have yielded a cash consideration to date in the region of 185 million dollars. The whereabouts or use to which these funds have been put requires clarification.

After reading the RAID/AFRONET reports one wonders if in the end, the nation got any money from the disposal of these huge national assets. But the sales had to go on.

Initially, Chibuluma South was part of the Nkana-Nchanga package included in the negotiations with the Kafue Consortium, but it was excised and sold separately to the Metorex consortium, at the time a mid-tier miner of platinum, cobalt, copper and nickel. The cash consideration, according to *Selling the Family Silver*, was $17.5 million with a commitment for future capital expenditure of $34 million. But the RAID/AFRONET report brings to light the following:

> At the close of bidding for the Chibuluma mine in February 1997, the Metorex Consortium openly acknowledged that it was being represented in its negotiations to purchase the mine by Francis Kaunda. The other bidder for the mine was the Kafue Consortium which wanted to purchase Chibuluma as part of the Nkana/Nchanga sale package. The following month, [F] Kaunda was appointed to handle negotiations over the privatization of ZCCM. Chibuluma Mine was split from the recommended sale package and awarded to Metorex on 31 July 1997. [F] Kaunda did not publicly terminate his connection with Metorex, nor resign from the negotiating team, nor exclude himself from negotiations over the sale package which included Chibuluma.

The murky purchase notwithstanding, Chibuluma turned out to be a very well managed and profitable small mine producing some 18,000 tons of finished copper per year and employing close to 800 people, almost entirely Zambian, unlike most of the bigger mining companies whose recruitment at senior personnel level is biased towards expatriates. In 2012, Metorex sold Chibuluma to the Jinchuan Group, a Chinese miner of base metals, but the predominance of Zambian management has continued: in April 2013, Chibuluma announced the appointment of Jackson Sikamo, a Zambian, as general manager, a first in this field.

Even though the original terms granted to the mining purchasers are now out of date, because after 2011 the Sata government made substantial changes to water down the exorbitant concessions granted by Chiluba and Mwanawasa, it is worth reporting them for the record. Both RAMCOZ and Chibuluma were granted more or less similar tax concessions (the concessions became more generous in later deals as a result of World Bank and IMF pressures and threats to withhold funds if certain deals were not completed by specific dates). For RAMCOZ and Chibuluma, the most generous concession appears to have been that each mine was deemed to be a new mine under the 1975 Act which allows 100 per cent deduction of capital expenditure in the year it is incurred (this presumably included the acquisition costs as well as all subsequent investment). Carry forward losses were permitted for a period of ten years, but there was no concession on the income tax rate, as far as I was able to ascertain – an academic point because, with the generous deductions granted, income tax would not have become payable during the so-called 'taxation stability' period of 15 years. (In the event Chibuluma commenced income tax payments in 2007.) The mineral royalty was reduced from 3 per cent of revenue (minus transport and smelting and refining costs) to 2 per cent, deductible against income tax. Other concessions included exemption from import duties above 5 per cent for capital items and 20 per cent for all other goods and materials, and, more significantly, VAT exemption for a period of 15 years, with arrangements that input VAT (the VAT that mines pay when they buy goods) be refunded by government the month following the submission of a claim. As there are no exchange controls in Zambia the two companies were allowed to operate bank accounts domestically and abroad and the government gave an undertaking that if exchange controls were introduced in the future the companies would be exempt up to the end of the 15-year 'taxation stability' period. In fact all concessions mentioned above were granted for the 15-year 'stability' period.

The mining privatization process was only completed in March 2000 with the simultaneous signing of agreements for the two biggest mining complexes: with Mopani Copper Mines for the Mufulira and Nkana mines and Konkola Copper Mines (KCM) for the huge Konkola complex, which included the Nchanga open pit, the Nchanga underground mine, the Konkola underground mine, the Nchanga Tailings dump, the Chingola refractory ores, the Nchanga leach plant, the Nkana Smelter and refinery and the Nampundwe pyrite mine near Lusaka, as well as Konkola Deep, a very large copper deposit that with an investment of several hundred million dollars would become the biggest mine in Zambia, producing over 200,000 tons of copper a year for 30 years. (KCM, under different ownership by that time, announced in November 2005 that the project would go ahead with an initial investment of $400 million.)

The Mufulira and Nkana mines and related assets were sold to Mopani Copper Mines, majority owned (73.1 per cent) by Glencore International AG, a Swiss metal trading company, at the price of $20 million cash and $23 million in deferred payments, $159 million new investment commitment and an additional 'conditional investment' commitment of some $200 million (*Selling the Family Silver*).

As I said, two years earlier the government had to turn to the Anglo American Corporation for the sale of the Konkola complex, because it had nowhere else to turn to after it mystifyingly rejected the Kafue Consortium's bid for it. The Kafue Consortium included three of the biggest names in the mining world: Anglovaal Minerals (AVMIN) of South Africa, Noranda of Canada, and Phelps Dodge of the United States as well as the British Commonwealth Development Corporation, a financial institution. The RAID/AFRONET report tries to make some sense out of the last minute collapse of the year-long negotiations with the Kafue Consortium:

> A year of protracted negotiations saw the replacement of ZPA/Rothschild by a GRZ/ZCCM negotiating team in apparent contravention of the Privatization Act; the refusal of the Government to accept a deal in June 1997 worth over $ 1 billion in cash, debt assumption and investment; the excise of the Chibuluma Mine from the overall Nkana/Nchanga package to be sold to a rival bidder; a collapse of the price of copper reflecting overproduction and continued repercussions from the Sumitomo Trading scandal; the failure of the government to conclude a deal worth a total of 700 million dollars it had accepted in October 1997; the onset of recession in Asia and Japan and further falls in the copper price; and progressively lower bids by the Consortium culminating in a reduced final offer in May 1998, which were flatly rejected.

The collapse of the Kafue Consortium deal stunned the country but it infuriated the multilateral institutions, which decided to withdraw balance of payment support. The immediate effect was that payment on some $235 million pledged in May 1998 was made conditional on a swift privatization of ZCCM. These pressures were a godsend for the Anglo American Corporation. With the collapse of the Consortium it knew that the government had exhausted its options and it used its advantage to the hilt. It set impossible conditions that needed to be fulfilled before going forward; it dragged its feet for a couple of years and ended up with a bargain both in terms of price and concessions. The *Economist* magazine summed up the deal:

> Anglo American, the original owners of many of Zambia's mines, will pay only 90 million dollars for three mines in one of the richest copper deposits in the world. Last year, Zambia turned down an offer worth nearly twice as much.

I summarized this very complex, one-sided deal in *A Venture In Africa* and I repeat it below even though it has since become irrelevant, because it is important to highlight the harm that the combination of excessive pressures from the international institutions and ignorance and incompetence from negotiating teams such as the GRZ/PNT negotiators can cause to African nations. Yet, despite the extraordinary benefits that Anglo American extracted, it would hand Konkola back to the government in 2002, contending that it could not manage to run the complex profitably. The conditions of the sale to Anglo were as follows:

The Anglo American offer, made through its Bermuda-based subsidiary ZCI (Zambia Copper Investments), was very complex and full of caveats and demands for changes in existing legislation, but, in summary, it appears that the Konkola Copper Mines Ltd was sold for a total of $60 million payable as to $30 million cash and the balance over six annual installments commencing in January 2006 (in other words full payment would not be completed until 2011), with a follow-up investment of $300 million. (The actual purchase price was $90 million [as the *Economist* correctly reported], but against that the government had to buy the ZCI shares in ZCCM for $30 million.) By comparison, the Kafue Consortium's offer had been $150 million cash with a follow-up investment of $1 billion. But, more importantly, it would not have included all the fancy concessions that the government had to make under pressure from Anglo ... It is important to highlight the inclusion of the tailings dumps and the Chingola refractory ores in the package. These are residues of decades of mining and, by the then available technology, inefficient metallurgical processing that contained some 380,000 tons of copper. With technological developments these residues can now be treated at very low cost, because they are lying on the surface. Anglo was aware of this bonanza. In 1999 it paid $130 million to buy the Kolwezi tailings in the Democratic Republic of the Congo. And, as I mentioned earlier, Bwana Mkubwa, [First Quantum's] similar operation in Zambia, is one of the lowest cost producers in the world because of them.

Apart from giving Konkola away, the government of Zambia made the following tax and other concessions: A flat income tax rate of 25% (instead of 35%) for a period of 20 years; KCM to be treated as a new mine under the 1975 Act [which allows 100 per cent deduction of capital expenditure in the year it is incurred, presumably inclusive of the acquisition costs as well as all subsequent investment]; carry forward losses for a period of 20 years; no withholding tax on dividends, royalties, interest and management fees paid to KCM shareholders, affiliates or third parties; royalties of 0.6% (instead of

3%) on the gross revenue of minerals produced (less transport and smelting and refining costs), deductible against income tax; exemption from rural electrification levy and excise duty on electrical energy; no customs and excise duty on all capital goods and only 15% (instead of 25%) on all materials; and total exemption from VAT with input VAT refundable within 10 days of submission of claim. In addition, the government of Zambia bound itself not to impose new taxes and not to increase the ones mentioned in the agreement for a period of 20 years. As regards the treatment of the foreign exchange earned from copper sales, KCM was granted similar concessions as those granted to Ramcoz and Chibuluma, with some additional privileges. The most important was that it only needed to remit to Zambia foreign earnings in order to meet local commitments if it did not already have kwacha available to meet such commitments. And for this purpose it was allowed to borrow kwacha locally up to 5% of the value of its annual sales revenues, which at mid-2006 revenues and rates would translate to some K100 billion [$25 million at the time: in other words it would not need to remit foreign exchange].

But the concession that affects the miners' lives most was the one relating to 'social assets and municipal infrastructural services'. While under an agreement with the Mineworkers Union (MUZ) KCM agreed to 'the provision or procurement of certain medical and recreational services and access to other recreational facilities', the government took over the provision of municipal infrastructural services in areas where KCM would operate. These included: water, sewerage, solid waste, domestic electricity supply, street lighting, storm drainage, roads, markets and cemeteries. By tradition in Zambia and many other parts of the world, the mine owners build housing for their employees and run the townships, including maintenance of all services, schools and hospitals ... but Anglo American baulked at the expense of running the townships.

According to the RAID/AFRONET report, the World Bank again came to Anglo American's rescue. It offered the government $37.7 million as a Mine Services Support package to cover the costs of financing some of the services in the mine townships of Nchanga, Nkana, Konkola, Mufulira and Luanshya – a band aid, of course, but it gave everybody the illusion of a solution while the problem remains unresolved to this day. In the end, the relevant municipalities have been landed with the task of servicing the townships, at an annual cost well in excess of the World Bank's $37.7 million. As they do not have enough revenue to cover the costs, the townships are neglected and the miners are angry.

The verdict about the mining privatization process must be that it was botched and intentionally so. Chiluba wanted to milk the mines for as long as possible and he employed many tricks to delay the privatization process. In the end the mines were sold at giveaway prices and some of the new owners lacked the expertise to operate them. The safety record of the industry, which was an example in Southern Africa, deteriorated, with a major accident reported almost weekly, some involving serious loss of life (an explosion at a new explosives factory killed 52 people in early 2005). And last but not least most of the proceeds from the disposals cannot be traced.

Did Chiluba do anything useful during his ten-year administration? Indirectly and without meaning to he did.

17. THE ZAMBIAN BUSINESS BLOSSOMS; THE ECONOMY DIPS

Chiluba cannot be given credit for overturning the One Party regime. That credit must go to the people of Zambia, because it is they in their own unique way that brought it about. And they achieved it in an amazingly peaceful fashion – food queues, a protest here, a strike there, a demonstration, a riot, a botched coup attempt, or two. And credit must also be given to Kaunda who grasped the message and bowed out; and to his colleagues who followed him, albeit many of them reluctantly; and to those who formed the Movement for Multiparty Democracy, Chiluba included, and kept it cool and civilized. But, Chiluba does deserve some credit despite his many faults. He stayed on message. He opened up the country, politically and economically, even though, at times, he did not seem to want to do it or know that he was doing it. The MMD deserves credit too, because, unlike UNIP, it did not try to regiment the society and did not issue diktats.

During the Chiluba administration the society emerged from under the shroud of the UNIP Central Committee dictatorship, with its obsession for controlling everybody and everything, and breathed openness for the first time in many years. And despite Chiluba's repeated blunders and vindictiveness particularly against Kaunda, optimism reigned. The media opened up too and dropped some of the sycophancy and servility towards the apparatchiks that it had been conditioned to bow to. Even though the economy was buffeted by the twin attacks of the IMF's structural adjustment and Chiluba's ignorant and overzealous implementation of it, business felt free and more optimistic. The abolition of the exchange control regulations and the establishment of the Lusaka Stock Exchange gave business a feeling of optimism that the time was ripe to embark upon new ventures. Endeavour and wealth stopped being considered antisocial and individuals felt free to grasp opportunities and try their hand at whatever came their way.

A major beneficial effect of privatization was that whole business sectors, previously reserved for state monopolies, suddenly opened up for competition. And with no exchange controls to ration foreign currency in order to satisfy the insatiable appetite of the parastatals and the fancies of bureaucrats and politicians, large numbers of Zambian airborne entrepreneurs, mainly women initially, blossomed. They would fly to South Africa with cash dollars in their pockets and return laden with suitcases of merchandise. They started out by distributing personally to random customers but as time went by to regular ones and later through shops and business premises. And, as they gained experience, in addition to South Africa they ventured further afield: to Dubai, and India and China and Hong Kong and Malaysia, and the range of merchandise expanded from fashions, to household goods, to kitchen equipment, to spare parts for vehicles and equipment, to electronics, builders' hardware and plumbing materials – the whole range that hitherto had been sold in shops owned by whites, Indians and newly arrived foreign enterprises. The foundation for all this was laid during Chiluba's administration, not by Chiluba or his government but by the entrepreneurial spirit of individuals. As time went by Zambian business took roots and it is still growing and expanding and we are now able to talk about SMEs and how to help them grow. And, in addition, we now have many large Zambian businesses that have grown from those humble beginnings and are now flourishing locally and in the region and internationally.

It is ironic that it was Kaunda who had launched the idea of a fast track for the development of Zambian enterprise with the Mulungushi reforms in 1968. But the many mindless twists and turns of the UNIP policies never gave it a chance to grow. The nascent Zambian enterprise was first shackled by the 'socialist revolution' when the national struggle changed from being 'a fight against poverty, hunger, ignorance and disease' to being a fight against 'capitalism and its offshoots' and later smothered by the 'One Party' doctrine, when, outrageously, the United National Independence Party declared itself 'supreme and the sole custodian of the people's interests' and the goal became the 'establishment of a humanist state where there will be no private enterprise'. In other words, the aim of Mulungushi reforms, which was to open a fast track for Zambian enterprise to grow, ran contrary to the later UNIP anti-capitalist thinking and became absolutely taboo in the 'humanist' utopia where private enterprise should not exist. To be fair, as I have already said, the rhetoric was a manifestation of UNIP's mania for controlling everything and everybody, and it was never followed by legislation to put any of that nonsense into effect. Even so, it did scare people and made them sit back. (I had personal experience: in order to help my neighbours who every December 'suffer' from overproduction of mangos, which rot and are thrown away, I decided to send an experimental consignment to London in the hope of establishing a market for them. The next thing I knew was a report from a friend that a senior UNIP grandee from the

Eastern Province was asking in political circles: 'Isn't Andrew making enough money out of his businesses and he now wants to take the food out of our mouth?' This gave my Zambian associates the opportunity to drop the project. They were not in favour of it in the first place and to be fair to them it was not a business proposition.)

But the laissez-faire policies of the Chiluba administration gave a chance to new initiatives to come to the surface and thrive. Many would-be entrepreneurs, who during the UNIP days whiled away their time in bureaucratic positions, afraid to use their savings in order to venture out because of UNIP's menacing rhetoric and its 'leadership code', grasped the opportunity to make a start. Many became successful and more followed and the numbers and the range of enterprises have been growing ever since. Zambian business is now firmly entrenched and nobody will dare touch it from now on.

The most shining example of what the Zambian entrepreneurial genius can, if left free, achieve, is the transport industry, which was reinvented by the Zambians, and is now completely in local hands and thriving. But, more importantly, it provided the seed for many new businesses, big and small. Its evolution was a joy to watch. It started during the last couple of years of the Kaunda era, when the government-owned United Bus Company started folding up. Poor management, inadequate controls and antiquated equipment took their toll and the company no longer had enough vehicles to service its routes. Zambian entrepreneurs spotted the opportunity and started buying minibuses to fill the gap. Pragmatically the UNIP era Ministry of Transport gave them 'road service permits' (needed in order to run public service vehicles) even though it was contrary to the doctrine of the day. But the Chiluba administration went one step further: it removed the customs duty on minibuses thus reducing the cost of a minibus, mostly imported second-hand from Japan, to between five and ten thousand dollars depending on size. So, minibuses replaced large expensive buses run in the colonial days by the British-owned Central African Road Services and later dilapidated ones run by the government-owned United Bus Company of Zambia. The owners were usually in full-time employment elsewhere. They would buy the first minibus which was then operated by members of the family. More minibuses followed. Sometimes they developed into a fleet financed by the profits of the enterprise. The minibuses that still dominate the city routes have now evolved into coaches for the intercity long-haul routes. And some operators have embarked on the long-haul freight services to Durban and Dar es Salaam. Or the minibus business was sold in order to provide the capital for a new venture not connected with transport.

All these achievements make a shining example of how home grown activities in harmony with the norms of the society can thrive. And they are all the more significant because they were made without official support, apart from the removal of import duties on minibuses by Chiluba. No outsider identified them and no government or other type of financing was involved. Individuals spotted the opportunity and started at the bottom, with personal and family money, and they succeeded through hard work along the lines of the rural Zambian tradition I encountered when I first arrived in the country in 1950 – self-help. From my later experience in INDECO, government loans were usually tapped by people with political connections. And very few borrowers ever intended to pay them back. The majority treated them as rewards for services rendered to political patrons. The same applied to the co-operative society grants and loans in those days, with the local UNIP branch chairman and the chairman of the Co-op being one and the same person cornering the co-operative's cash. And more recently funds from the Economic Empowerment Commission (EEC) appear to have suffered a similar fate.

But loans from established financial institutions and banks do not suffer this fate. Even though interest rates in Zambia have been the highest in sub-Saharan Africa for decades, and despite the reductions the Sata government achieved are still exorbitant, commercially contracted loans are serviced and the incidence of bad debts, though high, is not overwhelming like it used to be during my INDECO days. And the banks can still make obscene profits, higher than anywhere else. Chiluba's contribution to Zambian business development was that he created the enabling environment and did not try to interfere – a lesson future governments should take on board.

Unlike Kaunda who banned UNIP leaders and civil servants from having business interests, Chiluba encouraged them. Many may not think this to have been wise, but it was pragmatic. Despite the rhetoric, many UNIP leaders and civil servants did have business interests, and even though Kaunda may not have acknowledged it, he was aware of it. And, in those days, there were very few opportunities for investing personal savings, so opening family businesses made good sense. The problem arises only when civil servants operate in fields connected with their official duties, which invites corruption camouflaged as business deals and should be banned, and the culprits penalized and dismissed.

But the progress of Zambian businessmen should not be taken as an indication of Chiluba's overall economic success. The free market policies that caused the flood of foreign imports from South Africa and other countries destroyed many industries that had survived the gyrations of UNIP policies and the scarcity of hard currency. And the mindless importation of second-hand clothing which was allowed into the country with only nominal duty based on weight and not on value struck a fatal blow to the clothing industry, destroying some 200 clothing factories and tens of thousands of jobs.

The economic indicators of the period give a sorry picture. According to the *Education Characteristics 1990 and 2000 Censuses*: the GDP per capita at current US dollars in 1991, the last year of the Kaunda administration, was $418.54, while in 2001, the last year of the Chiluba administration, it was $349.65, a drop of 16.5 per cent. (So much for the structural adjustment programme that Chiluba followed uncritically.) Formal employment went down from 562,791 in 1990 to 513,512 in 2000, a 9 per cent drop in a decade. The literacy rate for the population aged 5 and above remained static between 1990 and 2000 at 55.3 per cent of the population. School attendance increased by less than 1 per cent between 1990 and 2000 from 25.8 per cent of the population to 26.7. Primary school attendance went down from 82.3 per cent to 79.1, while the secondary school attendance remained static at 53.9.

One can only conclude that the Chiluba administration from 1991 to 2001 was a wasted decade. But it was also a mean and nasty decade as Chiluba's vengeful streak surfaced time and again.

18. VENGEANCE AND CRUELTY AND FRUSTRATED AMBITION

Chiluba remained the darling of the Western countries for the whole of his first term despite many blatantly undemocratic steps, including a declaration of a 'state of emergency', incarcerations and medically proven ill-treatment and torture of detainees. He first turned his guns on Kaunda. He deprived him of his terminal benefits on the flimsy grounds that he was still involved in politics (in the process of handing over to a successor) and he had not therefore retired. Then, as I described earlier, he charged him with stealing government property. After Kaunda, he turned his guns on UNIP and its leaders. He arrested 26 senior members and charged them with 'planning to overthrow his government with the assistance of Iran and Iraq' (an unlikely duo). The 'Zero Option Plan', as the scheme was named, was supposed to have been hatched by two UNIP MPs, Cuthbert Nguni and Wezi Kaunda (son of the first president, Kenneth Kaunda). On 4 March 1993, Chiluba declared a state of emergency under Article 31 of the 1991 Constitution, which abolished the 'One Party' system and ushered in democracy. It did, however, preserve Sir Arthur Benson's brainchild, the Preservation of Public Security Regulations in its exact same wording in Article 31. (Sir Arthur must have laughed in his grave.) The 26 included, in addition to Wezi, his brother Panji, Kaunda's firstborn son and retired army colonel and also MP at the time; Rupiah Banda, former Minister of Foreign Affairs and future President of Zambia; Rabson Chongo, former Minister of Finance; and Lucy Sichone, a Rhodes scholar, veteran politician and chair of the UNIP Political and Legal Committee.

Some of the detainees were released early and only seven were charged with various offences against the security of the State, with Cuthbert Nguni and Wezi Kaunda charged additionally with treason. When they appeared in court Nguni could not walk unaided and the medical examination ordered by the court found that he and two others were tortured. Mercifully, the Supreme Court found that the emergency regulations were not valid and on 20 May all were released on bail, with Chiluba lifting the emergency on 25 May. Yet, despite all this he still remained the West's favourite. This emboldened him sufficiently to get rid of some of his critics within the MMD, including Emmanuel Kasonde, his Minister of Finance and architect of the economic liberalization and the removal of the exchange control regulations, and Arthur Wina, Minister of Education who openly accused Chiluba of corruption, inefficiency and of losing sight of the ideals MMD had aimed for when it came into office (*Africa Watch* publication, 10 June 1993).

During the Chiluba administration, the country saw a number of assassinations, a phenomenon never experienced in Zambia before. They all remained unsolved: Baldwin Nkumbula, son of the, by then, deceased ANC leader Harry, and former MMD minister who resigned citing growing corruption in MMD, died in a car accident under very suspicious circumstances; a lawyer who was investigating a case of fraud; a senior MMD official who was due to give evidence against the government the next day; Ronald Penza, the ex-Minister of Finance a few months after his dismissal from the cabinet, whose murder I described earlier. But the most callous amongst them was the assassination of Wezi Kaunda, the First President's third son and the most politically active amongst his children whom Chiluba had incarcerated and released in 1993. He was dragged from his car as he stopped to open his front gate on the evening of 3 November 1999, and shot four times. His wife was in the same car but the attackers did not hurt her. They pushed her out and used the car to escape. The police treated it as car hijacking, but most people believe it was a political assassination. After many hours in the operating theatre, the doctors at the University Teaching Hospital proclaimed that Wezi would survive. But he died from internal haemorrhage at 6 a.m. the next day. The family believes that somebody interfered with the tubes during the night. His father says: 'My son was assassinated twice.' The police never made any statement and none of these murders was ever solved. I saw Chiluba for the third and last time on the day of Wezi's funeral. He had sent for me and he asked me to convey to the family his shock and distress over the murder and assure them that he would leave no stone unturned until it was solved. He was planning to request the British High Commissioner for assistance from Scotland Yard. But nothing came of it.

Western eyebrows started rising when Chiluba changed the constitution to provide that only Zambians with both parents born in Zambia should be entitled to hold presidential office, thus declaring Kaunda ineligible to contest the 1996 election. By that time the Western countries started realizing that the Zambian Machiavelli had pulled the wool over their eyes for a whole presidential term of five years. But, after 1996, Chiluba ended up with an overwhelming majority in parliament, because, much to his delight, UNIP naively decided not to contest the parliamentary elections because of Kaunda's exclusion.

But Chiluba had not yet finished with Kaunda's persecution. On the night of 28 October 1997, a Captain Stephen Lungu, under the nom-de-guerre of Captain Solo (from the television series) and a major, Jack Chiti, attempted a coup. The coup failed and Lungu, Chiti and 68 soldiers were arrested within a couple of days. They were later charged with treason and 59 of them were convicted and sentenced to death on 19 September, the following year. Captain Lungu's sentence was later commuted by Mwanawasa, who succeeded Chiluba as president, to 20 years' imprisonment and he has since been released. Others, including Major Chiti were released earlier.

Chiluba, a mean and vengeful man who was ready to use any pretext to attack whomever he had a grudge against, grabbed the opportunity to settle old scores. His first targets were Kaunda and Roger Chongwe, his former Minister of Justice, a senior lawyer who after leaving the government was running a very respectable practice. He had also established a political party under the name of the Zambian Liberal Party. He had no particular ties with Kaunda, except that on 23 August they had been shot and wounded by the police when they were leaving, in the same vehicle, a political rally in Kabwe. Bullets grazed Kaunda's head and struck Chongwe in the cheek and neck. More to the point, neither of them was ever likely to get involved in a coup and in any case they were both away from the country at the time the coup happened. Chongwe was in Australia and decided not to return until years later after a change of government, but Kaunda, who was on a lecture tour in South Africa, returned the day before Christmas.

Christians the world over celebrate Christmas as a season of goodwill. And Chiluba kept bragging that he had declared Zambia a Christian nation. Yet, perversely, on Christmas morning, he sent his paramilitaries to arrest Kaunda and charge him with masterminding the coup. They surrounded Kaunda's house at 4 a.m., searched it from corner to corner and in the afternoon, they bundled him into a truck and took him to the Lusaka remand prison. They charged him officially and threw him into a cell already holding 19 others. Three days later, they flew him by helicopter to Mukobeko, the maximum security prison in Kabwe. There he was given a cell and a bed. But Kaunda promptly went on hunger strike, a weapon he had used time and again in the past. He declared that he would take no food or water until he went home. Kaunda is a veteran fighter and a very tough one and I have known him to fast voluntarily for prolonged periods. I thought that Chiluba had bitten off more than he could chew but, unexpectedly, he got out of that tight corner with the help of President Nyerere of Tanzania. When Nyerere heard of Kaunda's hunger strike, he flew from Dar es Salaam with his wife Maria and went straight to Mukobeko, where he persuaded Kaunda to end it. His approach was simple but compelling: 'Ken you are going to eat, or Maria and I are staying here to starve with you.' And Ken had to compromise, while Chiluba was shamed into sending him home, albeit after declaring his home a 'private jail'.

I do not think Chiluba expected it but the 'private jail' turned into a shrine: lots of sympathizers milling outside and many prominent people and friends paying their respects. I tried to visit a few times. The policemen on guard duty always had an excuse why I could not go in: he had other visitors; he was resting; the senior officer that had to grant authority could not be contacted – and 'come in the afternoon' or 'come tomorrow'. But, as I am white and they assumed I would not understand they warned each other in Chinyanja that 'this old man must not go through'. After a few attempts I gave up.

Kaunda was released in June 1998 on a 'nolle prosequi' order by the Director of Public Prosecutions after the intervention of Nelson Mandela who sent his Minister of Defence to procure a deal. Kaunda's lawyer, Sakwiba Sikota, felt let down by the release. He wanted a trial in order to prove Kaunda's innocence. But the nolle prosequi had become the hallmark of the Chiluba administration. (The Sata administration that followed two administrations later would use it even more frequently.) The thinking appears to be: 'arrest your enemies and your critics, real or imagined, charge them with whatever, preferably a non-bailable offence, incarcerate them for a bit, and then set them free on nolle prosequi: you made them suffer, you've had your revenge and you gave a warning to others'. What is sad is that the police are ready to carry out arrests on government instructions without question and the Director of Public Prosecutions, the Attorney General, and the other senior legal officers, are prepared to stand aside until they are given a nod by the government to issue a nolle prosequi while they know from the start that there is no evidence to support the charges. And the Law Association of Zambia does not raise strong enough objections to bring a stop to it.

But well before Kaunda's arrest, Dean Mung'omba had been arrested on 31 October 1997 in connection with the same Captain Solo coup. Dean, American educated and from a prominent family, had been one of the founder members of MMD and like many other intelligent members he became disgusted with Chiluba's ways. He broke away and formed the Zambian Democratic Congress, which made him a target for Chiluba's wrath. When he appeared in court on 4 November he reported that Captain Stephen Lungu had been so severely tortured that when he had been brought back to the detainees' cell at the Lusaka Central Police Headquarters they thought he was dead. Mung'omba himself had cuts and bruises on his legs, arms and hands. His lower lip showed bruising, and the back of his hands bore marks of cigarette burns. He described how he had been suspended on a metal bar by his handcuffed hands and rope-tied legs, and beaten by more than six police officers at a time, a technique called 'the swing' and commonly used by the police at the time. He also had electric shocks applied to his metal handcuffs. Judge Timothy Kabalata granted his appeal for medical treatment and ordered his removal from the Police Headquarters to the Lusaka Central Prison. Mung'omba described to the court three separate torture rooms in the Central Police Headquarters, where he estimated that up to 33 detainees had also been tortured. During his incarceration he contracted tuberculosis from which he died in 2005. Chiluba, the cause of it, did not seem troubled with any remorse and he had the nerve to attend his funeral much to the disgust of many in the congregation.

But he was bent on exploiting the abortive coup to the hilt and he had more scores to settle. For some reason he had fallen out with one of his closest confidants, Rajan Mahtani, a Lusaka businessman he had used for many years to carry out errands locally and internationally. Mahtani was charged in June 1998 that 'between July 1, 1995 and October 28, 1998 in Lusaka jointly and whilst acting together with others unknown [he] conspired to overthrow by unlawful means the government of the Republic of Zambia'. Mahtani applied for habeas corpus and was released on nolle prosequi, the Director of Public Prosecutions recognizing that he had no evidence to present to the court. Princess Nakatindi Wina, a prominent MMD member, one of the few female politicians of the time and wife of Sikota Wina, acclaimed freedom fighter and political leader, was also arrested. The reason for her arrest appears to have been that at Mahtani's habeas corpus hearing she testified that money she had received from his Finance Bank was for business and not for the purpose of preparing a coup. Yet she was charged with the same offence and incarcerated at Mukobeko, where she was tortured and had a miscarriage as a result.

Chiluba was very serious about revenge. And he was methodical about organizing it. A couple of years later he suspected his wife of many years of having an affair. He could not declare a state of emergency in order to punish the paramour so he invented a new non-bailable offence and passed it through parliament in a hurry: theft of a motor vehicle. He used it to arrest the wretched lover and keep him in jail to the end of his term.

With an overwhelming majority in parliament Chiluba schemed to change the constitution in order to run for a third term. He began early and methodically. First he issued an edict that no MMD official was allowed to start campaigning for the presidency until he said so. After that he announced that he did not want to stand for a third term but if the people demanded it he would feel obliged to bow to their wishes. Then he started a vigorous campaign through a number of cronies to get a movement pleading for him to stand, in the interest of the nation. Amusingly he even asked one of the televangelist stations in the United States to pray for him – a cynical explanation I heard at the time was that he believed that the American witchcraft is stronger than the African. But he did not want to rely entirely on witchcraft. He tried to buy the electorate, too. So he ordered the municipalities to sell all the houses they owned in all African townships of Lusaka, the Copperbelt and all the towns along the railway line to the sitting tenants. He set the prices at derisory levels, representing a couple of months' salary. The tenants who became homeowners were of course ecstatic. But the municipalities lost a huge chunk of their assets that generated rent income, which was financing their services. They tried to replace it by charging municipal rates based on a new valuation roll which the new tenants considered unacceptable. They refused to pay and Chiluba ordered that they should not. After that he ordered ZCCM to adopt the same scheme for the mining housing tenants and initiated a brand new one for the higher income voters. He called it 'The Presidential Housing Initiative', which he set up in order to build upmarket houses and sell them to middle income earners at knock-down prices. His popularity was soaring. The third term appeared within his grasp.

Yet, suddenly, it all collapsed because the people were outraged. They considered the third term as the thin end of the wedge and worried that it might turn out to be the precursor of another 'One Party State' situation. The people's indignation was marshalled by a newly formed organization named 'The Oasis Forum' put together by the Zambia Episcopal Conference, the Council of Churches of Zambia, the Evangelical Fellowship of Zambia, the Non-Governmental Organisations' Coordinating Council, and the Law Association of Zambia. The most spectacular aspect of the campaign against the third term was the wearing of green ribbons and the deafening honking every Friday afternoon. The outcry from the institutions, the churches, the professionals and the Oasis campaign scared him and he announced that he was never really serious about running for re-election.

With only a few months before the election his party ended up without a candidate and very little time to find one. And a combination of greed, ambition, and sheer lack of judgement would lead Chiluba to the wrong choice, which he must have regretted for the rest of his short life after that. He had been so confident about the success of his third-term bid that he did not seem to have prepared a Plan B. Now he had to find a candidate in a hurry and he wanted one that would do his bidding, because he had no intention of retiring. He planned to remain chairman of MMD and control his successor from that position.

I said many times that Chiluba was an expert manipulator. He had manipulated the ZCTU successfully for decades and his confidence in his ability increased during his term as president – it is easy to have it your way when vested with the powers of the office; nobody dares contradict or disobey you. He convinced himself that he could always have it his way, particularly with any recipient of the presidency lollipop that he was about to bestow. In the end, Chiluba stumbled upon Levy Patrick Mwanawasa, a lawyer from Ndola, the capital of the Copperbelt Province of Zambia. He had been his vice president for a couple of years at the beginning of his first term and even though he had some trouble with him (Mwanawasa had a car accident, which he considered an assassination attempt), he discounted that problem. The gift of the presidency, Chiluba thought, was so large that Mwanawasa would be eating out of his hands. In fact, exactly the opposite would happen. As things turned out Mwanawasa would bite the hands that fed him the presidency and just within a few months.

But the immediate job at hand was to win the election, and for this he had to market the candidate, to make him popular and electable. It was a difficult task. Mwanawasa was not a crowd puller, he was not a natural speaker (his English sounded like that of a peasant who had been to school for just a couple of years), and he was not comfortable with crowds.

The Copperbelt has the highest concentration of voters in the country so Chiluba decided to launch his successor in Kitwe, the Copperbelt's biggest and most central town. And he decided to use the opportunity to hand over the title deeds for the mining houses that he had given away in his quest for a third term. He would now use them in support of his chosen candidate. But the poor man was not up to it. Hugh Russell, the pen name of an amateur satirist who lived in Zambia at the time, sent a hilarious article to the London magazine *Spectator* on Mwanawasa's debut. It was published in the issue of 13 October 2001. I copy some highlights:

Mwanawasa spoke first. It was not a success. Perhaps it was his appearance, which is reminiscent of a subdued Joshua Nkomo. Perhaps it was his personal magnetism of which he has about the same amount as Roy Hattersley [the British Labour Party leader at the time]. Or perhaps it was the fact that he spoke entirely in English, which meant that after every halting and monotonous sentence, he was obliged to stop while an interpreter translated his remarks into the local language of Bemba. The problem here was that the interpreter was clearly a much more charismatic speaker than Levy himself. While Levy, sweated and stammered and muttered, the T-shirted interpreter gripped his mike and screamed out the message with great conviction and even greater volume. Certainly, those observers around me agreed that they would vote for the interpreter long before they would vote for poor old Mwanawasa.

Seated just behind the presidential candidate and smiling with apparent approval of his protégé's performance, was President Dr. F J Chiluba. And oh boy, what a contrast! This man really is the biz. OK, so you could make at least three Chilubas out of one Mwanawasa, but what he lacks in stature, the good doctor certainly makes up in style. His appearance was nothing less than dynamic. He was by far the best dressed man on the platform, opting for a neat but stylish safari suit with a casual open collar, in stark contrast to his sweaty colleagues in their suits and ties. A gold Rolex glittered on one wrist. A chunky gold bracelet with links like a chainsaw gleamed on the other. Something – diamonds? – twinkled at his cuffs. And his slim line sunglasses just had to have an Italian designer label on them. When he stood to speak, Chiluba's impact on the proceedings was no less impressive. True, the President is one of those men who are more visible sitting down than standing up but what he had to say was the sort of thing to make any one to sit up and listen …

The rest of the speech included some more surprising statements. Dr. Chiluba declared 'veni, vidi, vici', announced that he was a king and promised that in three to five years Zambia would be paradise. This last remark was greeted by the crowd with a roar that may have been approval, but might also have been disbelief. The speech made little or no reference to poor old Levy Mwanawasa, except towards the end when the President revealed that he had chosen Levy as his successor because Levy had never insulted him. And this certainly places Mwanawasa in a very small minority of political figures, in this country …

So is there any hope that the MMD and the Chiluba dynasty can be defeated? Well, yes there is. In fact it is hard not to feel that Mwanawasa and his mentor have lost before they've really started. The reason is this: Zambians have a highly developed sense of humor. They love to laugh at their politicians. And Mwanawasa, despite his impeccable credentials and his record of good work has given them too much to laugh at. His big mistake was to respond to the rumors that his accident had reduced his mental powers. He declared to the Zambian public that he was not; repeat not, a 'cabbage'. (For some unfathomable reason he in fact declared that he was a 'steak'.) The opposition press leapt on this declaration with whoops of joy. Soon one columnist was adapting the historic Zambian national slogan 'One Zambia, One Nation' to read 'One Zambia, One Cabbage'. Another writer accepted Mwanawasa's assurance that he was not a cabbage, but questioned whether or not he might be a cauliflower. And the jokes have spread among the general public. In the markets, giggling housewives no longer ask for a cabbage. They ask, of course, for a Mwanawasa.

2. President
Mwanawasa by Kiss
Brian Abraham

As Hugh Russell correctly perceived, Mwanawasa was not a natural for either politics or the office of head of state. He was a dreadful public speaker, and an appalling politician: he was impatient and quick-tempered and when cornered he had the propensity of uttering meaningless threats: once, responding to a criticism from Kenneth Kaunda, he told the First President of Zambia to shut up or he would be bruised. He would not normally have been able to win an election but he managed to scrape through because the opposition was split into four and, more to the point, because Chiluba, in his anxiety to secure a would-be surrogate at State House, put the MMD election machine into overdrive and employed every trick, legitimate and not so legitimate, in order to secure Mwanawasa's victory. In the event Mwanawasa only managed to secure 29.15 per cent of the vote against Andy Mazoka's (his main opponent and leader of UPND) 27.2. The election monitors both local and foreign declared the election flawed because of vote-rigging and faulty voters' rolls and the opposition cried foul and planned street demonstrations, which fizzled out after a couple of days. It also petitioned the results, but the High Court ruled three years later, in

February 2005, that the irregularities would not have altered the outcome. The MMD failed to win a majority in parliament, but Mwanawasa managed to concoct one anyway, pioneering a method that was to be perfected and used on a much greater scale by Michael Sata, the second president to be elected after his death: he appointed members of the opposition as ministers, and deputy ministers, thus securing their votes. Under parliamentary rules the MPs who accepted Mwanawasa's appointments had to resign and re-contest their seats. They did not on the grounds that they had not changed parties. They simply accepted the President's appointment in the national interest, they said. When their parties expelled them, they managed through a series of injunctions and other legal manoeuvres to hold on to their seats until the end of the parliamentary term.

Mwanawasa carried a big chip on his shoulder that was aggravated by the knowledge that his election was not accepted as legitimate by a large part of the population. He lacked humanity and he lacked humour, and would react fiercely at any hint of disdain, as a popular Zambian satirist found out.

Roy Clarke, who was running a weekly satirical column in *The Post*, under the pen name Kalaki (a vernacular corruption of Clarke – in most Zambian languages the Ls and the Rs are interchangeable) created a story over Mwanawasa's Christmas vacation in the Luangwa National Park. Its theme was the King of Luangwa's Christmas message to his assembled subjects: the animals of the Luangwa valley. The King, the Great Elephant Mwelewele (Bemba for useless) delivered his Christmas message to his subjects ('Distinguished elephants, honourable hippos, mischievous monkeys, parasitic politicians, bureaucratic buffalos and other anonymous animals') lampooning Mwanawasa's election and his government. A small sample:

> It was only you, my friends from the game park, who went out there and brought in 29% of the vote. The snakes of *Shushushu* [State Security Services] slithered into the ballot boxes and stuffed them with votes. The horrible hyenas were our trusted party cadres who chased away the opposition voters. Our reliable rhinos moved the ballot stations to unknown places in the forest. And our merry monkeys played hide and seek with the voters' cards ... I have nominated hippos to parliament and made them my ministers. I have appointed jackals as my district administrators and put the long fingered baboons in charge of the treasury. I have put the knock-kneed giraffe in charge of agriculture, the hungry crocodile in charge of child welfare and the red lipped snake in charge of legal reform. And best of all the pythons are now fully employed squeezing the taxpayers.

An apt allusion to Mwanawasa's election, of course, and a satirical portrayal of his government, intended to make fun, no doubt, of the President's Christmas sojourn, which he had pompously proclaimed as a 'working holiday'. But Mwanawasa did not have a sense of humour and would always go into a rage if he thought that he was being laughed at. The story was published on New Year's Day 2004 and by the end of that day Clarke had to go into hiding to avoid deportation.

Clarke is an Englishman who arrived in Zambia in 1962 as a student on vacation and returned to settle in 1965. In 1968 he married Sara Longwe, a Zambian well known women's rights activist, and by 2004 they had four children and four grandchildren. He had been writing his column for some ten years by then and he had been much more fierce in his mocking of Chiluba who, at least, had the sense to take it with equanimity. But Mwanawasa had a chip on his shoulder and was offended. So, despite his impeccable Zambian credentials, Clarke and his family went through a four-year nightmare fighting deportation. The Lower Court rejected the deportation order on the grounds that it would have split a Zambian family. Instead of thanking his lucky stars that the court gave him a way out, Mwanawasa's meanness was such that he appealed against the decision. It was not until 2008 that the Supreme Court confirmed the Lower Court's decision and the Clarke family could go to bed at night without the fear of a midnight police knock on their door.

As a politician Mwanawasa was clumsy and insensitive. In a speech he made at the funeral of 52 workers who died in an explosion at a Chinese explosives factory on the Copperbelt, he told the mourners that even though he was at the Copperbelt at the time, he did not go to the scene of the accident but returned to Lusaka on the instructions of his security officers, who were concerned about his safety. For a head of state to confess that he was around and did not go to visit the scene of an accident that killed 52 of his people because he was afraid about his own safety must be the mother of political blunder. By contrast, his arch-enemy, Chiluba, rushed to the scene immediately, and spent the period between the accident and the funeral visiting bereaved families and mourning with them.

And Mwanawasa would spend an inordinate amount of the nation's money, time, and effort in order to take revenge on Chiluba for the favour he did to him: handing him the Zambian presidency on a plate.

159

19. ZAMBIAN TRIALS AND THE LONDON DELUSION

The amazing thing about Mwanawasa was that he started off as the darling of the West and ended up as Zambia's patron saint of rectitude. The opinion of the West about every new president is usually a mixture of pious hopes and a misreading of the new arrival's personality, political standing, and real intentions, but, for the Zambian people, the West's view is irrelevant. The 'sainthood' was undeserved and had been promoted after his death by a local newspaper as part of an unremitting campaign against his successor. Mwanawasa branded his administration as the 'new deal government' – nobody knew what 'deal' he had in mind but he produced none. Later he introduced new labels: 'the anticorruption government', 'the government of laws', which increased the West's admiration.

He had to distance himself from Chiluba and his patronage as fast as possible, because he was conscious that the public opinion was right in believing that the election had been rigged in his favour by Chiluba and his cronies, a fact that had been confirmed by election monitors, both local and international; so on 11 July 2002, just over six months after he took office, he marched with a crusader's zeal to parliament to demand that his erstwhile patron's immunity be lifted. For greater effect, he organized a demonstration of thousands of party cadres who surrounded the outskirts of parliament shouting slogans and carrying placards against Chiluba, while Mwanawasa was addressing the House. He told the MPs that he had received evidence of 'suspected serious abuse of office, corrupt practices, and acts which generally endanger the security of the nation'. He enumerated them as follows:

Procurement of military equipment through a Congolese businessman he named as Katebe Katoto, aka Raphael Soriano whom he accused of being engaged in covert activities against the government of the Congo with the assistance of Chiluba. On Chiluba's instruction the Minister of Finance paid Katoto $20.5 million and signed a loan agreement between Katoto and the government of Zambia under which he would advance an additional $15

161

million in order to complete the deposit of $35 million required by the supplier. The loan was never made, the equipment was never supplied and when, some years later, Katoto was confronted by Mwanawasa's Minister of Finance, he informed the government of Zambia that the ostensible supplier had gone into liquidation. Mwanawasa told parliament that Katoto refused to disclose the identity of the supplier and, in any case, he had neither the capacity to supply the equipment, nor refund the money. Mwanawasa's conclusion was that the deal was a ruse conceived in order to swindle the nation. The 'phantom' supplier's identity emerged years later at a London trial which I shall cover later, as that of a Bulgarian Arms dealer, by the name of 'Teraton EAT'.

Zamtrop, a Zambian State Intelligence Services account opened with the London Branch of the then government-owned Zambia National Commercial Bank (ZANACO), through which numerous payments were made. While not alleging that all payments through that account were illegal, Mwanawasa reported that he was 'satisfied portion of them establishes a prima facie evidence that funds were embezzled or paid in suspicious circumstances'. He detailed the following: $1.1 million to Attan Shansonga, Zambian Ambassador to Washington at the time; $1.1 million to Chiluba's Swiss tailor, whom Mwanawasa named as Busile though he was later identified at the London trial as Boutique Basile of Geneva; $360,000 to V. J. Mwaanga, a former chief of the Intelligence Services and veteran politician who had also served as Ambassador to the United Nations and Minister of Foreign Affairs. Mwaanga's explanation according to Mwanawasa was that as a former chief of intelligence he was providing useful information to the Special Branch. A variety of smaller sums was paid to many others, including ministers, senior government officials, and many Chiluba family members (his daughter Helen received $90,000).

Mofed London and Mofed Tanzania, two real estate companies incorporated to handle ZCCM properties in England and Dar Es Salaam. Mwanawasa claimed that the former had appointed MISSL, a company belonging to Ambassador Attan Shansonga, as its manager and property consultant at a fee of £100,000 per annum and the latter had appointed Parkvale Ltd, a company belonging to a Mr Shimukowa, Chairman of ZCCM, in a similar capacity. Mwanawasa reported that revenue amounting to $300,000 raised from the sale of a shipyard belonging to Mofed Tanzania was never paid to the company.

Mwanawasa also reported a number of other incidents including the 'disappearance' of 67 tankers fully laden with fuel en route from Tanzania to Zambia. He concluded by informing the House that the offences he enumerated carried sentences ranging from five to twelve years' imprisonment and that in order to remove Chiluba's immunity parliament did not need to be satisfied beyond any rigorous standard of proof. He claimed that it could invoke its power as long as it felt 'that a strong case is made out' or that there is a public outcry that a prosecution is necessary, and quoted Article 43(3) of the Constitution that only requires that the contemplated proceedings 'would not be contrary to the interest of the State'. The opposition, which was baying for vengeance because it considered that the election had been stolen from it by Chluba's dirty tricks, voted with the government (even though Mwanawasa had been the beneficiary) and Chiluba lost his immunity by an overwhelming majority. A number of cases opened against him and about a dozen associates, which have been going through the courts and a number of convictions have been handed down but they have all been appealed. The result is that, by mid-2014 when this book went to the publishers, no sentence had yet been confirmed, 12 years after the sensational lifting of Chiluba's immunity.

The specific case against Chiluba, in Zambia, failed. After a series of legal challenges, starting with an injunction against lifting his immunity and a great deal of publicity over his more nefarious activities, he was eventually charged on 11 October 2004 with theft. Two directors of Access Financial Services, a finance company that handled a large number of the Zamtrop transactions, were charged with him. The specific charges were:

- Three counts, common to all accused, involving amounts totalling $323,030.
- Chiluba was charged separately with three additional counts involving a total of $184,886.
- The two directors were also charged separately with three additional counts involving $205,030 and K68,000.

All monies had been paid out through the Zambia State Intelligence Services Account held at the London branch of ZANACO under the name Zamtrop. In delivering judgment, almost five years later on 19 August 2009, the Lusaka Principal Resident Magistrate Mr J. Chinyama, obviously embarrassed over the long period the trial had taken, highlighted the twists and turns of the case, which included constitutional references to the High Court and late filing of defence submissions. Chiluba and his co-accused were acquitted on the three joint-charges. Chiluba was also acquitted on the three other separate charges against him, but the two Access Directors were found guilty of theft on the three separate counts against them.

163

There was political indignation over Chiluba's acquittal which was attributed to presidential interference. (By the time of the judgment, Mwanawasa had died and Rupiah Banda, his successor was known to be cultivating Chiluba as a political ally in the Luapula Province. However, I have read the verdict carefully at the time it was delivered and for the purpose of this book I am of the opinion that the verdict was sincere and the conclusions were arrived at after thorough study of the evidence and deep reflection.) As far as I could make out the grounds of Chiluba's acquittal hinged on his contention that funds withdrawn from Zamtrop and spent by him mainly on members of his family, were in fact his, deposited there by various donors since 1997. The Judge established to his satisfaction that private funds could properly be deposited in the Zamtrop account and could be withdrawn at the sole discretion of the ZSIS Director General. His conclusion was based on the evidence of Prosecution witness Reggie Phiri, the then serving Director General of ZSIS. According to the Judge's summing up, Mr Phiri had testified that:

> for operational accounts of the ZSIS, their management is entirely under the Director General who is the controlling officer. PW 19 [Phiri] found nothing wrong with putting private money in the Zamtrop account, whether or not it was for the President, since it was the Director General who decided what went into the account and he was not obliged to disclose the source of the money or its purpose ... I recall that when I looked at the Zamtrop statement, I saw and highlighted several payments that came into the account from sources other than the Ministry of Finance. I did state that their purpose was not stated and there is no evidence how they were expended. Those amounts came in, way before 2000 when the prosecution allege, and are supported by the statements of Mrs. Kaluba and Mrs. Benet that private funds for A1 [Chiluba] started to be credited to the 'picture account spreadsheet' [sic] in the Zamtrop account. In fact as I found and A1 stated these monies which included very large receipts came in as early as 1997 ... I have really exercised my mind on the issue and I am unable to stop entertaining the possibility that indeed accused 1 [Chiluba] may have been or was in fact entitled to those monies.

In his judgment, the Judge does not provide a reconciliation to show that the funds paid into the Zamtrop account for Chiluba were at least equal to the amounts paid out for his benefit, but as the sum involved was only around $500,000 and considering his statement above, he had obviously seen large entries, and may not have considered it relevant.

The two Access Finance directors were convicted on three counts relating to the theft of three lots of monies amounting to $205,030, K25 million and K43 million. As far as I understand it the monies originated from the Zamtrop account and were remitted to Access with instructions about their disposal from a firm of solicitors in London that had Zambian connections. As the directors allocated the sums to four specific accounts within Access, the Judge found that, in doing so, they 'permanently deprived the government' of their use and convicted them. As the case is still on appeal I cannot make any comments on the Judge's decision. However, I can highlight an interesting payment of $100,000 which according to the Judge 'ended up in RAZ account to allegedly pay back moneys used on account of the ZSIS'. (RAZ stands for RAMCOZ and this seems to corroborate the allegations that appeared in the RAID report about Chiluba's participation in RAMCOZ, as per Chapter 15.)

There were other cases against the directors of Access Finance as well as various others and most of them resulted in convictions. But they have all been appealed. The appeals were still pending mid-2014, when the manuscript of this book was sent to the publishers, so 12 years after Mwanawasa went to parliament, no convictions had yet been confirmed.

But the most perplexing legal action was a civil claim lodged in the High Court in London, on 6 October 2004 against Chiluba and 19 others. Two of the defendants were involved in a property transaction in Brussels and settled out of court conceding to the government of Zambia the relevant property, which consisted of two luxury apartment blocks. Unbelievably the apartments in question had been purchased on behalf of the Zambia State Intelligence Services as an investment! I guess intelligence services of other countries also have some sort of 'dark money' accounts in order to make payments they do not want to disclose and I suspect the original justification for the opening of the Zamtrop account was along such lines. But to use it to 'invest' in real estate in a European country where members of the Chiluba extended family appeared to reside could not possibly be without ulterior motive. Apparently the transaction took place in 1998 and it was financed by a cash down-payment and a mortgage. The mortgage had gone into arrears and the property was repossessed but the vendors redeemed it because they did not want their name mixed up in the affair and handed it back to the government. Even though the whole affair is highly suspect, it has never been clear whether Chiluba authorized or, more likely, initiated the purchase of the property in question, which according to a statement made in parliament on 24 January 2007 by Ms Lundwe, then Deputy Minister in the Vice President's Office, was valued at $8.9 million. (In the rulings made by the London Judge on 7, 8 and 11 June 2007 this turned out to be only $3,884,354.)

The claim against Chiluba and the 17 remaining defendants was heard before Justice Peter Smith between 31 October 2006 and 27 February 2007. The defendants were a mixed bag of Zambian public servants and businessmen, British-based lawyers and their legal practices, British and tax-haven registered companies, and a Swiss tailor, all of them involved in a multitude of transactions paid for through the Zamtrop account. The biggest single transaction however, which the Judge named as the 'Betti Katoto (BK) conspiracy' involved the Congolese Rafael Soriano, aka Katebe Katoto (reputed to be a relative of Chiluba's) and the mythical supply of arms to the Zambian Army for which the Ministry of Finance had advanced some $21 million.

As most Zambian defendants were facing criminal charges in Zambia over similar issues and their passports had been surrendered to the authorities, they were unable to travel to London for the hearings. In order to show fairness Judge Smith made a number of convoluted arrangements such as satellite video connection with the High Court in Lusaka ostensibly to enable the Zambian defendants to follow the London proceedings. He also arranged a two week sitting in Lusaka as special examiner to afford them the opportunity to present their defence. But, as far as I know, they all ignored both: the video connection and his visit. Chiluba turned the issue into a matter of principle: he refused to appear before a foreign court over issues that properly should be heard by the courts in Zambia and the Zambian defendants followed his example.

The London civil claim exposed a litany of transactions, many of them of dubious nature involving huge sums of money. They manifest wanton waste and extravagant tastes running into hundreds of thousands of dollars each and paid out of the national treasury through the Zamtrop account. Under the title 'Unusual Acquisitions' the Judge tabulated a number of payments to various people. I copy some below:

$1,209,400	Clothes from Basile Boutique, Geneva
$30,000	Cash
$450,000	12B Serval Road [presumably purchase of Chiluba's house]
$308,255	Payments to Chiluba's children for their education, accommodation etc.
$156,391	Cash for himself and various individuals
$179,000	Churches in America [to pray for his third term re-election?]
$725,000	T-shirts, baseball caps and other materials used in his second election campaign; also for the purchase of 1,200 bottles of Denis Ballet champagne, a fish skinning machine costing $15,000, etc.
$341,250	Credit card debt payment

$181,000	School fees
$371,149	Cash
$453,940	Cash
$250,000	Cash
$31,319	Cash
BF 590,934	Honda motorcycle

On the subject of the tailor, the Judge quoting the BBC said:

> The President (unlike the Emperor) needs to be clothed. FJT was known to be a stylish dresser. 'His suits speak of affluence, yet he presides over a country with millions barely scraping a living … But President Chiluba's suits are understood to be tailored by top designers in France and Italy … How much is spent on these clothes is a closely guarded secret. But many ordinary Zambians speculate that the figure has to be a mind-blowing one … It is not clear how many suits he has. But few people, even his closest aides, can remember seeing Mr. Chiluba in the same suit, or shirt, twice.

And he carried on with an itemized list of some of Chiluba's more spectacular clothing apparel seized by the Task Force, as opposed to the general list of trunks and suitcases that had appeared in the Zambian press previously. He described it thus:

> I saw some of the clothing at court … The items seized by the Task Force were considerable. First there were 349 shirts. A large number of these bore the FJT monogram on them and they were from virtually every designer outlet. Second there were 206 jackets and suits. A large number of these were from Basile bearing the FJT monogram. Third there were 72 pairs of shoes. A large number of these were hand made by Basile with the FJT logo. All were for FJT's unique personal specification (high heels). Many of them were in their original shoe covers and had not been used. There were a large number of other items. The full list can be found in bundle 17.2, page 217 et seq.

Delivering his verdict, Judge Smith divided the case into three conspiracies, along the lines of the Mwanawasa report to parliament when the latter sought the lifting of Chiluba's immunity in 2002: Zamtrop (the ZSIS account with ZANACO's branch in London), BK (the payment of some $21 million to Soriano-Katoto for the procurement of military equipment) and Mofed covering the ZCCM real estate companies in London and Tanzania. In his initial determination the Judge ordered:

3. President Chiluba
by Kiss Brian Abraham

- Chiluba, the Director of ZSIS Xavier Chungu and the former Permanent Secretary to the Ministry of Finance, Stella Chibanda to pay $26,345,316 for the Zamtrop conspiracy and $21,200,719 for the BK conspiracy, making a total of $47,546,035 each.
- The two Directors of Access Finance to pay $33,366,336 each, for the Zamtrop conspiracy with the Managing Director being ordered to pay an additional $21,200,719 for the BK conspiracy making his total $54,567,055.
- The Chairman of Access Finance: $62,279.
- The Meer Care and Desai, London Legal Practice and its two members: $7,021,020 for the Zamtrop conspiracy and $1,299,456 for the BK conspiracy making a total of $8,320,476, plus an additional sum to be calculated later.
- The London Legal Practice Cave Malik and its principal partner and his father: $8,282,812 for the Zamtrop conspiracy plus $452,043 for the BK conspiracy making a total of $8,734,855.
- Attan Shansonga: $3,035,639 plus a sum to be calculated later for the Zamtrop conspiracy.

- Boutique Basile: $1,209,400 for the Zamtrop conspiracy.
- Soriano: $21,200,719 for the BK conspiracy. (In this regard, the Judge revealed that although the President-Director of the Bulgarian purported supplier Teraton, Mr Peter Petrov, declined to give a formal statement he wrote a letter on 18 December 2006 confirming that the contract for the supply of arms to Zambia was never finalized and he never shipped any arms to Zambia or received any payment.)
- Finally, one respondent was found with no liability and the Mofed conspiracy was rejected.

But the Judge had not finished. On 11 June 2007, he made a further ruling adding interest and costs and deducting the value of realizations. I copy below the Judge's detailed determination relating to the Chiluba order. The reader will note that most credits refer to repossession of Zambian assets.

Summary of Liability – Dr. FJT Chiluba

	Liability Calculated With Interest Compounded Bi-Annually	Liability Calculated Including Additional Monies
Zamtrop Liability	$18,760,713.00	$18,760,713.00
Zamtrop Interest	$12,981,990.49	$12,981,990.49
Non-MOF Liability	$129,768.52	$129,768.52
Ditto	$50,610.14	$50,610.14
CM Receipts XFC/FMK		$154,990.00
Ditto		$54,255.54
CM Rcts 'one of our clients'		$79,995.00
Ditto Interest		$28,106.12
OOP Liability	$600,000.00	$600,000.00
OOP Interest	$219,362.82	$219,362.82
BK Liability	$20,200,719.00	$20,200,719.00
BK Interest	$8,609,743.53	$8,609,743.53
Less Jarban	$-1,336,725.84	$-1,336,725.84
Less Interest on Jarban	$-1,103,410.32	$-1,103,410.32
Less Lonrho	$-544,000.00	$-544,000.00
Less Interest on Lonrho	$-374,456.92	$-374,456.92
Less Monkey Fountain	$-37,696.34	$-37,696.34
Less Interest on M.F.	$-9,361.67	$-9,361.67
Less Siavonga	$-67,500.00	$-67,500.00
Less Interest on Siavonga	$-17,951.03	$-17,951.03
Less Lilayi Road	$-36,000.00	$-36,000.00

Less Interest on L.R.	$-19,161.16	$-19,161.16
Less Harptree	$-849,338.46	$-849,338.46
Less interest on H	$-32,883.04	$-32,883.04
Total	$57,124,422.72	$57,441,769.38

Judge's Note:
Credit for Serval road and chattels to be agreed/assessed following recovery

In summary, Chiluba's obligation was amended to $57,441,769; X. F. Chungu's and that of the former Permanent Secretary of the Ministry of Finance to $57,261,390 each; Attan Shansonga's to $4,400,684; Access Finance MD's $53,257,020; Access Finance Directors' $26,682,289 each; Access Finance Chairman's $100,575; Boutique Basile's $1,815,736; Soriano's $29,609,562, Cave Malik's $3,923,612; Meer Care and Desai's $11,135,665: in short, a cool total of $303,619,650!

I had difficulty in believing that the Judge intended a total payment of some $300 million, with each defendant liable to the full extent of his order, so I asked lawyer friends, and inevitably I received different opinions. Some believed that the London judgment constituted a civil contract and therefore all the defendants were held individually responsible to the full extent of the Judge's order. Most of them, though, thought that the order was limited to the assessed liability in respect of each individual. However, the argument is academic because none of the defendants, with the possible exception of Chiluba, would have been likely to have assets anywhere near the amount of the specific order against him, never mind the total. And even though I do not doubt that Chiluba had assets to cover the specific amount he was ordered to pay, I do not think that even he could meet the total.

But, more to the point, Chiluba's foreign assets and their location have never been identified, which makes the recourse to a London court an expensive 'wild goose chase'.

I did try to determine whether the government or its legal departments have a list of Chiluba's foreign assets and after many attempts for an appointment with the Director of Public Prosecutions, who had been the senior lawyer coordinating the case with the London legal team, I was asked to put my request in writing. I wrote on 12 September 2012, asking for an appointment in order to discuss the Chiluba plunder case and added:

I am particularly interested in obtaining a list of his foreign and local assets, if such list exists. I would also like to discuss the judgment of Mr. Justice Smith and its aftermath, and any other issue relating to Mr. Chiluba's administration that may arise out of our conversation.

I did not get a reply, so I turned to the former director of the Task Force, who had been in charge of the investigations before the force was disbanded. I did not get an appointment either. After trying a number of other sources, I came to the conclusion that such a list had never been obtained. Yet the discovery of the assets should have preceded the commencement of the case in London. The Mwanawasa administration should have employed international forensic experts to locate Chiluba's assets outside the country before it embarked on the London escapade, which cost the nation some $14 million in legal fees and travelling expenses, $11 million of which went to foreign lawyers. (These costs were disclosed in a statement to parliament on 26 November 2010, by the then Deputy Minister of Justice Todd Chilembo.)

The cost of forensic investigators would have been a fraction of the London legal costs and it would have helped the government decide whether the London case was worth pursuing instead of blindly embarking on a wild goose chase. The explanation the Mwanawasa government gave to the Zambian public that London was chosen because a London court's order was enforceable not only in the UK but all the countries of the European Union, made no sense without detailed information about Chiluba's foreign assets and their location. If, on the other hand, the government had employed investigators to locate the assets it would have been able to proceed with a criminal case against Chiluba in the Zambian courts and only resort to foreign claims against specific assets in the country they were located in, if those countries refused to register the Zambian judgment.

And the Zambian court was the only institution the case should have been assigned to. The Zamtrop and BK conspiracies cannot be remedied by foreign civil court judgments imposing spectacular monetary penalties, which do not have a chance of being collected. They were crimes and should have been prosecuted in a Zambian criminal court. The burden of proof may have been more onerous but a criminal court can impose other forms of punishment, to redress the harm to the society. The civil claim, particularly in London, was an expensive delusion. What can one say about those who conceived and promoted it? The ludicrous result of the course they followed was that the government of Zambia ended up spending a fortune in England in order to get a London court judgment to repossess Zambian assets, which were already in its possession! The reader will have noted that apart from the value of the Brussels apartment and, I believe, a tax haven company, totalling some $4.5 million, the repossessions incorporated in Judge Smith's tabulation above refer to properties in Lusaka, Ndola and Siavonga. The question is: Did the nation need to spend a fortune in London in legal fees and travelling expenses and 'per diems' for the 47 or so witnesses that had to be flown to London for the trial as well as the many accompanying officials, Judge Smith's and his party's trip to Zambia to sit as special examiner, satellite video connection during the entire trial, legal fees to highly qualified London QCs, and so on, in order to repossess properties in Siavonga, Monkey Fountain and Lilayi? Those had, in fact, been repossessed through action in Zambia, before Smith delivered his judgment, which in any case has never been registered in Zambia because the Zambian High Court refused to do it.

But let us analyse Judge Smith's verdict, of which he was obviously very proud: 'I hope this judgment will be given the widest possible circulation in Zambia,' he exhorted in his conclusion. He probably thought that the Zambian people should be eternally grateful to him and he wanted everybody to hear it. His first assessment was for $47,546,035 ($26,345,316 out of Zamtrop account and $21,200,719 paid to Soriano Katoto for the phantom military equipment) and the culprits involved were: Chiluba and three or four others in relation to Zamtrop and Chiluba and Soriano Katoto in relation to the military supplies. I can understand apportioning it amongst the participants and ordering them to pay the whole amount or according to their share of the loot plus interest plus costs. But why should a tailor from Geneva have to refund the sales proceeds from the clothing he sold to Chiluba which the Judge had seen and ridiculed in the part of his judgment I quoted above? His business was to sell clothes. He sold some to Chiluba and Chiluba received them as the Judge had verified, so he had to be paid; where the money came from was not his concern. And the solicitors and finance people, who may have provided the conduit for the transfer of the funds but just earned their normal professional fees? The Supreme Court in London must have thought along these lines too and allowed the appeals of the legal firm of Meer Care and Desai and its two partners, and Boutique Basile against Judge Smith's orders. (As far as I know these were the only two appeals lodged and they were both successful. The Zambian resident defendants ignored Smith's judgment.)

But the British High Commission (Embassy) in Lusaka treated Judge Smith's order as a major coup, and a major service to Zambia. They even brought a minor Royal from England to make the announcement, insinuating that Britain had in fact 'convicted' Chiluba. They also advanced the Queen's annual birthday celebration by a whole month in order to coincide with the announcement of the judgment. And they have been lobbying ever since for the registration of Judge Smith's order in Zambia. Mwanawasa submitted an application to the Zambian High Court for this purpose on 9 July 2007 and on 17 August 2010 Judge Hamaundu delivered his verdict. He refused to register the London judgment under the provisions of the 'Foreign Judgments (Reciprocal Enforcement) Act' because the 'United Kingdom was not one of the countries to which the Act applied' (in other words the UK was not prepared to grant reciprocal registration to Zambian judgments). The Judge advised GRZ that, if it desired to register the judgment, it should commence an action based on the principles of common law under the principles of 'Private International Law'. A lawyer friend clarified that the 'action' would be based on the London judgment because the judgment created an 'implied promise' on the part of Chiluba and the other defendants to pay the sums ordered by Judge Smith under the judgment.

As Judge Hamaundu's verdict was delivered during the Banda administration, many attributed it to Banda's protection of Chiluba. But even after Banda was succeeded by President Sata and the Chief Justice and his deputy were replaced, no new application was submitted for the registration of Smith's judgment. This drew the wrath of the British High Commissioner (Ambassador) to Zambia, who on 10 December 2012 was reported in the Zambian newspaper *The Post* to have made the following statement:

> A London court found Chiluba guilty of corruption involving around $46 million and the government of Zambia could demonstrate its resolve to rid the country of impunity by registering the judgment. The British government will help bring perpetrators of corruption to justice and recover stolen assets. The British government has zero tolerance to fraud and corruption.

And he went on to say that:

> The British government had been funding the Anti-Corruption Commission (ACC) for the last 20 years and it believed that the institution was a shining light among the Zambian government institutions.

I asked for details of the UK's contribution to the anti-corruption funding and I received the following response from the British High Commission:

> Since the late 1990s, the UK government, through the Department for International Development (DFID) has provided £9 million of support to the fight against corruption in Zambia. [£9 million over 20 years or so translates to £450,000 or $720,000 per annum, not a substantial enough sum to justify the High Commissioner's contention that it is the British contribution that made ACC a 'shining light among the Zambian government institutions'.] This has been in the form of financial assistance and technical assistance to

the Anti-Corruption Commission. DFID's current programme (2009–2014) is supporting the ACC to deliver the following results:

Involve 225,000 Zambian citizens directly in anti-corruption initiatives.

Successfully prosecute at least 70 persons for corruption in the courts and ensure administrative actions (dismissal, suspension, and recoveries) take place in an additional 200 cases.

Strengthen anti-corruption controls in 12 government ministries and agencies.

(How such requirements get implemented and how the results get quantified and verified is hard to imagine.) The letter continued:

The UK made no direct contribution to the costs of the Zambian government's proceedings against Chiluba in the High Court in London. However, DFID contribute GBP 1.4 million to a joint donor fund aimed at providing support for the Task Force on Corruption. The Task Force used these funds to prosecute cases in Zambia and the UK including the one against Chiluba himself, recovering more than $18 million to date.

(I do not accept the High Commission's contention that $18 million worth of assets were recovered and the reader can verify this in the details from Judge Smith's adjudication I copied above.)

In my view, the registration of Smith's judgment in Zambia will serve no useful purpose, apart from indulging the British amour propre. As the Zambian Attorney General of the time commented, 'to appeal the registration of the London judgment would be an exercise in futility'.

But what I find most disturbing is the tendency by many Western countries to disregard civil liberties when it suits them. The comment that Chiluba was found guilty of corruption by Judge Smith is one example. The case before Judge Smith was a civil claim and the verdict was an order for payment of liability assessed by Judge Smith; guilty verdicts are handed down in criminal courts and the case before Judge Smith was not a criminal one. A criminal case can only be tried in the country where the crime was committed and in the case of Chiluba the country was not Britain but Zambia. And as the onus of proof in a civil case is much easier an adverse verdict cannot be termed as conviction. The British diplomat was fully aware of this as much as he was aware of the principle that an accused is innocent until pronounced guilty by the courts. Yet he took a chance and made the comment regardless.

But there is a more disturbing example. In October 2005, six European countries, five of them members of the European Union, signed a memorandum of understanding with the Ministry of Finance, the Office of the President and the Task Force on Corruption in order to assist the Task Force financially to investigate suspected cases of corruption, bring the culprits to justice and recover government assets, a very laudable initiative. But it was marred by the following paragraph:

> The successful prosecution of these cases will depend to a large extent on the integrity and competence of the magistrate assigned to handle the cases. Whilst the Task Force has no direct influence over the assignment of magistrates to handle individual cases, it will be beneficial to have a few of the best magistrates designated to handle all the cases brought by the Task Force. The Deputy Director of Prosecutions should as far as possible maintain contact with the Judiciary on behalf of the Task Force, acting at all times within the limits of the appropriate behavior and ethical contact expected of the legal advisers on behalf of parties to litigation.

One wonders: Was this a vote of no confidence in the Zambian judiciary, or a cynical disregard of due process? Because, behind the convoluted language above, the glaring intention stands out as 'get a convenient magistrate who will convict the suspects regardless'.

But I shall cover the relationship between the government of Zambia and the Western countries in greater detail later. Let us first review the performance of the Mwanawasa administration.

20. Konkola: The Sale of the Century

In previous chapters I exposed in some detail the skullduggery over the privatization of the government companies in general and the mining companies in particular by the Chiluba regime, and the plunder of the proceeds he and others were accused of perpetrating. Though not fully quantified, they add up to huge amounts. But adding all of them together, they probably cost the country less than the 'sale' of the Konkola Mine, Mwanawasa's greatest blunder. He gave away the nation's biggest and richest mining complex for nothing and gave the new owners a present of some $2.5 billion in tax concession that he should have refused to make without demanding substantial additional cash. But let us start from the beginning.

The Anglo American Corporation handed Konkola back to the government early in 2002 and withdrew in indecent haste. The professed reason was not convincing: the price of copper was too low at 73 American cents per pound, against a break-even requirement of 80 cents, they said. (The market price at the time was 75 cents and according to Anglo it had no prospects of improving so the mine would continue losing money.) The withdrawal was more likely due to internal company politics that followed Anglo's hop, skip, and jump from its Johannesburg traditional home to London through Luxembourg and its Minorco subsidiary. The London new brooms must have wanted to demonstrate that Africa was the past. There were new more profitable pastures on the planet, which they intended to pursue, and they were not going to allow African companies to swallow resources in old operations for sentimental reasons. So they must have ordered immediate withdrawal from Konkola that had been losing money since they took it over. In view of the market conditions prevailing at the time, they could not find another buyer in a hurry, so they handed it back to the government, a move that met with general condemnation locally and internationally. Everybody was indignant that after they scuttled the Kafue Consortium deal and drove a tough bargain and secured obscene concessions, two years earlier, they just decided to walk away from the project. But the London directors were not going to change their mind and lose face. And as in their minds Konkola was worthless, they decided on a grand gesture of generosity: to donate their interest to the people of the Copperbelt through a trust whose mandate would be to prepare them for the eventual extinction of minerals. The official announcement read:

> It is also proposed that Anglo American will establish an independent entity, the Copperbelt Development Foundation (the 'Foundation') and will transfer to the Foundation for no consideration a 41.4% shareholding in ZCI. The Foundation will use income from ZCI to invest in projects aimed at diversifying the economy of the Zambian Copperbelt, contributing to the provision of health, education, and other social services on the Copperbelt, and mitigating the social impact of the eventual closure of the KCM mines. The balance of ZCI shares held by Anglo American will be transferred for no consideration to a management and employee incentive trust, intended to align the objectives of the new KCM management team and workforce with those of the new shareholders.

So, Anglo American got out of ZCI, which owned 58 per cent of Konkola, by bestowing its shares to two foundations intended to prepare the Copperbelt for the mining industry's eventual extinction (a death wish that, mercifully, is not likely to materialize for many decades to come).

The major shareholders must have kicked themselves over the withdrawal from Zambia when the price of copper skyrocketed within a couple of years, a development that Anglo, one of the oldest mining houses in the world was too absorbed in its migration upheaval to anticipate. And, gallingly for them, the price has remained high for more than a decade, reaching a level of $5 per lb for considerable periods. But the new blood in the now London-based Anglo American, foolishly, had no time for the extraordinary concessions their former South African colleagues extracted from the Government Privatisation Negotiating Team and seemed to be in a hurry to get completely out of Zambia, never to return. Instead, it embarked upon new investments in Chile, Brazil and other South American counties, on which it lost billions. The irony was that, in addition, the London Anglo had to eat humble pie on its predictions of the Zambian mining prospects, and unbelievably, in December 2012, it was back in Zambia: it took exploration licences in the North Western Province. But, by then, the original whiz-kids at the top had been replaced.

With the departure of Anglo, the Copperbelt Development Foundation became the biggest shareholder in ZCI, a Bermudan Public Company, whose second biggest shareholder was SICOVAM, a French public company that looked after the interests of a number of French shareholders. They were all destined to make a fortune of nearly $250 million out of their Konkola shareholding within a couple of years of Anglo's departure.

Amongst the number of new suitors, the Mwanawasa government chose a new investor interested in buying Konkola and in November 2004, it concluded a deal to sell 51 per cent of Konkola Copper Mines Ltd (KCM) to Vedanta Resources, an Indian-owned company listed on the London Stock Exchange. While some details of the deal became public, there was no official announcement of the full terms of the agreements and the concessions given to Vedanta. I tried to obtain copies of the agreements from the Mwanawasa government for my book *A Venture in Africa* but I struck a wall of silence. I was told by a senior official in the Ministry of Mines that the agreements were private and could not be made public. I asked how government agreements involving the sale of national assets could be termed 'private'. They involved a major national asset and they were entered into on behalf of the Zambian people and the Zambian people were entitled to know the terms, I observed, and pointed out that the 1969 agreements, when the Kaunda administration acquired controlling interest in the mines were tabled, debated, and approved by parliament. But the senior civil servants I spoke to tried to persuade me that it is in fact normal procedure that if the private party involved in an agreement made with the government did not want it disclosed the government should oblige. Sad but true. And I had a similar response from an opposition MP I tried to enlist for help. The reply was: 'Andrew, you know they will never release those agreements'. So there you have it: if the government does not want to do something, legitimate or otherwise, the loyal opposition of the time must acquiesce!

My own view was that the Mwanawasa government maintained this excessive secrecy because it had something to hide. And I persevered in my quest. I wrote to the then Attorney General on 2 November 2005, asking for at least the Anglo American agreements: acquisition of Konkola and termination. I never received a reply. I tried to get an appointment with him and made repeated visits to his office to the embarrassment of his secretaries, but with no success. But I did get information on the details of the main deal from the official announcement of the Zambia Copper Investments Ltd (ZCI) issued in Bermuda on 20 August 2004. The key terms agreed to were as follows:

Subscription by Vedanta for sufficient new KCM ordinary shares for an amount of US$25 million such that Vedanta obtains 51% interest in KCM. Accordingly ZCI will reduce its interest in KCM from 58% to 28.4% and ZCCM-IH will reduce its interest in KCM from 42% to 20.6%.

To enable Vedanta to subscribe for KCM shares, ZCI and ZCCM-IH will waive their pre-emptive subscription rights. As consideration for this waiver ZCI will receive a differed consideration of US$23.2 million from Vedanta payable over a period commencing on the completion date of the Vedanta investment and ending 31 December 2008 ...

Similarly, while ZCCM will not receive a deferred consideration from Vedanta, ZCCM-IH will receive as consideration for the waiver, US$16.8 million by way of a debt cancellation arrangement from GRZ (Government of the Republic of Zambia), whereby GRZ will cancel debt owed by ZCCM-IH ...

An undertaking has been given by Vedanta to support a feasibility study on the extension of the Konkola ore body by no later than 31 December 2006. Vedanta will contribute US$1 million towards the cost of the feasibility study.

(Those interested in greater detail will find the complete announcement as Appendix IV.)

The above figures match with the statement of the Chairman of Vedanta for the financial year ended 31 March 2005, who had reported the cost of the Konkola acquisition as follows:

In November 2004 we completed the acquisition of Konkola Copper Mines at a gross cost of $49.2 million.

But what did the nation get out of the sale of the Konkola colossus? The answer is zero. Out of the $49.2 million Vedanta reported as its cost, $25 million went to the new capital subscription, which gave it 51 per cent control of Konkola and against which it received the new shares. In other words the government of Zambia did not sell Konkola, it simply 'handed it over' to Vedanta, and the nation did not receive any money out of the 'handover'. ZCI received money amounting to $23.2 million for the diminution of its share in Konkola and one million went as contribution to the cost of the feasibility study. The only payment that would have represented cash for the nation was the $16.8 million that ZCCM-IH was due to receive for the diminution of its shares in Konkola from 42 to 20.6 per cent. But it did not and nobody is saying what happened to it. As the Mwanawasa government could not completely 'eclipse' it, the Ministry of Finance issued a credit note to ZCCM-IH against its debt to the government. I tried to obtain a clear statement from the then Minister of Justice (Mr Kunda) and, later, the Minister of Finance of the Banda administration (Dr Musokotwane) as to whether the funds were actually paid, but my letters remained unanswered. The question is: Did Mwanawasa waive the payment and not tell the nation about it, or did the payment go into somebody's pocket and remained unaccounted for, as so regularly happened during the Chiluba times, which the RAID/AFRONET reports I quoted earlier reveal (see Chapters 15 and 16)? The bottom line is: the Chairman of Vedanta in his statement does not mention it as a cost and the nation did not receive it.

But Mwanawasa's generosity to Vedanta knew no bounds. He proceeded to give it an additional present of some $2.5 billion by allowing KCM to carry forward all the tax losses 'incurred up to and including 31 December 2003'. These, according to the published accounts, amounted to $635,897,000. As the income tax rate for KCM was set at 25 per cent unchangeable for 20 years this means that KCM would not start paying income tax until after it made profits in excess of $2,543,588,000 (in short: two and a half billion dollars!). Additionally, under the provisions of the acquisition agreement, KCM is to be treated as a new mine under the 1975 Act, which allows 100 per cent deduction of capital expenditure in the year it is incurred, inclusive of the acquisition costs as well as all subsequent investment, and it can carry losses forward for a period of 20 years. When all this is taken into account, one wonders if KCM would ever pay taxes during the life of Konkola's various mines.

How could Mwanawasa commit this huge blunder at the expense of the nation, especially after the advantages and concessions that had been granted to the Anglo American Corporation and which were passed on to Vedanta undiluted? His legal practice, I understand, had been mainly commercial. He must have had some knowledge about the treatment of tax losses when companies change hands. His minister of finance, Ngandu Magande, was an economist and a banker and his minister of commerce Deepak Patel was an Indian businessman. And he had another adviser, a prominent Indian businessman in whom he publicly declared undying friendship who was also an accountant, and a close confidant, always by his side. Surely he ought to know that assessed tax losses had a 'present day value', which in normal commercial transactions would have been calculated and reflected in the purchase price. And that would have amounted to a few hundred million dollars. Why the World Bank and the IMF remained silent over the tax losses being passed on at the expense of the Zambian people remains a mystery. Both these organizations have offices in Lusaka and they were closely involved with the privatizations, albeit mainly in order to force the speedy completion of deals, which generally tilted the advantage towards the purchaser.

The Konkola deal was obviously a major coup for Vedanta, but what does that say for the government of Zambia? The French shareholders of ZCI, grouped together under Sicovam S.A. that held 33 per cent of the ZCI shares, were up in arms. They issued a statement describing the deal as 'the most outrageous and scandalous ever seen in Africa for decades'. And they had every justification in reaching that conclusion. Properly analysed the deal was blatantly unjust. This was proved just nine months later, when Vedanta agreed to pay $213.15 million for the 28.4 per cent balance of the ZCI shares, while it had only paid $49.2 million for the 51 per cent!

The price Vedanta paid for the acquisition of 51 per cent of Konkola valued the entire undertaking as of November 2004 at a derisory $96.5 million ($96,470,588 to be exact). (The calculation is based on the chairman's announced cost of acquisition of the 51 per cent. As he did not mention the $16.8 million of the ZCCM-IH credit note, and the government of Zambia has been coy about explaining why, I assume that Vedanta did not officially pay it.) Nine months later, in August 2005, Vedanta exercised its option to buy ZCI's 28.4 per cent remaining shares in Konkola and paid $213.15 million for it. On this basis, the value of the Konkola undertaking rose to $750.5 million ($750,528,169, to be exact) – an eight-fold appreciation in just nine months, which underlines the difference between an arm's length business negotiation and a cosy deal with a friendly and malleable president. The original deal was a real killing for Vedanta at the expense of the Zambian people, who are not likely to get any income tax out of Konkola until after 2025, assuming that the market price for copper remains reasonably high until then, and the government of Zambia gets a better handle on mining accounts.

I thought it was only fair to put these issues to Konkola and get their response for this book. I asked to meet the chief financial officer but I was being sent from pillar to post: 'the CFO was out of the country, I ought to see the commercial manager', and so on. It took a long time, but eventually I managed to get an appointment with the Konkola Director of Strategy and Business Development in the company's Lusaka office. In preparation I sent him the following email and questionnaire:

> I have been trying to get an appointment with your management in Chingola for more than a month. I requested to see Konkola Copper Mines' Chief Financial Officer and after a couple of telephone calls and explanations of the purpose for my request the lady I was communicating with told me that a more appropriate person would be the Commercial Director. After more abortive telephone calls I was referred to you. I've been trying to see you since before Easter and, on March 27, 2013 I was asked to state the purpose of my visit – hence this letter … I am now writing the history of Zambia since independence and I would like to discuss and obtain information/clarifications from you on the following:
>
> 1. The cost of the Konkola acquisition as reported by the Chairman of Vedanta in his annual report for the financial year ended March 31, 2005 amounted to $49.2 million. This represented $25 million for the acquisition of new

shares in order to give Vedanta 51% control, $23.2 million paid to ZCI for the diminution of its shareholding from 58% to 28.4% and $1 million contribution to the Konkola Deep feasibility study. Please confirm.

2. ZCCM-IH was meant to receive $16.8 million payment for the diminution of its shareholding from 42% to 20.6%. My research shows that ZCCM received a credit note for the above amount from the Ministry of Finance instead. I would like clarification as to whether your parent company paid the equivalent amount to the Ministry and when or whether the $16.8 million was waived and by whom.

3. On acquisition Konkola was allowed to carry forward 'all tax losses incurred up to and including 31 December 2003'. According to my research these amounted to $635,897,000. Please confirm or provide correct figure.

4. The acquisition agreement granted to Konkola a concessionary income tax rate of 25%. According to my calculation this would mean that Konkola would not start paying income tax in Zambia until after it made profits of $2,543,588,000. Please confirm or provide an alternative calculation.

5. Can you supply information on the amounts invested since acquisition?

6. Can you supply information on the amounts, if any, Konkola paid to the Zambian Revenue Authority in income tax and mineral royalties? Please do not include VAT and payroll taxes.

7. How many employees do you currently employ? Can you give a breakdown between local and foreign?

8. Can you supply the same information as at the date of acquisition?

9. Can you explain the criteria you apply before engaging foreign workers?

10. Konkola carries out a lot of its work through subcontractors. Can you give the same information about them as per 7 and 8 above?

11. Can you advise what is the total accumulated tax loss in Konkola's books, as at its latest Financial Year?

12. What is your current annual production of finished copper and what are your projections for the next five years?

Finally I would be very pleased to receive any other information you consider relevant. Conversely, I may have additional questions and subjects I would raise for discussion such as labor relations, utilization of local contractors and complaints appearing in the press from time to time about late payments to them etc.

Upon receipt of the letter, a meeting was promptly arranged and I met the Director of Strategy and Business Development on 12 April 2013. I was subjected to a two hour PowerPoint presentation of their current blurb, during which I was 'informed' that the Nchanga ore body is very thin, and extremely costly to mine. My interlocutor's view was that this must have been the reason Anglo American handed the mine back to the government in 2002, a point of view that ignores the fact that Anglo had been operating the mine since 1929, and that Jack Holmes who was leading the Anglo American team during the negotiations with the Government Privatisation Team had been working as an engineer at Nchanga itself (now Konkola) in the late fifties and early sixties, was promoted to the Head Office in Lusaka after independence and became a member of the board, all of which would suggest that Anglo American would hardly have been unaware of the nature of the ore body, and all other problems and advantages of the mine, one of the most profitable in the Anglo American's Zambian operations. The presentation dealt repeatedly with the difficulties of the Konkola ore body and its problems, and blamed the high operational costs of Konkola, on the nature of the ore body and the ore. The Strategy Director frequently expressed envy at the 'ideal conditions' and the large quantities of gold prevailing at Kansanshi that made First Quantum a highly profitable group. The thought that, maybe, First Quantum was a more experienced and efficient mining group did not seem to enter his head. Bearing in mind Kansanshi mine's chequered history of opening and closing down after a few years, over many decades under a series of previous owners, due to flooding and other operational problems I rather think that First Quantum's superior knowledge and expertise must be the explanation.

I was not able to get any comments on the acquisition costs and on the payment or otherwise of the $16.8 million that were due to ZCCM-IH on the debatable grounds that those were Vedanta issues. (The questions had been included in my email which he received before he set up the appointment; he had plenty of time to contact his head office in India or London and obtain the information. I take it that he did try and the head office did not give him permission to respond.) And I was not able to get any comment on the tax losses carried forward on acquisition, either. 'Unfortunately the records currently available only go back as far as 2006,' the Strategy Director told me with a straight face.

Vedanta has since gone on to invest, according to their pronouncements, $2.7 billion (a figure as per their blurb, which I was not able to check, though, as the reader will see later, the minister of mines revealed in May 2014 that the development did take place but its financing did not come from Vedanta but from Konkola funds and various other unreliable sources) for the further development of KCM. The main message of the blurb was to show the 'favours' Konkola is doing to Zambia: the largest private labour force (reported as 22,500 of which only 8,500 are employed directly, the other 14,000 represented workers employed by various contractors). A few weeks after our meeting, Konkola announced that it would be laying off 2,000 workers, which raised a storm of protests from the government and the mineworkers union, and it was finally retracted. The presentation also boasted about highest wages, highest corporate social responsibility contributions and complained about low labour productivity in comparison to other mines (a problem which Konkola should be able to solve by improving its mining methods), high electricity costs, increased royalties, etc. No information on direct taxes was disclosed. Over the six-year period 2006 to 2011 it paid just under $104.5 million in royalties. Sata and his Minister of Finance Alex Chikwanda must be congratulated for raising the royalties rate as is obvious from the following comparison: Konkola's 2011 royalty payment amounted to $36.5 million, while its 2006 (during the Mwanawasa administration) amounted to just under $3 million.

But the tax affairs of KCM are difficult to fathom. On 22 October 2013, the Zambian press reported that Konkola had not paid employees' PAYE (Pay As You Earn) deductions to the Zambian Revenue authorities for the years 2006, 2007, 2010, and 2011. The unpaid portion was reported to be 33 billion pre-rebased Kwacha (some $6.5 million); but in response to my query the company clarified that it amounted to 40 million rebased Kwacha ($7.5 million). On 28 October the *Post* reported that the Minister of Labour directed the company to pay the arrears from its own resources and not from the employees' future salaries. At the same time the *Post* reported that Konkola had another overdue tax amounting to 136.8 million rebased Kwacha ($25.8 million) for which it had asked for time to pay.

But that was not the end of Konkola's problems. As I said earlier its attempt to dismiss some 2,000 workers at the beginning of 2013 was vetoed by government. But in November the company announced a new lay-off of 1,529 workers who would become redundant because of its mechanization programme. The Minister of Labour vetoed the scheme, again. Then President Sata got involved and threatened to take away Konkola's mining licence, if the workers were dismissed. But the company appeared not to have taken the threat seriously and at a meeting with the Minister of Labour the CEO described the President's stance as 'political rhetoric'. All hell broke loose, after that. The *Daily Mail* reported on 9 November 2013:

> The Chief Executive of the Vedanta-owned Konkola Copper Mines (KCM) Kishore Kumar has fled Zambia after Home Affairs Minister Edgar Lungu demanded a meeting with him to discuss his 'rhetoric' jibe targeted at President Sata on Thursday. And Vice-President Dr. Guy Scott told Parliament yesterday that Government will take stern action against KCM for laying off 76 workers

and that 'Mr. Kumar has fled the country after realising the gravity of his careless, disrespectful, and arrogant statements against President Sata.' … Mr. Lungu [Minister of Home Affairs] warned other multi-nationals to take a cue [sic] from Mr. Kumar and respect not only the laws of the land but the country's leadership. 'Zambia is a sovereign country. We got our independence almost 50 years ago and right now we have an elected President, who is Mr. Sata. If you insult him, you insult those that elected him and the law shall deal with you regardless of whatever investment you have brought in and Mr. Kumar should have known this before he shot his mouth [sic].' Mr Lungu said investment or money shall not be used as a 'blunt instrument' to belittle the Zambian leadership or abuse Zambians.

On 11 November the government announced that Kumar had been declared a prohibited immigrant and the following day it was announced that a technical committee of officials from the ministries of Commerce, Finance and Labour and the Zambia Development Agency, had been constituted to evaluate the performance of KCM, with a view to recommending how the government should proceed. The following day, Mr Christopher Yaluma, Minister of Mines, Energy, and Water Development clarified that the Konkola management would be part of the committee. He expressed worries about the liquidity of Konkola and gave an assurance that the government's intention was to 'help it get back on track'.

While the government of Zambia was pondering how to help Konkola overcome its liquidity problems, its owner bragged that he was making $500 million profit per year since he took it over (way above Konkola's reported results). In a motivational speech he made to the Jain International Trade Organisation in Bangalore on 22/23 March 2014, Anil Agarwal, Vedanta's chairman, ridiculed Mwanawasa for receiving him as a mining magnate and giving him 51 per cent controlling interest for just $25 million while the mine was worth $400 million. He confessed that all he had at the time was $4 million. His speech in Hindi that circulated on YouTube in May 2014 accompanied by an English translation caused widespread anger and consternation in Zambia.

On 21 May 2014 Minister Yaluma revealed that the committee appointed the previous November determined that Konkola was on the verge of insolvency with total liabilities amounting to $1.567 billion exceeding its assets by $123 million, which made it unable to meet its obligations as they fell due. He detailed the obligations as bank loans, outstanding debts to local and foreign suppliers, unpaid cobalt and copper price participation to ZCCM-IH, deferred taxes and outstanding bank guarantees covering environmental liabilities arising from mining operations. He also revealed that Vedanta did not honour its obligation to inject $397 million into Konkola as foreign direct investment. According to the minister, capital projects totalling $2.8 billion were financed through Konkola's own cash flow, lease finance and short-term bank loans.

***

The international financial institutions and the Western countries who were singing the praises of foreign direct investment and the privatization did not seem to be put off by the huge concessions made, and the sharp practices resorted to during the disposal process; they both resulted in the nation receiving next to nothing from the disposal of its major assets. And the process continues with some new owners doing their best to avoid paying Zambian taxes. I shall cover some of their practices and their effects in a later chapter, but now I want to highlight how successful the mining companies have been in presenting a facade of corporate social responsibility to the Zambian public.

Kenneth Kaunda, the first president of Zambia and a zealot in the promotion of education was ecstatic over the expansion of Konkola that was explained to him during a visit in February 2012. He praised the company and dreamed that 'this type of investment will enable government to provide free education in Zambia'. And he added: 'Free education is not possible without you [investors] paying tax …' Little did he know that with the concessions Konkola and the rest of the mining industry enjoy, the taxation benefits from the industry were minimal and would have remained so for a couple of more decades, if the Sata administration had not taken swift action to increase the royalties, recognizing that firmer supervision of the mining tax evasion tactics would be a hard slog.

Courtesy of the Konkola PR department no doubt, Kaunda's comments made headlines in all the Zambian newspapers the next day, trumpeting the Father-of-the-Nation's approbation.

Even though most mining companies are publicity shy as regards their accounts and their profitability, they always make a big splash in the press when they donate to football clubs, sports events, and various charities. My own cynical view of such manifestations of corporate social responsibility is that they reflect a guilty conscience and their size is, usually, in inverse proportion to their income tax payments. I developed this view after many years of observation and I was amused to see recently a table setting out 'social payments and transfers by the mining companies of Zambia' prepared by the Extractive Industry Transparency Initiative: I copy the 2009 donations of the three highest payers and their income tax payment for the same year, converted into American dollars.

	Social payment (US$)	Income Tax (US$)
Konkola Copper Mines PLC	13,812,800	NIL
Mopani Copper Mines PLC	13,225,800	NIL
First Quantum	1,573,200	38,542,141

Need I say more?

***

The last agreement to be concluded was the sale (once again after the collapse of RAMCOZ) of the Baluba and Luanshya mines and a concession to develop the Muliashi North Deposit, near Luanshya. This sale was being handled by a committee of permanent secretaries, chaired by Dr Ngosa Simbyakula, permanent secretary to the Ministry of Justice at the time together with the RAMCOZ liquidators. The committee had already selected Anglovaal Mining (AVMIN), a very respectable South African mining company, as the preferred bidder. Dr Simbyakula, as chairman of the team, wrote to Gerry Robertze, AVMIN's boss, on 23 January 2003 informing him of the selection, and had followed up with a second letter on 3 February 2003, asking Robertze to travel to Zambia for the signing of a Memorandum of Understanding on 7 February. But Mwanawasa scuttled the deal two days before signing, and directed that Luanshya be sold to Enya BV, a Dutch investment holding company incorporated in 2002 with ambitions to become an international mining house. Enya used as the acquisition vehicle, a Swiss subsidiary under the name J & W Holdings AG, but over the years Luanshya ended up in the hands of the Bein Stein Resources Group (BSRG) and International Minerals Resources (IMR), in both of which Enya was reported to have a major interest.

Mwanawasa's action caused the departure from Zambia of the Anglovaal Group, which in 1998 had bought the Chambishi copper-cobalt plant and the Nkana Slag. It needed the Luanshya production for the Chambishi copper-cobalt plant and when it lost it through Mwanawasa's direct intervention it naturally came to the conclusion that Zambia could not be relied on. It sold the Chambishi plant to Enya for a cash payment of $6.5 million, transfer of a $25 million contingent liability and an additional payment of another $25 million over a period of five years, depending on cobalt prices and levels of production. According to the announcement at the time, AVMIN took a write-off of $90 million as a result.

Mwanawasa's intervention was a repetition of the RAMCOZ fiasco, when, in June 1997, a similar last minute intervention by Chiluba decreed the cancellation of the nearly finalized negotiations with another respectable

188

mining group, First Quantum, and the handing over of Luanshya to the Binani group. And it signalled a second odyssey for the unfortunate people of Luanshya and its mine. The new owners did not prove any more reliable than Binani's RAMCOZ; the mine closed down again in December 2008 and the Muliashi project which had been expected to start producing 60,000 tons of copper in 2010 was abandoned. In October 2009, the Banda administration finally sold Luanshya Mine to the China Non-Ferrous Metals Corporation (CNMC), for $50 million and an undertaking of an additional 'new investment' of $400 million. CNMC was selected from amongst four bidders, the others being Vedanta, the owners of Konkola, and two local bidders named EXCO Corporation and Luanshya Mineral Resources.

Over the years, it transpired that Enya's ultimate parent, the Kazakhstan Natural Resources Corporation, was owned by three Asian oligarchs. In its promotional literature of the time, it claimed to have operations in Kazakhstan, China, Russia, Brazil, and Africa (DRC, Zambia, Mozambique and South Africa). Its products were listed as ferroalloys, iron ore, aluminium, energy and some minor non-ferrous activities, i.e. a little of everything, hardly impressive credentials for the reliable copper miner that Zambia needed.

The Asian oligarchs eventually established the Eurasian Natural Resources Corporation (ENRC), which they floated on the London Stock Exchange, in 2007, raising substantial sums. It appears that they then proceeded to offload their Enya holdings on the new public corporation at 46 times the purchase price, according to the *Financial Times* of 11 May 2013, which attracted the attention of the London Stock Exchange and the UK's Serious Fraud Office (SFO). The *Financial Times* added that the Kazakhstan group

> is being investigated by the SFO over a range of allegations of fraud, bribery and corruption. A British law firm that had been appointed to conduct an internal fraud probe but was dismissed in March, 2013 stated that information from a whistleblower together with documentary evidence regarding the making of cash payments to African presidents was to be provided (including evidence that the payments had been sanctioned by a senior executive).

The *Financial Times* ended its report by stating that ENRC denied that there was evidence to back the allegations.

One wonders how people like Binani and Enya manage to corner African presidents, like Chiluba and Mwanawasa, and arrange to redirect nearly concluded deals away from recognized reputable companies to anonymous shells with little history and less previous experience in the industry to the detriment of the countries involved. I covered the sorry story of the Chiluba–Binani association in Chapter 16. It has now been fully investigated but little is known about the Mwanawasa–Enya one. It will be interesting to see if Mwanawasa's name will be on the list of African presidents who received cash payments from ENRC, assuming it ever gets published. Both Chiluba and Mwanawasa are dead now and cannot be questioned but maybe their associates and close advisors should be in order to safeguard against similar occurrences in the future.

Luckily, not all mining deals in Zambia had been a disaster. In August 2001, First Quantum bought the Kansanshi Copper and Gold Mine from Cyprus Amax, a wholly owned subsidiary of Phelps Dodge. It embarked upon a spectacular development programme that made Kansanshi one of the premier mining properties in Zambia. Kansanshi currently produces around 235,000 tons of copper a year (some 35 per cent of Zambia's total production); it is very profitable and from the record it pays its taxes faithfully. According to my research, in the six-year period 2006 to 2011 inclusive, its income tax payments totalled $1.055 billion, and its royalties $183.5 million. A record to be proud of and in the mining confusion of Zambia only matched in integrity by the Lilliputian Chibuluma Mine which paid $53 million and $12 million respectively over the same period, on an annual production of around 18,000 tons of copper a year, a very creditable performance indeed. Chibuluma and Kansanshi appear to be the better run and more reliable mining companies in Zambia. In addition to being good corporate citizens, the two companies are also diligent in their obligations to ZCCM-IH, their minority shareholder, paying small but regular dividends. Apart from these two and two small dividends of around $1 million each for the years 2007 and 2008 from Konkola, ZCCM-IH has not received dividends from any of its other mining investments in Zambia. One other successful mining company in Zambia has been Lumwana in the North Western Province, a greenfield project that was acquired in 1999 by Equinox Minerals; it started production in 2008 and in 2011 produced some 120,000 tons of copper. In 2012 Lumwana changed hands, when Barrick Gold of Canada took over Equinox Minerals.

But I have been absorbed in Mwanawasa's mining deals and strayed from the review of the rest of his performance.

21. FEW SUCCESSES AND MANY FAILURES

Mwanawasa's government had one major economic success. It managed to attain the benchmarks required of Heavily Indebted Poor Countries (HIPC) and Zambia qualified for foreign debt forgiveness in 2005, albeit after the IMF naively accepted 'commercialization' in place of the privatization it had demanded for certain large parastatals. (More about this strange concept later.)

I tried to get details of the composition of the Zambian debt but failed. The 'Completion Point Document' issued by the IMF does not give a breakdown and neither the Bank of Zambia nor the Ministry of Finance were able to give one either. The IMF's attitude is understandable. It would not have wanted to publicize the interest content of the debt, which I believe would have constituted its greatest part. And the Bank of Zambia and the Ministry of Finance would not have been able to produce reliable records going back so many years. Yet it would have been important to know the details of this notorious debt that many believe was wasted or went into the pockets of dictators. In Zambia, if one excludes the sums wasted on the ZIMCO bonds and the TIKA project, it was not. It built schools and hospitals and roads, of which we had next to nothing at independence. Defaults started with the oil price explosion and the collapse of commodity prices in the mid-seventies that lasted for some 30 years. And the debt ballooned with accumulated interest, over the 20 or so years it took the developed countries to make up their minds about what to do. In the meantime unpaid interest was accumulating or new loans were disbursed in order to cover the interest due, for the sole purpose of keeping the books of the World Bank and the IMF current.

As far as I know, only Oxfam made an attempt to research the third world debt though not its breakdown and its genesis. But it hit the nail on the head: in a 1996 report titled 'Multilateral Debt: The Human Costs' Oxfam accused the World Bank and the IMF of creating a 'bizarre financial circus in which more and more aid was being recycled in the form of debt repayment while the debt stock was increasing'. According to the report, a summary of which I saw in the *Financial Times*, Oxfam calculated that in 1993–4, $2.9 billion was provided through the International Development Association of the World Bank to the most indebted countries, out of which $1.9 billion was spent repaying World Bank loans! In other words the World Bank was disbursing new loans, so that the borrowers kept their obligations current and their interest obligation ballooned. According to Oxfam for every $3 lent under IDA, two went back to the World Bank in the form of debt repayments. And a large part of the balance went to the IMF for the same purpose. The result was, according to Oxfam, that debt repayments increased from $1 billion or 20 per cent of total debt service in 1980 to $3.3 billion in 1994.

But I must explain the 'commercialization' concept I referred to earlier. When governments get cold feet about policies they promised foreign donors to implement, and do not want to, they play a rearguard action instead of offering viable alternatives. In Zambia, the government was under pressure from the donors and the multilateral institutions to privatize the telephone and the electricity utilities before HIPC. As I said earlier it did not want to do it and the public, after the mining privatization experience, did not want it either. So after a lot of hand-wringing, the government created a new concept: commercialization. And it sold it to the IMF which accepted it enthusiastically. Its local representative, Mark Ellyne, was ecstatic. He told the *African Business* magazine of January 2004:

> What this essentially means is that the government will not sell any of the shares of state owned ZESCO to a foreign investor. They will cede complete control of the company to an independent, competent chief executive, appointed by an independent board of directors. Such people cannot be expected to do the government favours, as was the case in the past.

So the IMF accepted 'commercialization' as a suitable substitute to its demand for privatization and declared that the HIPC goals were attained. I assume that the people in Washington were not as naive as their Lusaka representative; they probably just closed their eyes and let the deal go through because they realized that it had to be done anyway. But, of course, the commercialization concept turned out to be just more of the same. The entities stopped being called parastatals but companies, which they always had been, and they operated 'profitably' and 'independently'. Profitability would not have been difficult to achieve; at the time they were monopolies after all. But how the second goal of operating independently could be achieved is hard to imagine. The theory is that they have independent boards and management but the practice is different. The companies are owned by government and it is the president who appoints the members of their boards and their chief executive officers. As far as ZESCO is concerned, when President Banda took office in 2008, he replaced the general manager; and as soon as President Sata took office in 2011 he immediately sacked the manager appointed by Banda and reinstated the manager Banda had sacked! The bottom line is that commercialization was the government's successful evasive action, which also satisfied the wishes of the electorate. ZESCO is still under government control, but many new electricity generation schemes are now undertaken in association with foreign investors. Distribution, though, is still the monopoly of ZESCO and it is still undercapitalized and efficiency suffers as a result.

***

The Mwanawasa government also boasted of some success in agriculture. With the help of reasonable rainfall, maize production increased and made Zambia self-sufficient in maize for a couple of years when production averaged around 1.2 million metric tons per annum. But rains failed and the 2004/5 harvest was down to an inadequate 866,187 metric tons. Zambia had to import maize again – back to the normal cycle. After that the annual production of maize increased somewhat, culminating in 1,211,566 metric tons in the 2007/8 season, the last of his administration. There was some influx of Rhodesian farmers in the first couple of years of the twenty-first century (courtesy of Robert Mugabe's land redistribution policies in next door Zimbabwe), that was hailed internationally as the agricultural salvation of Zambia. It was not. Most Rhodesians were actually tobacco farmers and their anticipated contribution to the increase in maize production never materialized and was not needed anyway. Peasant agriculture can cover the country's needs. But on arrival the Rhodesians had promised one acre of maize for each acre of tobacco and delivered neither. They turned to wheat instead because they found it more profitable. But the wheat production remained stagnant during the entire Mwanawasa period, culminating in 113,242 tons in his last season against 135,967 in the first year of his administration.

Both tobacco and wheat are irrigated crops and there have been concerns about overusing underground water resources. Contrary to general belief, Zambia does not have abundant water supply for agriculture. It does have two large river catchments: the Zambezi, that covers 75 per cent of the country (and includes the Kafue and the Luangwa tributaries) and the Congo (that includes the Chambeshi and the Luapula rivers). As the Water Board of Zambia highlights, the northern part of the country has a higher river density, while the southern part has more water 'which is confined to few large rivers making access difficult for most uses'. The major agricultural areas of the country are in the south and rely on small streams that dry up soon after the rains and never run in drought years. And irrigation dams that are springing up all over no longer fill up unless the rainy season is above average. Current levels of commercial agriculture generally manage to get enough water, but the peasants who live downstream struggle. In other words, very large scale irrigated agriculture can only take place alongside the big rivers, otherwise a huge investment would be necessary to pump the water from the river valleys to the plateau, a couple of thousand feet higher, over long distances.

Most Rhodesians were good tobacco farmers and they contributed to a large increase in production of Virginia tobacco, but by 2008, the last year of Mwanawasa's administration it tapered off to 17,005 tons. The Rhodesians were generously financed by Barclays Bank, which provided long-term loans at very low interest rates. The Zambian commercial farmers were aggrieved with Barclays' generosity to the Rhodesians and ascribed it to 'political motives', implying British government prodding. And there was discontent amongst the Zambian workers because many of the new arrivals were still Rhodesians at heart, with a 1950s attitude towards blacks, somewhat exaggerated by a feeling that Zambian workers are not as good as Zimbabwe ones. The Zambian workers complained of low salaries, substandard housing, and harsh treatment.

Very few Rhodesian farmers were still in Zambia a couple of years later. Either they were bad farmers and they failed, fleeing in the middle of the night leaving workers, creditors and the banks unpaid, or they were crooks, who took advantage of the generous loans and the absence of exchange control regulations and transferred their funds abroad and left in the middle of the night.

Peasant agriculture was neglected by Mwanawasa as much as it had been neglected by Chiluba, a phenomenon I attribute to their own urban upbringing as well as that of the majority of their cabinet – they knew very little about how people lived in the rural areas and what their real needs were. They only thought of urban amenities to offer rural people, such as electricity and telephones, instead of improved trunk and district roads, seed and fertilizer distribution, better produce marketing and most importantly a NAMBOARD style of pre-planting finance.

Four years after Mwanawasa came to power, at the end of 2005, lending rates in Zambia were hovering around 40 per cent per annum. In its 2004 Country Economic Memorandum for Zambia, the World Bank highlighted the problem:

> High lending rates have stifled private borrowing and undermined private investment and growth. At 8 per cent the ratio of private sector credit to GDP in Zambia is one of the lowest in Sub-Saharan Africa. In recent years commercial banks have preferred to invest in banks abroad and in government debt; by

mid-2003 such investments accounted for almost half of their aggregate total assets. Another 17.5 per cent of kwacha and foreign currency deposits are held in non-remunerated deposits with the Bank of Zambia. Commercial banks derive more than half of their income from government securities. About 15–35 per cent of their income comes from foreign exchange activities, including foreign exchange trading and fees on foreign exchange transactions.

But the Mwanawasa administration seemed oblivious and quite disinterested in the importance of the above statistics. Worse still and not highlighted in the World Bank report was that loans and advances, in other words local lending, amounted to less than 20 per cent of most banks' portfolios and of that only a small proportion was lent to indigenous Zambians. And the World Bank report went on to highlight that real interest rates in Zambia averaged 16 per cent per annum between 1994 and 2002, when they climbed to 18.8 per cent – perhaps the highest in Sub-Saharan Africa, an 'achievement' that the Mwanawasa administration should have been ashamed of.

But the Mwanawasa government carried on borrowing, blithely, issuing bonds and treasury bills month after month to some staggering totals like K5 trillion ($1.5 billion at the exchange rate of the time) for the year 2004. For the year 2005, the total stock of government bonds and treasury bills (after redemptions) increased by another staggering total of K3.45 trillion or $1 billion with an average interest coupon of over 20 per cent per annum. And the increase accelerated during 2006, with the bonds and the treasury bills (after redemptions) increasing by K450.45 billion and 694.74 respectively in the first six months of the year. As at 30 June 2006 the totals stood at: bonds K1.87 trillion and treasury bills 2.78 trillion, a record increase of 1.145 trillion in six months, against K885 billion for the whole of 2005 (Bank of Zambia fortnightly statistics).

Inevitably this size of government borrowing while at the same time copper prices were constantly rising attracted international speculation, particularly from hedge funds, that caused the Kwacha to rise. Unfortunately, the government persuaded itself that the rise was due to the landing of the much sought foreign direct investment and talked the Kwacha higher still: it publicized its desired target, K3,000 to the American dollar. It did not take very long for speculation to reach fever pitch. If the government wanted the Kwacha to rise to a parity of three thousand for one American dollar, when it was trading at 4,750, and at the time the price of copper was on the up, it did not need a genius to calculate that there was 35 per cent profit in the process. And government securities yielding around 17 per cent interest per annum at the end of 2005 gave an additional bonus to the transaction. So, foreign speculation accelerated. The government treated this as a sign of economic virility and initially it was encouraged in this naive interpretation by praises from various foreign diplomats. They changed their tune when they saw the disastrous effects the Kwacha appreciation was having on the country's non-traditional exports. Horticulture was the first to be hit, with many farmers who were producing vegetables and flowers for export to Europe ceasing production, because the export prices did not generate sufficient Kwacha revenue to meet their costs. But the biggest blow to the economy came from the failure of the cotton production, the mainstay of many rural districts. The cotton traders were unable to pay the peasant producers the pre-planting Kwacha price per kilo they had promised. The disappointed producers lost confidence and production dropped from 155,000 tons in the 2004/5 season to 118,000 the following year and only 55,000 in 2006/7. It took many years after the return of the Kwacha to its normal parity levels for the production to increase again, with cotton only getting back to six digit figures in 2010/11. Tobacco farmers had a similar fate. And the damage to the other 'non-traditional' exports of Zambia took as long to repair.

Mwanawasa never looked very healthy; he was grossly overweight but he did not seem to want to do anything about it. He suffered a minor stroke in April 2006 but this did not seem to make him change his habits and pay some attention to his weight. He was re-elected as president in September 2006 with 43 per cent of the vote in his favour. According to the Zambian constitution the president appoints his vice president after the election and this time he chose Rupiah Banda, an ex-UNIP politician from the Eastern Province. The Eastern Province had been the mainstay of UNIP after Kapwepwe's defection and a UNIP politician as vice president was an astute appointment.

Like most African presidents Mwanawasa had a punishing international travelling schedule, which he seemed to love. On 29 June 2008, he suffered a severe stroke for the second time while attending an African Union conference in Sharm el-Sheikh in Egypt. The Egyptian doctors managed to stop the brain haemorrhage and on 1 July he was flown to the Percy Military Hospital in France for further treatment. Announcements about his condition in Zambia were sparse and generally misleading. An announcement on 3 July 2008 purported to have emanated from the Zambian Embassy in South Africa reported his death, a false alarm that was swiftly denied. Mwanawasa died on 19 August 2008 and was buried on 3 September, his 60th birthday.

By that time the battle for succession was in full swing. Under the Zambian constitution, the vice president does not succeed, because he is appointed by the president instead of being elected by the people. He is allowed to act for a period of three months, during which time he must organize new elections.

Mrs Mwanawasa gave every outward sign that she wanted to stand and she used her husband's funeral for what many interpreted as a pre-election campaign. She decided that his body should be ferried to all provincial capitals so that the rural areas would have the opportunity to pay their last respects. Amazingly the Acting President acquiesced and allowed this huge unnecessary expense, making Zambian air force planes available for the purpose. But the political significance of this extravagance did not escape the attention of Michael Sata, the most prominent aspiring opposition candidate, who chartered his own plane and joined the airborne cortège. The gesture infuriated Mrs Mwanawasa who in Chipata confronted him and accused him of exploiting her husband's funeral for electioneering purposes. In the end Mrs Mwanawasa decided not to run and announced instead that her husband's wish was for his Minister of Finance to succeed him. The Lusaka rumour mill immediately concluded that she had made a pact with the Minister of Finance to support him to get elected provided he promised to bow out in her favour at the end of the term.

In the event Banda won the election with 40 per cent of the vote to Sata's 38. It was a neck and neck race, until the results of the remote parts of the Northern Province came through and gave Banda his wafer thin majority. Until then, as the interim results were coming in, Sata thought that he had been the winner and issued instructions regarding his swearing in ceremony. He did not want it at the High Court, which is the tradition but at the Independence Stadium. And he did not want the Chinese Ambassador to be present but he invited Taiwan to send a representative instead. He was very upset when at the last minute he lost, even though the election was declared transparent by the two monitoring teams, one from the African Union and the other from COMESA (Common Market of East and Southern Africa). He refused to accept the results and there were sporadic riots by members of his party in Lusaka and Kitwe. They fizzled out after a day or two.

The Banda administration started under very inauspicious circumstances.

22. 'Steady As She Goes'

Banda was sophisticated and suave, with a cosmopolitan background. He had read economic history at Sweden's Lund University and spent many years as ambassador in a number of countries, which included Washington as Ambassador to the United States and New York as Representative to the United Nations. He had also served as head of a couple of parastatals (government-owned enterprises) and Minister of Foreign Affairs. He had been a member of UNIP from the early days and he delivered the UNIP dominated Eastern Province to Mwanawasa and his MMD Party during the 2006 election. On Mwanawasa's death he automatically became acting president, with the constitutional mandate to organize elections within 90 days. He was later elected by the National Executive of the MMD as the party's candidate for the presidential election that followed, winning 47 votes against 11 cast for the then Minister of Finance who had been anointed by Mrs Mwanawasa as her husband's preferred successor. As I already said he won the election, but, in the final analysis, Banda's elevation to the highest position in the nation was pure luck. He had not been a rank and file politician, and, like Mwanawasa, he just happened to have been at the right place at the right time. Even though he had been in the upper echelons of UNIP for decades he never held a frontline position and never developed political instincts and rapport with the masses, a problem that surfaced time and again during his period in office. He was not a proactive person and for a politician he was unique: he was not much interested in attracting attention and publicity. He sat back and let the country get on without too much government interference or fuss. This engendered stability and confidence and resulted in substantial economic growth, something which his successors should note.

Investment, foreign and local, thrived, particularly the real estate sector and the construction industry. Shopping malls and housing estates, locally and externally financed, sprang up in Lusaka and other major towns. And there was an influx of businesses from South Africa setting up branches in Zambia, a not altogether beneficial development in my view; branches of South African businesses tend to displace smaller ones owned by Zambians, and damage

4. President Banda by
Kiss Brian Abraham

struggling Zambian industries, because the South Africans prefer to import South African products instead of buying locally. On the other hand it led to faster growth, and it was indicative of the business confidence Banda and his predecessor had generated. And he privatized one of the white elephants amongst the parastatals: the 'Telecommunications Company of Zambia' (ZAMTEL). ZAMTEL was sold in 2010 to the LAP Green Network, a company in the Libyan African Portfolio for $257 million and an undertaking for a further investment of $200 million, a sum that prudently, the Banda administration ensured was deposited in Zambia on takeover. The sale, which yielded almost twice as much as all the other parastatals sold by Chiluba, caused controversy because the valuation of ZAMTEL had been carried out by a Cayman Islands company, RP Capital Partners, which had been reported as having connections with one of Banda's sons. LAP Green improved ZAMTEL's operations, both landline and mobile, and according to its promotional literature it increased its subscriber base 600 per cent within a year. (Michael Sata, Banda's successor declared the deal corrupt and renationalized ZAMTEL when he came into office in 2011 but LAP Green sued and at the time of writing the case was still in the courts. On 25 March 2013 the Zambian High Court gave LAP Green permission to present evidence in London instead of Lusaka on the grounds that its witnesses had experienced intimidation by the authorities in Zambia and they were afraid to return. In fact ZAMTEL's last chief executive under LAP Green had been deported in August 2012.)

The Banda administration did nothing about increasing revenue from the mining companies despite the outcry over the concessions they enjoyed and the minimal rates of taxation. In my book *A Venture in Africa*, which was published in 2007, I suggested the introduction of a 'windfall profits' tax in order to redress the extraordinary benefits granted to the purchasers of the privatized mines by the Chiluba and Mwanawasa administrations. I pointed out that this measure had been frequently resorted to during periods of unusually buoyant markets, like the one the copper market was experiencing at the time and was still continuing to do so during Banda's regime and later. (Most mines had been sold at a time when the copper price was 75 American cents per lb, while in 2007 it was $3 and rising.) Many years earlier, the British government had imposed windfall profits tax in relation to North Sea oil and later on bank profits; the Australian government had done it in relation to minerals, the Chilean government in relation to copper. The then British High Commissioner (Ambassador) to Zambia took up the idea in the press, and the IMF and the World Bank followed. After long procrastination the Mwanawasa administration decided to act and introduced a tax, which had not been well thought through and was unduly onerous. But Dr Situmbeko Musokotwane, Banda's Minister of Finance, did not like the idea. He was persuaded by the mining companies that a windfall tax based on revenue was unfair. From his public pronouncements, it appeared that he may have been threatened that if he did not abolish the tax, Mopani and Konkola, two of Zambia's biggest mining groups, might shut down and go. So instead of modifying his predecessor's formula, he scrapped it and introduced a new tax, which he called variable tax, based on profits and not on revenue. In the Zambian newspaper *The Post* of 24 July 2010, he was reported to have said:

> When you tax revenue and not the profit you are basically closing the mines. Indeed this country still has a windfall tax but windfall tax on profits and not on revenues ... The windfall tax of 2008 would have led to chaos and social unrest on the Copperbelt and most key mines would have closed. Mopani Copper Mines would have closed, Konkola Copper Mines would not have completed their expansion programme ... do you imagine the social unrest and chaos on the Copperbelt? ... We need to be a little patient and in the next three to four years, mining taxes will be contributing one third of our GDP.

The Post ended its report by highlighting that 'last year Zambia earned 77 million dollars in mine taxes to the Treasury from total exports of 2.9 billion dollars' worth of copper!'

Musokotwane is an academic economist who does not know how business ticks and he appears to be too much of a hostage to his academic learning to try to find out. Mopani and Konkola obviously threatened him that they would close down unless he removed the windfall tax. He panicked and he succumbed. And they must have laughed behind his back at his gullibility and celebrated when he replaced the windfall tax with his 'variable tax based on profits' because they knew that they did not intend to show any profits (as the reader has already seen in Chapter 20).

If he had cared to examine the windfall tax Arthur Wina had negotiated with the mining companies in the 1960s he would have discovered that it was based on revenue and not on profits. Wina allowed the mines the entire profit up to UK£300 per ton, with anything above that to be shared fifty-fifty. As the price was £600 at the time, the mining companies that still earned substantial profits at the price of £300 per ton and an additional £150 per ton on top, were very happy. And the country prospered. A similar formula in the market conditions prevailing during the Banda presidency would have produced huge sums for the development of Zambia.

At the time Musokotwane caved in to the mines out of fear that they would close down and go, the market price of copper was above $4 dollars per lb and rising, against below 80 American cents when they were taken over. It rose to $5 per pound or some $10,000 per ton and stayed around that figure for a long period of time during his term as Minister of Finance. Even as late as mid-2014, the price was still hovering around $3. If Musokotwane had the slightest idea of how a businessman's mind works he would have known that no businessman packs up when the market is buoyant. He may decide to sell but only in order to take advantage of the buoyant market and dispose of his business at a very high price. In that case he will keep the enterprise going at full efficiency in order to get maximum price. Even the Grant Thornton/ECON report on the accounting irregularities of Mopani (see details in Chapter 30), which he received when he was still in office, did not make him reverse course.

***

On assumption of office Banda encountered a thorny problem in relation to Zambian Airways (not to be confused with the former state-owned Zambia Airways which Chiluba had put into liquidation in the early nineties), a privately owned and operated airline, which had developed a reasonably efficient regional network, and was the only competitor to South African Airways on the profitable Lusaka–Johannesburg route. Zambian Airways like most privately owned airlines in Africa was undercapitalized and ran into financial problems. It owed large sums to the National Airport Authority in passenger departure fees, which it had collected from its passengers but had not paid to the authority. It was also in arrears in employees' contribution to the National Pension Scheme Authority (NAPSA) and on a loan from the Development Bank of Zambia (DBZ), which is owned jointly by the government of Zambia and various international and regional financial institutions, with its management appointed by the government of Zambia. (I tried to get details of the shareholding from the Registrar of Companies but I was told that the file was missing, regrettably a frequent phenomenon in politically charged cases.) Banda was asked for government assistance in order to keep the company afloat on the grounds that it was the only regional Zambian airline and was performing a necessary service. He refused, probably coming to the conclusion that government participation was inappropriate (it would have caused an outcry amongst the international institutions and Western donors) and in any case the company was too far gone for redemption.

This appears to have put him at loggerheads with *The Post*, Zambia's only independent daily at the time, whose owner had bought a sizeable share in Zambian Airways a couple of years earlier. As a result *The Post* started a vilifying campaign against Banda and his administration: nothing Banda ever did was any good in the eyes of *The Post*. The attack became single-minded and relentless and intensified as Banda's term was coming to an end, leading to his eventual defeat in the election of 2011.

But Banda can boast of a number of spectacular achievements, particularly in agriculture: maize production increased from 1,211,566 tons in the 2007/8 season, the last of Mwanawasa's administration, to 3,020,380 tons in the 2010/11 season, the last of Banda's own administration. Similarly, production of wheat went up from 63,879 tons in 2007/8 to 237,336 tons in 2010/11, cotton from 71,821 to 121,908, Virginia tobacco from 17,005 to 27,146, ground nuts from 70,527 to 139,388, sunflower from 12,662 to 21,954, paddy rice from 24,023 to 49,410, sorghum from 9,993 to 18,458 and soya beans from 43,715 to 116,539 (source: Selected Social Economic Indicators 2010, Central Statistical Office). In short Banda almost doubled agricultural production, particularly peasant produced crops, like maize, ground nuts, cotton, sorghum and paddy rice.

Ignoring the subsidies, which have been going on for years and which are confined to maize, this amazing result seems to have been achieved mainly by ensuring that seed and fertilizer were delivered to the peasant farmers on time and that its distribution spread to a much greater number of farmers than before. 'This was the result of the establishment of "area development committees" set up by the Ministry of Agriculture to vet the farmers' input requirements,' Peter Daka, one of Banda's Ministers of Agriculture, explained. In this way the government was able to spread the available supplies to a much greater number of farmers, thus increasing the production. Distribution of seed and fertilizer before the onset of the rains at the end of October is critical and, perversely, governments seem to always miss this target. Peter Daka, who served as Minister of Agriculture for a considerable period, explained to me that he used to start working on the procurement early each year in order to ensure that supplies arrived by August to allow enough time for distribution to the remote parts of the country before the rains. But the main factor that influences the production of all peasant crops is pricing and marketing. Daka used the import parity yardstick in relation to the former and the Food Reserve Agency to buy all peasant crops instead of just maize, a task that before its abolition by Chiluba was performed by NAMBOARD. One additional success in agriculture the Banda administration achieved was that by the end of his term 97 per cent of the maize production was produced by peasant farmers.

Banda's successes did not end with agriculture. Formal employment also went up by 23 per cent, from 544,339 in 2008, Mwanawasa's last year, to 671,246 in 2009: a total of 126,907 new jobs. What was equally impressive was that 64,077 (half of the total) of those were created by the private sector, which as I said felt secure in the stability the Banda regime generated. And the per capita GDP increased from \$1182.65 in 2008, Mwanawasa's last year, to \$1425.31 in 2011, Banda's last year in office, though the major part of this increase must be attributed to the high copper price.

One additional initiative that was used to vilify him was the order for seven mobile hospitals, which were supplied and financed by China. The attack started in *The Post* newspaper, which accused Banda of wasting government funds and predicted that the vehicles would not cope on our district roads, that our standards of maintenance in Zambia were inadequate and the vehicles would end up broken down all over the country. The criticism was taken over by the Patriotic Front, then in opposition. Fast-forward to 2013 and the Sata regime: the Ministry of Health announced the successful operation of the mobile hospitals. They had treated 330,000 people since the first one arrived in 2011, and, in view of their success, the Sata government had placed additional orders, to raise the total to ten.

***

Banda's political performance was not as impressive. He had the propensity of shooting himself in the foot. As he never held a frontline political position, he stood aloof and did not have much of a feel for the masses and their views. In Chapter 19 I described in some detail both Chiluba trials, the civil case against him in London and the criminal one in Lusaka where he was acquitted, to the consternation of many in the country who attributed the acquittal to Banda's instructions. As I said earlier, I read the Lusaka judgment carefully and I am of the opinion that Judge Chinyama had reached his verdict to acquit sincerely and honestly, after meticulous study of the facts without any influence from Banda or any other political authority. I found his judgment well-reasoned and carefully considered. But, Banda had been cultivating Chiluba politically in order to get his support in Luapula (another political blunder: a more experienced politician would have kept his distance) so *The Post* and the opposition politicians immediately cried foul: Judge Chinyama's verdict had been dictated by Banda, they cried. And, naively, Banda reinforced their suspicions by making a press statement expressing relief at Chiluba's acquittal and thanking the Zambian people for accepting it calmly! A more experienced politician would have remained mum and, if pressed, would have said something about the independence of the judiciary. Again, fast-forward to 2013 and the Sata regime: on the occasion of Armistice Day, on 11 November 2013, President Sata gave instructions to build a mausoleum over Chiluba's grave!

***

Banda's administration lasted a short three years only, as his mandate was to complete Mwanawasa's term. A new election was held in September 2011 but he only managed to secure 35.42 per cent (987,866) of the vote. The opposition, Patriotic Front, under the leadership of Michael Sata won a convincing victory with 41.98 per cent (1,170,966 votes). A distant third was Hakainde Hichilema of the United Party for National Development, with 18.17 per cent (506,763 votes). In parliament, Sata's Patriotic Front secured 60 seats, Banda's Movement for Multiparty Democracy 55 and Hichilema's UPND 28. There were five Independents or representing minor parties and two seats remained vacant. Unlike many other African presidents who lost elections and refused to go, Banda gracefully bowed out following the tradition established by Kenneth Kaunda in 1991.

Sata's support came mainly from towns and there was ecstasy in Lusaka during his inauguration. In his inimitable populist fashion he had promised a job within 90 days for all unemployed and to double the salaries for everybody in low level employment. Youngsters were dancing in the streets in anticipation. Wherever I went during the first couple of weeks, I was confronted by youths asking my driver if I had doubled his salary.

Sata's term is only halfway through. It is proving to be both spectacular and controversial, more than any other president's so far, as the reader will see later. But one of his biggest challenges, like Banda's, turned out to be Barotseland.

23. A Protectorate (Within a Protectorate) Is Pampered ...

In Chapter 1, I described the genesis of the Barotseland Protectorate for the sole purpose of granting mining rights to Cecil Rhodes's British South Africa Company. (A senior chief on the periphery of Barotseland once gave me another reason: 'Lewanika needed British protection, because 30 of his predecessors had either been eliminated or dethroned and he was about to follow' he said.) But the protectorate status bestowed by the Lochner concession in 1890 notwithstanding, on its absorption into the Northern Rhodesia Protectorate in 1924, Barotseland became the Barotse Province of Northern Rhodesia, the senior British Protectorate to which it was attached. It was as late as 1948 that its protectorate status resurfaced, in a promise by the then Northern Rhodesia Governor Sir Gilbert Rennie and reaffirmed by the Conservative Colonial Secretary Harry Hopkinson as an inducement to secure the Paramount Chief's acquiescence to the Amalgamation of Southern and Northern Rhodesia that was under consideration at the time. The amalgamation was abandoned and the Federation of Rhodesia and Nyasaland was imposed instead, as I covered in Chapter 1. It was only then that the protectorate status of Barotseland was officially reinstated by a Special Order in Council, issued in 1953 the same year the Federation was created.

But the Northern Rhodesia Government simply ignored the reinstatement and carried on administering Barotseland as just another province of Northern Rhodesia, as it had always done. Civil servants serving in, say, Kasama were just as likely to be transferred to Fort Jameson (now Chipata) as to Mongu (Barotseland's capital). A provincial commissioner would change his title to 'Resident Commissioner' when serving in Mongu, but he was still reporting to the Secretary of Native Affairs of Northern Rhodesia and would revert back to being called provincial commissioner when he was transferred to, say, Ndola: all very practical and sensible.

But despite the inducement the Northern Rhodesia Government did not succeed in winning the unequivocal support of the Paramount Chief and the Lealui establishment or the Barotse people to the Federal cause. As Gerald L.

Caplan reports in his 1968 paper published in the *Journal of African Studies*, when Sir Gilbert Rennie, in April 1953, addressed a public meeting of some 500 people in order to generate support for the Federation only eight raised their voices in support. Even the Paramount Chief Mwanawina Lewanika was against it, but he was browbeaten and changed sides on Rennie's argument that 'since the Queen approved the Federation, opposition to it was tantamount to being disloyal to his protector'. Mwanawina's loyalty to the Crown would be exploited time and again during the Federal period, both by the Federal and the Northern Rhodesian governments, and would always bring him some reward. Their main target was the independence movement which was gaining strength; their hope was that Mwanawina's support in the fight against the nationalists was going to set an example for other chiefs to follow – the provincial administration of Northern Rhodesia being out of touch as usual: the other chiefs would do exactly the opposite; and the more the British mollycoddled the Barotse Chief the less the rest of the country trusted him. Nevertheless, the British administration thought that an inducement would do the trick and in the 1959 New Year's Honours list the Queen conferred a knighthood on the Paramount Chief who thus became Sir Mwanawina Lewanika III, KBE (Knight of the British Empire). They had hoped that this would secure his loyalty and cooperation but they got a surprise as Caplan explains in his above mentioned paper:

> Mwanawina was not yet prepared, however, to join with white racialists against black nationalists. Apparently at the urging of Godwin Mbikusita ... who had in 1959 become a member of the Federal Assembly supporting Welensky, the Paramount Chief renewed his demands for secession. When news of this leaked out, a tremendous uproar ensued. UNIP leaders agreed with the interpretation of the *Northern News*, a newspaper which supported Welensky [the Federal Prime Minister], that the decision revealed the Lozi Rulers to be as hostile to African Nationalism as to white domination. The Ngambela, Akabeswa Imasiku, hotly denied that secession was a reaction to the increasing likelihood of nationalist victory. Such a contingency, he asserted, was quite irrelevant, since 'we do not consider ourselves a part of Northern Rhodesia or as a protectorate within a protectorate ...' Above all Lealui's stand was intolerable to those UNIP leaders who were Lozi – not least perhaps because a number of them, particularly Arthur and Sikota Wina were themselves Lozi aristocrats with profound personal grievances against the Paramount Chief. On the initiative of these men the Barotse Anti-Secession Movement (BASMO), was formed in Lusaka late in 1960; their leaders spoke for the majority of Lozi in the towns along the line of rail who appeared to be antagonistic to the Lealui clique.

But the Chief ignored the protests and flew to London with his Ngambela to press his demand for secession directly with Iain MacLeod who was the Colonial Secretary at the time. This put MacLeod in a tight spot. He could not afford to upset the nationalists and he did not want to displease Mwanawina. So secession was out of the question, but Britain would ensure that his best interests would be taken care of, he assured the Chief. And he gave him another sweetener: permission to use the title of Litunga (Keeper of the Earth). In other words the British thought they had found the key to incentivizing the Paramount Chief in their favour: in 1948, they reintroduced the status of protectorate, which they made official in 1953, in 1959 they gave him a knighthood and in 1960 they allowed him to use the Lozi title Litunga. But they were wrong. What followed is succinctly summarized by Gerald Caplan and I quote it in full:

> The Litunga still demanded secession, while UNIP saw the new concession as part of an imperialist plot to divide and rule. With full Boma support, the Lealui government continued to provoke UNIP by persecuting its local adherents and deporting its organisers arriving from Lusaka, to which the nationalists reacted by intensifying their campaign to penetrate Barotseland. The more hostile towards Mwanawina UNIP became the more valuable an ally did he appear to Roy Welensky. Lifunana Imasiku, the Litunga's personal secretary and son of the Ngambela, claims to have met Welensky in Salisbury early in 1962. The Prime Minister suggested to him a plan for a new federation incorporating Southern Rhodesia, the Copperbelt, Katanga and Barotseland. Welensky is said to have offered to arrange a meeting between the Litunga and Tshombe but Mwanawina rejected the scheme, fearing it would alienate his white friends in Lusaka and London. Welensky was undeterred, however, and in February 1962 he put roughly the same proposition to Duncan Sandys, the Colonial Secretary: he would agree to secession of Nyasaland and North Eastern Rhodesia in return for a new federation in which Southern Rhodesia would provide the talent, the Copperbelt the wealth and Barotseland the labour as well as a co-operative African ruler ... Sandys apparently adopted the idea of a new Federation with Barotseland as its Bantustan. Accompanied by Godwin Mbikusita, who had become one of Welensky's two parliamentary secretaries he flew to Barotseland, conferred with the Litunga, and left with a signed document formally requesting Barotseland's secession from Northern Rhodesia 'while remaining within the Federation'.

Sandys later backtracked but even after his repudiation, as Gerald Caplan contends:

secession within or outside a federation remained Lealui's demand, as Godwin Mbikusita busily intrigued behind the scenes, encouraging the Litunga not to capitulate. Immediately thereafter, Welensky and Mbikusita were informed by R. A. Butler Deputy Prime Minister [who took over the portfolio of Central Africa], that, while Northern Rhodesia and Nyasaland would be permitted to secede from the Federation, Barotseland could not secede from Northern Rhodesia. The Lozi ruling class therefore considered that it had no alternative but to return for support to its erstwhile worst enemies – the local white settlers – against both the British Government and the threatening alien Africans [read the Zambians].

After the UNIP success in the 1964 election, Mwanawina flew to London to plead one more time for secession. But Butler told him bluntly that 'Britain could not afford to support Barotseland financially if it were divorced from Northern Rhodesia' (Gerald L. Caplan, 'Barotseland: The secessionist challenge to Zambia').

A. *Afternoon Bath* by
Adam Mwansa

B. *Akalela Dance*
by Petson Lombe

C. *Amalila* (Meal Time)
by Godfrey Setti

D. *Kimanyukunyuku*
(Colonial Pioneers)
by Stephen Kapata

E. *Business As Usual*
by Mulenga Chafilwa

F. *Icishiba* (Water Hole)
by Shadreck Simukanga

G. *Inkalata* (The Letter)
by Stary Mwaba

H. *Kakachema* (Herd
Boy) by Adam Mwansa

I. *Mandevu Market*
by H. Mulenga

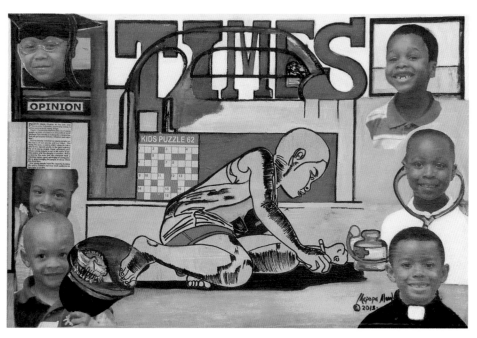

J. *Nganakula* (When I
Grow Up) by Mapopa
M'tonga

K. *Ovina Vimbuza*
(Dancer) by Henry
Tayali

L. *The Struggle Continues*
by Henry Tayali

M. *Ukusombola* (The
Harvest) by Flinto
Chandia

N. *Iminwe ya Gold* (Hands
of Gold) Frederick Chiluba
1991–2001

O. *Oyela Kumalo
Opatulika* (Saint Patrick's
Retreat) Levy Mwanawasa
2001–8

P. *Ifimalayo Fimofinefye*
(Same Promises Again
and Again) Rupiah Banda
2008–11

Q. *Ntungulu* (Ululation)
Kenneth Kaunda in
Retirement 2013

24. ... AND ABANDONED

All the toing and froing must have terrified the Colonial Office. They could not fathom what the Chief's next move would be – he had started making overtures to apartheid South Africa, Portugal, and Rhodesia – and as independence was approaching they needed to regularize their position and wash their hands of Barotseland for good. The last thing the British would have wanted was to grant independence to Northern Rhodesia and be landed with the Protectorate of Barotseland (a far from viable economic unit that they would have to support financially) any more than they had wanted to be landed with Nyasaland when they created the Federation of Rhodesia and Nyasaland (see Chapter 1). So, a few months before independence they engineered the 'Barotseland Agreement 1964' in order to absolve themselves of any obligations the Litunga, the Lealui establishment and the Barotse people may have thought Britain had towards them and at the same time to give them the impression they were taking good care of them by bestowing a special status for Barotseland in the yet unborn nation of Zambia.

The preamble to the agreement highlights the British worries:

> And whereas, having regard to the fact that all treaties and other agreements subsisting between H.M. the Queen of the United Kingdom of Great Britain and Northern Ireland, and the Litunga of Barotseland will terminate when Northern Rhodesia becomes an independent sovereign republic and Her Majesty's Government of the United Kingdom will thereupon cease to have any responsibility for the Government of Northern Rhodesia, including Barotseland, it is the wish of the Government of Northern Rhodesia and the Litunga of Barotseland to enter into agreements concerning the position of Barotseland as part of the Republic of Zambia to take the place of treaties and other agreements hitherto subsisting between Her Majesty the Queen and the Litunga of Barotseland.

I have not seen the Lochner treaty that bestowed protection on the Litunga in 1890, but I do not expect that it would have a provision for such a neat,

211

cost-free, exit clause such as: 'any obligations that may arise out of this, our promised protection, ceases to exist as soon as we farm you out to somebody else'. But they did have to farm him out to Northern Rhodesia so that they could pass on any possible claims to the future government of Zambia. In fact, according to the doctrine of decolonization legal responsibility for actions of the colonial administration would lie with its successor, in other words the government of the new nation. This policy was never officially announced and it was only indirectly admitted, 50 years after decolonization, when a group of Mau Mau fighters from Kenya won a British High Court ruling, on 5 October 2012, allowing them to proceed with a case against the British government for torture. The case was settled out of court in June 2013, with the British government agreeing to pay £19.9 million (some $30 million), in compensation to 5,228 claimants. William Hague, the British Foreign Secretary, while expressing regret (but no apology), emphasized: 'we continue to deny liability on behalf of the British government and British taxpayers today for the actions of the colonial administration'.

Be that as it may, the Colonial Office thought that Barotseland and the Litunga should not be left with the impression that the 'Empire' was abandoning them to the wolves. So it concocted the 'Barotseland Agreement 1964' and sold it to the Litunga as conferring a privileged position within Zambia. In reality it did not give him, or Barotseland, any different status or privileges from what other Zambian chiefs and tribes enjoy in their areas, even though the agreement pompously proclaims that he is 'authorised and empowered' to make laws for Barotseland in relation to the following:

> The Litungaship, the Barotse Native Government, the Barotse Native Authorities, the Barotse Native Courts, the status of the members of the Barotse Native Courts and the Litunga's Council, matters relating to local government, land, forests, traditional and customary matters relating to Barotseland alone, fishing, control of hunting, game preservation, control of bush fires, the Barotse Native Treasury, the supply of beer, the reservation of trees for canoes, local taxation and matters relating thereto and the Barotse local festivals.

Closer examination of the above 'powers' will reveal that all of them are routine rural issues that are also handled by every chief in his area, without special legislation. At first sight the authority over land stands out as a possible exception but an addendum to the agreement clarifies that:

> The Barotse memorandum has indicated that Barotseland should become an integral part of Northern Rhodesia. In these circumstances the NR Government

will assume certain responsibilities and to carry these out they will have to have certain powers. So far as land is concerned, apart from confirmation of wide powers of the Litunga over customary matters, the position is as follows: ... There should be the same system for land administration for the whole of Northern Rhodesia including Barotseland, that is, the Government Lands Department should be responsible for professional advice and services with regard to land alienation in all parts of Northern Rhodesia and that the same form of documents should be used for grants of land (i) for government purposes and (ii) for non-government and non-customary purposes. The necessary preparation of the title documents should be done by the Government Lands Department.

(The salient points of the Agreement and the addendum are included in detail in Appendix VI.)

In short, the Litunga's 'empowerment' over land, like any other chief's is confined to his traditional jurisdiction. He can regulate its use for his own people but the central government has the overall control, which it uses from time to time to alienate sections for other purposes, such as agriculture, national parks, tourism, mining, other commercial and industrial utilization, the creation of towns, and so on, a right that is exercised through the Ministry of Lands.

But the colonial government was more interested in ensuring that everybody understood that the past was dead and buried and that the Litunga accepted that he and Barotseland were going to be part of the 'unitary State of Zambia', as John Tilney, the then Under-Secretary of State for Commonwealth Relations, was at pains to make clear in the House of Commons during the debate of the Barotseland Agreement on 10 July 1964 (underlined italics are my emphasis):

The Committee will know that certain agreements were entered into between Her Majesty and the Litunga of Barotseland _which is part of Northern Rhodesia_ with respect to the administration of Barotseland. Her Majesty also formally assumed obligations under agreements concluded between the British South African Company and the Litunga during the period that the company was responsible for the administration of the Territory. Undertakings and understandings connected with these agreements have also from time to time been entered into.

These agreements, undertakings, and understandings did not in all cases clearly distinguish between rights and obligations of the Crown and the rights and obligations of the Government of Northern Rhodesia in relation to Barotseland. But following the conference, a new Agreement to which hon. Members have referred, the Barotseland Agreement, 1964, was entered into between the

Government of Northern Rhodesia and the Litunga, which was intended to define the relationship between the parties when Northern Rhodesia becomes independent and to supersede all existing obligations. *The purpose of this clause is to terminate all existing rights and obligations both of the Crown and of the Government of Northern Rhodesia under the existing agreements, undertakings and understandings except those arising under this Agreement.* Similarly, provision was made in the Uganda Independence Act 1962, terminating agreements between the Crown and the kingdoms in Uganda. The possibility of giving Barotseland the same sort of status within Zambia as the kingdoms had within Uganda was considered but the parties to the 1964 Agreement decided otherwise. *Under that Agreement, Barotseland, as the Right Hon. and learned gentleman said, is part of the unitary State of Zambia.*

I was very pleased to hear what hon. Members have said. I repeat what I said in the Second Reading debate. *We have not deprived the Litunga of power. It was a freely negotiated Agreement. We have honourably discharged our obligations* ... I am sure that this Committee will wish the Lozi people, under the rule of the Litunga increasing success, prosperity and happiness and that in *the unity of Zambia all will go forward in progress.*

During the debate A. Fenner Brockway, MP for Eton and Slough gave a generous testimonial that Kenneth Kaunda was a reliable person: 'I know Prime Minister Kaunda very well and I am sure he will carry out this Agreement in the letter and in the spirit,' he said and Sir Frank Soskice MP for Newport wrapped up as follows:

> I profoundly hope that the agreement, which I am sure will be honoured by Dr. Kaunda will put an end to the differences, which, unhappily, have arisen in the past over a considerable period of time, and that Barotseland and its inhabitants and the rest of Zambia – *for Barotseland is an integral part of Zambia* – will live happily together in future and that this Agreement will promote concord over many years.

'Amen' would have been appropriate, I guess, but 'they lived happily ever after' would not have been because the British equivocation over the years and Welensky's repeated attempts to draw the Paramount Chief into his schemes to maintain some sort of white federation in Central Africa carried with it the seeds of future conflict. But let me first explain Sir Frank's cryptic reference to 'the differences, which unhappily have arisen in the past'. Over the years the Litunga faithfully carried out the wishes of the provincial administration, which included banning the main nationalist parties, particularly ZANC and later UNIP from organizing and operating in Barotseland. That part may have been considered normal and routine for the period; most chiefs did the same under instructions from the local district commissioners, even though very few enforced it as rigorously as the Litunga. Many closed their eyes to 'unofficial' organizing. Apart from the many inconsistencies he displayed over the period of the Federation, the Litunga's greatest blunder was that he was persuaded to sponsor the establishment of the Barotse Peoples' Party (Sichaba) and fight the crucial 1962 election, in alliance with Welensky's United Federal Party, whose sole aim was to perpetuate white rule. The nationalists won and formed the first black government and Litunga was disgraced, when his candidates for the Barotse East and the Barotse West constituencies, F. L. Suu and G. M. Mukande, only managed 165 and 69 votes respectively to UNIP's Arthur Wina's 1,097 and Mubiana Nalilungwe's 688. And, in the pre-independence election that followed, UNIP won all 10 Barotse parliamentary seats.

The Barotseland Agreement 1964 was signed by Kenneth Kaunda as Prime Minister of Northern Rhodesia, Sir Mwanawina III, the then Litunga of Barotseland and Duncan Sandys, Commonwealth and Colonial Secretary. I am sure Kaunda signed because he considered it as part of the tidying up formalities for the forthcoming independence. If he and the other Zambian political leaders of the time had had the chance to reflect on the matter outside the overwhelming pressure of preparations for the forthcoming independence they would have refused to sign it because, as the debate in the House of Commons reveals, it was essentially a device conceived by the departing British Empire to formalize its exit and wash its hands of Barotseland and at the same time persuade the Litunga that it had his best interests at heart, by securing for him a special status in the new nation of Zambia. The problem was that the departing British civil servants made the Barotse people believe that the agreement did indeed give them a special status in Zambia and this would be misunderstood and exploited and cause problems in later years; hence the conclusion 'they lived happily ever after' would not have been appropriate.

It is obvious from the House of Commons debate that the British government recognized all along that Zambia as a nation could not possibly concede a special status for Barotseland, and that, after independence, it would have to administer it like any other part of Zambia – that is why expressions like 'Barotseland which is part of Northern Rhodesia'; 'under that Agreement, Barotseland, as the Right Hon. and learned gentleman said, is part of the unitary State of Zambia'; 'for Barotseland is an integral part of Zambia' kept recurring during the debate. And even though they knew it was not going to be adhered to they wanted to tell the Litunga: if the Agreement does not work don't blame us, you were part of the negotiations, and you

215

accepted it, hence the statement: 'we have not deprived the Litunga of power. It was a freely negotiated Agreement. We have honourably discharged our obligations'.

The unfortunate part was that Kaunda personally signed the agreement. He should have left it to the governor of Northern Rhodesia. If he had not appended his signature he would not have been accused of perfidy, as he has been. And, all things considered, Barotseland as a province of Zambia cannot possibly have a special status. It is the second smallest province in the country and if you exclude the Kaoma district which falls under a different chief not particularly enamoured with the Lozi connection, the figure for the Litunga's subjects would number some 700,000 in a population of 13 million, i.e. 5 per cent of the total. Chitimukulu, the Paramount Chief of the Bemba, can claim at least twice as many subjects spread over the Northern and Muchinga Provinces. And there are three or four other major chiefs, such as Kazembe in Luapula, Mpezeni and Gawa Undi in the Eastern Province, and Moonze and Mapanza in the Southern Province who can claim subjects of the order of 500,000 each, yet they were never promised or granted any special privileges; they never did ask for them anyway. The Barotse people must reconcile themselves to living within Zambia at par with everybody else. There is no majority tribe in Zambia and no tribe can claim dominance over the others. Similarly no tribe can claim special privileges. And the government of Zambia must avoid unnecessary pinpricks that make the Barotse people feel less equal, ignored, and downtrodden.

25. 'The Hateful Western Province'

The relationship between Barotseland and the government of Zambia has not been very smooth since independence. The first murmurs of dissatisfaction arose with the Local Government Act of 1965. It was intended to reorganize local government right through the country but the people of Barotseland took it as an affront. But the real 'kick in the teeth' came in 1968 when Kaunda decided that in furtherance of the 'One Zambia, One Nation' concept the names of towns and places with tribal connotation should change and Mankoya was renamed Kaoma and my 'home' town Balovale was given the generic name Zambezi. Although the same logic could not be applied to Barotseland, which was not actually called Loziland or Bulozi, its name was also changed to Western Province, a thoughtless gesture that offended the Barotse people. The people of Barotseland still talk of the 'hateful name: Western Province'. (Until the name was given to Barotseland, the Western Province of Zambia had been what is now the Copperbelt Province and I must confess that I am the one who gave it that name. I had just finished a meeting with Kaunda and he asked me if I could think of a suitable name for the Western Province because he was planning to give that name to Barotseland; everybody calls it the Copperbelt, I said and he agreed.) The final blow in the Barotse saga came with the abolition of the Barotseland agreement, which occurred in 1969.

Inevitably, Barotseland's 'special status' did not last very long in the Republic of Zambia and the Barotse agreement was officially abolished in 1969, when Clause 18 of the Independence Constitution was removed and replaced by the Constitution (Amendment) (No. 5) Act No. 33 of 1969. As I have already said, the main reason why the British included Clause 18 in the Independence Constitution was to safeguard the British South Africa Company's mineral rights and the mining companies' various concessions obtained during the Northern Rhodesian period. Even though BSAC's mineral rights were purchased before independence, the government proceeded with the referendum on 17 June 1969 and removed Clause 18. Its removal had the added advantage that it enabled the Zambian government to cancel the 'Barotse Agreement of 1964'. No one can dispute the impeccable process by which Clause 18 was removed. The referendum was properly held by a democratic government (four years before the imposition of the 'One Party State') and was approved by the electorate even though the task had the onerous hurdle of approval by 51 per cent of the voters on the roll, not just the votes cast. It must be said for the record, though, that Barotseland voted against its removal; and so did the Solwezi district, but I have not been able to fathom the reason for the latter.

Though there were murmurs of discontent nothing much came to the surface for many years. An explanation I heard in retrospect involved the existence of the continuous state of emergency during UNIP's period in power (initially excusable because of the Rhodesian liberation war and the incursions and acts of sabotage perpetrated by the Rhodesian army but, perversely, maintained after the liberation of Zimbabwe in 1980) that was used arbitrarily to incarcerate 'dissidents' without trial. I do not recollect mention of secession, though; the grievances were centred on the abolition of the 1964 Agreement. The first move that brought the matter to the surface was made in 1991, during the last few months of the Kaunda regime. The Barotse Royal Establishment must have come to the conclusion that Kaunda was going to lose the impending election and decided to start the ball rolling: it sent a letter to Kaunda on 16 March 1991 signed by the Ngambela and 17 *Indunas* (area chiefs) demanding restoration of the 1964 Agreement and strict adherence to 'The Barotse Authority' Ordinance of 1936. As the elections were getting close and Kaunda started thinking as a candidate, he responded on 1 August, assuring the Ngambela of his highest regard for the Litunga, whose 'wisdom he had utilized to administer the Nation in the capacity of member of the Central Committee of UNIP'. In a second letter addressed directly to the Litunga and written on 22 October 1991, one week before the election, Kaunda was even more accommodating: he 'appreciated the anxieties of the Lozi people' and suggested that they should best be discussed initially at 'professional level', that is, between lawyers. He suggested to the Litunga that he appoint his own lawyer, (at the expense of the government of Zambia) to start discussions with the Attorney General.

Kaunda lost the election and the Litunga appointed as his lawyers RMA Chongwe and Company who sent a letter to Chiluba, the new president, on 22 April 1992, complaining that the 1964 Agreement had not been honoured by the Zambian government, which 'watered it down through numerous laws without providing compensation by way of damages to the aggrieved party: the Barotse Royal Establishment' – a surprising point, because it implied that the Royal Establishment would have been happy with a monetary settlement. And the letter carried another convoluted statement, as follows: 'As if not enough, the Zambian Government through Parliament took over the assets of the Barotse

National Council through the Ministry of Local Government and Housing and the Litunga's treasury at the time amounting to 78.5 million British pounds, was forfeited to the State.' The letter ends by informing Chiluba that the Barotse Royal Establishment would suspend a legal action it had commenced against the government during the Kaunda administration to allow him time 'to discuss the matter with the Barotse people through their Royal Establishment'. (This was the first time I heard of such legal action and I have not been able to find any details.) A meeting followed between a Barotse delegation led by the Ngambela and various Ministers of the Chiluba administration, which never came to any conclusion as is obvious from a letter to the Litunga from Roger Chongwe, the Chiluba Minister of Legal Affairs at the time and founder of the eponymous law firm representing the Litunga.

Nothing concrete ever really surfaced after that and nobody ever paid much attention. But on 23 October 2010 a group calling itself the Barotse Freedom Movement, whose declared aim was to restore the 1964 Barotseland Agreement, organized a demonstration in Mongu, which was followed by disturbances. The demonstrators appear to have been the aggressors: they suffered no casualties while three policemen were injured and a police station was ransacked. This hardened attitudes and turned out to be the beginning of a serious movement for the recognition of the 1964 Agreement and/or secession that had been festering for some three years. Of greater importance politically was the outcry against the then president, Banda.

Michael Sata, at that time leader of the main opposition party, the Patriotic Front (PF), jumped at the opportunity to make political capital and early in January 2011 he spent ten days in Barotseland canvassing. On 8 January 2011, he made a speech setting out his and his party's position on the 1964 Agreement, which was destined to inflame the problem and elevate it from a moderate political demand to a hard line secession movement.

In a dispatch from Mongu, George Chellah of *The Post* reported Sata's speech:

The Barotse agreement is a valid agreement. How can you ignore an agreement that was signed sealed and delivered almost 47 years ago? There is no honest person who can deny the existence and validity of the Barotse Agreement. And those with honour and integrity honour valid agreements they have entered into whether they like it or not. The PF government will honour the Barotse Agreement without hesitation because we have no problems with it … Only crooks and dictators who want everything to be controlled from Lusaka can fear the Barotse Agreement. The Barotse Agreement was not about secession but a higher form of national unity.

Sata obviously intended his statement to be an attack on President Banda and increase his support amongst the Barotse people. It did not help him very much. The results of the presidential election that followed show him trailing third with 43,759 votes in his favour, behind Banda's 62,592 and Hichilema's 53,176.

When Sata made his extraordinary statement on the 1964 Barotse Agreement he may or may not have known that inflammatory flyers had been posted around Mongu a few days earlier, on 31 December 2010, calling for a big rally at the Royal village, Limulunga, for 14 January 2011. One of them signed by the 'Linyunga Ndambo Bulls' read:

> Come one come all to Limulunga Royal village on the 14th January 2011 where everything shall take place in style. Come and witness great miracles happening. The Hour has come when there will be bloodshed and streams of blood flowing into the plain on this day. The Palace shall be on fire if His Majesty the King will not allow us to succeed on this day. Non Lozis pack and go.

Another also signed by the same group:

> Bemba and Nyanja in all government departments, you are all informed that we don't want to see you on 31st January 2011. Go to your Native Homeland. This is our Native Homeland, Barotseland. Failure to follow this instruction you will be killed like chickens.

And a circular issued jointly by Linyunga Ndambo and the Barotse Freedom Movement asked that

> all radio stations, hospitals, schools, colleges, hotels, motels, guest houses, households, buses, taxis, night clubs, bars, taverns etc., stop playing music, jingles, etc., in Bemba and Nyanja or any other languages spoken in Northern Rhodesia.

The rally did take place despite police refusal to issue a permit and it degenerated into a riot during which two people died, many were injured and 120 were arrested. The ferocity of the behaviour of the police may have had something to do with the casualties they suffered in the hands of the demonstrators the previous October.

Sata is the quintessential populist. He will always say what his audience wants to hear and quixotically he seems to get carried away by his own words and wills them to be true. At least, in his mind, at the time he is speaking, he is convinced that what he is saying can and will be done. But, like most populists, he does not essentially feel bound by what he says and is ready to change course if he realizes that the line he had been pursuing is likely to displease a greater body of opinion than the one he had been trying to gratify, or cause some other upheaval. By that time he would have achieved his immediate goals, anyway. And on Barotseland he did change course. A few weeks after he was elected president in September 2011, he appointed a Commission of Inquiry into the Mongu riots and the grievances of the Lozi people, under the chairmanship of Roger Chongwe, whose legal firm had represented the Litunga on the dispute over the agreement in 1992, while he was serving as Minister of Legal Affairs in the Chiluba government. The Chongwe Commission reported at the end of February 2012, dutifully recommending what it must have thought was the wish of both Sata and the Litunga: that the Barotse Agreement should be restored. But Sata, as President of Zambia had changed his mind and in a press statement carried by *The Post* on 29 February 2012 he spelled out the reasons why, perhaps not very articulately, but certainly very graphically. In essence they represented the thinking of every Zambian president before him, Banda included:

> I would be very reluctant to advise my government to reinstate the Barotse Agreement because by doing so, that is opening the Pandora's Box. All the Provinces, Mpezeni will come that we also want to secede. Chitimukulu will come we want to secede, the Tonga will have a Paramount Chief and they want to secede and there will be secession within government and secession within Provinces because Nsengas would not want to be ruled by Mpezeni, so those are some of the difficulties we have to bear in mind. First of all you have not told me what benefit the Barotse agreement gave the Barotse people ... What is in that Barotse agreement is a self-government, which used to be in the Native Authority, but because the people of Barotseland at Independence were so organized that when they went to England, they campaigned for a separate rule to maintain their native authority, it was more of a native authority not Barotse agreement.

In conclusion he wondered from which resources the people of Western Province would raise taxes even if they were granted secession. After Sata's statement, the Barotse Royal Establishment called a meeting of the Barotse National Council, which took place at Limulunga on 26 and 27 March 2012. The resolutions display a very hard line attitude and a determination to secede, as well as a very unrealistic appreciation of the hurdles that lie ahead and the chances that any international body would take seriously the Barotse demands. It mandates the

Barotse Government to immediately formalize the Declaration of Dispute with the Zambian Government on the basis that the Zambian Government has violated and unilaterally abrogated the Unity treaty [a wishful misrepresentation of the 1964 Agreement, I presume] whose purpose was to bind the two territories of Barotseland and the rest of Zambia, and also notify the SADC, AU, Commonwealth and United Nations of the fact ... The Barotse Government is mandated to within 30 days, request the United Nations to oversee the transition process ... and within 30 days to put in place a transition process leading to taking over all functions in Barotseland and the election of the Katengo Legislative Council ... [and] to immediately engage the Zambian Government with the sole purpose towards self-determination for Barotseland within the shortest possible time under the auspices of the United Nations.

The resolutions are signed by the chairman and seven members of the council and confirmed by the Ngambela and Mukuluwakashiko (Prime Minister and Senior Councillor of the Litunga). The council also mandated another meeting by the end of June, 'to receive reports on progress'. Since then the Barotse Royal Establishment has declared that it is happy with the status quo and the secessionists have remained out of the headlines.

But when I visited Barotseland in March 2013, most people I spoke to were incensed with Sata's attitude and the treatment he gave them when he invited them to Lusaka for what he had declared when he met them 'would be the beginning of a dialogue over the Barotseland Agreement and the general development of Barotseland'. From the minutes kept by the Barotse delegation, that have been availed to me, it appears that the meeting was a bit of 'a dialogue of the deaf' with Sata declaring that he was not prepared, or able under his oath of office to discuss the dismemberment of Zambia, and every delegate declaring that there was no solution other than secession. However, from the minutes, it appears that the delegates came away with the impression that Sata's stance indicated that he had not yet decided how to deal with the issue and was probing in order to determine possible solutions. They concluded: 'it is also quite clear that further consultations with other sections of the Barotse society will be necessary' and declared:

The Conclusion to the Barotse problem lies more in the hands of the people of Barotseland than the Government of Zambia. Given the chance the Government will continue to carry on with cosmetic solutions that serve its needs and not of Barotseland. There is acute need for authoritative and democratic approach by the people of Barotseland in their engagement with Government on the matter if a lasting solution is to be determined.

A Delphic oracle? It sounds like one: a little threat to go it alone and a little hope for a lasting solution. But most mature people I met in Barotseland (I met no one from the Royal Establishment) seem to think that a determined dialogue and willingness to give and take and understand each other will produce results. No doubt more agitation will follow, but one must hope that in the end realism and common sense will prevail and a compromise will be reached. On my part, I feel confident that this will be so. Most activists I met are mature, highly intelligent, educated people and none of them uttered a single slogan during long discussions with me. Their arguments were articulate and well-reasoned.

But I see no solution other than the wholehearted inclusion of Barotseland in the Republic of Zambia, at the same level as everybody else, with its dignity intact and holding its head high. Let us forget the nonsense of the 'Western Province'. Barotseland is Barotseland to its people as much as Lubemba is to the Bemba, and giving it any other name officially will not change their feelings, or make them less or more Zambian. And let us remember that first and foremost we are all Zambians. Despite disparate origins and backgrounds, our people who moved from their tribal lands to the urban centres learned to live together in unity. Whatever we have achieved so far is the culmination of everyone's combined effort and the Lozi people were part of this process, as a matter of course, not as a result of Barotseland's protectorate status. Their contribution was equal to that of everybody else.

My visit to Barotseland and my contacts in the rest of the country, which include many Lozi who live in Lusaka, left me in no doubt that currently (2014) opinions are polarized and emotions are very high. But, equally, I came to the conclusion that deep down not many are ready to walk into the unknown. An equitable solution that takes care of everybody's sensibilities will be greeted with a sigh of relief. What is needed is dialogue in order to analyse and digest the issues and reach dispassionate conclusions, based on logic and common sense. And the dialogue should not be at Zambian government–Barotse Royal Establishment level but amongst people from Zambia and Barotseland (including the activists) who can think the problems through. The aim should be to reach a consensus, on a course of action that takes care of the Barotse concerns but maintains the integrity of Zambia and the dignity of Barotseland as an integral part of it. Maybe the initiative should come from the civic society (even though it has to be funded by the Zambian government, unless some international donor steps in), such as organizations like the Oasis Forum, some of the churches with strong roots in Barotseland and NGOCC. This is an issue of enlightenment and persuasion amongst peers. No immediate government action is necessary except the withdrawal of the 'hateful Western Province'

223

name that offends local sensibilities and the restoration of its proper name: 'Barotseland'. Maybe President Sata who likes to meddle with provinces and districts can take up this initiative soon. No doubt, with the advice of the civic bodies other initiatives will need to follow.

As I said, the solution uppermost in most activists' minds is secession. They have persuaded themselves that there is oil and mineral wealth in Barotseland and that investment in their extraction has been held back by the government of Zambia. A very simplistic argument went like this: 'Do natural resources stop at borders? There are diamonds in Angola, just the other side of our border and there is oil in Cabinda, which is not that far away. And there are copper and other minerals on the Copperbelt. Why shouldn't there be in Barotseland? If we were independent we would open our borders and investors would come to explore.' This view is very widely held and obviously forms the basis of the logic behind the Barotse National Council's mandate to the Royal Establishment to declare a dispute with the government of Zambia that 'will lead to self-determination within the shortest possible time under the auspices of the United Nations'.

But, can independence be attained? Let us remind ourselves that one of the reasons why the British refused to keep Barotseland as a protectorate after Zambia's independence was because they considered it economically non-viable and it would be costing them money. And let us understand that neither the United Nations nor any other international body will want to encourage the emergence of a new small poor country, because they fear that it may end up as a failed state, like Guinea Bissau, or Somalia, or the Central African Republic. I agree that in regard to Barotseland such danger is, currently, remote. Barotseland is a reasonably homogeneous region and secession is not likely to cause civil war, or attract invasion. And the Litunga and the Barotse Royal Establishment are held in high regard. But it will be very poor and the international bodies are wary of poor countries because poverty breeds discontent and discontent breeds unrest and coups; or, at best, poor countries end up needing handouts. And who can say that the deference towards the Royal Establishment will remain after prolonged poverty? And that some hot-heads will not decide to take over because they will think they can do better? And this leads us back to the original argument: the failed state. Another factor that will make the international bodies hesitate over Barotseland's independence is the fact that it is too small: just 700,000 people, or if the Nkoya are included 900,000 who are currently not suffering from persecution or oppression or facing genocide.

The secessionists are relying on the United Nations, the African Union, the Commonwealth, and SADC to help Barotseland get international recognition. But for the reasons I indicated above I doubt that any one of those organizations or their member countries will want to give Barotseland recognition. There is a precedent for this in Africa: Somaliland, which broke away from Somalia on 18 May 1991, has not yet been recognized by any other country, despite the fact that it is itself peaceful while the country it broke away from is a dangerous mess. I checked Somaliland on the internet and I got the following description of it: 'Unrecognized by any country or international organization, self-declared, de facto sovereign State.' With that kind of status can a country attract foreign investment? Like Somaliland, Barotseland will not and the dream of future independent prosperity will turn into the reality of perpetual poverty.

To me, life within Zambia appears to be the realistic alternative and as I have already said, in such a case Barotseland has to be at par with every other province of the country. We must be very careful not to be waylaid into interim half-baked solutions, such as autonomy or other 'privileges' in order to appease current firebrands. The effect of such appeasement will be to sweep the problem under the carpet for a little while. But it will flare up within a very short time, in different forms. And, worse, it may infect other parts of Zambia. Whatever we do we must find a forever solution.

The Barotseland problem like most of the problems of Africa is a colonial hangover. The British South Africa Company needed a piece of paper in order to access copper which it believed was abundant along the Kafue River. It got it from Paramount Chief Lewanika and it reciprocated by giving him a number of privileges. (It also, arbitrarily, extended his territory a couple of times through an 'Order in Council' by giving him suzerainty over areas the British South Africa Company wanted to exploit.) Many studies and myths, written before and after independence, created a large Lewanika empire sometimes extending all the way to Mozambique and a long way into Angola. But in the Colonial Office's 'Northern Rhodesia Report for 1929' (Appendix I) which was written within living memory of the genesis of the protectorate, the description is much more modest:

> The Barotse under Lewanika enlarged their kingdom by conquering one or two
> of the surrounding tribes, such as the Bankoya and the Balovale. Beyond these
> limits their authority was both nebulous and ephemeral.

The British colonial administration that followed increased the privileges of the Litunga depending on the favours it wanted to extract from him from time to time. None of those privileges trickled down to the common man in Barotseland who, in reality, had the same status as everybody else in Northern

Rhodesia, out of which we made Zambia together, even though we only started getting to know each other some 100 years ago. Colonialism put us together and we assimilated. We went to school together, worked together, fought together, and got our freedom together: we emerged as Zambians. We did all this together and together we are now sharing the fruit of our efforts in independent Zambia. And we must face the future together and the hardships and problems that, no doubt, lie ahead and any benefits or setbacks that will follow.

Nobody can deny that the blessings of Zambia are shared equally amongst its entire people, without discrimination. Proportionately there are as many Lozi working outside Barotseland as there are Bemba and Ngoni and Tonga and Ila and Lunda and Luvale, living outside their tribal areas. And proportionately the Lozi are equally represented on the various Zambian political and civic bodies as the other provinces. And proportionately, there are as many successful Lozi entrepreneurs and professionals and successful members of the thriving middle classes as there are from any other part of the country.

When the people who live in Barotseland say they are neglected they are not saying something new. They are simply echoing what most people from the rural areas of Zambia are saying. And they are right and their brothers and sisters in the rest of the rural areas are right too. But this is the unfortunate by-product of our economy, which has a first world component in the form of the mining industry while the rest of the country is third world. Unfortunately this leads to a political imbalance too. The urban people live in greater concentrations, and they have better facilities generally available to them, but particularly better education. And they are more vocal and carry greater political weight. They attract greater attention from governments especially since 1991, when the cabinets have been mostly composed of urbanites with little knowledge of the rural areas. This is a serious handicap in our development and needs to be rectified and its solution will benefit Barotseland as much as all other remote parts of the country. In the meantime the pattern remains: high levels of development come with the discovery of minerals. In earlier chapters I described how neglected the North Western Province had been. This is not the case in the eastern part of the province any longer, because copper has been discovered there.

The government needs to look earnestly into finding ways of improving the economies of the rural areas for the benefit of the people who live there: eight million out of a total of thirteen million for the whole country. And this will yield a dividend for the rest of the country too because prosperity in the rural areas will go a long way towards solving the unemployment problem of the towns. Many must have observed by now that whenever employment opportunities improve in the urban areas, the numbers of unemployed increase, because employment opportunities attract rural people into the towns like a magnet.

Michael Sata, the President of Zambia since September 2011, unlike his three immediate predecessors has rural origin and grass root support. And he has, so far, shown genuine desire to do something for the rural areas, though, in my view, the subdivision of rural districts he created is wasteful and even though popular, does not solve the problem. The rural areas need a complete new system of administration that gives local people greater say in the running of their affairs. Such a system would also go a long way towards rectifying the neglect that the rural areas, including Barotseland, feel. I agree with President Sata that any concessions given to the Litunga will raise equal demands from the other major chiefdoms of Zambia. And the government of Zambia cannot yield to demands based on Victorian concessions and dated systems of government.

But there is one element of Barotseland that may provide the common thread for the reorganization of our rural system of government. The Litunga's chiefdom and the Barotse Province have the same boundaries, which does not apply to any other Zambian chiefdom apart, perhaps, Chitimukulu's. So a radical reorganization of the rural administration on a provincial basis can take care of the Barotse demands without creating the anomaly of special privileges and, at the same time, provide the impetus for the renaissance of our rural sector.

The rural administration, in any case, is a complete mess after all the tinkering that has taken place over the years. It needs root and branch reorganization that will introduce a unified administration capable of focusing on local development. The project will be complex and sensitive with both political and administrative implications. I am sure that we can tackle it on our own, but outside help may be useful. The goal must be true decentralization in order to empower the rural areas to make their own decisions on their development. This is an issue that has been tackled before by many countries with rural populations and the United Nations Development Programme may help us locate suitable individuals to help us set it up. But I must clarify what I mean by 'help'. We need guidance about what can be done and what results it can achieve and what methods we need to employ. But the end result must be to empower the rural people to take direct care of their needs. We must bear in mind that any such reorganization is of major importance to us and to the future of our country, so we must ensure that we provide the local input by attaching eminent locals who are immersed in our way of life and governance, so that we do not end up with a foreign-conceived plan that will prove unworkable because it does not fit within the norms of our society and the thinking of our people.

I shall come back to this subject when I review the district subdivision scheme that Sata announced in 2012. But let us first review his performance during his first two years in office.

26. BA MWINE ZAMBIA: 2011

Many years ago, when I was still relatively young and active and travelled, I met Margaret Thatcher at a social gathering outside London. 'Ah! You are from Zambia!' she said loudly for everybody to hear. And in an imperious tone she continued: 'Do you know my friend Kenneth? You must tell him that he reshuffles his ministers too often. He must give them time to learn their jobs.' For some reason, when one is out of the country and is confronted with mindless criticism of home, especially in that tone of voice, the instinctive reaction is to go on the offensive. 'Don't you Mrs Thatcher?' I asked much to the embarrassment of my hosts. She did not answer. She turned to my wife and started talking about summer holidays.

So, is Michael Sata, the President of Zambia since September 2011, in good company? The answer is: No. Thatcher's and Kaunda's reshuffles may have been frequent but Sata's are supersonic. In my long international career as a journalist and businessman I cannot think of any other country where ministers and generals and senior administration officials were changing positions at such high speeds, except during the Second World War, when countries were at the final stages of impending collapse under the advancing forces of Hitler. But Zambia is, like it has always been, peaceful and stable in what is now a peaceful region.

The trouble with frequent reshuffles is not just that ministers don't get time to learn their jobs, as Mrs Thatcher surmised. It is that they get terrified. They do not want to lose their job and suffer the public ridicule that follows high level dismissals, after tenures as short as a few weeks sometimes, and conclude that to keep it they must avoid doing anything that the boss might disapprove of. And as they are not sure of what he will like and what he will not they do nothing because that is the safest way to not displease him. But this means that little thinking and planning is generated at ministry level. They mostly sit back and wait to be told what to do. This encourages the boss to improvise and pronounce his own policies which many times have not been fully considered.

The next stage in this environment is competition for the boss's favour and this creates a climate of servility and sycophancy and undeclared civil war within the senior ranks, with everybody trying to show greater loyalty than his colleague. Everybody accuses everybody else of disloyalty and betrayal and is ready to dig a dagger into his rival's back. The country went through this experience in the later years of the Kaunda administration during the apogee of the UNIP Central Committee's power as 'guardian of the people's interests'. It eventually led to the paralysis of the 1980s and the ousting of UNIP in 1991. But it cost the country some 15 years of stagnation and the people great hardship. In Chapter 11, I highlighted some of the excesses that resulted from the unchecked powers of the Central Committee, which can be used as a yardstick for what could happen in similar situations in the future. They can be classified into two main categories: (1) demand for uncritical obedience to the president, the party and the powerful within, and (2) false accusations of disloyalty against those who are suspected of not toeing the party line, or against whom powerful members have an axe to grind – this category usually includes, the cleverest and the most competent members who consider it their duty to take initiatives and speak their mind, in other words the people who should not be persecuted but cherished. During the UNIP Central Committee's unchecked powers, the country experienced meanness and vengeance, not only against perceived wayward members of the party but against successful individuals labelled enemies of the 'party and its government' because of their success and social prominence and their refusal to 'join the herd'. Many different sanctions were applied: expulsion from the party and dismissal from government positions, pressure on employers not to give them jobs, or to dismiss them, and for those operating internationally withdrawal of their passports. Bad-mouthing and back-stabbing were always part of the process. The bottom line was to hit their livelihood, in order to make them conform and make others toe the line. Under these circumstances most intelligent people who can make their own way usually drift away and leave the country.

When this stage is reached, the leader has already become hostage to his inner circle. All those who were likely to tell him the truth have already departed and those who remain are feeding him with what he wants to hear. It happened to Kaunda, a few years after the 'One Party State' was introduced and he was kept in ignorance of the level of discontent that was building up in the country. I know because I watched it and warned him many times. From his responses it was obvious that he did not believe it because it was so different to the information he already had; and he probably thought that it was some sort of sour grapes on my part.

But in those days, UNIP was constitutionally entrenched and Kaunda appeared happy to bestow extraordinary powers to 'the Party and its Government'. And he was comforted by the thought that elections were a charade and he and UNIP would be re-elected anyway, perhaps for ever. The PF cannot afford that degree of self-deception. It was democratically elected, it has to face re-election in 2016, and I don't think that the country has the stomach for another 'One Party State' experience, as it has shown when Chiluba attempted a third term. Sata, who had been Chiluba's campaign manager for the third term attempt, must be well aware of the country's indignation and unremitting resistance to even the slightest whiff of 'one party'. Yet, unlike the post-Chiluba MMD, the PF appears to be trying to elevate the party above the government and new policies are frequently proclaimed from the party secretariat instead of the relevant ministers or the president. Most of them are inconsequential but in January 2013, the Secretary General announced that the party would soon introduce a new policy 'in order to make education more relevant to the needs of the people'. The core element of this policy appeared to be greater prominence of the local languages in the national curriculum, an experiment that Tanzania attempted some years back, burnt its fingers and abandoned. But it smacked of cheap party-misplaced 'patriotism'. We experienced the phenomenon before. When those in power lose their grip, they resort to slogans such as patriotism and maintenance of 'our culture and traditions' in order to retrieve it. When it happened during the Kaunda administration, UNIP had in reality lost the support of the people and its grandees formed a ring around Kaunda and fed him lies and kept him out of touch. He had become their hostage – an eventuality that Sata should guard against.

Sata came into office after ten years in opposition (2001–11), as head of the 'Patriotic Front', a party he created after he was passed over as Chiluba's successor. Before that he had a full ten years (1991–2001) of uninterrupted career in MMD as a senior minister in Chiluba's cabinet, after a short sojourn in junior positions in the 'One Party' UNIP government. On his inauguration he declared to the country and the world at large that Zambia had been the victim of years of corruption and mismanagement, particularly under the Banda administration. He had zero tolerance towards corruption, he said, and he was going to clean up and put right all deals done by Banda, and one by Mwanawasa as it turned out. He made no mention of any of Chiluba's many deals that needed correction. And he proceeded to appoint a number of commissions of inquiry over a number of deals and issues. The Western powers cried Amen and applauded. But many prominent Zambians were uneasy. They felt that the choice of ministers as chairmen of most of the commissions, most prominent among them the then Minister of Justice, pointed to predetermined conclusions.

Neo Simutanyi, Executive Director of the 'Centre for Policy Dialogue' charged that the commissions were a waste of public funds and added that the President should have allowed the investigative wings to do the job rather than waste taxpayers' money on commissions. He also urged Sata to stop embarrassing the various commission chairmen and his ministers in public. He advised him to first study their reports before making any statements on the outcome, adding that attacking the chairmen of the commissions at the time of the presentation of the report tended to confirm that the President had a predetermined conclusion in mind.

Simutanyi's comments about predetermined conclusions must have been prompted by the 'Finance Bank' affair. Sata had appointed a commission of inquiry to look into the seizure of Finance Bank by the Bank of Zambia in December 2010. He announced the appointment on a Friday and on the Monday that followed he ordered that the bank be handed back to its previous major shareholder, without waiting for the commission to investigate and report. The South African newspaper *Mail & Guardian* carried the story under the title 'Zambian Politics trip up FirstRand':

> South Africa's FirstRand Bank was taught the harsh reality of doing business in politically polarised Zambia when it attempted to expand its portfolio by acquiring one of the country's major commercial banks, Finance Bank Zambia Ltd ... Finance Bank was taken over by the Zambian reserve bank, the Bank of Zambia, and then handed to FirstRand to manage, with longer-term prospect of an outright purchase ... Finance Bank is politically sensitive because its executive chairperson, Rajan Mahtani, is a close ally of Sata – a kingmaker who mixes business with politics, which often lands him in legal battles after changes in ownership. 'There is nothing on paper, no document of sale for Finance Bank and I am directing the Ministry of Finance to take the Bank back to its owners immediately,' Sata said when he fired the central bank governor, Caleb Fundanga, who had presided over the repossession and sale of the bank ... Ex-Governor Fundanga, a renowned economist, refused to discuss the deal, saying only that the Bank [of Zambia] acted within its mandate, in order to protect the interest of depositors and creditors and to ensure stability of the banking sector as a whole. In a government gazette notice of December 31, 2010, announcing the takeover, the Bank of Zambia cited weak corporate governance and risky management systems that perpetuated the wanton violation of Zambia's Banking and Financial Services Act and compromised Finance Bank's solvency ... There was evidence that a tender to purchase [sic] the bank was advertised and five financial institutions applied: First Alliance Zambia; Exim Bank Tanzania; I and M of Kenya; and JM Capital, Quantile and FirstRand of South Africa. FirstRand which was already managing Finance Bank won the tender.

Simutanyi's admonition to Sata to stop embarrassing his ministers in public arose from the President's habit to attack not only ministers, but senior civil servants, and many others, who happened to be around on public occasions, with or without apparent reason. Sata would always receive commission reports in front of the television cameras and the commission chairman, in his presentation, was expected to give a brief summary of his findings in order to give Sata the opportunity to brag about being proved right. On one occasion, the chairman of the commission appointed to investigate the purchase of scanners by the Zambia Revenue Authority for the inspection of freight vehicles at border posts did not perform to Sata's expectations, correctly assuming that the report is confidential until the President had reviewed it and made a decision on whether to release it to the public and in what form. This infuriated Sata. *The Post* described the scene under the title 'Inquiry on ZRA annoys Sata':

[Kingsley] Chanda, who used to be Zambia Revenue Authority Commissioner General but was fired during Levy Mwanawasa's presidency, presented the Commission's report ... he kept quiet about the findings and recommendations, opting to go straight into reading the terms of reference before handing over the document to the President. The visibly upset President Sata wondered why Chanda was not disclosing the findings and openly rebuked him: 'You said nothing in your speech, there is nothing for me to comment, other than to direct the Minister of Finance to bring the report to Cabinet ... because you are economizing on the truth. We don't know why we appointed you' ... President Sata quickly called for the National Anthem to be sung and thereafter walked out. As he walked out President Sata remarked while pointing at Finance Minister Alex Chikwanda: 'next time don't recommend such people to me'.

Events would prove Simutanyi right. The cost of the commissions proved a complete waste of public funds. Apart from the publicity generated during the presentation of some of the commission reports and some 'off the cuff' remarks made by Sata, none of the reports were ever made public and no announcement was ever made on whether the government accepted or rejected any of the recommendations.

Sata's position with regard to Barotseland shifted from his public statement of 8 January 2011, in Mongu, to the inevitable position that Barotseland is part of the 'unitary state' of Zambia as the reader will have already seen in Chapters 23, 24 and 25. The Minister of Finance announced in August 2013 that he was very satisfied with the performance of ZANACO, the government-owned ailing bank that Mwanawasa had sold to RABOBANK of Holland, and 'let bygones be bygones' or words to that effect, so that issue was adroitly buried. The decision of the commission in relation to the Finance Bank, as I said earlier, was pre-empted a couple of days after it was set up and the Minister of Justice who had been appointed chairman of most of the commissions was dismissed. In short, most issues and non-issues that the commissions were appointed to investigate were skilfully swept under the carpet.

Sata seemed to revel in opportunities to pillory his officers in public, even those he had just appointed to high positions. One such victim was the First Inspector General of Police he had appointed immediately after taking office. The occasion was unrelated to the police. Sata was addressing army officer-cadets at the commissioning parade in Kabwe on 23 December 2011 and he used the occasion for a scathing attack on the unsuspecting Inspector General who happened to be present. *The Post* reported:

> During the commissioning parade of officer-cadets, in Kabwe yesterday, President Sata taunted Inspector General of Police Dr. Martin Malama saying he had failed to control people inciting violence in Western Province and those who wanted to secede: 'I am very disappointed Commander in Chief,' he said addressing the Army Commander. 'You are aware that people in Western Province are inciting to create a State within a State and my Inspector General of Police is smiling … The gun is to protect Zambians but prevention is better than cure. Let us not wait Mr. Inspector General because they are looking for office[r]s in Western Province. They have appointed a Prime Minister and you are smiling. What type of Inspector General are you?'

Needless to say, the hapless IG, who had been promoted to the position from the post of Copperbelt Commanding Officer immediately Sata came to power, lasted only a few weeks in his new job. While he was still unpacking his furniture that had just arrived from the Copperbelt to Lusaka he was dismissed.

But Sata's method of governance is unique to Sata and outside the norms one has learned to expect from a head of state. He is a restless person and always expects centre stage. If there is nothing new to do he will pick on something close by, hence the revolving doors for ministers, secretaries to the cabinet, permanent secretaries, and other senior officers and the constant reallocation of government departments to suit the 'talents' of new appointees, which seems to have produced unusual combinations such as 'Ministry of Community Development, Mother and Child Health' or 'Ministry of Education, Science, Vocational Training and Early Childhood', or progressions from 'Ministry of Information, Broadcasting and Tourism', to 'Ministry of Foreign Affairs and Tourism' to 'Ministry of Tourism and Arts', or 'Ministry of Local Government,

Housing, Early Education and Environment' to 'Ministry of Lands, Natural Resources and Environment Protection'. How many files and in what condition survived these migrations only future registrars will know.

And Sata is an exhibitionist par excellence. In this vein he picked a white man as his vice president. It had the desired effect: 'there are only two countries in the world that have a black President and a white Vice President: the United States and Zambia,' the American Ambassador opined, much to the delight of Sata, no doubt. But according to the Constitution of Zambia, in order to qualify as a president, a person must be a Zambian citizen and both his parents must be Zambians by birth or descent, qualifications that the present incumbent does not fulfil. So the white vice president cannot act in the president's absence. A senior black Zambian minister is appointed to act when Sata is out of the country on one of his many trips. The acclaimed Zambian satirist Kalaki (Roy Clarke) in his weekly column attempted a more comprehensive job description: 'The Vice President in charge of Cutting Ribbons, Funerals, and Miscellaneous Ceremonials'. In reality, the vice president's main duty is to direct the Patriotic Front's parliamentary business as Leader of the House and answer parliamentary questions every Friday, during parliamentary sessions. Also to oversee the numerous by-election campaigns that Sata had generated since he took office. In the process he became the chief apologist and militant propagandist of the Patriotic Front and its policies.

Some decades back, the UNIP government announced the Ministry of Decentralization in order to 'bring government to the people'. The result was jobs for rural cadres as district governors or 'district secretaries' (they were renamed district commissioners by Chiluba) and their staff, whose task was to preach Kaunda's 'Humanist Gospel' paid for by the central government. Since then, it has become routine: the party in power appoints the district commissioners and the opposition parties complain about the unfair advantage that this corps of taxpayer-paid cadres in official positions gives it. In opposition, Sata was particularly fierce over this issue and on assuming office he dismissed all the Banda appointed district commissioners and other officials. Moreover, in callous disregard of the hardship that it would cause their families, he ordered them to vacate immediately not only their offices but their houses as well. The unfortunate officers, whose only crime was to belong to a different political party, were not given any time to arrange relocation for themselves and their families to sometimes distant places of origin, or find new schools for their children.

Sata, quite correctly, declared that the positions should go to line civil servants. But, the announcement did not prevent him from appointing his own party cadres instead. In fact the local cadres were falling over each other to fill those posts. So much so that in Mpulungu there was a demonstration against the appointed district commissioner, because he was not local but hailed from Mbala, a town some 40 miles away. This upset the party's local cadres, so the district commissioner was withdrawn 'for deployment in the foreign service' according to the official announcement. A similar incident occurred in Chibombo where the district commissioner was declared a foreigner. He was in fact local, born in the area and a PF cadre in Ndola for some time; his family, however, hailed from Zimbabwe though it had been in Zambia since the Federal days.

On the rural administration front Sata made what many thought a spectacular leap forward: by the end of 2013 he created 31 new rural districts. He also created one new province, Muchinga by taking away six districts from the Northern Province. (Muchinga includes his birthplace Mpika but he graciously placed the capital at Chinsali, Kenneth Kaunda's birthplace.) And he transferred the capital of the Southern Province from Livingstone to Choma on the grounds that it has a more central location. The creation of the new districts increased the size of the rural administration by some 50 per cent, from 59 rural districts to 90 and the total number of districts to 103 when the large towns are added. It also reduced the average number of inhabitants of a rural district from 136,000 to 89,000. The measure was highly praised not only by those living in the various new districts but also by many Western diplomats, who applauded its decentralization potential without calculating the size and the probable cost of the units that have been created. If the average population has now reduced to around 89,000 this means that after you deduct the provincial capitals and some other large districts in the Eastern and Northern Provinces which average above 200,000 (Chipata's population is nearly half a million) you end up with the majority of the smaller districts at around 50,000 and some even smaller ones, like Luangwa district which according to the 2010 census numbers has a population of just 24,304, Chavuma 35,041 and Milenge 43,337. No doubt many of the newly created ones will fall into the latter category.

It has never been made clear whether this huge expansion of the district administration had been a properly planned decision, taken by the cabinet after submission by the Ministry of Local Government and consultation with the affected ministries such as Lands, Energy, Communications and, last but not least, Finance or whether it was ordered ad hoc, during Sata's tours as a by-product of his populist enthusiasm. The problem is that each district has two parallel administrations: the elected one under the district council and the government one under the district commissioner. Can we afford such a wasteful system for the administration of such small numbers of people? Since the government has already introduced the 31 additional districts, it will not be willing to backtrack and abolish them. The least it should do now is to merge the two administrations and achieve savings in that fashion. And it needs to embark upon drastic staff reductions. Otherwise there will be huge costs in both capital investment and recurrent expenditure, which it will not be able to meet, and it would run the risk of ending up with 31 shanty towns instead of the shining district headquarters that the people of the relevant areas expect. This has already happened in Milenge, a new district that Chiluba created in Luapula in 1997.

A report in the *Post* of 24 April 2013, under the title 'Milenge Civil Servants squatting in villages', paints a desperate picture. The district commissioner gave a disturbing account of the living conditions: the only accommodation available to his staff were three houses, out of a total of ten owned by the district council and each one was shared by three to five officers including himself. Most other members of staff were 'squatting' in huts in the surrounding villages, he said. I have no doubt that Chiluba made Milenge into a district in 1997 in order to gratify his constituents who, 16 years later do not seem to have derived much benefit from it. With the Milenge precedent in mind, are officers appointed to the newly created districts facing a 20-year odyssey before they settle down?

The capital costs needed to accommodate and provide offices for all the newly created provincial and district headquarters will be huge. Just consider the personnel required to man Muchinga Province under the current establishment standards: one minister, one deputy minister, one permanent secretary, at least two undersecretaries, a number of assistant secretaries, senior principals and many clerical officers and junior personnel. The same number of people is already employed in respect of the Southern Province, but their transfer from Livingstone to Choma will require equivalent infrastructure as that for the new Muchinga Province. I'll hazard a guess that the cost of the administration buildings, the office furniture, the equipment, the vehicles and so on will run to a few hundred million dollars for each province. And the alienation and the preparation of land (or its purchase from commercial farmers in places such as Choma), and the construction of roads and housing for the many senior and junior officers will cost at least as much. The capital investment for each district will be a lot less but there are 31 of them, and some, like Pemba, Zimba and Chisamba, are in the middle of farming blocks where land will have to be purchased from surrounding farmers at very high costs. In regard to Chisamba, the eventual decision entailed complete relocation to Chief Chamuka's area, which means that its development will start from scratch: clearing the bush, building roads, finding water, supplying electricity and all other services a town needs, before the building of offices and housing can begin. Putting everything together, my guess is that the total capital investment needed for the 'decentralization' programme will cost two or three billion dollars. Can the nation afford tying up so much money to accommodate a bloated bureaucracy, which in the final analysis this project really is? So far the only official allocation of funds for this project is K204 million (approximately $39 million), for infrastructure, in the 2013 budget and K550 million ($90 million) in the 2014 budget, a drop in the ocean in relation to the needs. If Milenge district in Luapula is anything to go by, it will take years before many of the new districts get the infrastructure and the houses and offices. But, as a senior government official said to me, since it started the 'new-districts' project has created its own momentum and it will materialize gradually, over a period of time, never mind how long that will be. And come to think of it by that time the population will have grown to justify it, because it looks that, like Milenge, it will take two or three decades, at least.

Capital costs aside, the recurrent costs will also be heavy. As I said, each district has two administrations: a government one, reporting to the president under a district commissioner and officers from all major ministries and departments and a district council reporting to the Minister of Local Government headed by an elected district chairman and a district secretary, with duties similar to those of a mayor and a town clerk, the latter appointed by the Minister of Local Government. District councils are expected to cover their expenses from property rates, personal levies, licence fees and other levies they are allowed to raise, though the central government has a say on the levels they set for them. In addition they receive central government grants for water, sanitation, health, fire, road services, police, agriculture, and primary education, but these account for a very small portion of their budgets. The councils are chronically short of funds and they cannot afford to provide any meaningful service to their communities. Many are in arrears in salary payments to their staff, some as long as 18 months. (In Lukulu, a remote district in Barotseland, the council salaries are reputed to be six years in arrears. Yet at a recent visit Sata split the district into two.) They will be in an even worse position in the future, after their boundaries have been shrunk and some of their revenue sources transferred to a newly created district. And the small councils will only be able to raise negligible revenue, but their overheads will be almost as great as those of the larger councils.

The local government has been driven to this parlous state by constant government interference since 1991. In 1992, when Sata was the Minister of Local Government in the Chiluba administration he decreed the retirement of all staff with more than 22 years of service. The move was presented as an effort to reduce the staff levels of local councils, though many thought that the step was taken because the Chiluba administration believed that the older employees of the rural councils were UNIP supporters and wanted to get rid of them. Be that as it may, the measures burdened the councils with huge retirement bills and deprived them of experienced officers while the numbers ballooned again with inexperienced recruits. In 1993, the structural adjustment programme decreed no central government fund transfers to local government. In 1995, Chiluba ordered the sale of government houses below market price and gave wholesale exclusion from the payment of rates to a large number of institutions. The personal levy Act of 1994 set extremely low maximum-minimum levels for personal levy. In 1996 the government withdrew vehicle licencing from the councils, which deprived them of a major source of revenue. And the council staff complain that the district commissioners' departments, i.e. political bureaucracies not rendering any service to the communities, are generously funded while the councils lack the funds to provide the services they are mandated to do.

In short, the scheme was already unaffordable before the new districts were added. With them the situation became 50 per cent worse and the government would be well advised to merge the establishments of the district councils and the district commissioners, regardless of the fact that the political affiliation of each service may differ in some districts. It must also take care to control the numbers of both. If it plucked enough courage to do this it would achieve great savings in both the capital investment and the recurrent expenditure. The district commissioners' establishment should be pruned to skeleton staff that can be accommodated in the district council offices, and the council staff should also be trimmed in order to avoid duplication of duties. These and other economy measures should be introduced urgently if Sata does not want to be remembered for creating 31 shanty townships instead of new district headquarters in the country.

The creation of a new province and the creation of 31 new districts have proved hugely popular. Smallish areas and medium size villages have mutated to districts and district capitals and their residents anticipate the grandeur that goes with it and they love it. And no doubt the Patriotic Front expects the project to create large numbers of jobs, which will go some way towards fulfilling the chimeric expectation it created during the election campaign, of jobs for everyone within 90 days of its election to power. So scrapping it at this stage is inconceivable but downsizing it along the lines outlined above, or any other way, is an economic imperative. But rural districts, whole or subdivided, are still governed from Lusaka. The district commissioners are party organs reporting to the president. And the district councils, though elected, do not have any teeth: their activities are constrained by the paucity of their treasuries. In other words the decentralization aspect of the project is just wishful thinking and the method of running dual administration over small districts is expensive and wasteful but, worse, it does not add to the development of our rural sector.

Somebody in government must have been conscious of this state of affairs and on 9 April 2013, the Minister of Local Government announced 'the Approval of the Revised National Decentralization Implementation Policy'. A three-column, page-length advert was published in the press on 23 April 2013 in order 'to guide all stakeholders on its implementation'. After announcing that the 'vision' is to promote 'a decentralised system of governance within a unitary state' and that the 'mission statement' is to promote 'decentralised and democratically elected systems of governance which enhance community participation' it spells out the objectives as follows:

> To empower Provinces, Districts and Communities in order to achieve effective Social Economic Development;
>
> To promote people's participation in democratic governance at the local level to enhance Local Government;
>
> To promote cooperative governance with the national government, provincial administration, Provincial Assembly and local authority to support and enhance the developmental role of Local Government;
>
> To promote the participation of Chiefs and other traditional leaders in governance and the preservation of culture and heritage whilst respecting cultural diversity;
>
> To coordinate gender mainstreaming programs in the councils in order to promote gender equality; and
>
> To develop and manage human resources, in order to enhance individual and organisational performance.

The advertisement does not give any details of the functions intended to be passed on. The phraseology is: 'the government shall decentralize some functions with matching resources to districts, which shall perform these functions through democratically elected councils'. The process appears to be that the Cabinet Office 'shall provide leadership and facilitate the devolution of some functions to the Provincial and District levels', while the 'Ministry of Local Government and Housing through the Decentralization Secretariat will also continue to guide all stakeholders in the implementation of the policy'. In short, the government is thinking about some decentralization, but it has not yet decided about what to decentralize and how.

Perhaps President Sata can consider something really radical instead: a fundamental change that can shift the rural development initiative from remote Lusaka and hand it over to the rural people who are directly affected. To be cost effective it has to be at provincial level, in order to encompass large areas and large numbers of people. The role of the provincial government will need to be redefined and enhanced to enable it to service the real needs of its people and their development. The most important and urgent economic sectors to be tackled are agriculture and, in order to make it work smoothly, communications. The most critical recurrent input is the annual purchase of seed and fertilizer and their timely distribution to the farmers. While the Banda administration managed to get its act together and through timely distribution increased the production of peasant crops, particularly maize, spectacularly, as I reported in Chapter 22, the PF administration was not as successful. The 2011/12 maize crop dropped to 2,852,687 tons against the 3,020,380 tons under Banda the year before. But the input distribution for the 2012/13 season was a hit-or-miss affair with some areas not receiving any inputs until the end of the rainy season. As a result the crop dropped to 2.53 million, a reduction of some 17.5 per cent below Banda's last year. The projection for the 2014 crop was anticipated by government to be a record breaking 3.35 million tons but the Farmers Union announcement put it at 2.7 million, some 20 per cent below the government estimate. If, instead of Lusaka, provincial officers were responsible for the input importation and distribution the whole exercise would be more efficient not least because those responsible would be members of the local communities who interface with local farmers daily and they will come under their direct pressure. As the decision making will be at provincial level, local businessmen may be used for this purpose and they will also be under a similar sort of pressure. Extension services would also become more relevant and more efficient because the performance of the extension officers will be more tightly controlled at provincial level. Similarly, the road network needs to be determined locally and it needs to remain open right through the year regardless of the weather; emergency repairs during the rainy season need to be carried out expeditiously in order to keep the communications open. If the responsibility is theirs, rural people are very resourceful and capable of many band-aid solutions using local resources.

The real cost of maize production in remote areas is high because of the high cost of delivery of inputs. The cost of mealie meal is higher still because, often, maize has to be transported to some major town for milling and then returned. According to the *Times of Zambia* of 22 October 2013, the Zambian Cooperative Federation announced that it commissioned the Development

Bank of Zambia to raise $21 million for the establishment of 25 milling plants in rural areas, a very useful and worthwhile initiative, that would reduce the cost of mealie meal in the rural areas. I hope the Federation will involve rural companies or local businessmen in this project and I would recommend that in smaller areas, cheaper plants to be operated by local businessmen should be also encouraged. Other sectors such as education and health will be more efficient if they are supervised locally by people who have a direct interest in their results, while they are guided by educationists from the Ministry of Education and medical doctors and Public Health Officers from the Ministry of Health.

The big problem will be the composition of the provincial administration. Not much will be achieved if it remains the same with a minister and deputy minister in charge, appointed by Lusaka. They will always defer to the central government because their own aspiration will be to secure a Lusaka posting. If the aim is to transfer responsibility to the rural people the government should start thinking about provincial councils, whose composition will be shared between elected officers and local chiefs. And the provincial permanent secretary's primary duty must be to serve the provincial council and its chairman; in other words his primary focus must be the interest of the province in which he serves. (A second permanent secretary can be appointed for the provincial minister whose duties, I assume, would be to disseminate government policies through the district commissioners.)

But, I realize, I am treading on dangerous ground: this process may produce a situation where in a province, the opposition party can be in the majority. Is that so dreadful? In the United States it is routine, with half the state governors belonging to the opposition party, and it works. Perhaps I should clarify here that I am not advocating a federal structure, which would be expensive and unsuitable for a small country like Zambia, and which Zambia cannot afford. But, I am not a constitutional expert, and I must clarify that what I have in mind are administrative arrangements not constitutional changes.

If the government tackles the empowerment of the provinces seriously, it will, at the same time, solve the Barotse problem. Sata was right when he said that if he gave the Litunga any form of special powers he would end up facing the same demand from every other major chief in the country. Barotseland is a province, and it is inhabited mainly by Lozi, but also by Nkoya, Mbunda, Chokwe, Luvale and some smaller tribes. To this extent, it has the same characteristics as every other province in the country: the Northern Province is inhabited mainly by Bemba but also by Namwanga, Mambwe, Lungu, etc. and every province in Zambia has a similar make-up. In other words, the common characteristic of our rural areas is not only the chief and the variety of tribes. It is the province that personifies the uniformity of our rural areas. Any reorganization of the rural administration must, therefore, take place at provincial level so that nobody can look over his shoulder and complain that he has been overlooked. Instead of tinkering with districts let us consider seriously how to empower the provinces in order to look after the development of their people. But I must again emphasize that if we seriously believe in the development of the rural sector, we must shift the decision making on rural issues there.

And we must stop thinking, like the colonial authorities did, of powers of the Litunga and the chiefs. The powers of the chiefs are traditional and well entrenched and they should not be interfered with. When we start thinking of powers for the rural people through provincial councils comprising elected members and some ex-officio traditional leaders the solution will be easier. And the developmental goal will be enhanced because the focus will be on the immediate economic necessities that will dominate the agenda.

Now on to another of Sata's initiatives: the finances of another very popular project he announced are as dicey as those of the new districts. The project was announced in September 2012 and was named 'Link Zambia 8000'. It involves the construction and rehabilitation of 8,200 km of roads at an estimated cost of \$5.63 billion (announced as K28.15 trillion at the time); a more realistic budget would have been based on a cost of \$1 million per km, which would raise the total estimate to \$8 billion, way above what the National Treasury can afford in the foreseeable future. But the project itself is too ambitious and can be trimmed down. For example, some of the proposed roads lead to extremely isolated areas where traffic density is low and need not be paved. The 2013 budget contains an allocation 'for road infrastructure' of K3.434 billion of which 3.07 billion (some \$585 million) was allocated to the Link Zambia 8000 project, and a beginning has already been made with great fanfare. According to the Sixth National Development Plan the allocation for 2014 was projected to be K6.760 billion (some \$1.275 billion), but the 2014 budget allocation amounted to K5.127 billion (some \$850 million). The Development Plan allocations for 2015 and 2016 amount to K10.61 and 7.53 billion respectively, making a total allocated for the whole project of K27.97 billion or some \$4.6 billion, which would mean some 55 per cent completion by 2016, not a bad target for such an ambitious project, if in the end it can be achieved. The allocation in the 2014 budget is a little short of the target and one hopes that the balance will be covered in supplementary estimates as and when more funds are secured. The Sixth National Development Plan allocations for 2015 and 2016 look optimistic, but some of the roads are sorely needed and one hopes that the projected funds will be secured.

But Sata is unstoppable. In 2013, he started another road initiative: 'Pave Zambia 2000'. This is meant to pave the township roads using concrete blocks, an equally desirable project because the roads of most townships turn into streams and waterholes in the rainy season and dust bowls in the dry season. But where the money is going to come from is again a mystery. There has been talk of the Road Development Agency issuing a $1.5 billion bond, but even if it were successful the amount aimed for is just a drop in the ocean; and as the commodity prices drop and the international commodity market tightens, its success is becoming very uncertain.

One must hope that donor countries will follow China's example and step in. The Export Bank of China has already started offering finance for sections allocated to Chinese contractors operating in Zambia. I shall step on dangerous ground again, and put forward the suggestion that maybe the Western countries should be asked to consider converting their annual budget support into undertaking the construction of specific sections of 'Link Zambia 8000'. I need to confess here my own very cynical view of the budget support that they have, so generously, been giving us over the years. I do not want to sound ungrateful but I always felt that their contribution did not really benefit the Zambian people but the mining companies. My reasoning was that if the budget support was not available to them, Ministers of Finance would have no other way to balance the budget and they would have to put pressure on the mining companies. But 'our cooperating partners' plugged the hole year after year and the mining companies were left off the hook. To its credit, the Sata administration has already taken the initiative to make the mining companies pay more, and it does not seem to be too shy to squeeze even harder. And it does not need to increase the taxation rates in order to achieve this. It can do so easily by plugging the loopholes in the financial reporting of the mining industry.

As I said earlier, in Finance Sata made two astute appointments in Alex Chikwanda as Minister of Finance, and Michael Gondwe as Governor of the Bank of Zambia. Chikwanda, who has an economics degree from Lund University of Sweden, is both a veteran politician and a successful businessman. He served in the Kaunda administration in various capacities, including that of Minister of Finance in the mid-seventies. The 2012 budget, which he had to announce after less than three weeks in office, may have been largely prepared by the Banda regime, but bearing in mind the timidity of his predecessor the increase of the mineral tax from 0.6 per cent to 3 per cent has his signature. The first full year budget he produced for the fiscal year 2013 was characterized by pragmatism and concern for the improvement of the economy in general and the Zambian people in particular with special emphasis on the business sector. Even though the scandal of the tax evasion by some of the major mining companies had only become prominent at the beginning of 2013, the budget, which he announced in October 2012, had already taken the first step towards focusing the mining taxation on revenue rather than their 'never-likely-to-be-revealed' profits: he doubled the mineral tax from 3 per cent to 6 per cent.

And the Bank of Zambia under Michael Gondwe chipped in with its own contribution. In the chapters covering the performance of the Chiluba and Mwanawasa administrations I highlighted the scandal of the interest rates that prevailed during their period in office. And in Chapter 21, I highlighted the concern of the World Bank that reported our real interest rates as the highest in Africa averaging 16 per cent per annum over the period 1994–2002 and 18.8 per cent per annum after 2002 when Mwanawasa took over. The Banda administration remained equally unconcerned over the interest levels. The Bank of Zambia governor who served under both Mwanawasa and Banda sat back and let this state of affairs fester. His feeble response, not unlike that of the Banda Minister of Finance, was that he could not interfere with the market. (Not unlike the Minister of Finance, he did not take into account that what he called 'the market' consisted of the few banks operating in Zambia at the time which had a common interest in keeping the rates high. As it turned out, the parent companies of the biggest foreign banks operating in Zambia then did not hesitate to manipulate international rates like the Libor. In 2012, Barclays was the first international bank in the world to be fined by the United States Federal Reserve $460 million for manipulating the Libor rate. It was followed by Standard Chartered which between August and December 2012 paid fines to various United States regulators amounting to $667 million.)

Like Chikwanda, Gondwe decided that exhortations were not going to get him anywhere and he took the bull by the horns: he announced a Bank of Zambia base rate of 9 per cent and allowed the banks to fix their lending rate within a band of 9 percentage points above it. By the end of 2013, the maximum bank lending rate had crept up to 18.75 per cent, the base rate having been increased to 9.75 per cent. On average, this reduced the lending rate in 2012 to 16.1 per cent as against the 2011 average of 23.6 per cent: a drop of roughly one third. And Gondwe, out of concern for the small businessman and the private borrower, who were exploited with usurious interest rates in excess of 100 per cent, fixed the maximum microfinance rate to 42 per cent and all others to 30.

Another major achievement of the Zambian finance duo was the successful issue of the first ten-year Zambian Eurobond, in December 2012, amounting to €750 million at an interest rate of 5.625 per cent. The issue was oversubscribed and as the credit rating of Zambia remained high right through the first half of 2013, a new issue was being contemplated. However, conditions deteriorated during the latter part of 2013 with one of the major rating agencies putting Zambia on negative watch. In April 2014 a new one billion dollar ten-year bond was again successfully subscribed but at the very high interest rate of 8.625 per cent.

On the questionable side, the Ministry of Finance and the Bank of Zambia, in 2012, prohibited all internal foreign currency transactions 'in order to safeguard the Kwacha against a downward trend', which they declared to be against the country's interests. For a start I cannot see why a mildly depreciating Kwacha would be against the national interest, especially when one of our aims should be to promote 'non-traditional' exports, which consist mainly of agricultural products. They should remember that one of their predecessors, in 2005, pushed the Kwacha to unsustainably high levels and as a result he destroyed the cotton industry which had become a major factor in the economy of the rural areas, especially the Eastern Province and the western districts of the Central Province. Cotton production has since recovered but it took many years before it reached its previous levels. In view of the history of the exchange controls that plagued our economy until the mid-nineties, any action that would be interpreted by the market as a prelude to their reintroduction will have the opposite effect. Which is exactly what happened: despite the threats and exhortations, since the introduction of the new regulations, the Kwacha depreciated by some 10 per cent and it was on a downward trend at the end of 2013. The reason is simple: businessmen worried that exchange controls may be reintroduced play it safe and convert their spare Kwacha into dollars and externalize them, before it happens. But the major factor usually affecting the parity of the Kwacha is the availability of dollars, and in this the closer scrutiny of the mining companies' export earnings, which the finance authorities of Zambia put forward as the reason for their action, is justified. Inevitably, the Minister of Finance backtracked when the Kwacha hit 6.5 to the dollar in the middle of March 2014 having lost roughly a third of its value from the time the regulation was introduced.

During its first couple of years, the Sata administration had been looking over its shoulders raking the past, examining allegedly dubious deals made by its predecessors, Banda and Mwanawasa, stirring the political, judicial and administrative pots and ending up producing more of the same. It concentrated its efforts on major public works, many of which are indeed useful and some sorely needed but in the process it increased the budget deficit, which in the 2014 budget is projected to climb to 8.5 per cent of GDP, setting alarm bells ringing amongst Zambia's cooperating partners and the rating agencies, as I said earlier. Politically it focused on how to increase its power, and how to emasculate the opposition using methods that would have made the UNIP Central Committee of the eighties proud.

27. THE CIVIL SOCIETY GETS UNEASY

In October 2012, Sata raised a wave of indignation when he declared that in government he discovered that the Public Order Act, which he thought a repressive law when he was in opposition, is in fact a good law and should be preserved. 'When you are in government is when you realize that there will be no government when there's no sanity in society. There will be no government when there's no order in society,' he said attributing social order to the oppressive remnant of an old colonial 'Order in Council' that seeped into the Zambian statutes. The Law Association of Zambia was up in arms:

> 'It is clear to us that the Public Order Act as it stands today is subject to manipulation and has been arbitrarily used to stifle freedom of assembly,' said James Banda, LAZ President. 'Accordingly our considered view is that such a law cannot be allowed to grace our statute books and our litigation team will shortly file an appropriate application to challenge this colonial law. [It did and lost, at least the first round as the reader will see later.] The decision to litigate is necessary to remove any tension which is mounting as a result of the arbitrary application of this archaic law. It is necessary in a democratic dispensation such as ours to ensure that fundamental freedoms are not left to the whims and caprices of a few individuals wielding state power,' he concluded.

But it was not just the Law Association of Zambia that was upset. According to *The Post* Suzanne Matale, the General Secretary of the Council of Churches of Zambia, expressed equally strong objections.

> For me, it came as a huge surprise that the President had to retract his steps on the Act because the Public Order Act is a repressive Law. It needs to be changed so that it is not used to victimize people that have divergent views on issues. The Church does not shift goals and we are going to keep championing for this Act to be changed ... The Public Order Act was one that the President had called evil ... It is very sad that they should begin to negate on many issues that they did not like before. Now they praise them

249

and I think that this is a huge problem because we want to see development ... Now, one year down the line we are still waiting to see improvement in the areas they promised.

But discontent and indignation spread over a much wider variety of issues and this prompted the Zambia Episcopal Conference to circulate a Pastoral Statement which was read in all Catholic churches on 3 February 2013. The irony about this was that Sata is a devout Catholic ostentatiously exhibiting his devotion at every opportunity (he would govern according to the Ten Commandments he declared at the time of his inauguration) and the Catholic Church had supported him during the 2011 election campaign. But as we experienced over the independence struggle in Zambia the Catholic Church is not shy in going public in support of human rights, and civil liberties, as the Episcopal conference epistle testifies.

I'll introduce the issues raised in the circular and give the Episcopal Conference's position in conclusion.

Prevailing Political Environment

After the reintroduction of democracy in 1991, political parties took backstage in the governance of the country leaving the president and the ministers in the forefront. Even though the MMD Party had a National Executive Committee that was frequently mentioned, no individual member of it was particularly discernible as having any role in the governance of the country. But, Sata elevated the secretary general of the Patriotic Front to rank number three in terms of protocol, after the president and the vice president. He also installed him in a separate office and gave him staff to handle the affairs of the party, something that has not been in existence since the UNIP Central Committee was eclipsed. A few months later, he sacked his minister of justice and handed his portfolio to the party secretary general, thus giving him greater prominence. Many in the country saw this combination as the thin end of the wedge and came to the conclusion that Sata's ultimate aim was the reintroduction of a One Party State. Vitriolic statements and harsh treatment of the opposition parties and their leaders reinforced that impression. The Episcopal Conference takes up the issue:

Unfortunately, looking at what is happening around us, it would seem to us, that the ideals of a politically plural society have not been fully understood and appreciated by those who aspire for political leadership in our successive governments. This can be seen by the high level of political intolerance that continues to characterise our political environment, especially the intra-party and interparty relationships ... We appeal to our leaders across the political spectrum to demonstrate maturity, dignity, and magnanimity in the way they exercise their leadership and in the manner they relate to each other.

Yet after the episcopal circular the persecution of the opposition became a lot more intense.

By-elections
On assuming office, Sata decided to petition the results of all parliamentary seats won by opposition parties at astronomic costs in legal fees and, more importantly, court time. Very few resulted in gains for his party. The Episcopal Conference:

> Much as we acknowledge that there are by-elections occasioned by deaths of office holders we are also seeing more and more by-elections motivated by greed, individual interests, and a selfish propensity for political dominance. This is being done without care, serious prior consideration of the views of the electorate and sensitivity to the colossal amounts of money these by-elections are imposing on the economy.

Lack of Political Integrity among our Leadership
The Public Order Act was not the only issue over which the PF government changed positions after it came to power. An equally important one was enticing opposition MPs to join the government by offering them positions as deputy ministers. When such offers were made, the temptations (status, ministerial salaries and perks, cars, houses and allowances) were too great for targeted members to resist. By the middle of 2013, the PF had an overwhelming majority in parliament, despite starting the parliamentary term as a minority government. And Sata had 81 ministers and deputy ministers on the government benches out of a total parliament of 158. Mutale Nalumango, a former Deputy Speaker of the National Assembly, was indignant. In a statement to *The Post* on 15 March 2013, she contrasted Mwanawasa's equivalent measures in 2002, which she attributed to the need to fill cabinet positions because he did not have the numbers on his party's benches. She made the point that the end result of Sata's indiscriminate appointments of opposition members as deputy ministers, whose function is mainly cosmetic, was in order to secure their vote in favour of his government, which she characterized as killing democracy and taking the country back to the One Party State. The Episcopal Conference's admonition:

> Another concern ... is the lack of political integrity amongst our leaders. Many of them seem to find it easy to change positions on policies for personal

gain, expediency, or convenience. We have seen leaders subscribe to particular principled positions when in opposition only to repudiate those positions when accorded the instruments of power ... We appeal to the conscience of each of our politicians and call for a new era of good political leaders, who are consistent in their avowed principles, truthful and committed to the wellbeing of the public.

The Public Order Act

I covered the issue earlier and the comments of the Law Association and the Council of Churches of Zambia. The Episcopal Conference:

> Maintenance of Law and Order cannot only mean preventing opposition political parties from exercising their basic rights to freedom of assembly. The unfair restriction of people's liberties is breeding dangerous discontent. We call upon the Government to embrace the spirit and letter of democracy before the Nation is plunged into chaos. The Public Order Act, in its current form, has no place in our statutes. It is both repressive and anachronistic. It needs to be repealed.

The Barotseland Situation

I covered the issue extensively in Chapters 23, 24, and 25. The Episcopal Conference:

> We are aware of a climate of intimidation and serious human rights violations currently prevailing in the Western Province: abductions of citizens; arbitrary arrests and individuals being subjected to long periods of interrogations, even torture. These acts are totally unacceptable. They must stop forthwith ... We reiterate the call we made in our Pastoral Statement (29 January 2012) for the current administration to work with all stakeholders towards creating a more conducive environment that would lead to the amicable resolution of all matters surrounding the Barotseland situation.

Human Rights

The police had been very arbitrary in handling opposition party rallies and demonstrations, and sometimes innocuous visits of party leaders to markets and meetings. But there have also been arbitrary deportations. One of them was of a Rwandese priest in Chadiza in the Eastern Province who had been accused of making a sermon critical of the government. The deportation was clandestine and his parishioners only learned about it after he contacted them from Rwanda. It was not just the Church that was livid; many organizations were up in arms. The pressure built to such a crescendo that after many weeks Sata himself intervened and brought the priest back to Zambia. But deportations carried on especially of people whose business interests were in conflict with those of people close to State House or other senior functionaries. The unfortunate victims were not given a chance to apply to the court for protection. One of them, the Nigerian chief executive of Chilanga Cement (the Zambian subsidiary of the French company Lafarge) was driven to Ndola, 180 miles away, and put on the plane by the police before he even had a chance to contact his company never mind organize his private affairs. The practice in the past had been to serve potential deportees with an order from the immigration authorities or the Minister of Home Affairs giving them a few days' notice to leave, which gave them the opportunity to make legal representations and sort out their private affairs. The Episcopal Conference:

> Despite having instruments and institutions designed to promote and protect human rights, the human rights situation in Zambia is deteriorating in a manner that is causing worry. Examples include the arbitrary use of power by Government officials; intimidation and threats of arrest against leaders and individuals who speak against government; deportations and even threats to our own Catholic priests for sermons seen as critical of government.

The Judiciary

Almost immediately after his inauguration Sata started attacking the judiciary, accusing the judges of incompetence and corruption. He retired the Chief Justice and his deputy and replaced them with two lady justices of the Supreme Court. According to the Zambian Constitution the chief justice has to be confirmed by parliament. She was not because she was over the retirement age of 65 but she carried on acting while Sata was dilly-dallying over her replacement. The Deputy Chief Justice chose to retire. But the most contentious issue, which destabilized the judiciary and upset the country was the suspension of two high court judges and a justice of the supreme court. *The Post* reported the news as follows:

> President Sata has suspended three Judges over their alleged professional misconduct and has since appointed a tribunal to investigate them. But Supreme Court Judge Philip Musonda, who has been suspended with High Court Judges Charles Kajimanga and Nigel Mutuna, wondered why the matter was not taken to the Judicial Complaints Authority first. President Sata suspended the three Judges over their conduct in a civil case involving the Development Bank of Zambia as complainant and The Post Newspapers Ltd., Mutembo Nchito [a prominent lawyer who was appointed by Sata as Director of Public Prosecutions]

253

and JCN Holdings Ltd., as defendants. The tribunal comprises Malawi High Court Judge Lovemore Chikopa as chairman and members that include Justice Thomas Ndhlovu and retired High Court Judge Naboth Mwanza and Chipili Katunasa as secretary. Addressing journalists at State House President Sata said his administration would work hard to fight corruption in all government institutions. 'In this regard I have received credible complaints against their Lordships, Justices Philip Musonda, Charles Kajimanga and Nigel Mutuna and have accordingly decided to appoint a tribunal to investigate allegations of misbehavior or incompetence of the said Judges pursuant to the powers vested in me under the Constitution ... The said judges will accordingly be suspended pending the recommendations of the tribunal in two months' time. With respect to Justice Nigel Mutuna the Tribunal shall generally inquire into his conduct in relation to the manner he presided over the hearing and determination of the case of Development Bank of Zambia – v – The Post Newspapers Ltd., JCN Holdings Ltd., and Mutembo Nchito ... The circumstances under which Justice Mutuna heard the matter without formal order from Justice Albert Mark Wood, pointed to a conspiracy with Justice Philip Musonda and Justice Charles Kajimanga to defeat and subvert the course of justice ...' On Judges Musonda and Kajimanga President Sata directed the tribunal to inquire into the manner in which the duo interfered in and illegally retrieved ... the cases of Development Bank Zambia – v – The Post Newspapers Ltd., JCN Holdings Ltd., and Mutembo Nchito and Finsbury Investments Ltd. – v – Antonio Ventriglia and Manuela Sebastiani Ventriglia from Justice Albert Wood.

The unfortunate part of this imbroglio was that the reason for the judges' suspension was alleged 'misconduct' in relation to two cases involving close associates of the President who had played a very substantial role in his election: the editor of *The Post* newspaper, and the lawyer who had handled the cases against Chiluba both in Zambia and London and whom Sata appointed as Director of Public Prosecutions, an appointment that raised many eyebrows and some protests. Finsbury Investments was the investment vehicle of Rajan Mahtani, the Indian businessman and major shareholder of the Finance Bank (I covered how Sata, on assuming office, handed it back to him in Chapter 26). The Ventriglias, an Italian family that operated a terrazzo business in Ndola for decades and had branched out into cement manufacture under the name of Zambezi Portland Cement, had a dispute with Finsbury for some years. Zambezi Cement appeared to have obtained part of its financing through a syndication put together by Mahtani's Finance Bank. The details are murky but it appears that Mahtani used the opportunity to acquire a large shareholding in Zambezi and the dispute appeared to be over which party had control of the company. The dispute was before the courts, as Sata stated in his press conference, but the Ventriglias were unceremoniously bundled out of the country in November 2012 by order of the Minister of Home Affairs, Edgar Lungu, who issued a deportation order on the grounds that their stay in the country 'was illegal', a statement that raised eyebrows bearing in mind the years the family had been in the country, the successful terrazzo business they had run for decades and the fact that their children who were also deported had been born in the country. Yet Lungu said that their conduct was found to be a danger to 'the peace and good order of Zambia contrary to section 34 (1) (E) of the immigration and deportation Act'. Upon their departure Mahtani appointed his own manager for Zambezi Cement and installed him on its premises. What followed was unseemly: though in exile, the Ventriglias through their Lusaka lawyers obtained a writ of possession; but even though it was signed by the Chief Justice herself the sheriff was not able to serve it because the police surrounded the plant and would not let his bailiffs enter. The authorities sat back while the police maintained their blockade and Mahtani kept his manager in place. One by one, all members of the Ventriglia family were deported, including the sons (in their forties) who had been born in Luanshya. It is against this background that the Episcopal Conference wrote:

> For some time now there has been persistent discourse on the state of the Judiciary in Zambia with respect to its independence and impartiality. This situation has undermined public confidence in this institution. There is need to restore confidence in this important arm of the government. There are also many unresolved questions of public interest that have been left hanging and unanswered by the Executive. For example, when shall we see progress on the much talked about reforms in the judicial system? What is the current status of the Judge Chikopa [the Malawian chairman] Tribunal that was appointed last year? Why do we still have an acting Chief Justice and Deputy Chief Justice? When are these structural issues going to be resolved? These and other questions need answers from the Executive because the Nation deserves to be informed to avoid unhealthy speculation and rumours.

The Constitution-Making Process

Constitution-making has become a never-ending saga that one might take as a bit of a joke if it was not so serious. We are still operating on the 1996 Constitution, which was introduced by Chiluba at the time that he had an overwhelming majority in parliament because UNIP the opposition party at the time refused to participate in the election, after Kenneth Kaunda's disenfranchisement. Since then, both Mwanawasa and Banda appointed constitutional commissions. They both promised a new constitution before the 'next election' but they never produced one. The main reason is the universal demand for a rerun if the elections do not produce a president with 50 per cent plus one majority. As they were both aware that they were unlikely to get over 50 per cent of the vote in the first round, they dilly-dallied, worried over the uncertainty of the results of the second round. (The reader will remember that in 2001 Mwanawsa was elected with just 29.15 per cent of the vote; and the irony for Banda was that he lost the elections while Sata did not get the over 50 per cent majority, so a rerun might have given him another chance. Perhaps Sata should note.)

Sata, in opposition, was very vocal about the delay and he made a promise that when elected he would finalize a new constitution within 90 days of assuming office. (Ninety days was Sata's benchmark: within that period he would give everybody a job and would double everybody's salary, so why not produce a constitution within the same period?) Needless to say that he did not deliver and the Episcopal Conference decided to remind him of his promise:

> Up to now, a people-driven democratic constitution continues to elude us as a nation. This is in spite of colossal amounts of money and time that have been gobbled and wasted on the exercise. The Patriotic Front (PF) in their pre-September 2011 election campaign promised the Zambian people a new constitution within ninety days of their accession to power. Today, sixteen months down the line, little progress, if any, seems to have been made on the constitution. There are public misgivings on the current constitution-making process, in part due to the following reasons:
>
>> The refusal of the current administration to give the constitution-making process a legal framework that would protect the process and the content.
>>
>> The uncertainty, the lack of a road map and a predictable timeline on the process has also led to doubts about the sincerity of government on the Constitution. From the time the Technical Committee started work several deadlines for completion of the process have been promised and missed. Currently, we have a new deadline of 30 June 2013. We hope that this new milestone will be upheld and honoured. [It was not.]
>>
>> The non-publication of the projected budget for the entire constitution-making process ... is unacceptable because it goes against the need for Government accountability on expenditure; Government needs to exhibit transparency on this matter.
>>
>> Uncertainty on the referendum question: The people of Zambia deserve better. We need a categorical assurance of a referendum by the Executive

because that is what the Zambian people want and this is what they were promised by the current administration.

The publication of the Technical Committee's report missed many deadlines and in the middle of November 2013, when it was ready, the Minister of Justice issued instructions that the Committee should sign only ten copies for delivery to the 'Appointing Authority' (the President) and to nobody else. The Committee considered this instruction to be against its mandate and sought a meeting with the President, while the civil society went up in arms. The *Weekly Post* of 15 November 2013 reported:

> Civil Society was in uproar. It has continuously called for a proper road map for the constitution making process and some NGOs took this latest development as the final proof that government is manipulating the new constitution. Many wondered what government was trying to hide, including Transparency International (mockery), Open Society Foundation (sabotage), Young African Leaders Initiative (hypocricy at its worst) and Caritas Zambia (provocative). They were supported by the Law Association of Zambia (suspicious).

The Need for More Consultation

I have already written extensively on the issue of rural administration with the establishment of Muchinga Province and 31 rural districts and the absence of any information regarding the capital costs or the recurrent expenditure they will absorb. I also wrote about the PF diktat on new education policy. These issues worried the Episcopal Conference; it said:

> In the recent past, we have seen unprecedented Government decisions and actions being made by way of decrees. This has especially been the case when the government has announced the creation of new political boundaries and governance structures. We appreciate the noble objectives behind these decisions, mainly to enhance participation in the governance system and make services more easily accessible to citizens. However, though the constitution gives power to the Republican President to make decisions even by decree, it is desirable and sometimes necessary to consult as this facilitates prior understanding and appreciation of issues and guarantees success at implementation stage.
>
> Another case of the absence of consultation is in the areas of education. The Government–Church relationship in the education sector is governed by the Education Act. As major stakeholders in the education sector, we are dismayed by the growing tendency for unilateral pronouncements, circulars, and directives coming from government functionaries. Some of these directives have

far reaching consequences in the manner we run our schools and sometimes border on matters of policy. Government would do well to consult with key local partners and stakeholders ...

In the area of Health ... it is disheartening to see major decisions such as realigning of our medical institutions to new government ministries taken without consultation. [This must refer to the transfer of the department of 'Mother and Child Health' out of the Ministry of Health and into the Ministry of Community Development.]

It is our fervent hope that the government will do some objective and serious introspection in this area and act to carry everyone along when important decisions are being made.

Registration of All Mobile SIM Cards

The last issue the Episcopal Conference pronounced on was a government order for the registration of all mobile telephone SIM cards. The ostensible reason was to prevent criminality but everybody suspected that the real reason behind the order was to monitor people's private communications and spy on their political views, something that was widespread during the 1980s. And the government did not stop there. A couple of weeks later the Global Voices Advocacy reported that the government had engaged Chinese experts to install a secret internet monitoring facility in the country, at the cost of $1.8 million. At the same time it was learned that Sata had authorized the State Security Service to monitor the telephone and online communications of anyone living in Zambia if ordered to do so by the Attorney General. This intrusion in people's private lives, infuriated many citizens. The most articulate critic was Elias Chipimo, leader of the rather small but highly principled National Restoration Party (NAREP). He warned that 'slowly and surely Zambia was becoming a police state where there is growing erosion of all the gains of democracy Zambians fought so hard to reintroduce when they successfully brought down the one party state' and he continued: 'It seems that those days are now looming and we must fight tooth and nail to ensure that they never return.' According to Mr Chipimo all internet service providers had been visited by a team composed of officers from ZICTA (Zambia Information and Communications Technology Authority), the Office of the President (State Security Services or *ShuShuShu* in urban slang) and the Chinese contractor and asked to provide detailed diagrams of their networks with a view to installing splitters that would direct duplicates of all traffic to government. Even though the engagement of a Chinese contractor to monitor all internet activity had not broken out at the time, the Episcopal Conference in its pastoral letter was equally alarmed by the registration of the SIM cards. Its Pastoral Statement was no less direct:

We take note of the call by ZICTA for all mobile phone users to register their SIM cards with service providers or risk having them deactivated. According to ZICTA the move is meant to deter criminality ... While the intention to control criminality and abuse of communications technologies is noble we call upon the Zambian Government to put in place legal guarantees for the protection of personal data and privacy.

The circular was signed by the President of the Zambia Episcopal Conference (ZEC), Archbishop of Kasama and Apostolic Administrator of Mpika, Ignatius Chama; the ZEC Vice President and Bishop of Ndola, Alick Banda; the Archbishop of Lusaka, Telesphore Mpundu; the Bishop of Livingstone, Raymond Mpezele; the Bishop of Monze, Emilio Patriarca; the Bishop of Chipata, George Cosmas Zumaile Lungu; the Bishop of Solwezi, Charles Kasonde; the Bishop of Mongu, Evans Chinyama Chinyemba, OMI; the Bishop of Kabwe, Clement Mulenga; the Auxiliary Bishop of Chipata, Benjamin Phiri; the Apostolic Administrator of Mansa, Michael Merizzi; and the Bishop Emeritus of Mansa, Aaron Chisha.

But the civil society representations fell on deaf ears. The Sata administration completely ignored all the issues raised and, if anything, its attitude hardened.

28. Arrests, Incarcerations and 'Nolle Prosequi'

By-election campaigns became more frenzied, as the PF determined to win them at all costs and the other parties did their best to stop it. In the process there were frequent confrontations amongst cadres of the various parties some of them resulting in many injuries. A by-election for Livingstone Central that took place barely a month after the Episcopal circular I summarized in the previous chapter became so violent that the Electoral Commission had to postpone polling for a couple of weeks. Tempers needed to cool after a PF youngster was killed in a confrontation between PF and UPND cadres in the Libuyu township of Livingstone. The government seized the opportunity to pin a charge of murder on Gary Nkombo, the Mazabuka Central MP, who was leading the opposition UPND by-election campaign, and lock him up.

I interviewed Nkombo, who informed me that his arrest took place in the middle of the night after a turbulent evening. According to his story, PF cadres attacked the UPND campaign office during the early evening, throwing stones. He made a number of attempts to contact the Minister of Home Affairs who was also in Livingstone at the time but he failed and late in the evening he received a police 'call out'. He arrived at the police station at 11:30 p.m., where he was arrested. He was not given any reasons for his arrest and when he asked, Nkombo says, the arresting officer's response was that he had instructions to do so. Nkombo also claims that before his arrest he was punched by a PF minister within the police station.

Nkombo reports that he was kept in detention for four days, without charge and when he was eventually taken to court, the police proffered a charge of murder and tried to join him with seven others who had already been charged for the Libuyu incident despite the fact that Nkombo was nowhere near Libuyu when the fracas took place. The magistrate rejected the attempt of joining charges as being outside his jurisdiction, and ordered that Nkombo be properly charged within 14 days, but before the end of the period he was released on 'nolle prosequi' from the DPP, a process that was started by Chiluba, but the frequency of its use increased under the Sata administration.

Two years after the general election, petitions challenging the 2011 results were continuing and by-elections were becoming more controversial and violent, not least because by mid-2013, the winning streak of the Patriotic Front seemed to have run out. The opposition parties started winning most of them with substantial margins, as the result of the by-election of the Mkaika constituency in the Eastern Province, which took place on 5 September 2013, indicated: the PF candidate came a distant second with 1,712 votes to the MMD candidate's 9,054. A few weeks earlier, by-elections in three other constituencies produced similar results. As some winning candidates in those constituencies had been the previous incumbents, the PF made an attempt to prevent petitioned losing incumbents from ever standing again. It tried it in three constituencies (Malambo, Petauke Central and Mulobezi) where by-elections were due to take place in August 2013. This produced a series of court injunctions, appeals, counter injunctions, and so on, with the result that the by-elections kept being postponed. On 3 July 2014, the Supreme Court finally announced that MPs whose elections were nullified were allowed to re-contest their seats.

With political tensions rising the PF administration became very intolerant of criticism and started targeting vocal opponents. But opportunities to incarcerate opposition leaders under a murder charge like Nkombo's are rare and the Public Order Act can only be used to deny mass protests, demonstrations, and election rallies by opposition parties. A handy alternative to harass critics and other vocal opponents turned out to be the Drug Enforcement Commission (DEC). It was established under the Dangerous Drugs (Forfeiture of Property) Act of 1989 and reconfirmed when the Act was replaced by the Narcotic Drugs and Psychotropic Substances Act, Chapter 96 of the Laws of Zambia, in 1993. The Act bestows power on the commissioner 'whenever he has reasons to believe that there is reasonable cause to suspect' that an offence under the Act has been committed to 'authorize a drug enforcement officer or a police officer' to enter premises, search and arrest persons, break open and examine any article, break open any outer or inner door, forcibly enter premises and detain every person there until the premises have been searched. He is also entitled to arrest anyone he considers a suspect.

None of the procedures mentioned above requires a court order. According to Brebner Changala, one of the victims of such a search, the officer who arrested him had a pad of printed warrants in triplicate, pre-signed by the DEC Director General, from which he filled one out in his presence and handed him a copy. The problem with such a procedure, if it is commonly pursued, is that it transfers the final judgement on possible culpability from the commissioner to a junior officer.

Changala, a successful self-made Lusaka businessman (he received the UK Trade and Investment Award for Small Businesses in 2004) who had set up a chalk manufacturing facility in Lusaka and was supplying blackboard chalk to schools since the year 2000, had been an outspoken civil rights activist and he may have upset Patriotic Front elements because of his frequent protests against human rights violations. He first lost his contract to supply chalk to government schools and at 3 a.m. on 7 August 2013 his house was invaded by nine DEC officers who arrived in six cars. After filling in and handing him the search warrant, they proceeded to make havoc of his house and office, confiscate his computers, iPads, his children's laptops and video games and then arrest him and incarcerate him; and their first act on arrival was to confiscate his mobile phones and disconnect his landline so that he could not communicate with either his lawyer or a friend, Changala said.

They carried out a thorough search of the house until 9 in the morning when they moved to his office, which they finished searching at 12 noon. Apart from taking away a number of documents of a political nature and his computers and other electronic gadgets I mentioned above, they also removed a packet containing 59 pills of Vermox, a children's deworming medicine that his sister had forgotten in his house. They took him to the force headquarters for interrogation after which they released him. They rearrested him and his sister the next day, kept them both in custody for the entire weekend and on Monday, 12 August, they took them both to court and charged them for possession of psychotropic drugs. The magistrate set the hearing for 20 August and as the offence is non-bailable, they were taken back to jail. The day before the hearing was due to commence the police took him and his sister back to the court and withdrew the case on a nolle prosequi order from the DPP.

But Changala's civil liberties were not the only casualty of this saga. His company, Brebner School Chalk Ltd, is now moribund, operating at 10 per cent capacity. He had to dismiss 68 workers, half of them in Monze, a small town some 150 miles south of Lusaka, who were digging gypsum, the school chalk's main ingredient. And who supplies the chalk now? It is imported from South Africa, or India, or China, of course. This is not the way to encourage local industry and create the jobs the PF had promised the electorate. President Sata should find out who the culprits of this outrage are and punish them severely. And he must make it clear to his party that Zambian industries and Zambian jobs are sacrosanct; under no circumstances should they be jeopardized by low level apparatchiks who want to settle scores or silence their critics, real or imagined.

Two journalists, one in Lusaka and one in Kabwe who were suspected of writing for the *Zambian Watchdog*, an internet publication that had been blocked from all Zambian internet service providers on government orders, received similar treatment. Another victim was Clayson Hamasaka, a lecturer in Journalism and head of Media Studies at the Evelyn Hone College in Lusaka. He had been dismissed from his position a year earlier, and he attributes his dismissal to a visit of the UPND leader to the college at a time of student protests triggered by an outbreak of a gastric epidemic at the school. He believes that the authorities suspected him of organizing the visit. Hamasaka informed me that on 9 July 2013, his house was also searched by the DEC, 'looking for drugs and anything else criminal'. No drugs were found but his laptop was taken away, he was arrested, and was 'warned and cautioned' on suspected seditious practices, but finally charged on 23 July with possession of obscene material, which the police claim they found on his laptop. He denies the allegation and the case was continuing when this book was sent to the publishers.

This pattern of ruthless attacks on the opposition and other critics of the regime was reminiscent of the UNIP dictatorship period and its attacks on those it declared as dissidents. The intense activity manifested discord within the higher echelons of the Patriotic Front, not an unexpected event, considering the free hand Sata gave to the party secretariat. By mid-2013 a group led by the Minister of Defence started a campaign of 'reconfirmation' of Sata as the sole candidate for the 2016 election, a move that many interpreted as an indication that senior leaders were elbowing for the top job. Uncharacteristically, Sata sat back while the trouble escalated. It took a predictable course: two factions led by senior party dignitaries started accusing each other of undermining the boss's re-election in 2016. The rivalry spilled over into the daily press with the Minister of Defence and Minister of Justice (who was the party Secretary General at the same time) exchanging insults and accusations of disloyalty to the President and the party. And it spread amongst the cadres, with different groups supporting different patrons resorting to fights and causing injuries to each other. It all looked like a repetition of the 1980s, which was the beginning of the end of Kaunda's period in office. When Sata eventually stepped in, he dished out Delphic oracles instead of quietly imposing his authority and restoring discipline and common sense. His statements could be interpreted as meaning: 'if anybody feels strong enough to take me on, let him step forward'. Nobody would dare do that, so instead the skirmishes between the two factions intensified, with frequent cadre demonstrations demanding the dismissal of the Secretary General, which tends to indicate that in the last quarter of 2013, the Patriotic Front was as much at sea as the other parties it had managed to destabilize since it took power two years earlier.

While the cadres were fighting each other the hierarchy dropped any pretence of unity and started hurling dirt at one another, exposing underhand activities that the 'other side' was supposed to be involved in. The most outspoken was the Secretary General and Minister of Justice. According to *The Post* of 28 September 2013 he said:

> Most of my colleagues are busy flying out of the country almost every week. They are busy doing business in their government offices. They are busy acquiring tenders to prop up their businesses which were failing when they were in the opposition. I don't do any of those things … The genesis of what you see in Lusaka is about the policy we put in as a party to kill the culture of MMD: of Party members extorting money from business operators …, collecting illegal levies in markets …, engaging in invasion of other people's property, for example land … Those who have grouped together against me have seized on these measures and are saying to our party membership: 'you would have been OK; you would have been selling land today in Lusaka; you would have been extorting money or levies from business operators; you would have been levying marketeers had it not been for the fact that we have a secretary general like Wynter Kabimba, who is against these measures.'

In short: most of my colleagues are taking advantage of their positions in government to enrich themselves and they are extortionists and crooks; I am the only clean one around, and I am persecuted because I am trying to maintain decency, while the others are corrupt, they are using their positions to get rich and they encourage the PF cadres to do the same. What was amazing about this outburst was that the Secretary General did not seem to care that he was in fact attacking the very foundation of his own party's existence and Sata's greatest boast: the fight against corruption. In normal circumstances the inevitable follow-up would have been for him to resign or get sacked. Instead he received wholehearted support from the Vice President. According to *The Post* of 30 September the Vice President said:

> The real issue is that current events are in fact an attack on his [Sata's] leadership, intended to undermine his power … These people are bent on dividing the Party … They are after Michael Sata's power if not his job … They are tearing him up – on one side there are his lieutenants of many years who have done so much to put him in power … We made the PF work because of Wynter, me and the boss [Sata] and other dedicated people. In the hard days we made it work, even when others were hammering us. Yes, he [Secretary General Wynter Kabimba] is my friend. But the fact is that it would be a serious loss to the PF, and the President most particularly.

Sata was in New York attending the United Nations General Assembly opening session when all this was happening. A few days after he returned, on 8 October 2013, he issued an anodyne statement repeating that, personally, he was not desperate for endorsement. He warned 'those who have been establishing parallel structures aimed at promoting their peculiar agenda to stop confusing the Party', because their 'machinations which are grounded in malice and dishonesty ... have the potential to weaken the cohesion of the Party'. Finally, he urged the 'loyalists' who serve in his administration to concentrate on the 'development agenda'.

Conclusion? Round one appears to have gone to the Secretary General who had been Sata's 'blue-eyed boy'. But if I know anything about squabbles within political parties in Zambia, many more rounds will follow.

In the meantime, Sata did nothing to shake his party out of its vengeful mode and its continuous attack on civil liberties and its opponents' human rights, which is what the examples I mentioned earlier indicate. So much so, that the intra-PF cadre fights that became the order of the day also spread against the leaders of the opposition. The most despicable incident was the manhandling of Hakainde Hichilema, the leader of UPND, near Chitimukulu's Palace in Kasama district. It happened at a police roadblock, which many think was set up specifically for Hichilema's visit.

The incident annoyed the recently elected Chitimukulu who had granted the appointment and who issued a strong statement of condemnation. Instead of trying to calm the controversy, the Sata administration proceeded to add insult to injury: 'The Chitimukulu had not yet been gazetted, which means that he has not yet been recognized by the government' (or words to that effect) declared the Minister for Chiefs and Traditional Affairs, which many took as a suggestion that Chitimukulu was not to be acknowledged until the government gazetted him officially and that the UPND leader had no business visiting him. (It later emerged that Sata had another candidate in mind.) This incensed not only the Chitimukulu but the Bashilubemba (the Bemba Royal Establishment). They warned the Minister of Chiefs to stay out of the issue because she is not Bemba royalty. And in typical Bemba hauteur they declared, according to the *Times of Zambia* of 25 September 2013: 'Our job ends with appointing and installing; ifya gazette ifyo fyabo' (implying that gazetting is a government eccentricity and irrelevant as far as they are concerned). And according to *The Post* of 24 September they asked:

> Before Professor Nkandu Luo or any other persons became either minister or the President was there no Chitimukulu? Who constitutes Chitimukulu? Is it the government or is it the Bemba people themselves? They must stop provoking us.

They need to own up and apologise ... It is in the interest of the PF Government to recognise the Mwine Lubemba (Chitimukulu) who had been legally selected by the rightful organ of the Bemba people: Bashilubemba. And there is no one who is above Bashilubemba. Bashilubemba's position has been there before the Colonial Government.

And in the ultimate display of overflowing Bemba self-confidence and superiority they warned the government that if it maintained its stance over the recognition of the newly installed Chitimukulu, the Bemba chiefs would sever ties with it and stop recognizing it. (*Daily Nation*, 26 September 2013). However, Bemba pride notwithstanding, it is not easy to ignore the might of government. On 22 November 2013 the *Zambia Weekly* carried the following:

The Bemba Royal Establishment (Bashilubemba) has – reluctantly – agreed to discuss succession wrangles with President Sata. Earlier this year the traditional leaders installed Henry Sosala as Paramount Chief Chitimukulu Kanyanta Manga II of the Bemba People in Kasama against the directive of Government. Since then government has deployed 500 paramilitary police officers in Kasama District in general and at Chitimukulu Palace in particular, which resulted in the Bashilubemba refusing to show up for a meeting at State House. This week after a seven day ultimatum to comply, the Bashilubemba announced that it was ready to dialogue [sic] with government.

After Hichilema and Chitimukulu the PF's wrath turned on Dr Nevers Mumba, the MMD leader, who was charged with defaming the President in comments he made during a radio interview. He responded in an open letter to the President, claiming that his remarks contained nothing different to what leaders of the opposition usually say in such type of political interview, and quoting some of the President's similar comments when he was in opposition. But the case against him was proceeding.

At the end of 2013, the PF was rattled but the civil society remained quiet. The Law Association of Zambia (LAZ) did take up the case of the constitutionality of the Public Order Act and the case was heard by the High Court in April 2013. On 23 October 2013, Judge Evans Hamaundu rejected LAZ's application, finding that the act does not contravene Articles 20 and 21 of the constitution, as claimed. The LAZ appealed the verdict to the Supreme Court, and the appeal is pending.

LAZ had also taken up the issue of the 'temporariness' of the Chief Justice who had been acting for more than a year, and, even though her nomination had been rejected by parliament in February 2013, she had not been replaced.

At 69, she was past retirement age, which in Zambia is 65, and the contention was that the President's power to extend the term of a justice of the supreme court is limited to one single extension of up to seven years in the position he or she occupies when reaching retirement; no promotion is allowed. In relation to the 2013 temporary incumbent, LAZ contends that her term as justice of the supreme court had already been extended by President Banda in 2009 for a period of three years which ended in April 2012, and President Sata was not entitled to grant a further extension never mind a promotion to chief justice that he effected on 14 June 2012, according to LAZ. At the end of August 2013, LAZ gave President Sata an ultimatum to regularize the position, within one month; he failed to respond.

On 23 September 2013, LAZ filed a claim in the High Court against the Attorney General as first defendant and the acting Chief Justice as second defendant asking the court to declare her appointment illegal, null and void. And for greater effect a number of members of the Law Association of Zambia, some clad in their court robes, marched from the LAZ offices to the High Court, a distance of a couple of miles accompanying the chairman of the litigation committee, who filed the claim. The issue seemed to be developing into a major legal confrontation, with 18 law firms filing to represent the acting Chief Justice and 12 to represent the Law Association of Zambia.

In the meantime the Chikopa Commission had been prevented from sitting through a series of injunctions petitioned by the Zambian judges it had been appointed to investigate and indignation was building up in the country that Chikopa had been in Zambia for more than a year and a half and he was costing a fortune in fees and accommodation. As he is a serving Malawi judge, questions were also raised about his position within the Malawi judiciary after such a prolonged absence and the fate of the cases he was handling there prior to his departure for Zambia.

According to *The Post* of 6 September 2013, Grace Manyonga, the secretary of the Non-Governmental Organisations Coordinating Committee (NGOCC), accused the PF government of being 'unresponsive and intolerant of divergent views and unwilling to be accountable to the people that voted it into office'. Her comments revolved around the government's attempt to force all NGOs to register under the NGO Act, which they fear is intended to gag them. NGOCC represents 24 civil society organizations, prominent amongst them being the Council of Churches of Zambia, the Zambia National Women's Lobby, Women for Change, and Transparency International.

And in reviewing the government performance for the year 2013, the Zambia Episcopal Conference, at a press conference held in Lusaka on 26 January 2014, noted 'with deep concern' that the strides Zambia could have made continue to be negated and eroded by governance arrogance of the '"know it all" type'. It proceeded to review the status of the issues it raised in its pastoral statement which was read in all Catholic churches on 3 February 2013 and noted that there are many unresolved issues and negative developments that are taking the country many years backwards. It continued:

> In our similar statement at the beginning of 2013, some of these governance concerns were raised; for instance: the hostile political environment; the high incidence of by-elections; the lack of political integrity among our politicians and leaders; the selective application of the Public Order Act by the Zambia Police Service; the deteriorating human rights situation in our country; intimidation and police repression with regard to the Barotse issue in Western Province; the stalled constitution making process.

Its comments were particularly strong in relation to:

- 'Abusive and biased' application of the Public Order Act, describing the political environment as 'characterised by manipulation, patronage and intimidation of perceived government opponents';
- 'The vast sums of money that have gone and continue to go into holding of by-elections,' which could have given Zambians many schools and hospitals; the failure of progress over the 'constitution making process after a spirited start in November 2011' which it compared to 'the Inquiries Act whereby the President and the Cabinet sit to cherry-pick what they think should be in the constitution';
- The threat to the food security that had been escalated by the late delivery of farming inputs particularly fertilizer for the 2013/14 farming season;
- The threat to the status of traditional leaders; in this regard it advised that traditional affairs and conflicts related to succession should be resolved by set customs, procedures and systems within the traditional structures;
- The delay in the enactment of the Freedom of Information Bill lamenting at the same time the highly polarized media environment along political preferences, which 'deeply undermines' the integrity of the media;
- The tendency of 'government by decree' as manifested by the creation of a multitude of new districts and the decision to use local languages as a mode of instruction at lower primary schools; it stressed that it was unjust and in violation of human rights to force children to learn in local languages that are not their native language and urged the government to immediately withdraw the policy and engage in consultations on it.

The ZEC statement handed out to the press was signed by the same Catholic church dignitaries who signed the pastoral statement of January 2013, and which appears in Chapter 27. Sata and his party received it in the same deafening silence they did the year before.

But as he is already halfway through his term, he has to start tackling these problems and many others in a hurry in order to secure his re-election in 2016, and more importantly, his legacy. First and foremost he has to restore discipline in his party.

29. PRESIDENT SATA AND HIS FUTURE LEGACY

All Sata's headaches in the second half of 2013 stemmed from the central committee of his party. Central committees had been relegated to backroom status by all three presidents (Chiluba, Mwanawasa, and Banda) of the MMD era, because of the oppressive rule perpetrated by the central committee of the 'One Party' State. Unfortunately, the Patriotic Front Central Committee had been given undue prominence by Sata, so much so that its secretary general had assumed the role of co-manager of the country alongside Sata and his vice president. Apart from a handful of individuals the rest of his cabinet was mostly ignored. And it gave senior party apparatchiks the feeling that, like the UNIP Central Committee of old, they are the true guardians of the people's interests and that their duty is to maintain the dominance of the Patriotic Front. It is their excessive zeal that caused the interparty conflicts that the country experienced during the first two years of Sata's regime, which I described in some detail in Chapter 27. But in the process the secretary general alienated a large part of the cabinet, many members of which resented his arrogance and concluded that he was amassing too much power and decided to cut him down to size.

The rivalry culminated in the intra-party conflict that the Patriotic Front experienced towards the end of 2013. Sata appeared to have decided that his best option was to sit back and let the various factions fight it out until they exhausted themselves, a course that Kaunda had taken many times during his administration.

There is also something else reminiscent of the UNIP era that Sata has to watch: a docile press and an overbearing inner circle he inherited from his political campaigns. Of the three major dailies in Zambia, two are owned by the government and the third that had become successful because it had been the only uncompromising independent daily in the country for a couple of decades dedicated itself to Sata and the Patriotic Front body and soul. There is a very thin line between professed acolytes, and sycophants. Each one has his own agenda, but their collective praise and adulation forms a curtain between the leader and the public, and prevents him from getting a direct feel of what the country's real thinking is. Sata should not have had to wait for the civil

271

society's representations (Chapter 27) to hear the people's misgivings about his policies and behaviour. With a more open press, and fewer sycophants around, he would have known about it earlier and done something to correct it, before it needed to be spelt out in great detail by the civil society. And by listening to his party apparatchiks and ignoring the civil society representations, as completely as he has done twice, he risked losing a large measure of support in the country.

Sata must shake himself free from old associates who line up for rewards for past services. This is imperative for the success of his fight against corruption and it will also be in his long-term interest as well as that of those involved. And he must not allow his party to take sides in the business disputes of his friends. He must wash his hands of their cases and allow the legal processes to take their course. And for equity's sake he must instruct that the counterparties who have been deported return to the country to handle their side of the litigation.

But first and foremost the President must make his peace with the judges and the Law Association of Zambia. It was a mistake to attempt to import a foreign judge to sit in judgment of them. It demeans the Zambian judiciary and it demeans the nation. He must not allow his inner circle to accuse our courts of being corrupt. Those who accuse others of being corrupt are usually assumed to deserve the same label, a view that was particularly strengthened after his own secretary general's outburst when he accused many of his senior colleagues in cabinet of extortion and of abusing their positions in order to enrich themselves, and of encouraging the party cadres to do the same. And if all the judges are corrupt, who is going to replace them? Not foreign judges from Malawi or elsewhere. They will be replaced by colleagues from the Law Association of Zambia, of course. And why would they be expected to be of different ilk if they will come from the very body the rest of the judiciary that stands accused came from in the first place? We cannot go on accusing each other of corruption. We only give ourselves and the country a bad name because when all is said and done, nobody believes that the accuser is less guilty than the accused.

The excessive persecution of the opposition parties and other protesters is obscene and it is counter-productive at the same time. The PF does not need all the opposition MPs to cross the floor in order to govern, especially if the process means that Sata has to pack half of parliament on the government front bench at tremendous cost to the nation. I believe that at the end of 2013 there were 81 ministers and deputy ministers in government; in other words, 51 per cent of parliament was sitting on the government front bench. I do not want to overstate the point. But whether opposition MPs are sitting on the Patriotic Front benches or on those where they belong, Sata can still govern and he can do so better if the opposition does not feel persecuted and its opinions are respected.

Persecuting the opposition leaders and incarcerating them, regardless of the fact that in the end they are released with a 'nolle', can prove harmful to the government in the long run. Just in case he has forgotten it, I would like to remind President Sata that when he was in opposition he received his biggest popularity boost from Mwanawasa who put him in jail when he expressed support for the Chililabombwe striking miners. His unjust incarceration nauseated the public and increased Sata's support. He should ask himself if what his government is doing to the opposition parties now is likely to have the same effect. Party cadres obsequiously cheer and rejoice when opposition leaders are sent to jail, for no real reason. But the general public finds it revolting and sympathizes with them.

The bottom line is that if he carries on the way he has been doing, the opposition parties and many members of his own party that have been kicked around during the infighting may band together in a new political movement, as happened with the MMD in 1990. If forced into a corner the country is capable of repeating that feat. And the infighting within the PF that has been taking place since the middle of 2013 makes this a very serious possibility. Zambia has proved that it has inexhaustible patience with the antics of its politicians but once it decides 'enough is enough' it throws them out. It did it to Kaunda. And it did it to Chiluba over the third term. When the opposition is pushed against the wall, like it had been in the late eighties, the only alternative it has is to band together and take with it disgruntled members of the Patriotic Front as well.

The politicking that has taken over the Patriotic Front has become the major preoccupation of the party and all the media that support it. Nobody seems to pay any attention to anything else. There is little coverage of national issues. The main preoccupation of the media is to report who said what about whom. Inane statements by obscure politicians about equally obscure rivals make headlines, so that the prowess of one clique in the Patriotic Front can be praised and its opponents vilified. I know some editors personally; many had notable careers and they are capable of better. I am amazed at the tactics they employ and I hope they snap out of it; if for nothing else, for the sake of the young journalists who are coming up now. What example are we setting for them to follow?

Sata has already showed that he is tough and can make bold decisions. A prime example was the abolition of subsidies to the price of fuel, and even more courageously, to the price of mealie meal. He faced students' riots and many other protests as a result but he did not budge. But there is a lot more cost-cutting he will have to do. And a lot more careful thinking needs to be done on how to utilize our meagre resources to relieve the suffering of the poorest of our people while at the same time we set up structures that will help us to move forward at a faster pace and on firmer ground than hitherto. Our needs are many, but our resources are few. We have to ration them carefully in order to achieve the best results while at the same time we maintain a record of fiscal prudence and the confidence of the international financial markets. Above all we must avoid overextending ourselves financially to the brink of bankruptcy, like we did before. The President of Zambia and his minister of finance have the power and the duty to make sure we do not.

And he must be vigilant. He must avoid being lulled into complacency, by half-baked optimistic plans that are announced by some of his senior ministers from time to time, which are designed to show progress achieved or in the horizon but do not stand up to a logical test. Such plans are usually accompanied by extravagant claims of high employment prospects intended to please him and thus enhance the relevant minister's status. A prime example of this was the ridiculous projection of 500,000 jobs to be created by planting trees. But there are others. On 18 October 2013 an official announcement claimed that the Patriotic Front created 326,480 jobs. It lists some unexceptional, believable numbers under various sectors, but 53 per cent of the total, i.e. 174,052 jobs are attributed to jobs created in arts and entertainment. The Zambia Labour Force Survey 2012 issued by the Central Statistical Office, reports total employment in the 'Arts, Entertainment and Recreation' sector in 2012 as 10,267 (Table 8.5). This means that on the basis of the announced numbers, employment in the sector increased 16-fold, adding 163,785 new jobs within a few months, a highly improbable achievement.

But the most exaggerated claim came from the Ministry of Tourism and Arts, when it announced to the press on 23 September 2013 that tourism would create 300,000 jobs in the two-year period 2013 and 2014. Sata must ask the ministry to substantiate this claim and have the Ministry of Finance and Planning or his own staff vet it (he must consider employing a financial analyst at State House to vet his ministers' boasts). Their immediate response is likely to be: 'It is not possible.' Employment in tourism is not reported separately in the employment statistics. But there is an item called 'Accommodation and Food Service Activities', which is a near enough definition. Under this item the total employment in the industry in 2012 was 62,671 of which 29,574 was in the formal sector and 33,097 in the informal sector. (Zambia Labour Force Survey 2012, Table 8.5, Central Statistical Office.) In other words employment in the sector is expected to increase five-fold over a 24-month period, another statistical impossibility.

But let us analyse this further: the main employer in tourism is the hotel industry. According to my estimates a hotel the size of the Intercontinental in Lusaka (224 rooms) creates some 650 jobs: around 500 directly and, with luck, say another 150 (30 per cent) indirectly as a result of the multiplier effect it will have on other sectors: restaurants, nightclubs, tour operators, travel agents, buses, taxis, curio craftsmen and sellers and so on. In that case, in order to create 300,000 jobs we need to build 461 (say 450) Lusaka-Intercontinental size hotels around the country. But 450 x 200-bedroom hotels will create a capacity of 180,000 bed-nights; multiply this by 365 days a year and you will find that 450 hotels will create an annual capacity of 65.7 million bed-nights. Assume that a visitor will spend six nights per visit (average between business visitors and tourists) and you will come to the result that we would need nearly 11 million visitors every year staying for six nights each to fill them; or, if you assume that only 60 per cent occupancy is needed in order to keep the hotels viable, we would still need 6.5 million visitors per annum to keep them going. Such astronomic figures are simply not attainable. And last but not least, has the ministry given any thought to how much such a project will cost, where investors will come from and whether we have arguments to persuade them that such large investment in our tourism is viable and sustainable? And how long will it take to build the hotels? (Definitely not by the end of 2014; by that time not even the architectural plans would reach the drawing board.) Sata needs to bring his ministers down to earth regarding some of their expectations and the information they put out to him and the public before they and his party lose all credibility. (That financial analyst at State House is needed urgently.)

After the manuscript had been sent to the publishers, Sata announced a new initiative, which, according to the announcement, will generate 'one million jobs within five years' by recreating the industrial Development Corporation of Zambia (INDECO) that I managed in the early years of independence. Not enough is known about the project yet for in-depth analysis, but I thought that I should say a few words about it.

When we inherited INDECO the business sector in Zambia was entirely composed of foreign and settler businesses both of which thoroughly distrusted Zambia, the Zambians and the Zambian government. They had all been strong supporters of the Federation and they consoled themselves for its loss with the slogan 'Independence was for the blacks but the money is still ours'. And in that spirit they employed every trick in the book to keep the Zambians out of the business sector, as I described in detail earlier. Opening the sector to Zambians became INDECO's mission. This was later reinforced with the proclamation of the Mulungushi reforms in April 1968, whose purpose was to open a fast track for the development of Zambian business in a two-pronged attack: (1) regulatory changes and (2) acquisition of control of a number of companies (see Chapter 6). The foundation for development of Zambian enterprise was thus laid and Zambians started making inroads into the business sector. But the political authorities changed their minds. The 'One Party' regime proclaimed a new goal: the creation of a humanist utopia where there would be no private enterprise, thus turning its back on private initiative and destroying any attempt to encourage the Zambian entrepreneurial spirit. It also brought the parastatal sector under direct control of the 'Party and its Government', which, unfortunately, translated into nepotism, opportunism, corruption and inefficiency. Chiluba rightly dismantled it, albeit corruptly, and, unwittingly perhaps, resuscitated the Zambian private enterprise by abolishing the UNIP leadership code and the exchange control regulations. Zambian enterprise has since grown into a major component of our economy (see Chapters 16 and 17).

And this makes the new project INDECO redundant. We needed INDECO when the business sector was entirely in foreign and settler hands and out of bounds for Zambians. Now it is dominated by Zambians and most of the settlers who remained, though they have not yet assimilated, are more ready to fall in line with Zambian aspirations. Any measures we plan to take from now on must be geared towards encouraging the Zambian business to grow and expand in new directions. In the process it will create many new jobs, without the government having to invest new funds that, in any case, it does not have.

It is now time for the government to review the extraordinary privileges its predecessors granted to foreign direct investment in the mid-nineties and the first decade of the twenty-first century and create a new set of incentives that will apply equally to local as well as foreign investment in order to encourage local business to innovate and expand in new directions. And Sata should consider disposing of some of the businesses still in State hands. It seems an established tradition now that government businesses are chronically short of working capital and inefficient as a result. Many Zambian private businesses are capable of taking them over and making them more efficient, but as the process involves the disposal of national assets, the sales must be transparent and aim to fetch the highest price for the nation, be it from a local or a foreign buyer. The process is likely to yield large sums of cash that will go some way towards funding some of Sata's ambitious projects – such as the 'Link' and the 'Pave' Zambia, the new districts, the universities, and so on – that will otherwise languish unfinished for many years to come.

And apart from providing incentives to big business to grow, we must also turn our attention to assisting SMEs and small scale businesses. They can create many jobs in both the cities and the rural areas, where they are most needed. As the reader will see in the chapters that follow, I shall be examining a few ideas that might assist small scale business and small farmers, in both peri-urban and rural areas, to develop.

In short, we must focus on assisting local private enterprise to grow and create jobs and we should refrain from another experiment with a new parastatal sector that in all likelihood will end up corrupt and inefficient like the last one. But let us now assess what we have, what we can get, and what we need most.

Part IV

Taking Stock

30. Copper: Our Boon and Our Bane

Copper has always been the mainstay of the Zambian economy and it has always given its people their biggest headaches. Apart from the sorry tale of neglect and oppression of the people of Zambia during the colonial period, the concept of the Federation of Rhodesia and Nyasaland that caused so much disruption in the progress to independence and set back the country's progress by a whole decade would not have been attempted without the copper mining industry to excite the greed of the white settlers. And it provided the financial backbone which was used to develop a white dominated society that was determined to subjugate the owners of the land for its own long-term benefit, which it intended to drag out for decades if not centuries. Even in its final moments, when the Federation had lost the battle for existence, its prime minister floated the idea of dismembering the country and amalgamating Barotseland and the Copperbelt with Southern Rhodesia and Katanga in order to prolong the white domination of the wealth of the region.

Naturally the employment policies of the mining companies were designed to favour their white employees: generous salaries, lavish accommodation and social facilities, education and training for their children, and, most important of all, job reservation. The African employees remained untrained and unskilled and underpaid: a deliberate policy that kept them on the lowest rungs of the employment ladder, so that the plum jobs would remain reserved for the European mineworkers.

(On at least one occasion, though, the rejection turned out to be for the benefit of the rejected. Valentine Musakanya, who was educated at Kutama (St Francis Xavier College) in Southern Rhodesia and passed matric in solid subjects such as Latin, English, Physics and Chemistry, applied to train as an electrician at Nchanga mine where his father was working. He was rejected because the company did not accept black apprentices at the time. But he went on to read Philosophy and Social Science by correspondence with the University of South Africa and rose to the position of the first secretary to the cabinet and head of the Zambian civil service, after independence.)

279

Even in the late fifties and early sixties, when independence was around
the corner and the number of high schools increased and educated young men
became available for training in skilled jobs, the mines shunned them. They did
the same with university graduates. As late as 1966, when I was the CEO of
INDECO I personally recommended for appointment a young Zambian (who
knowing the discrimination in the industry had the guts to study for a PhD
in metallurgy at the University of Newcastle) to the management of the Anglo
American Corporation. Six months later, completely demoralized, he walked
into my office and told me that he was still on a 'familiarization' course and that
at the time he was driving a crane at Nchanga mine. Another young graduate
friend, with a degree in chemistry from the University of Salisbury, who had
joined the Nchanga mine a couple of years before independence, had been
appointed in the mines' education department, to teach basic English to adult
miners; he left and joined the civil service, immediately after independence.
The mining companies were so beholden to the European Mineworkers Union
that they were afraid to plant Africans as equals among them.

'African advancement' had been a sore point in Northern Rhodesia for
decades prior to independence, and continued to remain so in Zambia. It had
been broached as far back as 1940 by the Forster Commission, which had been
set up to report on disturbances on the Copperbelt, during which 17 African
workers were killed when soldiers of the Northern Rhodesia Regiment opened
fire on them during a strike. In his report Sir John Forster, QC recommended
that:

> The mine Managements should consider with representatives of the
> Government and the Northern Rhodesia Mine Workers Union [established in
> 1936 to represent the interests of the daily paid European workers; the African
> Mineworkers Union was not formed until 1949] to what positions not now
> open to him the African worker should be encouraged to advance.

But, the Northern Rhodesia Government effectively vetoed the idea on the
grounds that white mineworkers who had enlisted for war service had been
promised their jobs back on their return. The government stated:

> During the war, some dilution with African Labour has been accepted, but
> it would be impossible to maintain Africans in posts previously occupied by
> Europeans to the exclusion of previous holders returning from the war.

What this extraordinary statement admits is that African workers, as far back
as the forties, were capable of performing jobs reserved for the Europeans and

they were doing so during the war, when the Europeans were away fighting. Yet, the industrial colour bar that existed before the war was officially reimposed in a new agreement between the European Mineworkers Union and the companies immediately after the war ended. It bluntly provided that no African could be engaged in a job performed by a European. Lawrence Katilungu, the President of the African Mine Workers Union tried very hard to break it in the 1950s with a series of strikes, demanding higher salaries. His theory was that if the African workers started costing them too much the mining companies would have to train them. But he was not successful.

On independence, we thought that, at long last, we would be able to shape the industry and make it respond to the needs of the people it had held back for decades. But neither the mine owners nor the European Mineworkers Union were prepared to give way. This led to a series of strikes and severe unrest on the Copperbelt; so in 1966, President Kaunda appointed a commission of inquiry to look into the problems of the mining industry. It was headed by Roland Brown, Attorney General of Tanzania at the time. The conclusion of the Brown Commission was that there was wide dissatisfaction with the conditions of service laid down by the companies. He proceeded to give the following graphic description:

> The counsel of the mining companies complained in his closing speech, with some justification, that no one had a good word to say for his clients. Many of the witnesses who gave evidence before us, particularly the individuals who came forward on their own initiative, attacked the mining companies in extravagant language, making complaints which were frequently exaggerated and sometimes wholly without foundation. We take this to be an indication, not of a desire to mislead the Commission, but of the depth of feeling aroused. We also think that it shows that dissatisfaction is of a very general kind, dissatisfaction with the shape of things in the industry which the individual worker has difficulty in expressing in any other way than by over-emphatic and sometimes distorted complaints about specific points of grievance. What has led to this sad state of affairs? Essentially it is a matter of disappointed hopes. In 1964, when the African worker felt confident that his right to equal treatment could no longer be challenged he was asked to accept policies which seemed to imply the reverse … The good faith of the companies is not accepted by the workers in the industry. This is regrettable but must be faced. It is a consequence of the deplorable history of African advancement during the Colonial era.

As Brown said, African advancement was not faring any better since independence. Long before the Brown Commission was appointed, the government had established a Zambianization Committee comprising of representatives of various ministries, including the ministries of Labour, Mines and Education as well as the African and European Mineworkers Unions and the mining companies, in order to put direct pressure on the industry for faster progress on African advancement. The companies, together with the European Mineworkers Union, showed willing but were determined not to budge. They engaged various types of consultants from South Africa who produced sophisticated sounding schemes and charts to impress the committee that they were indeed trying but they had to ensure that the safety of the mines and the levels of production were not put in jeopardy. The result of their 'efforts' is highlighted in the following projection they gave to the Brown Commission:

Numbers employed and projected:	31/3/1966	1/1/1970
Unskilled	28,617	26,868
Part Skilled	8,431	9,028
Semi Skilled	—	893
Skilled	—	163
Junior Supervisors	2,976	3,198
Section Bosses	1,636	2,653
Shift Bosses & Foremen	62	578

In other words the mines with tongue in cheek were proposing, over a period of four years from 1966 to 1970, to reduce the number of unskilled workers by just 1,749, and promote 597 to part-skilled positions, 893 to semi-skilled positions, 163 to skilled positions, and increase the junior supervisors by 222, the section bosses by 1,017 and the shift bosses and foremen by 516; an upward movement of just over 5,000 in a labour force of over 40,000. And they tried to persuade the commission and the government that they needed four years to achieve this pitiful target.

The Brown Commission did an admirable job in analysing every aspect of human relations in the industry. It even offered two alternative solutions to the problem of change houses and toilets which, of course, before independence were racially segregated. After independence the segregation basis changed from race to rank but, as very few black miners were being advanced, the perception of racial segregation remained. The commission's suggestion was: either adopt alphabetical separation in the use of the various facilities, or use salary scales as the guide.

Is it any wonder that the government lost patience with them and in 1969 sought controlling interest? I covered the history of the acquisition of 51 per cent of the Anglo American and Amax owned mines in great detail earlier. I was the protagonist in those negotiations and any comment I make will be perceived as biased, but it is a subject I keep thinking about and I am satisfied in my own mind that the deals achieved were the best for the long-term interest of the nation. They would have led to an accelerated Zambianization of the mines at both the operational and managerial levels that in the final analysis meant that Zambians would have acquired sufficient in-depth knowledge of the industry not only to run the mining operations efficiently, but also to handle its finances, in other words to attain complete control. The 49 per cent foreign shareholders of the time who had fought fiercely for the continuation of the Federation and lost would have adjusted to the new circumstances after they lost the latest battle for control of the mining companies and for the continuation of white superiority. The Zambian government control and joint management solution would have served the best interests of the nation as well as those of the then owners, which is the essence of desirable and successful foreign investment. In modern parlance: to operate in the best interest of all stakeholders. But this was not to be. Within a short four-year period the mindless abrogation of the agreements followed in August 1973. It burdened the National Treasury with a huge outflow of $230 million partly paid from the national reserves and the balance of some $125 million through a short-term borrowing at the exorbitant interest rate of 13 per cent, in order to buy the outstanding acquisition bonds (ZIMCO bonds) whose market value at the time was $110 million and enrich a British wheeler-dealer and his Zambian accomplices to the tune of some $100 million plus.

But worse followed: political control of the industry which coupled with the collapse of the commodity market, a consequence of the oil price explosion of the period, led to the industry's terminal decline. I must, though, again, highlight one positive achievement of that period: the very large investment in education and training of Zambians. While the management of the industry was dominated by UNIP (the only political party allowed at the time) and some of its puppets a large investment was made in educating young Zambians locally and abroad. The final result was that a Zambian workforce emerged with the skills of running the operations as efficiently as in any other country, assuming they received the necessary inputs, which unfortunately they were not able to get because political demands had priority over the foreign exchange ZCCM generated. (I have already covered the plunder and the demise of the industry by the Chiluba regime and its 'sale' to new unknown operators at giveaway prices under pressure from the foreign donors and the international financial institutions.)

These gyrations disrupted the stability and the cohesion of the industry as it had developed during the period between the government's acquisition of 51 per cent and the abrogation of the agreements: the 49 per cent owner-managers and the mineworkers may have been adversarial but they were familiar with each other. They had a good measure of each other's breaking point and they would not cross that line, which made for industrial stability. If the arrangement had continued, Zambians would have taken charge not only of the operations but of central management and they would have ended up running the industry. (The career of Anderson Mazoka at the highest echelons of the Zambian Anglo American is indicative of what could have happened with many other senior Zambians if changes to the agreements came about through negotiations instead of the abrupt cancellation divined by Tiny Rowland and his cohorts.) After the abrogation, the balance tipped in favour of the mineworkers. They were politically powerful and usually got their way, the management always yielding to their demands in 'the interest of industrial peace'. With the privatization industrial relations moved back to square one. The new owners, with only a couple of exceptions, are novices in mining and they are novices in the country. They do not know our capabilities and they are more comfortable with their own people. They import workers for jobs that have been done by Zambians for three or four decades. Inexplicably the government seems to be content to allow them to do so. I was shocked when I heard from government officials that they issue work permits to foreign bricklayers because their output is higher than what their employers can get from Zambian bricklayers.

If they had checked they would have found that the greater productivity of some of the foreign workers is due to ten-hour working days, which is against the Zambian labour laws that their employers ignore, like they ignore our tax laws and many others. And the bureaucrats do not seem to realize that the 'cost advantage' of foreign workers to their employers is not our concern. Our concern is to secure jobs for our people. It is now a common sight in Zambia to see foreign workers driving tipper trucks, graders, and road rollers, while the Zambian workers are shovelling dirt on the side like they did in the fifties, a phenomenon we fought against and eradicated with independence. And some of these foreign workers instead of returning back to their country at the end of their contract manage to get residence permits and settle permanently. Some even set up stalls in the markets in competition to our marketeers.

The government must take this problem seriously and enforce much stricter rules regarding employment of foreigners. In the course of my research I found to my horror that we still have a government Zambianization committee. It is chaired by the Deputy Minister of Labour who can call a wide variety of organizations to appoint representatives. And, to my surprise, from discussions with various bodies, some accept it as a wonderful idea. The reader will remember the tricks the then mining companies and other foreign employers played in order to avoid Zambianization; I have no doubt that the current ones do just the same. We had to put up with it 45 years ago but we have come a long way since, and we must now stop 'pussyfooting' with Zambianization committees over this matter. It is time to put our foot down and say no to foreigners coming to take jobs from Zambians. And the current productivity of our workers should not be a factor in this regard. Productivity is a factor of discipline and that is the responsibility and the prerogative of the employer to enforce. And it is also a factor of skills and if some workers' skills need improving it is in the interest of the employer to do so with training, which will give him immediate benefits and at the same time help enhance our labour standards.

In short, it is time to declare that certain jobs are reserved for our citizens and people born in Zambia, and under no circumstances should investors be allowed to import foreigners to perform them. And that should not be negotiable and the unions should be encouraged to report any contraventions they come across, not to Zambianization committees but to the immigration authorities and the labour offices who should be directed to take immediate action to stop it.

But this is not the only sin of the new mining companies and the various contractors. In the international commodity market Zambia has developed a reputation of being a very high cost producer of copper. Based on my knowledge of the industry and the still relatively high grades of our ores, I had difficulty in swallowing this accusation, but in the course of my research I have found the reason. Some mining companies inflate their production costs in order to avoid paying taxes. In previous chapters I gave some examples of this phenomenon, highlighted by international NGOs and others and they all reveal practices aimed at Zambian tax evasion. The two mining groups most frequently associated with criticism, both in the Zambian press and the international investigative NGOs, are Konkola and Mopani. They both seem to be publicity shy, except when they distribute 'lollipops' to communities, to football clubs and charities.

Despite the privileges and tax advantages they have secured, some new mining groups are hell-bent on siphoning huge sums out of Zambia, using a variety of methods. In 2009, the Zambia Revenue Authority commissioned Grant Thornton, an international accounting group, and ECON Poyry, a Norwegian consulting and engineering group to do a 'pilot audit of the operational costs, revenues, transfer pricing, employee expenses, and overheads' of Mopani, one of the major mining companies on the Copperbelt and a subsidiary of the Swiss commodity trader, Glencore. The investigating team came to the conclusion that the reported numbers relating to all the above items are in doubt and highlighted the following:

- At least $50 million of the reported labour costs for 2007 was unexplainable.
- Fuel costs had doubled between the period 2005 and 2007, even after the increase in production had been accounted for.
- Mining costs had increased extravagantly and the difference was outside the boundaries of the cost analysis. The same applied to the insurance, security and safety, admin costs and spares.
- Residual costs increased by $205 million from 2005 to 2007, which was attributed to the increase of scrap metal amounting to $266 million. The audit team also reported that it was unable to match the general ledger data with the trial balance data and offered the hypothesis of 'high variance costs the cause of which was not easily discernible!'

The most disturbing finding of the team was a significant problem of pricing, caused by long-term contracts with the parent company. It also found that the hedging pattern was not normal and surmised that this was done deliberately in order to move taxable revenue out of the country, a process that it explained as follows:

> A company that only wants to move revenue out of a country will want to 'hedge or enter into a long-term contract at the most favourable LOW point; such a hedge is usually established at the bottom of the cycle. By doing it this way, a company that wants to move revenues out of tax jurisdiction makes sure that it makes losses both when prices are rising and when they are coming down ...'
> [As the transaction is placed with the parent company, which makes the true hedging, the method gives the opportunity to the parent to make the profit while the Zambian company is making a loss and thus reduces its Zambian tax liability.]

Apart from the hedges an even more worrying aspect is the scrap inventory, which was carried in the company's books at $266 million. I made a quick calculation and came to the conclusion that this represented some 40,000 tons of copper, a quantity unlikely to have ever been available in Zambia, which raises a number of questions: the scrap was obviously bought outside Zambia; it would not have been shipped to Zambia, because it would not make sense as there is no local market for it. The purpose of buying it is difficult to understand, because to the best of my knowledge no customer will accept scrap in substitution for primary copper, if for some reason the company had a production shortfall. The existence of such a huge quantity of scrap raises many questions: How did the company's auditors in Zambia verify it? How did they verify the purchase cost? Did the transactions originate from the company in Zambia or its parent? If the latter, did the local auditors accept certification from the parent or from independent third parties? Did they check foreign warehouse receipts? And last but not least did they obtain a satisfactory explanation from the company that such transaction was necessary in the ordinary course of business?

The investigating team highlighted that Mopani is allowed to carry forward losses up to ten years and that at 2008 it was still carrying forward a $72 million loss assessed in 2000. It also reported that the company is allowed to write off 100 per cent of expenditure on mining, prospecting and exploration which for the two years 2007 and 2008 amounted to US$260 million and US$371 million respectively bringing the total accumulated tax losses to US$703 million.

Mopani paid no income tax in the six-year period 2006 to 2011 inclusive, a fact that has not been denied by the company. It only paid royalties which according to my research amounted to $85.28 million, of which $2.6 million was paid in 2006 and $28.5 million in 2011. (The figures I received from the company directly show no significant difference: it reported its total royalties for the period as $96.2 million, with the payment for 2006 being $3 million and $23.1 million for 2011. The significance of the comparison of the 2006 and the 2011 payments? The 2006 to 2010 payments were at the derisory rate of 0.06 per cent of roughly the cost of production, in force during the Mwanawasa and Banda administrations; in 2011 the Sata administration increased the rate to 3 per cent and in 2012 to 6 per cent.)

Mopani's chairman at a press briefing in April 2013 contended that during the six-year period 2007 to 2012, the company paid to the government $420 million in taxes. (According to the information I received from the company it paid $412.8 for the period 2005 to 2011.) The chairman did not give a breakdown for the $420 million and the journalists did not ask any questions. (The company did not give a breakdown of the 412.8 million it reported to me, either.) But the contention that the payments constitute company taxes must be dismissed. It is a ploy invented in order to exaggerate the contribution of the mining industry to the economy of Zambia and impress the Zambian public. Konkola adopted the same method. The figures include every bit of money mining companies pay to government or other national bodies; they include the 'Pay As You Earn' tax they deduct from their employees' wage packet every month, which, as everybody knows, represents their employees' tax and not their own; import duties, VAT, licence fees, vehicle registration fees, property rates paid to municipalities, etc., none of which comes under the category of company tax. And the fact that they are reporting it as company tax is another indication that they are trying to hide the fact that in reality they pay very little or no income tax. I stand by my statement that for the period 2006 to 2011 (probably the same six-year period that the chairman was talking about) Mopani paid either $85 million or $96 million in mineral royalties only, and no income tax.

Such antics not only confirm the reports that now surface frequently that some Zambian mining companies are misreporting their earnings in order to avoid taxes, but they also indicate that their reported production costs are exaggerated. Naturally I wanted to get Mopani's side on these issues and its response to the Grant Thornton/ECON report for the purpose of this book. I contacted the Zambian chairman by phone and followed up with an email setting out my questions:

> Thank you for your prompt response to my telephone call. As I explained, I am in the final stages of writing the above book and would like to discuss with you a number of issues pertaining to Mopani. I give below a typical questionnaire I go through with the mining companies:
>
> 1. Please confirm (or correct) that Mopani Copper Mines Ltd. combines the old Mufulira and Nkana mines. It is majority (73.1%) owned by Glencore International AG. Its cost was $20 million cash and $23 million in deferred payments, a commitment of $159 million new investment and an additional 'conditional commitment' of $200 million. [Source: *Selling the Family Silver*]
> 2. Have the commitment and the additional commitment taken place, when and how much? Can you supply information on the amounts invested since acquisition?
> 3. Who owns the balance of the share capital?
> 4. Was Mopani created as a new company after acquisition of Mufulira and Nkana? If not what was its name before and what was it engaged in?
> 5. What were the income tax and mineral tax rates at acquisition and what are they now?
> 6. Can you supply information on the amounts, if any, Mopani paid to the Zambian Revenue Authority in income tax and mineral royalties? Please do not include VAT and payroll taxes.

Then I repeated the questions I asked Konkola about employment criteria and statistics, relations with the mineworkers union and the government Zambianization committee. I asked about the accumulated tax loss and current and projected production levels and concluded:

> I take it that you are aware of the Grant Thornton/Norwegian report. Do you have any comments? If not can you please explain the reference to US $266 million in scrap copper: origin, quantity and purpose. The report is very critical

of your hedging policies. Can you make a comment? The National statistics of 2010 show Switzerland as the number one export market for Zambia, taking 51% of our exports. Can you make a comment?

I received the following reply: 'We will respond to your questionnaire as soon as we can. I would suggest that we meet when our response is complete.' I heard nothing and on 20 April 2013, I sent the following email: 'Are you going to be in Lusaka next week, and if so can we meet?' I received a reply on 22 May apologizing for the delay and explaining that Glencore's PR Department had been busy following the recent merger with Xstrata. I responded that I needed a reply by the middle of June as at that time I had to deliver the first manuscript to the publishers. On 6 June 2013, I received a large package consisting of a 114-page blurb on Glencore and a memorandum to the European Investment Bank (EIB) in response to the Grant Thornton/ECON report, which emphasizes the fact that the ZRA characterized it as 'confidential, preliminary and an incomplete draft'. The response does not answer the specific questions I posed and completely ignores the issue of the hedges and the scrap inventory, the most important issues in my email. In fairness I include Mopani's report to EIB in its entirety as Appendix VII for the interested reader.

In addition the package included an eight-page document with a two-page addendum under the title 'Written evidence submitted by Glencore International Plc (April 2012)'. It does not specify where it was submitted. It provides some general information about Glencore and it substantially copies the Mopani document in Appendix VII. It reports that since Mopani has been taken over it paid $425.1 million in taxes, royalties, and 'other dues to Government' which it defines as 'Pay As You Earn (PAYE), Mineral royalties and Import, Customs and Excise Duty. Mopani also pays Import VAT and Reverse VAT as well as property taxes on a monthly basis.'

As the reader will see later, the 'Africa Progress Panel' (APP), an organization headed by Kofi Annan, the former secretary general of the United Nations, in its report on the same subject highlighted the fact that 'the total tax paid by the Zambian mineworkers is higher than the tax paid by the companies they work for' (*Financial Times*, 10 May 2013). Yet the government of Zambia allows Mopani and Konkola to classify PAYE payments as company payments when in addition to Annan, everybody knows that they represent employees' income tax. The same applies to property rates which are paid to the town councils and not to government. Either the Minister of Finance or the Minister of Mines, or both should put their foot down and stop the mining companies from misleading the public. They can order that PAYE payments must be reported by their proper name: employees' income tax payments or not at all.

And there is another indication that something is really wrong. According to the National Export Statistics of 2010 (the latest available) Switzerland is Zambia's number one export market receiving 51 per cent of our exports. Switzerland has no copper manufacturing industry. The large percentage of our exports that are reported as going to Switzerland would indicate that substantial quantities of Zambian copper are first sold to companies in Switzerland before reaching their final destination, which tends to confirm the claims of underpricing that the international investigations reported. It is of course common knowledge that Mopani is a subsidiary of Glencore, which is based in Zug, but Konkola's Director of Strategy and Business Development did say during our interview that Konkola also sells part of its production to the Lucerne-based Trafigura, another major international oil and minerals trader. Trafigura's name has in the past been connected with international scandals such as oil for Iraq and dumping of toxic waste in Cote d'Ivoire; it has also been banned from doing business in Malta. In 2012 the Zambian press reported that some ministers were under investigation over a contract for the supply of oil to the government-owned Zambian oil refinery. Both Glencore and Trafigura are offshoots of Marc Rich (née Marcell David Reich), the Israeli–American commodities trader who was indicted by the United States on federal charges for tax evasion, and illegal oil deals with Iran during the hostage crisis. He was living in Switzerland and after the indictment did not return to the United States even after he received a presidential pardon from Bill Clinton in 2001. China with huge copper manufacturing capacity comes a distant second on Zambia's export league taking 20.2 per cent of our exports (Selected Social Economic Indicators 2010, Central Statistical Office).

In the meantime reports about the plunder of Africa by international investors, particularly mining companies, have become fashionable and new ones are constantly surfacing. A more recent one by the Washington-based group Global Financial Integrity (GFI) estimates that in the ten-year period between 2000 and 2010 Zambia lost $8.8 billion to crime, corruption, and tax evasion. According to the report issued by GFI, Dev Kar – an economist and co-author of the report – attributes the biggest part of the loss, which is equivalent to 50 per cent of Zambia's GDP to multinational copper mining operators whom he accused of robbing the country of the opportunity to advance. 'The money could have been used to build hospitals and schools and lift the economy out of poverty,' he said. Though I do not doubt that African countries and particularly Zambia lose a lot of money to crime, corruption, and tax evasion, I have difficulty in accepting the accuracy of such specific assessments.

His co-author, Sarah Freitas, reported another very specific estimate of $4.9 billion of Zambia's lost funds that 'could be traced to trade "misinvoicing", part of which arises from "importers, pretending to pay more to foreign companies than they actually do". Freitas is wrong in this conclusion. Over-invoicing had been common in Zambia – and may still be in countries where exchange control regulations exist – and the official exchange rate is grossly overvalued, while the market rate is a small fraction of the official rate. At that time, over-invoicing was taking place in order to convert the Kwacha into hard currency, mainly dollars. But since Zambia abolished the exchange control regulations in the early nineties, it stopped, because it is no longer necessary and it costs too much. Overpricing carries with it the burden of higher import duty because the duty is levied on the over-invoiced price. The duty averages some 25 per cent of the landed cost and as money can now be transferred freely, I cannot see why anybody would want to pay a 25 per cent premium in order to convert his Kwacha. Exchange control evasion is, therefore, no longer a factor and tax evasion has remained the only reason for siphoning funds out of the country. This narrows the range of evaders to exporters, most prominent amongst them the mining groups; they make huge profits, they have foreign parents and have the incentive and the capability to pursue it through under-invoicing exports not over-invoicing imports. Freitas concluded: 'Zambia's GDP was US $ 19.3 billion in 2011. Its per capita GDP was US $ 1,413. Its government collected a total of US $ 4.3 billion in revenue. It can't afford to be haemorrhaging illicit capital in such staggering amounts.' Bearing in mind Freitas's uninformed comments about over-invoicing, some of these reports should be taken with a pinch of salt.

But a more reliable and interested observer studied this matter too. According to the *Financial Times* of 10 May 2013 Kofi Annan's Africa Progress Panel reported that 'transfer pricing [the transactions made by multinational companies and their subsidiaries] costs Africa billions of dollars annually and many governments have given excessive tax concessions in order to attract foreign investment'. As an example it highlights the fact that the total tax paid by the Zambian mineworkers is higher than the tax paid by the companies they work for. And it highlights that the Congo lost $1.386 billion over the two-year period 2010 to 2012, as a result of undervaluation of state assets (of which $725 million was attributed to the Eurasian Natural Resources Corporation, the erstwhile owners of Luanshya mine I reported on earlier).

Hoping to introduce some measure of scrutiny, APP called for G8 and G20 countries to require full public disclosure of the beneficial ownership of companies bidding for mining concessions or face penalties; and for Canada, China, and Australia to support transparency standards in line with those recently adopted by the USA and the EU. Annan told the *Financial Times*: 'we firmly believe that Africa could dramatically improve the lives of its people if they can ensure that they get a fair share of the revenues generated by the extractive industries and use the revenues to invest in its people, in education, in health, in infrastructure and other things'.

The international institutions heaped praise on both the Chiluba and Mwanawasa administrations for their successes in attracting foreign investment. But does the word 'attract' apply to the privatization of the mining sector in Zambia? We were giving the mines away and in the process many potential takers came sniffing. And we endowed the lucky ones who were selected with incentives and privileges that sacrificed the country's income for a couple of decades. The winners of the Zambian mining bonanza do not seem to have the slightest appreciation of our generosity but proceed to use every trick in the book to minimize their tax liability to the country, as it is detailed above.

We have enough examples of tax evasion to conclude that there is plenty of income we can generate by plugging the loopholes in the reporting of the mining industry. And we can do it on our own, though we must understand that we shall encounter strong reaction from the companies and a vigorous public relations campaign against the exercise. In order to silence them and preclude accusations of persecution that will inevitably be made, my view would be to engage international consultants to carry it out. The Grant Thornton/Econ of Norway 'pilot' report revealed a large number of potential leakages, not all of which have been looked into thoroughly and in sufficient depth to deliver incontestable figures that would support legal action. But an official Ministry of Mines/ZRA combined mandate carried out through international consultants can produce the figures on which tax assessments can be based and penalties can be imposed if irregular practices are revealed. ZRA and the Ministry of Mines have very wide powers of inspection and investigation if my memory serves me right (I was permanent secretary of that ministry in the late sixties, and I was chairman of both Nchanga Consolidated Copper Mines and Roan Consolidated Mines in 1970). But if it does not, new legislation should be enacted urgently to create them.

We could and we should have got more income from the existing mines during the last few years when the market was buoyant. The Mwanawasa administration made an attempt, albeit a misguided one, but the Banda administration negated it due to the timidity of its Minister of Finance. In 2013 the commodity markets stalled and copper was hovering at around $7,000 a ton, a price not to be sneered at, but way below its peak of $10,000. Let us hope that it will revive soon – though the indications in 2014 look negative – but the long-term solution to our over-reliance on copper must be the diversification of our economy. The subject comes up regularly and is immediately followed by suggestions to increase the value of our copper exports by converting a proportion into products such as cable, sheets, etc. It sounds a good idea but we should not rely on it. Copper exported in any form other than raw material would encounter heavy transportation costs, and import tariffs. And starting up cable factories requires huge capital investments and expertise. Such factories exist in abundance in the developed world and China, the major consumers of copper and other primary materials. As a rule manufacture takes place where the demand is and it is unrealistic to expect cable manufacturers to translocate to Zambia. It is more economic and efficient for them to expand or diversify from their existing base, rather than start from scratch in a landlocked country, some 2,000 miles from major ports and many more thousands from the markets. In any case, we have had a cable factory in Zambia, ZAMEFA, which has been operating since the late sixties supplying the regional market, which I understand is in the region of 10,000 tons per annum, an infinitesimal proportion of our total production of copper.

Adding value to copper does not diversify the economy of course. We have to look to the other sectors for diversification with the full knowledge that we are unlikely to create a copper equivalent; and we are not going to be able to generate huge amounts in export earnings. But we can raise the standards of living of our people through increased local production and conserve foreign exchange through import substitution. And the resulting prosperity will attract investment in the manufacture of consumer products that cater for the needs of the local market, as well as that of our nearest neighbours. And we can make a start by banning salaula (second-hand clothing), which killed our garment industry that was employing many tens of thousands of workers.

But agriculture must remain our priority.

31. FARMERS AND CHARCOAL BURNERS AND MARKETEERS

President Sata has been dangling land to investors in every country he visited since his inauguration. He offered it to the Japanese and to the Koreans and to the Chinese and to some European countries too. I hope they do not take him up on it. If we learned nothing from Zimbabwe next door, we should at least remember the land issue and try not to bequeath a similar problem to our grandchildren. Sure, we have plenty of land to spare at the moment. (If we distributed the land of our country to every man, woman and child they would get nearly 15 acres of arable land each. Our Nigerian and Malawian friends would only get one and a half acres each and some of that may be sand in a desert or water in Lake Malawi.) But our grandchildren will not have as much land to spare, as we do now, because their numbers will have grown. Maybe we are not good farmers now and very few of us have the money to farm except at subsistence level. But our grandchildren can be good commercial farmers if we start doing something serious about it now.

President Sata and everybody in public life should bear in mind the country's current employment picture:

> Total Employment: 5,499,673 of which only 847,420 (15.4 per cent) is in the formal sector, while 4,652,253 (84.6 per cent) is in the informal sector.
>
> Total Employment in Agriculture: 2,872,331 of which 87,420 (3 per cent) in the formal sector and 2,784,911 (97 per cent) in the informal sector.
>
> (Source: 2012 Zambia Labour Force Survey, Table 8.5, Central Statistical Office)

In other words, agriculture is the main activity of our people and represents 52.2 per cent of total employment, formal and informal. More importantly, only 3 per cent of those employed in agriculture are employed in the formal sector, while 97 per cent, an overwhelming majority of our people are in the informal sector, that is peasant farmers. It is idle therefore to expect to occupy our unemployed in the formal sector. The easier solution is to expand employment in the informal sector, which already employs 84.6 per cent of our people.

Earlier on I praised President Sata for making the tough decision of withdrawing the subsidies on maize. That decision needed greater courage from him than any other political leader, because the withdrawal of the mealie meal subsidy will affect the main body of his political support: the politically powerful urban workers. But, as the above figures show, the peasants, who have lower political clout, are in the majority. They are much poorer and we must make every effort to help them get out of poverty.

We can start by distributing land to them instead of looking for foreigners to buy it. After the Zimbabwe debacle, we must always have at the back of our mind that if foreigners get it now they may decide to cling to it, even after their lease expires, and this will cause friction in the future. Instead of selling land, Sata should embark on a system of nationwide distribution of land to the peasants along the lines of Kanakantapa and Kasenga, near where I live, outside Lusaka. These two 'resettlement' schemes started as part of the 'Back to the Land' Kaunda initiative in the seventies and eighties. They have been around long enough to show results; and I have been in the area since it began so I can see the difference land makes to the life of people. The farmers around me are not rich. But they work very hard and they make a living. They feed their families and they send their children to school and they are able to cover secondary school costs, away from our area where we only have basic schools. Kasenga and Kanakantapa and the many other similar settlements around the big cities and towns of Zambia began slowly but they have worked and they are working. Lusaka is within reach for the vegetables and potatoes and onions and sweet potatoes and chicken and goats that people produce; also for the beef and milk, which they mostly sell directly to consumers, which makes it beneficial to both sides: the farmers make more money and the consumers save because the prices are lower than they are in shops. But the mainstay of peasant agriculture is maize and the acreage is increasing every year.

The farmers on the perimeter of major cities could expand and diversify if they had access to tools that are more productive than the hoe and the bucket and the sweat of their brow. Walking tractors with their various attachments and trailers, and pumps and small irrigation units would enhance the productivity of rural agriculture. And animal drawn implements would be even more efficient. But in order to move to the next phase of development, agriculture needs financial attention.

There are plenty of financial institutions in the country, big and small; but the small commercial banks are focusing on the same commercial and industrial sector that the big banks cover. If they turn their attention to the small farmers, they will make more money. They can charge higher rates, which will make them more profitable even after the inevitable higher debt delinquency they will face. But they can mitigate that risk too if they team up with implement suppliers. And if Sata does proceed with land distribution to the peasants, he will make the banks more comfortable and more enterprising because they can lend on the security of the land. All these factors are not going to emerge overnight. Progress will be slow, but let us make a start with the land distribution.

I know that in the rural areas, people have access to land under the traditional system. But what I am advocating is giving them individual title, so that they know that the land they cultivate now belongs to them and it will be there for their children and their grandchildren; and as they develop it they can use the title as security to borrow money for further development.

In the meantime the Input Support Programme needs rethinking. It was based on import parity equivalence and it is too expensive. We must admit that it has achieved its purpose: we are self-sufficient in food now, but we produce surpluses which are too expensive and we cannot afford. We must wean our farmers away from dependence on it but we must be very careful not to disrupt the system abruptly and end up having to import food again. Let us remind ourselves of our agricultural goals: we must cover our needs and adequate safety margins; and if we have surpluses for export, they must have been produced at a cost that will allow us to generate some profit when we export them to neighbouring countries such as D R Congo. But, equally importantly, our production should be accomplished by our peasant farmers, who have no way of securing pre-planting finance. Until we give them title to their land and train the financial institutions to finance them this is a task that the government has to perform. It has to organize the financing of the system and it has to reconcile itself to the fact that it may lose some money in the process. The Food Reserve Agency can be empowered to do the financing, with the mandate that it must deduct the cost from the value of the harvest it will receive, in the full knowledge that initially bad debts may turn out to be heavy. When the farmers have title to land, the financial institutions can be prevailed upon to take over the task. It will be a mammoth task, but Sata will be remembered as the greatest reformer in Zambia if he introduces it.

But we also need to train our farmers to achieve higher yields and introduce better farming practices. Extension services should be revamped and the extension officers should be equipped for greater mobility, by the provision of bicycles and motorcycles at village and district levels, and larger vehicles at provincial level. And their mandate must be to transition the peasants from some of the traditional methods to more sophisticated techniques. And also guide them towards additional crops that are needed locally. (The beer consumption in Zambia, for example, is very high and the breweries have to import large quantities of malt from outside. Sorghum and millet can be used for this purpose and they have both been peasant crops for generations.) And groundnuts make another valuable crop; they used to be exported successfully in the past. With encouragement it can be done again. Cotton, another successful peasant crop, is doing well and its international marketing appears to be in capable hands.

***

Is charcoal agriculture? It is forestry, of course, but we must turn it into peasant agriculture in order to save the trees and in order to save the industry; and I mean: the charcoal burning industry. We are all self-righteously up in arms at the destruction of our forests by those we call 'vandals' who cut the trees in order to make charcoal. But let us look at the facts: charcoal and firewood are still the main fuels for the township people who comprise more than half of the urban population. And it is the only fuel for the peasants and the rural towns. According to the 2010 statistics, 51 per cent of urban households use charcoal for cooking and 6 per cent use firewood, while 14 per cent of rural households use charcoal and 84 per cent use firewood (Selected Social Economic Indicators 2010, Table 6.3, Central Statistical Office).

How are we going replace that? With fancy tin stoves that use grass that European manufacturers improvise in order to get credits against their factories' carbon emissions? And let us remember that charcoal burning is a major industry. Many hundreds of thousands of people are making a living out of it: the woodcutters who cut the trees and turn them into firewood; the charcoal burners who make the kilns and turn the firewood into charcoal; the transporters who carry the charcoal to town either in rickety trucks or on bicycles; and the market vendors who sell it. Do we want to throw all these people out of their jobs? It hurts to see the destruction of the forest. But without charcoal three quarters of the population will not be able to cook or keep warm during the winter. And I can see no alternative fuel that will be acceptable to the populace and at the same time provide the employment levels that charcoal does. The industry has to be preserved and the forests have to be protected. There are solutions and we must find them. And they must be Zambian solutions: we must turn charcoal burning into peasant agriculture that will grow its own trees.

We need fast growing trees; not as industrial plantations (it would be a crime to clear additional areas of forest for this purpose), but in order to distribute them to the peasants to plant around villages to replace the trees they have already cut down. Early in 2013 the government announced a tree planting campaign and boasted that it will create half a million jobs! And many people laughed and I laughed with them (do jobs grow on trees?). But if we take the tree planting seriously and source fast growing species and make nurseries in every district we may not create half a million new jobs but we shall certainly save more than that by saving the charcoal industry of our country. And the peasants will benefit, because they will be growing the trees and they will be selling them to the charcoal burners when they are mature. Or turning them into charcoal themselves.

***

If we think hard and seriously we can find home grown solutions to most of our problems. And a home grown solution is an African tradition. African societies have always been taking care of themselves with the means available to them within their own norms. We have to build on what is already functioning and as the base broadens the people will find their own ways to expand it in new directions. This is what I believe happened in Nigeria, where in the seventies this huge nation of traders operated from markets and sidewalks and tiny shops. From that base, Nigeria has now developed into the most sophisticated entrepreneurial nation in Africa. So, which way forward for Zambia? Local enterprise has made tremendous strides since independence. There is a base and we can build on it. But let us first review the base.

In the early years of independence, we thought that programmes aimed at promoting local enterprise must have two arms, one rural and one urban. But now the make-up of the country is uniform, and any variations are only a matter of scale. The centres of the major cities have all the signs of urban prosperity: shopping malls, fast food shops, shiny new automobiles, chic ladies, and smart-suited gentlemen, going about their daily business. The shopping malls were initially dominated by South African distribution chains, but many Zambian-owned boutiques have now also moved in. They are serving the middle classes, probably between 20 and 30 per cent of the urban population.

But the overwhelming majority of the people live in the townships and the ever increasing shanty towns where unemployment is high. Many trek to town every day in search of work and they do anything to earn their daily bread. Street vending is a convenient occupation and many turn into 'mishanga boys' (a term coined in the early eighties referring mainly to vendors who were selling cigarettes by the 'stick' instead of full packets but used generally for all those involved in what was called 'black market' trade during the time the country was experiencing shortages of essential commodities) offering food and vegetables and fruit but also items such as shoes and clothes and toys and belts and sunglasses and SIM cards and mobile telephone chargers, at every set of traffic lights. The merchandise is obviously not theirs (they would not have the funds to buy it; it probably belongs to a shopkeeper and their remuneration will be a commission on what they sell). It is a tough life but at least they can make a plate of food at the end of the day; the alternative would be hunger. Others make a stall at any convenient street corner or sidewalk. They join the corps of marketeers, some of whom are able to pay for their wares. There are established markets in every city of Zambia, but as unemployment ballooned so too did the number of vendors, now spread wherever they can find space and customers.

They sell everything: building materials, doors and windows, clay bricks and concrete blocks, sand and stone and cement and furniture and beds and desks, and chairs and tables and plumbing and electrical materials and electronic goods, and motor spares and many others. They duplicate the range that is available in the shops and the industrial areas at very much lower cost and greater accessibility. As there is a market in every neighbourhood, customers do not need to travel to get service and they usually carry their own baskets and bottles. They save on transport and they save on packaging and they can buy smaller quantities than those pre-packed and sold in shops, which makes it more affordable: a family can buy cooking oil in a Coca-Cola bottle, enough for the evening meal, if that is all it can afford. As most of the merchandise sold at the markets is locally produced, the markets support large numbers of people:

- Small farmers within accessible distance from the main towns produce and also transport their vegetables, potatoes, onions, chicken etc. on bicycles or on ancient vehicles that only the ingenuity of African poverty can keep on the roads (and a token of appreciation to the traffic officer, who will overlook its condition and the absence of a 'certificate of fitness').
- Technicians and artisans who make construction goods and furniture and who depend on the marketeers for their distribution.
- Women and children who compete with industrial quarries breaking stones to different sizes with hammers.
- Jobbers and small contractors and their labour force who build houses and fences and small buildings and carry out maintenance and repairs in the townships as well as the main towns. Some of these contractors are engineering graduates from the University of Zambia with experience in the construction industry. Because they have no capital they undertake contracts on a labour only basis and help the client with the procurement of materials. They produce quality work at a fraction of a building contractor's cost.

I hope I put across to the reader that the markets are major economic engines that provide gainful occupation to many people who would otherwise have difficulty in making a living. And I hope the reader understands that their spreading all over town is market driven and provides a useful service, and no one should feel that their existence demeans us, or our towns or our country. But where the marketeers take over whole streets the municipalities have to intervene and bring about order; there are areas where sidewalk vendors block the entrances of shops and destroy their business. The shopkeepers have to be protected not only by the municipalities making sure that their entrances remain free but also by providing sanitation services: regular refuse removal is sorely needed. The municipalities have to find ways to finance the sanitation services they need to provide. For this they have to be pragmatic. They have to forget licensing and just levy a small fee (daily or weekly) for the space a vendor occupies. The fee may act as a catalyst to reducing the large numbers of vendors, in addition to financing the sanitation service.

Another way of reducing the overcrowding of vendors in the streets is by the government banning the importation of salaula. They are an eyesore and they take the biggest space. But more damagingly they destroyed the textile and clothing industries of the country and they caused the loss of tens of thousands of jobs. There are many people who make a living out of selling salaula. But without salaula we can generate many more jobs in textile mills and factories making new clothes, which will be selling in regular shops through shop salesmen. The end result will be that the total employment numbers will increase.

And if we are really serious about assisting the poorer people in our midst, we must find ways of assisting the small businesses in raising finance. I am not about to advocate any form of direct government financial assistance, because we know from experience (ZANACO under government control, Citizens Economic Empowerment, DBZ of old) that government financial institutions succumb to political pressures and end up with uncollectable loans. But we can incentivize the existing banks and other financial institutions to carry out the task.

Many readers may be smiling with incredulity. But it can be done. Our banking industry is obscenely profitable, especially our major banks. It must be persuaded to service not only the small and medium enterprises but also the very small ones; and not just the businessmen, but the farmers too. They can be assisted by the Bank of Zambia to do so, by being allowed somewhat higher lending margins on certain types of business, and by the release of a part of their non-remunerated deposits with the Bank of Zambia against certain types of loans. And what do we expect from them? To tailor the right type of service their small customers need. To do that they must listen: to the transporter who wants to buy a minibus, a coach or a tipper truck; to the furniture maker who wants to buy machinery to improve the quality of his products; to the contractor who wants to buy cement mixers, and other construction machinery or a small quarry, or loading equipment; to the information technology expert who wants to run a computer bureau or sell computers, mobile telephones, software and other electronic goods; to the motor mechanic who repairs vehicles in his backyard and wants equipment for a workshop; and to traders of every kind, from produce buyers to importers of mining and engineering supplies; and to the farmers whose needs I detailed earlier.

Before I close this subject let me warn against a possible development. Major banks may band together and offer to set up a jointly held institution for this purpose. This would be a sop and it should not be accepted. There will be endless wrangles about it. Its capital will be inevitably inadequate and when additional capital will be needed it will be difficult to achieve a consensus in order to raise it. There will be conflicting opinions on the performance of borrowers, which will create unnecessary problems with the borrowers and may lead to foreclosures. The authorities must insist that individual banks provide this kind of service directly so that the performance of the borrowers and the relevant department is judged within each bank. In that case the performance of the department will be judged within the overall performance of the bank and patience or otherwise displayed accordingly. It will also be easier for the Bank of Zambia to grant individual incentives if needed.

Sata has expressed concern about the development of the Zambian business sector and I hope he will give these suggestions some thought. But he has also shown a welcome interest in education. He has already started a campaign of spreading universities around the country and recently laid the foundation stone of a new university in Palabana, near where I live.

32. 'To Learn and Learn More from the Learned'

(From 'Ithaka', a poem by Constantine Cavafy)

We do need more universities in Zambia but, before that, we need to improve education at elementary and secondary level, in order to make sure that when children reach each of the several transition levels, they have been properly prepared to pass to the next one. And when they leave high school, they have been properly prepared for further studies, or at least their standard compares favourably with that of the other countries around us. Currently it is appalling and this was starkly highlighted in the 2012 Southern and Eastern Africa Consortium for Monitoring Education Quality (SACMEQ) when Zambia ranked 13th out of the 14 countries in reading and 12th in mathematics. We should have been expecting it: the high school pass rate in mathematics has recently gone down to 39.3 per cent and the pass rate in English is even lower still at 35.5 per cent, a dismal picture.

That the quality of education in Zambia is very low is obvious from the statistics. According to the 2011 Educational Statistical Bulletin, the latest available, the picture was as follows:

Total number of schools: 8,993 (8,362 for grades 1–9 and 631 for grades 10–12)

Total number of students: 3,730,530 (3,478,898 for grades 1–9 and 251,632 for grades 10–12)

Total number of teachers: 77,961 (65,014 for grades 1–9 and 12,947 for grades 10–12)

Pupil Teacher Ratio: 49.6 for grades 1–9 and 25.3 for grades 10–12, as per the bulletin (though, according to my calculation, it is 53.5 and 19.4)

This results in the following very worrying figures:

Enrolment in grades 1–9 totalled 3,478,898 while enrolment in grades 10–12 totalled 251,632, in other words only 1 in 14 children make it to secondary

303

schools and of those only 90,031 obtained a certificate, i.e., only 1 in 39 children enrolled in grades 1–9 are likely to get a grade 12 certificate.

The pass rate is particularly low and more so in all science subjects, because of a shortage of science teachers; very few are available (and most of them are now 50 years old and above) because the Zambian universities seem unable to get enough students in science subjects. Out of a total university student population of 17,026 in 2009, only 152 were enrolled in the Schools of Mathematics and Natural Sciences.

In Chapter 4, I highlighted the deplorable neglect of African education by the colonial authorities, which prompted the government of Zambia to give it top priority at independence and I described the lengths it went to in order to spread education throughout the country. A shining example of the zeal with which our first government pursued education was the speed at which the University of Zambia was established. Preparations started in March 1963: three months after the first African government in Northern Rhodesia (a coalition between UNIP and the ANC) took office. By January 1964, a plan had been formulated and a provisional university council was appointed – all this occurred many months before independence. Harry Nkumbula, the ANC leader, who was the Coalition's Minister of Education, deserves credit for this early initiative. After the 1964 election when UNIP won an overwhelming victory Nkumbula was replaced by John Mwanakatwe, who pursued the university initiative with equal zeal. By July 1965, just nine months after independence, a vice chancellor had been recruited from Canada and on 17 March 1966 the first intake of students started work at the Ridgeway Campus, using the buildings of the Oppenheimer College for Social Research. The foundation stone for the Great East Road Campus was laid in July 1966 and the university moved to its main campus in 1968. Within the same period, primary school enrolment doubled, while the secondary school enrolment increased threefold. And as the years went by the numbers of schools spread all over the country, enrolment multiplied and the quality of education attained a very high standard. But the stagnation of the 1980s set in, followed by the Chiluba years and the many mindless experiments with various economic policies I described earlier in the book. New facilities to keep pace with the population increase were no longer affordable, the old buildings could not be maintained, and education had to make do with dilapidated school buildings, overcrowding, shortage of teachers, and lack of books. And the administrations that followed never tried to do something about it.

The reality is that investment in education has not kept pace with the growth of the population. There are not enough school buildings, and many of the older ones are in dilapidated condition because they were built half a century ago and have never been properly maintained. In order to cope, many schools built 'temporary' classrooms of dubious quality and also introduced double and triple shifts for the lower grades. Such stopgap measures became permanent and, of necessity, teaching time has been curtailed and learning has suffered.

In other words, after the initial enthusiasm of the early years of independence, which saw education blossom both in scale and quality, it has been put on the back-burner and it has remained there for decades. And the secondary education seems to have been given an even lower priority than the elementary. The pursuit of large numbers in elementary schools intake is strong, encouraged perhaps by the effort to attain the millennium development goals. But not much thought seems to be given to the higher levels, which produced the lamentable results I have already highlighted.

The Ministry of Education does not get adequate funds to build new schools or maintain the existing ones; the 2013 budget allocation for education infrastructure amounted to K663.3 billion (some $126 million). And it does not get funds to run the existing schools properly, either. There had been a small increase in the education share of the budget under the Banda administration, when, in 2010, it rose to 19.9 per cent of the budget (equivalent to 3.5 per cent of the GDP, up from 2.9 per cent in 2006) but, under Sata, in the 2013 budget its share fell back to 17.5 per cent of the budget ($1 billion for recurrent expenditure and the $126 million for infrastructure I mentioned earlier). In the 2014 budget, though, there was a big improvement in the allocation, which increased to 20.2 per cent of the budget distributed as $1.385 billion for recurrent, $162.5 million for primary and secondary infrastructure and $76.8 million for university infrastructure, a good start for an education renaissance.

But instead of just concentrating on the main problems of our education system, the Patriotic Front is tinkering at the edges, as I indicated in Chapter 26. It plans to reorganize the education system and introduce only local languages as a medium of instruction up to the 5th grade, instead of the current practice under which the medium of instruction is English from the beginning, with the local language being an optional extra. I have already expressed my reservations over this course of action but I would now like to expand on the risks it entails particularly in view of the dismal results I highlighted earlier.

My concern is that to promote the local languages at the expense of the English language, which is the most widely spoken Western language in Africa and the language of technology worldwide at the same time, will disadvantage all our children who go to government schools and it will reduce our rural people to a 'second class' citizen status, unable to compete with their urban brothers.

JICA, the Japan International Cooperation Agency, in a report under the title 'Basic Education Analysis' published in August 2012, provides the following details of the project:

Teach Grades 1–4 in local languages: Cinyanja, Cibemba, Citonga, Kikaonde, Lunda, Luvale, and Silozi.

Provide Academic and Technical Paths after Grade 8 (to Grade 12).

Rearrange subjects: for example geography, history, and ethics are integrated as social science.

Teach Information and Communication Technology skills in primary education classes using ICT in secondary education.

English will remain the official medium of instruction beginning Grade 5 up to tertiary.

According to the JICA report all preparations, such as printing and distribution of the new syllabus, development, and publication of teaching materials, orientation of the relevant officers and so on should be completed within 2013 and the introduction of the new curriculum was expected to start in January 2014. (It did.)

The worrying aspect of this system is that it will handicap the children from the rural areas. In the urban areas, most children get some degree of familiarity with English at a very early age because it is widely spoken in all the towns. So, if they only start learning it at school in grade 5, they can still catch up because of that familiarity; it will give them adequate proficiency to manage through life even if they do not go beyond grades 7 or 9, as most of them will probably not. But in the rural areas, grade 7 children will only get three years' instruction in English which does not give them enough basis on which to build and this will be a handicap in later life, because it will curb their mobility and confine them to the rural areas where they grew up, or shanty towns and menial jobs if they move to towns. We must also remember that in the urban areas there are many private schools, whose standards are higher than those of government schools and all of them provide instruction in English. Government school leavers are already at a disadvantage in comparison to the many urban private schools and the new system will only increase the gap.

The next major innovation of the new system is the choice from two streams after grade 7: academic or technical. Both these measures need rethinking. Can a person as young as 12 or 13, or his parents, make such a decision at that age? And what is the definition of a technical path? For the majority it will obviously mean vocational training, which means, at best, it will lead to a trade school. The probability is that children from poor families with poorly educated parents will end up in the technical stream which in the final analysis means they will end up as unschooled artisans. They will not know enough English to compete with children who attended government or private schools in the towns and they will not be accepted in trade schools.

Perhaps the government has time to rethink this policy. But a lot of money has already been spent in the preparation, printing, and distribution of the new syllabus and teaching materials. It would have been better spent on the rehabilitation of schools and training of teachers.

The zeal with which the early administrations pursued education seems to have evaporated. It is not only the lower and secondary education that have suffered, but the universities have been neglected too. In 1970 the University of Zambia (UNZA) had 1,000 students and Schools for Education, Humanities and Social Sciences, Natural Sciences, Law, Engineering and Medicine. By 1980 it had 4,000 and in 2011 the number rose to 16,330. As few buildings have been added the university is now breaking at the seams. The lecture rooms are overflowing but, worse, student accommodation is in a deplorable state, with students camping on rooftops and on verandas. Similar conditions obtain at the University of the Copperbelt (CBU), which was established in 1978, initially in Ndola but later in Kitwe at the Riverside Campus of the Institute of Technology. It is also overcrowded, with 8,907 students in 2011. The students' facilities are worse than those of Lusaka causing frequent confrontations with the university authorities. The vice chancellor complains that the students prefer to squat in hostel corridors, the university chapel or the canteen, or share dormitories and beds at the main campus, but refuse to go to outside hostels that the university has secured.

There are two other government-sponsored universities: the Mulungushi, which in 2011 had 2,688 students and the Nkrumah Teachers' Training College in Kabwe with 523 students which in 2011 was elevated to university status. In total, there were 28,448 students enrolled in the above mentioned four universities: 17,332 men and 11,116 women. In addition, there is an Open University in Zambia with some 4,300 students and in 2012 the government also elevated the Mukuba and Chalimbana Teachers' Training Colleges to university status. At the same time it announced the establishment of a number of new universities, notable amongst them those in Chinsali, Lubwa, Livingstone, Mansa and Mongu, but these are still at an embryonic stage. And early in 2013, Sata laid the foundation of a new university at Palabana in Chongwe district, as I already said. I do hope that the government made its calculations correctly and it has adequate funds to complete and equip the new universities it is starting. Otherwise the money would be better utilized to repair and expand facilities of existing institutions of all levels, even if this would mean that students will have to move a long way from home for their education.

The Evelyn Hone College (named after the last governor of Northern Rhodesia) in Lusaka has proved a very successful institution offering diploma courses in a variety of technical subjects as well as arts and public administration. In recent years a private education sector has emerged and is flourishing. It covers all levels from kindergarten to university and it is capitalizing on the inadequacy of government schools and the poor quality of education many offer. A large number of private schools are of very high international standards, but there are worries about the standards of some of the intermediate ones, particularly those that specialize in attracting pupils who failed to make the transition at grades 7 and 9.

There are also many private technical colleges, as well as eight private universities, some of them with tongue twisting names such as LIUTEBM 'Livingstone International University of Tourism Excellence and Business Management'. The government does not exercise much control over the private sector education except at registration and their licence renewal stage. And even then, that is confined to examining physical facilities, and getting information on their curriculum and lecturers' qualifications. However, a new act, the Higher Education Authority Act will set standards for all public and private institutions, ensure continual improvements in the quality of learning and qualifications and protect students from unregistered providers. It will also enable students to transfer between institutions locally and abroad: a very commendable initiative that will protect our children and their parents from wasting hard won family money on unscrupulous entrepreneurs who have neither the capability nor the intention of educating them. I do not want to give the impression that I am against private education. On the contrary, I applaud it. Private education is useful at all levels, but particularly so at the higher levels. It saves government huge amounts in both investment and annual expenditure, which would otherwise have to come out of the national budget. But its standards must be regulated and rigorously supervised.

We have many needs but education should be given top priority. The greatest leap in our development occurred because of the zeal with which the first Kaunda administration embarked upon setting the foundation of a sound educational system of the nation. The results of the many years of neglect are now visible in our society and they are harming our progress. We need to catch up by strengthening the base. Laying the foundations for new universities may be glamorous, but they will not be much use if we do not have students with the educational standards to fill them up. (Assuming we have the money to complete the buildings in the first place.)

Our problems are many. It is hard enough having to think them through, but we are constantly bombarded with gratuitous advice from all directions. We must persevere and find our own solutions and not be diverted by 'well-meaning' advice, which abounds.

33. Many Critics and Many Suitors

Some years back, the following joke was making the rounds of Lusaka: 'During the colonial days we had one governor: the British Governor of Northern Rhodesia. Now we have many: we have a governor from the IMF, a governor from the World Bank, one from the United States, one from the European Union, Britain, France, you name it. Is it any wonder we are going around in circles?'

I do not want to sound ungrateful to the many countries that have indeed helped us in difficult times (and carry on generously doing so) but I often wish that they were not always so dogmatic about what is good for us. We are not as knowledgeable and experienced as they are. And our society is not as advanced as theirs. We are plodding along and so far we may not have produced miracles, but we did not produce major disasters either. Sometimes I wish we were less patient than we are but when I think of the stability our inexhaustible patience has brought I rejoice. Intuitively, we know what is good for us. In any case, try as they may, these well-meaning and generous friends are not likely to succeed in making us after their own image, and they had better make a note of that.

In the developed countries, diplomatic representatives do not comment on the economic and social policies of countries they are accredited to. In Africa they do and I guess they take the view that they spend a lot of their taxpayers' money in aid so they have the right to do so. But I wish they were more careful about it. Their comments, usually in praise of one government initiative or another but often based on inadequate knowledge and superficial interpretation of the issues, stifle local debate. The foreign approbation or disapproval is usually solicited by the press and is aimed at serving a specific political purpose. It may inhibit opposing views from emerging in public but it does not change the fundamentals, or the people's basic views, which are often outside the grasp of foreigners. One striking example was the praise heaped on the Mwanawasa government when his minister of finance pushed the Kwacha to the astronomic, for the period, level of 3,000 to the dollar. The policy was foolhardy and caused the decimation of horticulture and tobacco, but worse, that of the cotton industry which lasted for nearly a decade and impoverished the peasants of the Eastern Province and the western districts of the Central Province. If they had remained silent local views in opposition would have surfaced. And, in 2012 and 2013, they have been praising the creation of many districts as a decentralization programme. Why don't they leave it to the people of Zambia to decide whether the programme is affordable, how many years it will take to generate the funds for its implementation and what the district 'decentralization' is likely to achieve? They are the ones who will be around to find out, while the present day diplomats will have been redeployed many times over and will probably have forgotten about Zambia by then.

But the foreign embassies are not the biggest culprits. Various itinerant specialists, who pass through our borders on attachment to one ministry or another, spread dangerous doctrines. Earlier in the book I described a similar phenomenon in the early years of independence and the eccentricities of Professor Mars and Robert Oakeshott. At that time we did not have a record for them to criticize; they just wanted to lead us into the ideal society of their fantasies. Now, it is different. We have 50 years of history behind us; in the opinion of some of these erudite itinerants we have wasted them and they go to great lengths to tell us how we squandered opportunities and what we should have done instead.

Along the lines of the 'many governors' joke there has been a cliché circulating in Zambia for some 20 years: 'At Independence our per capita income was three times higher than that of South Korea and now it is 40 times lower' (a misinterpretation of the pontificator's convoluted calculation, which I explain later. On a direct comparison basis, it is only 14 times lower). The 'Zambia–Korea' theory is included in a book published by the John F. Kennedy School of Government of Harvard University under the title: *Promoting and Sustaining Economic Reform in Zambia*. The book was edited by Catharine B. Hill and Malcolm F. McPherson. A chapter written by McPherson titled the 'Historical Context' has an appendix under the title 'South Korea and Zambia compared' which includes the following:

> It was noted in the text that Zambia's leaders had never attached a high priority to economic growth. For South Korea it was the opposite. Students of South Korea's economic history regularly make the point that rapid economic growth was the main factor legitimising the regimes of its otherwise unsavoury leaders … As noted in the text, in 1965 South Korea's per capita income measured in US dollars was roughly one third of Zambia's [Zambia 294 dollars, Korea 106]. At that time South Korea was widely seen as one of Asia's 'basket cases'. By contrast, Zambia was the rising star of Southern Africa [it never was; with UDI and the civil wars in the surrounding countries, we were struggling to make ends

meet]. As seen in Table 2-2, the per capita income of South Korea (measured in PPP terms) in 1998 was 12,270 dollars while that of Zambia was 860 dollars. (The non-adjusted data show a similar gap.) That is, relative to Zambia's income, the average income in South Korea increased by a factor of forty [sic] over a period of 33 years … [This convoluted calculation that was made in order to achieve a more spectacular effect means that South Korea's per capita income grew 116 times between 1965 and 1998, while Zambia's grew only 2.9 times, which means that Korea grew 40 times faster than Zambia.]

The table itemizes a number of spectacular differences I do not intend to bother the reader with, except to highlight a couple I consider most relevant. First the size of the economy of each country, in 1998:

Zambia: 3.2 billion dollars, South Korea: 370 billion.

What is amazing is that this number did not ring warning bells and make McPherson review the argument that he was pursuing. In 1998 the population of Zambia was 9.5 million and the population of South Korea 46.287; if McPherson had taken the trouble to compare the size of the two economies in 1965 instead of their per capita income, he would have found that the economy of South Korea at $3.042 billion in 1965 was three times larger than Zambia's, which was $1.029 billion because our population at the time was 3.5 million and Korea's 28.7 million. McPherson continues:

Since Zambia's natural resource base is inherently richer than South Korea's the fundamental difference in economic performance largely reflects the development strategies pursued by each country. South Korea chose to emphasise export-oriented growth. From the late 1960s onwards Zambia promoted import-substituting industrialization.

In short: it is our fault. We were not clever enough to pursue what was best for us. First, let us examine the statement 'Zambia's natural resource base is inherently richer than South Korea's', a factual statement which is undeniable. But our natural resource was just one product: copper. We were rich in the late 1960s because the Vietnam War created high demand for copper that pushed the price up to $2 per lb calculated at 1992 dollar equivalent (Daniel Edelstein, *Metal Prices in the United States: Copper*). But by the end of the seventies the oil price explosion caused the collapse of the international commodity market and the price of copper dropped to below $1.50 per lb and after the Sumitomo scandal in 1995/6 to below $1 per lb

313

and it remained there until 2005. And how could we have built 'export-oriented growth', when, after UDI, we had to resort to airfreighting copper, the only export product we had, to the ports in order to ship it to the market? And we did not have any other industry to speak of and we are landlocked in the middle of Africa with our traditional trade routes cut by UDI and civil wars raging to the south and east and west (Rhodesia, Mozambique, South West Africa (now Namibia) and Angola) and a failed state (Zaire, now the Democratic Republic of the Congo) to the north. And could we have promoted industrialization when we had no industrial base because the Federation had directed it to Southern Rhodesia and our internal market was three and a half million people of which two thirds were living on subsistence agriculture? And, last but not least we had no private capital or skilled labour, except in the mining industry.

McPherson was resident advisor to the Zambian Ministry of Finance for four years (1992–6), yet he did not seem to be aware of the state of Zambia's economy (except for the story of copper on which he based his argument in order to condemn us) or education at independence. Another punch below the belt from MacPherson:

Female adult illiteracy in 1997: Zambia 33 per cent, Korea 4 per cent.

At independence female adult illiteracy was almost total; as the reader will remember from Chapter 4, we had only 77 women with high school education, 480 with junior high and only 27,980 others with any education at all. To have reduced female adult illiteracy to 33 per cent in 33 years was an achievement: after all most mothers and grandmothers aged 50 and older in 1997 would have been illiterate at independence because they were in their late teens and older at the time.

But McPherson ignored the most important reason why South Korea and Zambia do not bear comparison: history. The history of South Korea goes back to 1200 BC, in a region whose history goes back 5,000 years. We are a young country of just 50 years, with less than 100 years of gestation before that, under a colonial and Federal regime that was racist and oppressive because it was dominated by apartheid minded Southern African whites. During that period education and training were denied to us. We could not possibly bear comparison even with many countries within Africa, never mind South Korea. As Ricardo Hausmann, the director of Harvard's Centre for International Development said, 'Growth is driven by knowledge at the level of society' – Korea had 3,000 years of it and at the time we committed the cardinal errors he diagnosed we had just about 100. Another factor that McPherson did not mention is the economic advantage South Korea derived in the aftermath of the Korean War and the superpower rivalry in the region.

It would have made little difference to Zambia if McPherson published his outlandish views in an academic book only. Very few would have read them in Zambia and those who might would have been of a level to view them critically and reject them. But he had to show how clever he was while he was still in Zambia so he spread them far and wide, and the comparison with Korea has now become the 'standard of our incompetence', talked about by all and sundry, particularly by many young Zambians.

But the advice that influenced the development course of Africa mostly came from the international financial institutions in the nineties in the form of structural adjustment programmes. The primary concern in Zambia at the time was the high inflation rate and I have already covered the way it was tackled during the Chiluba era. Apart from the fiscal measures, the core of the advice was to open our market to foreign goods and foreign investment. We did and we attracted foreign goods that flooded our markets to the detriment of our emerging industries; we also attracted foreign investment of varying quality and value. I have already written extensively about the disposal of the mines and the concessions and the privileges the new owners demanded and received and the arrogant disregard of our laws by many of them particularly with regard to taxation, environment protection and labour regulations. What benefits did we get? A temporary relief from the ZCCM losses, which were mainly due to the low price of copper in the international market, as Anglo American Corporation's abandonment of Konkola in 2002 indicates, but a huge opportunity loss because we sold the mines at the worst possible point of the market cycle and made huge concessions to boot. We did get increased copper production, but not increased taxation. We got no increase in formal employment.

We had a huge contraction in fact as the employment statistics indicate. According to the Labour Force Survey of 1990, formal employment in the mining sector amounted to 61,540. In 2000 this had dropped to 36,463 according to the same statistics, of which only 22,000 were working for companies belonging to the Chamber of Mines according to its promotional pamphlet intended to advertise the industry's contribution to the Zambian economy. This was being projected to reach 31,575 in 2006 and 35,199 in 2009. The Zambia 2012 Labour Survey puts it at 67,608; in other words mining employment took 20 years to overtake its pre-privatization level and obviously did so as a result of large investment in new mining properties, such as Lumwana and Kansanshi. There has also been very high activity in mineral exploration that seems to have revealed a couple of minerals we did not know we had, as well as the possibility of oil in the North Western Province. All these point to possible increased economic growth in the future, assuming the economies of the Western and Asian worlds hold, even though in 2013 their prospects looked precarious. None of these projects will materialize soon if the commodity prices remain stagnant as they are doing mid-2014, because of reduced demand from China.

During the last decade, mining and related industrial development in Zambia, combined with the growth of the Chinese and other Eastern countries' markets, have attracted investment from China, India and Korea. The highest profile is that of China, which the European countries view with a jaundiced eye. To be fair, the Chinese are different people and we are not used to their ways. But in the final analysis, as foreign investors go, there are no major differences between the goals of the Chinese and those of the other foreign investors. They all try to maximize their benefits and this we should accept as a fact of life and set up regulations and policing to safeguard our interests. The Chinese tend to bring more workers from China to work for them than others do, but, as I already said, it is up to us to ensure that they scale that down.

So far the Chinese seem to have concentrated on mining and contracting, especially road building. They tend to bring low level Chinese labour to do jobs the Zambians have been doing for years. But we can (and should) make them stop, by enforcing more strictly our labour laws. One interesting development that made headlines in the international press recently was the establishment of a Chinese-owned shoe factory in Ethiopia. The explanation was that it can produce shoes for Europe, more cheaply than they can be made in China. This indicates pragmatism that can be very beneficial to Africa in the future, if it persists. China dominates the world market for low priced goods (such industries no longer exist in the Western world). If, and when, production in China becomes too expensive, and Chinese business is prepared to transfer it to Africa the benefit will be in skills development as well as employment and taxation. In Zambia they have already acquired a number of 'Zambia–China economic zones', a concept that I have viewed with scepticism so far but which I am ready to cheer if enterprises within the zones commence manufacturing for exports.

There is a lot of backbiting of the Chinese in the Western press, but we should remain neutral. The Chinese are foreign investors like everybody else. Many of them, no doubt, may end up settling in Africa. But so did (and still do) whites of many nationalities and many Indians and other South Asians. The days are gone when they could attempt to subjugate the continent in the way the colonial powers of Europe did in the seventeenth and eighteenth centuries, and as late as 1884, when Bismarck organized the Berlin conference. It cannot happen anymore. We may have malleable governments but I cannot think of one likely to relinquish its powers in favour of a foreign country, or that would be able to survive if it did. And if our generation managed to fight for our freedom and got it, I do not think that future generations will be unable to safeguard their national interest.

Foreign investment inevitably brings new immigrants and apart from the Chinese we are attracting many from other parts of the world, but particularly the Middle East, South Asia and many whites from South Africa. Immigrants from the first two are mainly low level businessmen and they engage in small and medium enterprises. They do provide a useful addition to our industrial base but many are holding back the progress of our people who only recently started occupying those levels of business. They also tend to recruit from among members of their foreign families instead of employing, training and promoting Zambians, a practice that the Ministry of Labour and the immigration authorities should try to control.

From South Africa, we mainly get branches of white South African companies, who are piggybacking on their black government to spread into Africa. Currently they employ many South African whites in senior positions and they give preference to South African products ignoring and often undermining local suppliers. But their future is somewhat tenuous and will depend on how long their prominence within South Africa will last.

***

I covered above a number of pressures that we have to contend with and I think, as time goes by, we are getting better at managing. But there are times when we shoot ourselves in the foot, either directly or through the various African and regional institutions we are members of. In 2009 the Southern Africa Development Community (SADC) persuaded the 14 countries in the region to become members of the SADC common market (a South African plot to take over the regional market, if you ask me). And we enthusiastically joined: after all didn't the European Union start as the European common market? I froze when I first heard about joining SADC and I told friends in government that our industries would be unable to compete with South African products coming in duty-free and many would close down. 'Don't worry,' I was told. 'We have taken care of that. We do not need to remove all duties at once; we have until 2012 to phase them out.' Unfortunately I was right and many of our smaller industries are indeed facing hard times and some have closed down. (I have recently heard that the African Union presented a proposal for an African Passport to be introduced by all its members and I was very pleased to hear that Michael Sata, the Zambian president, rejected the proposal outright. I have no doubt that the South Africans will oppose it too. They want to sell their goods duty-free but they would not want our unemployed to descend on them looking for work!)

But it is not just South Africa we have to contend with in relation to trade. The EU also wants duty-free import for its products (or at least 80 per cent of them) and it has been dangling 'Economic Partnership Agreements' (EPA) to Africa for about a decade. They look very much like one-sided type of deals: they are touted as 'Aid for Trade', but whereas 'Aid' is undefined, 'Trade' is pretty specific: some 80 per cent of European exports to be allowed duty-free. And in the meantime, the 'Common Agricultural Policy' is in full force and subsidizes European agriculture to the tune of some $75 billion a year, effectively blocking out African agricultural products from the European market. The Europeans have not been very successful in selling their EPA concept. So far only ten African countries have signed and Zambia is not one of them. I hope it does not.

What is surprising is that the Europeans still persevere. They have to compete with the American generous African Growth and Opportunity Act (AGOA) which offers African products preferential access to the American market, and the Chinese who do not ask for any agreement because they know that their products are the cheapest in the world markets, anyway.

34. Epilogue

We have come a long way. And we have achieved wonders. When I look back to where we started from and where we are now I feel proud. And I rejoice at many things that younger people do not probably even notice, because they, quite naturally, take them for granted now; at the same time I am angry at many other things we could have accomplished and we have not and I guess younger people are, and have every right to be, angrier. In a previous chapter I gave a pretty dismal picture of the state of education in the country. We could have done better and we should be angry with ourselves for allowing it to deteriorate to the level it did. But people of my generation who lived through the distant past of colonial neglect must be excused for looking at the state of the nation with some degree of satisfaction and pride.

Some months ago I was travelling early in the morning between Kasama and Mpika, a distance of some 130 miles, on my way back to Chaminuka. Along the road kids were rushing to school (the road is studded with schools): all of them in freshly laundered uniforms (the older boys wearing ties in the middle of the bush!), books in their satchels, running to school and playing and laughing. And I smiled and felt happy. (Of course they would not look the same on the way back with dusty shoes and crumpled clothes and the older boys' ties loose and their collars open – a privilege of their age.) I am painfully aware of everything I said about the state of our education. Yet, happy kids rushing to schools make a picture of optimism and hope. The schools they are going to may be somewhat dilapidated and some of their desks broken. But at least we have schools and teachers now. At independence we had very few and certainly none to see in villages along trunk or district roads. Now we don't just have village schools; we also have village kids whose parents can dress them in clean uniforms and make them look like every other school-going kid in the world. (A few years ago I had a visit from an old British friend who had been a district officer in Kabombo and Balovale (now Zambezi) in the fifties. We witnessed together a similar scene between Zambezi and Chavuma and he was astonished. 'I used to plead with mothers to send their children to school in those days and they ignored me,' he said. But what did they call 'schools' in those days? A thatched hut, and one or two teachers, that would take a few children through sub-A and sub-B, and maybe end in standard II with no prospect beyond? And they were so few and so far apart that children had to walk for many miles every day to get there, or they had to spend Monday to Friday at the school, sleeping on the ground under a blanket they brought from home, and feeding on the little food they managed to carry with them on Monday. The mothers quite rightly did not consider that the hardship was justified for a school of that type that would make no difference to their children's future, and they ignored it.)

I am sure that today's kids' parents are not as sanguine as I am. They expect better schools with better facilities and better results. Why should they put up with schools that are old and dilapidated and so overcrowded that they have to teach in shifts, with too few teachers who are overworked? Why should they put up with standards that place Zambia at the bottom of school results in the region, as I described in an earlier chapter?

This kind of contradiction pervades every aspect of life in Zambia. Driving through Kalingalinga, in Lusaka, and seeing the array of building materials and builders' hardware, and furniture and other products, most of them made in the area or around Lusaka, is very satisfying. The products on sale by the side of the road cover the needs of the jobber and the small contractor and the householder. Many people make a living out of them: people who did not exist at independence, because no one was being trained or given the opportunity to make them. But, while people of my generation may be pleased with what they see, younger people, including those who make them now would not be as pleased. They work in their backyards, in the open air, with few tools and no facilities to give their product a better finish or produce a better range. They can say that 50 years after independence, they should be further ahead with better workshop facilities producing better products. But some of them who started at Kalingalinga have moved on and many of those who are struggling today in the open air will follow and others will take their place. Kalingalinga is a microcosm of our society and a mirror of its progress.

And driving around the towns, in the well-to-do areas, and seeing the impressive new houses that Zambian architects design for the middle classes and the chic ladies and smart gentlemen and their busy lives, also gives a good feeling. No Zambian owned a house liked that or lived in one before independence. And the many businessmen who run big and small companies, and the many professionals, lawyers and judges and doctors and lecturers and professors and senior government officers and all the other members of the middle classes did not exist before independence as I highlighted at the beginning of this book. And the rest of the middle classes who live all over the country in equally comfortable homes, with water and electricity and gardens did not exist either.

But away from the town centres and the well-to-do are others who live in very high density areas and still others who live in the squalor of the shanty town, many without jobs and in abject poverty. Yet, the high density areas and the shanty towns are buzzing. There are markets and small shops and schools and churches and children playing and people rushing about. And the unemployed do not just sit around wallowing in misery. They roam the towns looking for work or something to do. They hang outside contractors' yards in the hope of getting 'piece work' that will give them a plate of food for a couple of days. And, by mid-morning, when their hopes for that day have faded away they walk around the towns hoping that something else will turn up. And they try again the next day and the next. And somehow they manage to earn a living; otherwise they would have gone back to the village, where at least there is always a plate of food.

Many try their luck in the markets, as porters, as cleaners, as tyre menders, car washers, bicycle repairers, or odd-jobs men for a bit of money; and if they are lucky some shopkeeper will give them some goods to sell in the streets or at a corner stall. The middle classes dislike market stalls in every corner and street vendors roaming about, because they soil the towns and, in their view, they demean them and our nation. They should accept, instead, that we are a poor country and be proud that so many people do not stand around lamenting their fate and their misery, or take to crime, but roll up their sleeves in the time honoured Zambian tradition of self-help and try to make a living; and they are not angry with society about their fate. The job of the marketeer and the vendor is hard. They work in the open air in the sun and the wind and the rain and the heat and the cold and they barely make a living. The vendors at the traffic lights have the hardest job. They carry their wares in their hands all day long, constantly running back and forth to catch a customer rushing through in his shiny car. And when the traffic lights change and the customer rushes off and they miss a sale they shrug their shoulders and smile and they run for the next one.

I am proud of them all and I am even more proud of our minibuses, our Zambian invented and wholly owned industry that is providing a comprehensive transport service to every corner of each town and its outskirts and is thriving. Its owners are happy, and its drivers and its 'call boys' (Zambian term for the conductors whose main task is to shout for customers) are happy too. And it is pleasing to hear that the Sata government made arrangements with the Chinese for the supply of a couple of thousand new buses to be distributed to minibus operators in order to improve their service.

And the rural people? They are making good progress too, and they are bridging the gap that existed between them and the towns along the line of rail. The major rural towns now have most of the facilities of urban living. Chipata in the east, Mongu in the west, Kasama and Mansa in the north, and all the towns between, all the way to Lusaka and Livingstone, as well as Solwezi in the north west have well stocked shops, workshops, contractors, artisans, markets, small lodges for the travellers, and a very impressive construction boom to boot. It is heartening to see so many new houses and shops and offices under construction in all those towns. Most trunk roads are now tarred or will soon be under the Link Zambia 8000 project, and local bus services are running within the bigger towns and their periphery. And the peasants in their villages are now above subsistence level, even though they still have to rely on government for agricultural inputs. As I said earlier, their lives can improve faster with more enlightened land policy and decentralization. All in all the countryside is managing much better now than it used to do.

We could have made much greater strides, but when we started life as a free nation, too many obstacles were thrown on our path. The biggest was UDI and I covered its effects in great detail in this book. But the civil wars that were started in the countries around us, by the racist regimes of Rhodesia and South Africa, took their toll too. And our noble support for the liberation struggles in Southern Africa cost us dearly, but we do not begrudge our contribution. We are proud of it.

Yet despite all the drawbacks we faced in the early period after independence, we made great progress, because we were all united in the common purpose of coping with the adversities that besieged us and bridging the development gap left behind by the colonial and Federal neglect. We stumbled when the politicians started fighting each other and some of them became more preoccupied about how to dominate, instead of how to improve the lives of the people. And we went through a decade and a half of a 'One Party' regime before the people rose up and shouted 'enough', and threw the culprits out. The prime focus of the Chiluba regime that followed was the enrichment of many of its leaders but in the process it left the people to their own devices and Zambian enterprise started breathing again. And despite the many harmful fiscal measures Chiluba introduced in compliance with the structural adjustment programme, the society surged forward. The Mwanawasa and Banda regimes continued on the same lines and the economic awakening of China and the demand for raw materials it generated gave a lift to the price of copper and our economy thrived.

The inevitable conclusion is that the country made faster progress when its people were allowed to use their own initiative. And it regressed when the main preoccupation of those in power was to maintain their dominance and in the process they tried to regiment the people's thinking and curtail their initiative. This is a message that Sata must take on board. The political picture halfway through his term is bleak. All three main political parties, PF, MMD, and UPND, are broken and lack direction. The rest of them are so small that in their present form they do not count. There is a political vacuum over the country that will inevitably be filled.

If Sata cares about his legacy he must fearlessly throw the bad eggs out of his party; he must put a stop to his party's politicking and infighting and turn his full attention to the needs of the country. During the election campaign he spoke about the levels of unemployment, the low wages, the poverty of the peasants; and the many other needs of the nation, some of which he started tackling. He is still conscious of the high unemployment rates, as is obvious from some of the overoptimistic communiques that come out of State House regularly announcing exaggerated numbers of jobs created and to be created, as I highlighted in a previous chapter. He still has half a term ahead of him in order to do something about it: something real that will produce short-term relief and lay the foundation for long-term progress. It is going to be a tough job. But he can do it. And he will always be remembered for it if he does.

Appendices

Appendix I

Northern Rhodesia Report 1929

COLONIAL REPORTS—ANNUAL.

No. 1516.

NORTHERN RHODESIA REPORT FOR 1929.

(For Reports for 1927 and 1928 see Nos. 1410 and 1470 (Price 1s. 8d. each) respectively.)

LONDON: PRINTED AND PUBLISHED BY HIS MAJESTY'S STATIONERY OFFICE.

(To be purchased directly from H.M. STATIONERY OFFICE at the following addresses: Adastral House, Kingsway, London, W.C.2; 120, George Street, Edinburgh; York Street, Manchester; 1, St. Andrew's Crescent, Cardiff; 15, Donegall Square West, Belfast; or through any Bookseller.)

1931.

NORTHERN RHODESIA

ANNUAL REPORT, 1929.

PREFACE.

The territory known as the Protectorate of Northern Rhodesia lies between longitudes 22° E. and 33° 33' E. and between latitudes 8° 16' S. and 18° S. It is bounded on the west by Angola, on the north-west by the Belgian Congo, on the north-east by Tanganyika Territory, on the east by the Nyasaland Protectorate and Portuguese East Africa, and on the south by Southern Rhodesia and the mandated territory of South-West Africa; comprising in all an area that is computed to be about 287,960 square miles. The River Zambezi forms the greater part of the southern boundary; its two main northern tributaries are the Rivers Kafue and Luangwa. With the exception of these river valleys, the territory consists of a table-land varying from 3,000 to 4,500 feet in height, though in the north-eastern portion, and especially in the vicinity of Lake Tanganyika, the altitude is greater.

The little that is known of the early history of Northern Rhodesia is very fragmentary and is gleaned from the accounts of the few intrepid travellers who penetrated into this unknown territory. The curtain of obscurity lifts for a moment when we read the diaries of the Portuguese Governor of Sena, Dr. Lacerda, who led an expedition in 1798 from Tete into Kasembe's country, close to the eastern shores of Lake Mweru. He was followed in the early 19th century by two Portuguese traders, Baptista and Jose, who brought back stories of the great interior kingdom of the Balunda, which extended from Lake Mweru to the confines of Barotseland and included the whole of the country drained by the Upper Congo and its tributaries. This kingdom is reputed to have lasted from the 16th to the 19th century. Very few historical facts are known about it, but the name of Muati Yamvo, (in Lunda: Mwantiyamvwa) the dynastic title of the Paramount Chief, is associated, like Monomotapa, with many half-legendary stories. Neither of these expeditions was of any very great geographical value and it was not till 1851, when Dr. Livingstone made his great missionary journeys and travelled through Barotseland and visited the Victoria Falls, that the civilized world had its first authentic information of Northern Rhodesia. Other and later explorers who brought back stories of the barbarism of the natives, of the wealth of game, and of the glories of the Victoria Falls were Serpa Pinto, Cameron, Selous, and Arnot.

From the very early days when the hordes of migratory Bantu swept southward from Central and Northern Africa, Northern Rhodesia has been subject to constant invasion from stronger tribes on its borders, so much so, that the vast majority of the present native population, though of Bantu origin, is descended from men who themselves invaded this country not earlier than 1700 A.D. One or two tribes, numbering now only a very few thousand, such as the Masubia of the Zambezi, are all that remain of the inhabitants of Northern Rhodesia prior to that date. Though the story of these invasions has passed into oblivion, their traces remain in the extraordinary number and diversity of races and of languages in the country.

At the present time statistics are available of seventy different tribes resident in the territory, of which the most important are the Awemba (108,665), Achewa (75,058), Angoni (51,004), Awisa (49,030) in the Eastern Districts; the Barotse (65,250), Batonga (94,546), Balenje (37,662), Balala (40,880), Balovale (32,672), Bakaonde (35,397), Baila (21,486) in the Western Districts; and the Asenga (62,294) and Alunda (60,761) members of which are resident in both Eastern and Western Districts. There are said to be 30 distinct native languages in use, of which Chiwemba and Chinyanja have been adopted for educational purposes in the Eastern Districts and Chitonga (closely allied to Chila) and Sikololo in the Western. In addition to these, Chinyanja is in use as the official language of the police, and is probably the language most generally spoken by Europeans; it is, in reality, a Nyasaland language—the word means "Language of the Lake"—but it is also spoken to some extent round Fort Jameson.

The chief invaders of the early part of the 19th century were the Arabs from the north; the Angoni, a branch of the early Zulus who fled from the oppressive tyranny of Tchaka and who settled in the north-east of the territory; and the Makololo, an offshoot of the Basuto family, who, in the beginning of the 19th century, fought their way from the south through Bechuanaland (Botswana) and across the Zambezi under the noted Chief Sebitoani; they conquered the Batoka, the Basubia, and the Barotse and founded a kingdom which was distinguished by a comparatively high degree of social organization.

The duration of the Makololo kingdom was short. Soon after the death of Sebitoani, the Barotse rebelled and massacred the Makololo to a man. The influence of their occupation is still to be seen in the Sikololo language, which is largely spoken amongst the tribes near the Zambezi. The Barotse under Lewanika enlarged their kingdom by conquering one or two of the surrounding tribes, such as the Bankoya and the Balovale. Beyond these limits their authority was both nebulous and ephemeral. In the year 1890 Lewanika asked for British protection and on the 27th June the Barotse Concession was signed, by which Lewanika recognized the Protectorate of Queen Victoria and gave to the Chartered Company certain mining and commercial rights over the whole of his dominion. Lewanika, on his side, received a yearly subsidy of £2,000.

During this time the slave trade established by the Arabs continued unchecked. Its baleful influence had gradually spread from the shores of Lake Nyasa and Tanganyika over the whole territory; but with the establishment of a Government post at Abercorn in 1893, the slave trade in this part of Africa received its first serious check. In each succeeding year more Arab settlements on the Lake shore were destroyed. Sir Harry Johnston defeated the Arab Chief Mlozi at Karonga in 1894, and the last caravan of slaves, which was intercepted on its way to the east coast, was released at Fort Jameson (Chipata) in 1898. Even after that, bands of slave raiders were occasionally encountered on the north-east boundary, and skirmishes with them took place as late as 1900; but with the final establishment of the administration of the British South Africa Company the slavers quickly disappeared from the country.

The status of the conquered tribes under Lewanika's dominion was that of a mild form of slavedom [sic]. This social serfdom was brought to an end by an edict of Lewanika, who in 1906 agreed to the emancipation of the slave tribes. Previous to 1899 the whole territory had been vaguely included in the Charter granted to the British South Africa Company, but in that year the Barotseland-North-Western Rhodesia Order in Council placed the administration of the western portion of the country by the Company on a firm basis; and this was closely followed by the North-Eastern Rhodesia Order in Council of 1900 with similar effect. The two territories were amalgamated in 1911 under the designation of Northern Rhodesia, and the administration of the Company (subject to the exercise of certain powers of control by the Crown) continued until 1924, when, in terms of a settlement arrived at between the Crown and the Company, the administration of the territory was assumed by the Crown, and the first Governor was appointed on 1st April, 1924.

The currency in use consists partly of English coinage and partly of notes of the Southern Rhodesia issue of the Standard Bank of South Africa and Barclay's Bank (Dominion, Colonial and Overseas) both of which have branches and agencies in this country. The coins and notes of the Union of South Africa are also current at par. English weights and measures are employed.

There are considerable climatic differences between various parts of the country. The Zambezi, the Luangwa, and the Kafue Valleys experience a much greater humidity and a more trying heat than do the plateaux above 3,500 or 4,000 feet. The hottest months are October and November before the rains break, when the mean maximum is 97° in the Zambezi valley stations and 85° at plateau stations. The mean maximum for the eight months of the hot season (September to April) is approximately 90.3° with a mean minimum of 64.5° while the corresponding figures for the four months of the cold season (May to August) are 78.7° and 46.6° ...

GENERAL.

The illness of His Majesty the King was a subject of grave concern to the people of Northern Rhodesia, who, in common with the rest of the Empire, observed Sunday, 7th July, as a thanksgiving day for his happy restoration to normal health.

A strike on the Rhodesia Railways occurred in February and traffic was at a standstill for nearly three weeks, but the government had been able to take preliminary measures to provide for the maintenance of essential services and, although considerable economic loss and general inconvenience to the public were incurred, food supplies were nowhere exhausted. The strike occurred in the middle of the rainy season and some apprehension was felt lest the roads might become impassable, but special work was promptly undertaken and in spite of the increased volume of traffic, through communication on the Great North Road was maintained.

The Earl of Athlone, Governor-General of the Union of South Africa, accompanied by Her Royal Highness Princess Alice and Lady May Cambridge, visited Livingstone from the Victoria Falls in October, and Sir Jose Bebiano, G.B.E., Portuguese Minister for the Colonies, passed through the Protectorate in June on his return from opening the Benguela Railway.

Towards the close of the year an archaeological expedition under the leadership of Professor Cipriani arrived in the territory. They propose to embark during 1930 on an exploration of several areas which are reported to contain relics of palaeontological interest.

The year was for the natives a period of progress and prosperity. Rapid mining development reacted throughout the territory, and the economic situation of natives is steadily improving. The average number of natives in employment during the year was 62,500, of whom over 22,000 were employed in mines. The labour situation was generally satisfactory, though certain employers (notably farmers) complained of periodical shortages.

To natives, the most important event of the year was the passing of the Native Authority and Native Courts Ordinances. It was found impossible to put into practice the system of indirect rule based on these Ordinances before the end of the calendar year but the Chiefs and people were fully informed of the terms of the Ordinances, and appear to welcome the change. Movement into Reserves continues slowly in the railway line area, and is almost completed in the East Luangwa Province. Movement in the Tanganyika Province will commence in 1930.

The native population of the territory is now estimated at 1,298,651, an increase over the 1928 figure of 36,679 or nearly three per cent. Immigrants into Northern Rhodesia in 1929, exclusive of natives, numbered 1,861, of whom 1,646 were British subjects. The following comparative figures of immigration, exclusive of visitors, are indicative of the increasing progress being made by the territory:

1923	1924	1925	1926	1927	1928	1929
260	438	474	756	1,038	1,066	1,861

The majority of these immigrants were absorbed by the mining areas, the white population of Ndola increasing from 1,775 at the end of 1928 to 4,247 at the end of 1929.

Seventeen persons were deported, six being criminals, and eleven being indigents. Of these deportees one was a native. No figures of emigration are

329

available. Accurate statistics of native immigration are not available, but at least 4,000 appear to have entered the country during 1929 for purposes of domicile, apart from the large number who came to seek employment on the mines. The majority of these immigrants came from Mozambique and Angola.

FINANCE.

It is satisfactory to be able to record that the financial year 1929–1930 showed a surplus of revenue over expenditure of £117,762, thus exceeding the result of the previous year, when the series of annual deficits was broken for the first time within the financial history of the territory. The expansion in revenue has been well maintained and reflects a constant development of the resources of the territory with a consequent increase in the prosperity of both Europeans and Natives. Townships in the mining areas have continued to grow and considerable revenue was derived from the sales of Government land therein for which competition remained keen. Following the expansion in revenue, expenditure also increased but was kept in check by the exercise of strict economy.

The revenue from all sources for the year amounted to £672,289, an increase of £130,683 or 24.12 per cent, over the previous year …

Appendix II

The Mining Agreements
Draft memorandum to the Cabinet by
H.E. the President as Minister of State Participation, October 1969

1. I recommend to Cabinet that approval be given to the agreement negotiated with representatives of the mining groups, the salient points of which are the following:

   (a) GRZ through Indeco will purchase 51% of the net book value of the RST and AAC mines as at 31st December 1969. It is estimated that the figures will be approximately as follows:

	Value (Km)	GRZ Cost (Km)
RST Mines	165	84
AAC	245	125
Total	410	209

   Further details on the valuation are given in paragraph 2.

(b) Payment will be made in the following manner:

(i) RST: over a period of 8 years at an interest rate of 6% pa

(ii) AAC: over a period of 12 years also at an interest rate of 6% pa

The payment is subject to certain variations depending on the size of Indeco's dividends. A detailed explanation is given in paragraph 3.

(c) A management, sales and consultancy agreement will be entered into with the existing groups along the lines explained in detail in paragraph 4.

(d) The groups will be reorganized so that two new operating companies will be formed, one to be called Nchanga Consolidated Copper Mines Ltd. to absorb the mines of Nchanga, Rhokana, Bancroft and Rhokana Copper Refinery. Indeco will hold 51% of the shares of this company and a new holding company in the AAC group will hold the remaining 49%. Another new operating company to be called Roan Consolidated Copper Mines will be formed to absorb the mines of Mufulira and Luanshya and the Ndola Copper Refinery. A detailed explanation of these reorganizations is given in paragraph 5.

(e) GRZ will give the following guarantees:

(i)   That during the duration of the bonds the level of taxation will be no higher than it is at present (see paragraph 6)

(ii)   That the dividends of the 49% shareholders can be freely remitted during the duration of the bonds (see paragraph 7)

(iii) That the liquid assets of the present holding companies will be disposed of in the manner set out in paragraph 8.

(f) GRZ will undertake to introduce the legislation required for the enactment of this agreement. Amendments will be required to the Companies Ordinance and the Income Tax Act in particular. Also it is recommended that Zambia becomes a signatory to the International Convention for the Settlement of Investment Disputes. Further details of the legislative changes required are given in paragraph 9.

2. Valuation. The assets of the operating companies have been valued at book value in accordance with the guidelines I laid down at Matero on 11 August. Non-mining assets such as loans to Zambian and Malawi governments have been excluded from the purchase price and also assets held in Rhodesia. Included in the valuation is the net asset value of certain subsidiaries and associated companies such as the Copperbelt Power Company, Mine Air Services Ltd., Ndola Lime Company and Mining Timbers Ltd. It is expected that for the purpose of the takeover, RST assets will be valued

at approximately K165 million and AAC assets at K245 million of which Indeco will purchase 51%. The exact value will be determined when the accounts are drawn up as at 31 December 1969. Indeco will have the right to supervise the drawing up of these accounts.

In order to give the Cabinet some idea of the degree to which this deal is favourable to Zambia, I wish to make comparison with the 51% takeover of Anaconda Mines by the Chilean government. We are buying 51% of mines with a rated capacity of 750,000 tons per year. The total value is approximately K410 million. This means that we are paying K545 for every ton of capacity; the Chileans are paying K630 per ton of capacity. What is more this price difference understates Zambia's advantage in this matter since Zambian mines have a greater degree of vertical integration. A much higher percentage of Chilean copper is exported unrefined so the purchase price in the Zambian case includes a greater element of refining capacity. The second check is to relate the valuation of K410 million with one year's post-tax profits. At a price of K850 per ton the post-tax profits of the mining groups are approximately K102 million. In other words we are buying the mines at a price, which is equivalent to only 4 years earnings. The Chileans are paying a price, which is equivalent to 8 years earnings. Such a takeover on one of the World's stock markets would have produced a value equal to 11 to 13 times one year's earnings. As can be seen from the Attachment, Indeco will be retaining K7.6 million at a price of K850 per ton after it has paid out instalments on the bonds. At K900 per ton Indeco will retain K12.3 million a year. The Attachment shows the surpluses accruing to Indeco after repayments are met, at different selling prices. These funds can be used for industrial and mining development and this means that the revenue of the government, which will not be reduced by this whole exercise, can now be concentrated even more on rural development.

I therefore submit that the valuation negotiated by the government representatives is extremely favourable to Zambia.

3. <u>Payment of the Compensation.</u> As I indicated at Matero on 11 August, the Zambian Government does not have the money to buy the shares for cash nor even to make a down payment. Payment will be made out of future dividends paid to Indeco. In other words the companies themselves are in effect lending us the money to purchase their shares. In recognition of this debt, Indeco will issue bonds to the tune of 51% of the value of the two companies. These bonds will be guaranteed by the Government. The bonds will be repaid by way of an annuity at 6%, the period being 8 years in the case of RST and 12 years in the case of AAC. In the case of RST the annual repayment will be approximately K13.6 million per year and

K14.6 in the case of AAC. There is a provision for accelerated repayment. If Indeco's dividend is such that 66% of this dividend exceeds the amount of the annuity repayment stated above, then Indeco will in fact pay out the higher amount. Thus it is possible, if the price is consistently high over the next few years for the bonds to be paid off more quickly than was stated. For this provision of accelerated repayment to come into force the price must be as high as K925 per ton. At this price Indeco will be retaining K14 million after payments of the two sets of bonds, which can be used for further industrial and mining development. Put quite simply, we pay more rapidly only when we can afford to do so. In the case of RST this rule will apply from year 2 onwards and from year 3 onwards in the case of AAC. This means that if years 1 and 2 are years of high dividend Indeco will not have to accelerate the repayment thereby allowing it to accumulate a reserve against the possibility that in later years its dividend is less than its repayment obligation. It will be noticed that the terms of the repayment are slightly more favourable to RST. This is deliberate since RST is a more profitable company than AAC, a fact which is not reflected in its book value and so it was thought right to make some allowance for this while still remaining within the framework of book value. The bonds will be expressed in dollars and will be guaranteed as fully and freely convertible.

4. <u>Management consultancy, sales and buying.</u> There will be 11 directors for each operating company of whom 6, including the chairman will be elected by GRZ, and 5 will be elected by the mining groups. The mining groups will have the right to nominate one of their numbers as the Managing Director subject to the consent of the government directors. The Managing Director will be responsible for carrying out the instructions of the Board and for the running of the company.

The RST and AAC groups will be retained as the managers and sales agents of the Zambian mines. Both groups will form separate management companies, which will be registered in Zambia. These companies will assist the Managing Directors in their task of putting into effect the policies and directions of the Boards. This assistance will include financial commercial and technical management directed towards the optimization of production and profit; in addition it will include the supervision of management information services and computer facilities. The management companies will also provide on a consultancy basis, certain specialized services such as engineering design and supervision of construction and commissioning. They will also provide facilities for the recruitment of expatriate staff. These companies will provide by way of secondment the top manager and specialists. It is proposed that only those who were known as non-represented will be employees of these companies. Below this level all expatriates who were formerly represented by ZEMA (Zambia European Mineworkers Association) will be employees of the operating companies. The management, consultancy and sales agreements will in general last as long as the bonds are unpaid. However some of the duties contained in the agreements, e.g. sales and recruitment can be terminated before the bonds are fully repaid so as to allow the operating companies to move into the various fields as and when they feel capable of doing so. There is a separate buying agreement by which the two groups will be the exclusive purchasing agents of the operating companies and this agreement will last until 1974 with the possibility of renewal. In other words the minimum time for the duration of RST's management, consultancy and sales contract is 8 years and 12 years for AAC (assuming the accelerated provisions do not come into force). This compares very favourably with the situation in the Congo where Gecamin has tied itself to a 25 year contract with SGM which is a Belgian concern.

The fees for these various contracts are as follows:

Sales	0.75% of gross turnover (Congolese mining company Gecamin is paying 4.5%)
Management	0.75% of gross turnover plus 2% of profits post mineral tax but before income tax
Purchases	1.75% of the value of purchases
Engineering consultancy	3% on the value of capital projects for which consultancy is provided by the two groups
Recruitment	15% of the first year's salary, of anyone recruited; this to include all costs.

All these fees except the management fees are being paid already to various agents or associated companies and so do not represent a net addition to the costs of the operating companies. All these arrangements do is to ensure that the existing groups receive the exclusive contracts for these various functions. Only the management fees represent a net addition to the costs of the operating companies. These amount to about K8 million for the two groups together at a price of K850 per ton. It is estimated that about 45% will remain in the country either as local costs or as taxation on the profits of the management companies. These fees compare very favourably with those paid in similar circumstances in other parts of the world, as I am confident that the two groups concerned have the technical knowhow and the resources to keep our mines in the position where they are at present that is in the forefront of world mining.

5. Company reorganization. Soon after I invited the two groups to sell their shares to the State it was made clear that this referred to the shares of the mining operating companies not of the holding companies. Thus Indeco would not acquire 51% of the industrial and commercial interests of the holding companies. As part of the agreement it is the intention of RST to amalgamate all their mines into one company to be called Roan Consolidated Copper Mines Ltd. and AAC to amalgamate all their mines into a company called Nchanga Consolidated Copper Mines Ltd. Both RST and AAC as holding companies will cease to be Zambian companies incorporated under our own companies ordinance; for example instead of Amax and other shareholders holding shares in RST (a Zambian company) which in turn holds shares in Mufulira and Luanshya Amax will hold shares in a reconstituted RST, which will be an American company which holds shares in Roan Consolidated Copper Mines, which will be a Zambian company. All that happened is that the holding company which is sandwiched between the parent company and the operating company has changed its country of incorporation. From Zambia's point of view this makes no difference whatsoever to such matters as taxation, remittance of dividends, share quotations, etc. A similar arrangement is to be made for AAC.

The incorporation of the holding companies outside Zambia benefits the two groups without harming Zambia's interests. This is because they do not then have to pay tax twice on their profits but only once in Zambia and not a second time abroad. This has been agreed on the common sense principle that we are able to do the companies a favour at no cost to ourselves. The externalization of the holding companies as legal entities must not be confused with the externalization of the funds of those companies. The externalization of these funds is to be in accordance with the reinvestment agreement, which is discussed further below in paragraph 8.

It is proposed that the reformed holding companies should hold a certain minimum percentage of the shares of the operating companies; in other words, they are limited to the extent to which they can sell part of their 49% to other shareholders. The purpose of this is to ensure that those companies to whom we entrust the management of our mines also have a sizeable financial stake in them. This would provide a guarantee of the efficiency with which the management is carried out.

6. Taxation. The taxation of the copper mining companies in Zambia is already, probably, the highest in the world. For example the rate in Chile varies from

mine to mine but is generally between 40% and 55%. The current rate in Zambia is 73%. In view of our development needs we cannot afford to lower this rate even though it would make repayment easier. It is proposed, however, to guarantee the companies that taxation will be no less favourable than it is now while there are still bonds outstanding. This allows for the possibility of a different method of assessment but represents a commitment not to increase the overall level of taxation. In the recently negotiated deal between the Chilean government and the Anaconda mines, similar guarantees regarding dividends and taxation were given. This provision of a guarantee as to the level of taxation does not apply to customs and excise duties. The only stipulation here is that such duties are non-discriminatory with respect to the mining companies.

7. <u>Dividends.</u> As I indicated in my speech at Matero, the exchange control regulations permitting remittances of only 50% of the profits will now fall away. Therefore it is proposed to guarantee the free convertibility of the dividends of the "B" shareholders so long as the bond is unpaid. Since the size of the dividends varies in the same way as our export earnings it means that if our foreign exchange earnings are low the amount paid out as dividends will also be low and if our reserves are high then we are in a position to allow a high remittance of dividends. The attachment shows the foreign exchange implications of this deal. It will be seen that at a price of K850 per ton during the years in which compensation is being paid foreign exchange outflow is only slightly higher than it would be under normal conditions. In other words we are succeeding in buying 51% of the mines from foreign investors while only increasing the foreign exchange outflow by a mere K1 million a year. At any price higher than K850 the foreign exchange outflow is less than it would have been although Zambia is at the same time purchasing 51% of the mines. After completion of the repayment our foreign exchange position is of course immensely improved.

8. <u>Liquid Assets of the holding companies.</u> At the date of takeover of the operating companies the holding companies, which are not being taken over will be left with a large amount of liquid assets, which we do not wish to take over as part of the nationalization. These came from dividends, which were paid by the operating companies to the holding companies, which the latter have been unable to remit owing to the 50% of profits rule. As has been mentioned before these holding companies will be externalized as legal entities and this section is intended to deal with the way by which the liquid assets of these companies are to be dealt with. It is proposed that

these funds should be the subject of reinvestment agreement. This would mean that half the amount would be treated as new foreign investment though in fact it will not go through the process of being remitted and returned to Zambia. It will be invested in new joint mining ventures or in the operating companies and since it will rank as foreign investment the interest and dividends earned on this money will be remittable. The other half of these liquid assets will be allowed to be remitted over a two-year period. By virtue of these reinvestment agreements it will be possible to open up one or more of the areas where extensive exploration has been completed such as Baluba and Chambishi underground. RST has already indicated that they are willing to go ahead with these two mines.

9. <u>Legislation required.</u>

   (a) The companies have requested that the agreement should be submitted, in the event of a dispute, to arbitration at the International Convention for the Settlement of Investment Disputes. This means that Zambia must become a signatory to the World Bank Convention on the Settlement of Investment Disputes between States and nationals of other States. I shall be submitting a separate Cabinet memorandum shortly recommending that Zambia does become a signatory. Briefly the Convention provides a forum for conciliation and arbitration in the event of a dispute. It is an administrative council on which each signatory nation has one seat. Unlike the next best alternative, the International Chamber of Commerce in Paris, the large majority of signatories are underdeveloped countries and since each country has one vote on the Council, which is responsible for the appointment of arbitrators, the Convention is not dominated by big business. I believe the case for becoming a signatory stands independently of these mining proposals since by doing so Zambia would testify to its faith in fair and reasonable resolution of disputes in a manner not subject totally to the arbitrary behaviour of the host government.

   (b) Enabling legislation in the form of changes in the Companies Ordinance will be required in order for this deal to pass through unimpeded by a small group of minority shareholders.

   (c) It has been agreed that stamp duties and transfer duties arising out of the reorganization should be waived and an enactment to this effect should be made.

   (d) It has also been agreed that amendments to the Income Tax Act should be made to ensure that on amalgamation of the mining companies into one operating company no relief from taxation, which would have been enjoyed before the reorganization would be lost. In particular it is desired that accrued losses should still be carried forward for income tax purposes.

(e) It has also been agreed to introduce an amendment to the Income Tax Act exempting interest on the Bonds from Taxation in Zambia.

(f) It has been agreed to amend the Fifth schedule of the Income Tax Act so that the existing mines get the same benefits as new mines with respect to the taxation relief arising from the writing off of their investment. This should act as a considerable incentive to new investment, which the expansion of our mining industry requires.

10. Cabinet is asked to advise whether the recommendation in paragraph 1 should be accepted.

Appendix III

Abrogation of the Mining Agreements
Kenneth Kaunda's Press Statement, August 31 1973

After the preliminaries, the President's speech went on as follows:

In the last three and a half years the working relations with our partners in the mining industry have been good. However, certain provisions in the agreements have proved detrimental to our national interests. I would like to refer to some of these:

1. Effective control. The effective control of the industry was vested firmly in the minority shareholders.

2. Power of veto by minority shareholders. The minority shareholders have power of veto in respect of a wide range of actions and decisions. These include the winding up of operating companies and disposing of assets or granting of any of its concessions, mining or other substantial rights to others, enlarging the companies' activities, making any financial commitment, borrowing of money, appropriation in respect of capital expenditure or expenditure for exploration or prospecting, etc.

3. Formula for redemption of Bonds. The agreement provides for a fixed minimum amount to be paid each year of ZIMCO bonds, irrespective of profitability of the companies. They also provide for acceleration of the redemption of bonds when profits are high. But there is no provision for extending the period of bond redemption during lean years when there is a sharp decline in the profits due to decline in the price of copper or natural disasters like in the cave-in at Mufulira mine in 1970.

338

4. <u>Financial disadvantages.</u> <u>Exchange control.</u> The minority shareholders enjoy preferential treatment in respect of exchange control regulations, which permit automatic externalization of profits, dividends, management and sales fees.

5. <u>Taxation.</u> The agreements provide that RCM and ZCCM will not be subjected to any increase in mineral taxes, export taxes, income taxes royalty payments, withholding taxes, or any other revenue measures as long as any of the bonds are outstanding. The two companies are allowed to write off all their capital expenditure in full in the year in which they are incurred. Prior to these agreements capital expenditure incurred was spread over the life of the mine.

6. <u>Utilization of profits.</u> The agreements provide that profits from the mines cannot be used for non-mining activities. In other words, the mining companies cannot be forced to use mining profits in the interest of the Zambian economy if the minority shareholders would prefer to use that money out of Zambia as dividends. Our experience in the last three and a half years has been that they have taken out of Zambia every ngwee [penny] that was due to them. A major part of the capital for expansion programs of both companies has been obtained from external borrowings and not from internal profits. You may be interested to know that right now my government is being asked to approve an external borrowing by the two companies of about 65 million Kwacha!

7. <u>Sales and marketing.</u> The agreements give the minority shareholders the sole and exclusive right to provide sales and marketing services for the metals and minerals at a very high fee.

8. <u>Management and consultancy.</u> The agreement also states that the minority shareholders will provide sales and marketing services for a large fee.

    Although most of this work is performed in Zambia the minority shareholders have entered into separate arrangements with non-resident companies for reasons best known to themselves, but not comprehensible to us.

9. <u>Zambianization.</u> There is of course the vital question of Zambianization in the mining industry. The agreements made no provision whatsoever on this vital issue. And of course related to this matter is that of recruitment, which was left entirely in the hands of the minority shareholders, again at a high fee to themselves.

    I mention all these to show some of the problems we have experienced with the agreements as presently constituted. Countrymen, we cannot allow this situation to continue. It has to be changed. But let me assure you and the rest of the world once again, that as a Party and Government we will always endeavour to find reasonable and honourable solutions to our problems in accordance with our philosophy of humanism.

However we still have the task of completing the program started at Mulungushi on 19th April 1968 in order that the people of Zambia may have effective control on the affairs of their economy. In accordance with the mandate given to me by the nation, I decided that with immediate effect:

- Outstanding bonds should be redeemed.
- Steps should be taken to ensure that RCM and NCCM revert to the old system of providing for themselves with all the management and technical services which are now being provided by the minority partner.
- A new copper marketing company wholly owned by the government should be established here in Zambia.
- The Minister responsible for mines shall be the chairman of RCM and NCCM.
- The government will appoint the managing directors of both RCM and NCCM.
- Mindeco shall cease to be the holding company for RCM and NCCM
- The Minister responsible for Finance will hold shares in RCM and NCCM for and on behalf of the government.
- The rest of the mining operations which are not connected with RCM and NCCM will continue to be administered by Mindeco and the status of Mindeco therefore will be equal to that of RCM and NCCM.
- Normal taxation provisions and exchange control regulations will apply to RCM and NCCM and the Minister responsible for Finance and the Governor of the Bank of Zambia are instructed to take appropriate measures.

He then announced the appointment of an implementation committee under the chairmanship of Humphrey Mulemba who was both Minister of Mines and Chairman of the Economic and Finance Committee of UNIP's Central Committee.

Author's Memorandum to Kaunda
Dated 19 September, 1973

When we met yesterday afternoon you asked me to let you have a memorandum with my comments on the mining agreement. Taking the various comments raised so far my comments are as follows: (When I quote articles of the various agreements I refer to the NCCM agreements, but parallel articles exist in respect of the RCM agreements).

1. Management. It is true that the minority shareholders can nominate the managing director, but in fact he can only be appointed by resolution of

the Board. Since the government directors are in the majority, they have in fact a veto over his appointment. Similarly, article 76 D (i) of the Articles of Association provides that the removal of the Managing Director may be effected "at any time by a resolution of the majority of the Directors", i.e. by Government. In effect therefore the government can refuse to appoint or if it has appointed it can remove any director who does not comply with the wishes of the Board. In that case the minority shareholders will have to find a replacement who should ideally be a strictly professional mining man whose interest lies in the technical efficiency of the operation.

2. <u>Limitation of powers of the Board.</u> It is true that article 102 of the Articles of Association of NCCM provides for the limitation of some of the powers of the directors but this is only aimed at ensuring that the companies remain essentially mining companies and do not diversify in other areas which may prove against the interest of the minority shareholders. Similarly, that the majority shareholder does not arbitrarily use the funds to further its own interests to the detriment of the minority. I would like to add that these are standard provisions in all companies where there is a substantial minority.

3. <u>Borrowing powers.</u> Article 104 does indeed limit the powers of the directors but Clause 104B defines the limit as being twice the amount of the share capital. The paid up capital of NCCM is K253 million and RCM K121 million, therefore the borrowing powers of the directors extends to K506 million and K242 million respectively. Adding the reserves that each company could capitalize, the borrowing powers of the directors could in fact extend to K730 million for NCCM and K394 for RCM. It will be seen that these figures are so large that they are unlikely ever to be needed.

4. <u>Dividends.</u> Clause 118 (B) defines dividends payable each financial year as being the "aggregate amount equal to the consolidated net profits of the company and its subsidiaries for each financial year as shown in the audited accounts of the company in respect thereof after deduction therefrom of: appropriations in respect of capital expenditure and expenditure for exploration and prospecting and of reserves for necessary working capital, having regard to market conditions and short term liquidity requirements of the company, as may in each case be approved by the directors" Clause 118 (B) (iii). In view of the above the government directors could reduce the dividends to any amount if they insisted that the entire capital expenditure was appropriated out of profits and made adequate provisions in respect of exploration, prospecting, working capital and liquidity, depending on market conditions.

5. <u>Reinvestment by RST and Anglo.</u> Not only could the directors under the agreement reduce the dividends but in addition they could demand

from RST and Anglo an investment contribution of K15 million and K12 million respectively "from funds not subject to exchange control" (i.e., in foreign exchange) "for the development of existing or new mining ventures in Zambia considered to be commercially viable by the Board including the Baluba and Chambishi underground mining projects" (see Clause 17 of the mining agreement with RST and Clause 9 of the supplemental heads of agreement with Anglo). To the best of my knowledge the Board has so far failed to make recourse to this clause which could have augmented the foreign exchange reserves of the country by K27 million.

6. Acceleration and deceleration of Bond repayments. While there is an acceleration clause in the agreements, the interesting fact is that conditions have never reached the point where it could be invoked. The reason is that the acceleration clause was used as a carrot to obtain the concession from the minority shareholders to pay for bond redemption only a small proportion of the dividends in the first year of operations. It had been calculated that in view of the buoyant conditions of the copper market, which were not expected to last for more than about a year, it was more advantageous for Zimco to retain a substantial portion of the dividend initially. Events proved that this assumption was correct. The Board should subsequently have reduced the dividends to the minimum. This would have kept the profits in the hands of the companies and thus increase the net asset value of Zimco. Zimco then could have borrowed externally against its enhanced net asset value and thus pay the bond redemption externally without affecting the Nation's foreign exchange position.

7. Exchange control and taxation. Despite the provisions that the above regulations should not become less favourable during the duration of the bond redemption it is interesting to note that in fact the companies' dividends were substantially below the "30% of capital, 50% of profit formula", which applies to all foreign companies. The taxation undertaking was given because the taxation was already so high that added to the government's shareholding of 51% it brought the government's share of the profit to 87% of the total.

8. Capital allowances. The allowance to write off the new capital expenditure in the year it is incurred is not part of the agreements. It was a separate provision to the Tax Act, which followed as a result of the new Mining Act, which came into force in 1970. The old capital expenditure is still written off over the period of the life of the mines. Immediately after Independence the write off period for capital expenditure was set for five years. However, as this had not attracted new mining investment

and as the new Act provided for total taxation of 73% of profits plus participation which raised the government's share to 87%, it was decided that new capital expenditure should be written off in the year it was incurred in order to ensure that new investors recoup their investment before they start paying tax. It is important to emphasize that the write off of the capital expenditure in the manner described is not tax relief but postponement of tax.

9. Management and sales agreements. The fees in respect of the management agreement are too generous in present circumstances. However, this was the best we could extract in the very tough negotiations of 1969. I do not think that the minority shareholders themselves expected this agreement to last its full term of 10 years. The same agreement covers provision of engineering services. The fees in respect of the latter are indeed very competitive. If the engineering services agreement was entered into with any of the other international organizations, such as Bechtel, Brown Roote, Sir Alexander Gibb etc. we would have to pay substantially more for the services.

10. Zambianization. In view of the overall direction of Mindeco and the existence of a special government department it was not thought necessary to include any special provisions on Zambianization in the agreement.

Appendix IV

The Tika Project
Parliamentary Statement by the Minister of Mines, Mufaya Mumbuna, on the Tika Project, 5 March 1981.
Summary and Comments by the Author.

After explaining the origins of TIKA in 1972 (the minister explained the origin of the acronym as 'Technical Industrial Kalumbila Associates' amid roars of laughter from the members) he informed the House that the 'project was initiated as a Party scheme' and, according to the official record of the debate, continued:

As is normally the case with any new major project of this nature, external funding had to be obtained as the resources of the Party were limited. By agreement, Tika Limited was to obtain international funding for the project and assistance to secure these loans was to be accomplished by contracting the work to international firms.

The project was planned in three parts and was assigned to three major firms for execution. The companies were Energoprojekt of Yugoslavia, Mannesman

Demag of West Germany and Pullman Swindell of the United States of America. All three firms entered into a series of agreements with Tika and altogether to the best of my knowledge sixteen agreements are in our possession. There may be more agreements which I am not aware of – concluded and accepted by the Tika Board of Directors.

The Directors of Tika included hon. H. Mulemba MCC (member of the central committee); hon. D. Lisulo, MCC; Mr. L. M. Lishomwa who was permanent secretary at that time; Mr. P. S. Chitambala MCC; Mr. B. R. Kuwani, Governor of the Bank of Zambia at that time; Mr. F. M. Walusiku, Deputy Secretary to the Cabinet; Mr. P. K. Chiwenda and Mr. L. J. Mwananshiku ...

The financing of the Tika project was secured from three sources: Demag responsible for the construction of the smelt shop, continuous casting plant and rolling mill obtained their financing through KFW and AKA of West Germany ... Energoprojekt's responsibility was for mining equipment, beneficiation plant and pelletizing plant and they planned their financing through Soberi SA, a Belgian banking consultant. Both Demag and Soberi were successful in obtaining loan commitments for their respective sphere of responsibility – they got their money. Pullman Swindell and Kuhn, Loeb, Lehman Brothers – a financial consultant firm made several representations to the United States Exim bank in an effort to obtain financing for the HYL plant. The Exim bank ultimately declined to make the necessary loan to Tika despite repeated efforts ...

The pursuit of a loan from Exim Bank had extended over a long period during which Tika Limited was paying for the on-going work which Pullman Swindell had undertaken through a letter of credit from the Bank of America, via the Bank of Zambia, while KFW/AKA funded the Demag fabrications on a reciprocal basis.

(Here, the Minister's language is confusing and I take it to mean that the Bank of Zambia opened a letter of credit in favour of Swindell through the Bank of America, and that KFW/AKA disbursed to Demag, with recourse to the Bank of Zambia.)

Charmingly, the Minister proceeded to confess that:

the production of components by the contractors continued resulting in having some components in transit, others at warehouses and yet a few others at port of embarkation. In 1976, on Tika's instructions Pullman Swindell began to phase out its work so as to reduce the drain on Tika Ltd. In brief, failure to obtain the Exim bank loan and loans from other sources caused the integrated iron and steel project to be suspended. This left a number of work items incomplete, materials and equipment scattered all over Europe and the United States of America and several administrative and technical problems involved.

By this time, 1976, a sum of approximately K17 million ($20m) had been spent in foreign exchange by way of part payment for work carried out and also K2m locally for work accomplished (civil works at Chisasa).

The spiralling world inflation together with continued recession led to severe constraints in organizing external funding. This coupled with organizational difficulties, namely non availability of suitable personnel and increased local costs led the government to transfer the project from the Party to the Ministry of Mines in 1977.

The Minister went on to explain that the estimated cost of the project spiralled from the projected K50 million in 1973 to K65m in 1974 and K260m in 1979, when he recommended its closure. He reported that creditors had given the end of 1980 as the deadline for payment of their outstanding claims, failure of which would lead them to take legal action. He went on:

> It is also understood that several of the items which are lying at a number of stations around Europe and USA have been incurring storage charges. These cannot be released and sold until such time as the amounts due are settled.
>
> The total anticipated claims for the Party – complete units and for servicing of the loans – is in the order of K40 million. In addition, interest and storage charges are payable. The ruling interest rate, both in Europe and USA is exorbitant and I am not in a position to say what would be the actual total cost that would be payable by Zambia, especially if we delay …
>
> Having said all this I would like to point out that most of these goods belonging to Tika are stored in several warehouses. They will require to be sold and money realized … However, it must be remembered that many of these components and equipment were manufactured for a specific plant in Zambia and, therefore, may not find a ready market. Probably most of these could be sold only as scrap in which case the amount realized would be minimal in comparison to what they cost.

Adding up the amounts paid, the outstanding claims of K40 million and interest and storage charges would indicate that the best part of $100 million went down the Tika Chisasa drain, though at the time figures as high as $150 million were rumoured. The whole expensive effort ended up as 'scrap' lying around various warehouses in Europe and America as the Minister candidly admitted.

Appendix V

The Konkola Deals
ZAMBIA COPPER INVESTMENTS LTD.
(Registered in Bermuda) JSE code: ZCI ISIN:
MG9884321240 ("ZCI" or "the company")
THE INTRODUCTION OF A STRATEGIC EQUITY PARTNER FOR
KONKOLA COPPER MINES PLC
AND FURTHER CAUTIONARY ANNOUNCEMENT

1 Introduction

Further to the cautionary announcements published over the period 16 May 2003 to 23 July 2004, Rand Merchant Bank ("RMB") is authorised to announce that ZCI, the Government of the Republic of Zambia ("GRZ"), ZCCM Investment Holdings plc ("ZCCM-IH"), Konkola Copper Mines plc ("KCM") and Vedanta Resources plc ("Vedanta") (collectively, "the Parties") have reached agreement on the terms of an investment by Vedanta into KCM (the "Vedanta investment"), subject to the fulfillment of certain conditions precedent set out in paragraph 4 below ("conditions precedent").

2 Background and rationale for the Vedanta investment

Concomitant with the exit of Anglo American plc from ZCI (and indirectly KCM) in September 2002, the KCM shareholders and GRZ embarked on a process to ensure the long-term sustainability of KCM. It was agreed that the introduction of a new strategic equity partner was the most appropriate route to follow to secure the future of KCM and to address two key issues, namely:

- the provision of technical expertise and management experience; and
- funding support and financial stability for KCM

The introduction of a new strategic equity partner would therefore address the management and capital constraints of the business.

A bid process was therefore initiated in October 2002 and bids were received in February 2003. After due consideration of the bids received, Vedanta was selected as the preferred bidder by the KCM board and endorsed by GRZ. Vedanta is an international mining and metals group ("the group") with zinc, copper and aluminium operations in India and two copper mines in Australia. It listed on the London Stock Exchange plc in November 2003 and has a current market capitalization of approximately US $ 1.4 billon. Vedanta holds its interests in its operations through two subsidiaries, Sterlite Industries (India) Limited ("Sterlite") and the Madras Aluminium Company Limited. Sterlite is Vedanta's principal subsidiary company and is currently listed on the Bombay Stock Exchange. Vedanta's copper operations are owned and operated by Sterlite, which holds majority stakes in the group's zinc business, Hindustan Zinc Limited, and the group's principal aluminum business, the Bharat Aluminium Company Limited. Vedanta has also recently embarked on a major capital expenditure programme of approximately US $ 2 billion to significantly expand its operations,

3 Detailed terms of the Vedanta Investment and associated arrangements
The key terms of the Vedanta investment that the Parties have agreed to are as follows:

- The subscription by Vedanta of sufficient new KCM ordinary shares for an amount of US $ 25 million such that Vedanta obtains a 51% interest in KCM. Accordingly, ZCI will reduce its interest in KCM from 58% to 28.4% and ZCCM-IH will reduce its interest in KCM from 42% to 20.6%;
- To enable Vedanta to subscribe for KM shares, ZCI and ZCCM-IH will waive their pre-emptive subscription rights. As consideration for this waiver, ZCI will receive a deferred consideration of US $ 23.2 million from Vedanta, payable over a period commencing on the completion date of the Vedanta investment and ending on 31 December 2008. The schedule of deferred payments is as follows:
  - two million, three hundred and twenty thousand US dollars (US$2,320,000) on the completion date;
  - five million two hundred and twenty thousand US dollars (US$5,220,000) on 31 December 2005;
  - five million two hundred and twenty thousand US dollars (US$5,220,000) on 31 December 2006;
  - five million two hundred and twenty thousand US dollars (US$5,220,000) on 31 December 2007;
  - five million two hundred and twenty thousand US dollars (US$5,220,000) on 31 December 2008:
- Similarly, while ZCCM-IH will not receive a deferred consideration from Vedanta, ZCCM-IH will receive, as consideration of their waiver of US $ 16.8 million by way of a debt cancellation arrangement with GRZ, whereby GRZ will cancel debt owed by ZCCM-IH to GRZ;
- In the event that the free cash flow (after sustaining and project capital expenditures) of KCM is negative at any time during a period of nine years after the completion date of the Vedanta investment, then Vedanta will guarantee and be responsible for providing or securing the necessary additional funding required by KCM to immediately fund to the extent of the negative cash flow up to but

not exceeding a cumulative amount of US $ 220 million ("standby funding commitment"). Should this standby funding commitment be provided by Vedanta in the form of equity, it will be not dilutive to the existing shareholders;

- Vedanta will contractually undertake not to exit KCM prior to 1 January 2008. Thereafter if it wishes to exit, Vedanta is required to provide a twelve month notice period during which time it will provide management to KCM and it will pay an exit fee equivalent to the following year's budgeted capital expenditure (as adjusted for any over or under spending of capital expenditure in prior financial periods), with its standby funding commitment terminating on the exit date;

- Vedanta has agreed that KCM will set aside a portion of its future annual free cash flow to create a cash reserve so that the shareholders and GRZ have assurance that as cash is accumulated in the reserve, KCM has dedicated funds available to fund its environmental and terminal benefit obligations;

- An undertaking has been given by Vedanta to support the feasibility study on the extension of the Konkola ore body by no later than 31 December 2006. Vedanta will contribute US $ 1 million towards the cost of the feasibility study;

- Should the KCM board determine to proceed with further development of the Konkola ore body, Vedanta will be responsible for securing the debt finance necessary in accordance with typical market practices for similar projects. In addition, Vedanta will be required to contribute whatever equity is required by KCM to secure the debt funding. ZCI and ZCCM-IH will be able to follow their rights but should they decline to do so, the additional equity will be contributed by Vedanta on a dilutive basis;

- Vedanta will have a call option in favour of Vedanta over ZCI's shares in KCM, exercisable on either a positive development decision on the Konkola ore body or the achievement by Konkola mine, a division of KCM of 3 million tonnes per annum ("tpa") of ore production for four consecutive quarters. The exercise price will be the prevailing fair market value for ZCI's KCM shares as agreed to between ZCI and Vedanta or, failing agreement as determined by an independent investment bank;

- If the KCM board determines not to proceed with the further development of the Konkola ore body, then ZCI and ZCCM-IH will have a call option over Vedanta's shares in KCM, exercisable on or after 31 December 2009 at the prevailing fair market value of such shares. However, if Vedanta can

348

demonstrate at any time, before the exercise date of the call option, that an additional five years production for the period from 2013 to 2017, at 175,000 tpa of produced finished copper utilising the existing KCM mining licence and adjacent areas is achievable, then in those circumstances the exercise date of the call option will be deferred for a period of five years, such that it may not be exercised prior to 31 December 2014; and

- GRZ will continue to own one special share in KCM, which will allow GRZ to vote at KCM shareholder meetings under certain circumstances as specified in the new KCM articles of association and which will become effective on completion. For example, the consent of GRZ shall be required for any material change in the nature of the business of KCM.

The resulting ownership structure subsequent to the Vedanta investment will be as follows:

Vedanta:	51%
ZCCM-IH:	20.6%
ZCI:	28.4%
GRZ	Special Share

On the basis of Vedanta becoming the new controlling shareholder of KCM, GRZ has also agreed the terms of a new development agreement with KCM, which regulates the legal and fiscal framework under which KCM operates in Zambia. In addition to providing legislative certainty to KCM for the agreed stability period, the development agreement has certain incentives which will benefit KCM if the KCM board decides to proceed with the further development of the Konkola ore body.

At present the board of directors of KCM consists of three ZCI appointed directors, two ZCCM-IH appointed directors and one GRZ appointed director (with limited voting rights). On completion of the Vedanta investment the board of KCM will be reconstituted and consist of five Vedanta appointed directors, two ZCI appointed directors, two ZCCM-IH appointed directors and one GRZ appointed director (with limited voting rights).

4 Conditions precedent

The Vedanta investment is conditional upon the fulfillment of, inter alia, the following conditions precedent:

- Approval of the Vedanta investment by the ZCI shareholders by way of an ordinary resolution requiring the approval of 75% of ZCI shareholders present or represented by proxy at the meeting;
- Approvals by the JSE Securities Exchange, Paris Bourse and the South African Reserve Bank of the circular to shareholders;

- A waiver by the Securities and Exchange Commission of Zambia of the requirement that Vedanta make an offer to ZCCM-IH and ZCI for their shares in KCM and the consent thereto by ZCI and ZCCM-IH;
- The consent of certain KCM debt providers to the Vedanta investment;
- The signature of a management agreement for the provision of certain services by Vedanta to KCM; and
- Upon satisfaction of the above conditions precedent, the execution of a new shareholders agreement governing the relationship between the Parties, the execution of a new development agreement between KCM and GRZ, the execution of the call option agreements between Vedanta, ZCI and ZCCM-IH and the adoption by KCM of new articles of association.

5 Warranties

ZCI, ZCCM-IH, and KCM have provided certain warranties to Vedanta normal in a transaction of this nature.

6 Opinion

RMB has been appointed by ZCI to prepare a fair and reasonable opinion in respect of the terms and conditions of the Vedanta investment. This opinion, together with the opinion of the board of directors of ZCI, will be contained in the circular to shareholders.

The board of directors of ZCCM-IH is of the view that the Vedanta investment is in the best interests of ZCCM-IH shareholders, who will continue to benefit from ZCCM-IH's 20.6% retained interest in KCM, and thus share in the future development of KCM's assets.

7 Documentation

A circular, which is subject to the approval of the JSE Securities Exchange South Africa and the Paris Bourse, giving details of the Vedanta investment and containing a notice of a general meeting of ZCI shareholders is being prepared and will be posted to ZCI shareholders by no later than 4 October 2004.

8 Financial effects of the Vedanta investment and further cautionary announcement

The financial effects of the Vedanta investment are in the process of being finalised. Full disclosure of the financial effects, including the effect on net asset value per share, net tangible asset value per share and headline loss per share, will be published shortly. Accordingly, shareholders are advised to continue to exercise caution when dealing in the securities of the company until such time as a further announcement is made containing the financial effects of the Vedanta investment.

By order of the Board,
Bermuda 20 August 2004

Sponsor and Independents Advisor
Rand Merchant Bank (A division of FirstRand Bank Limited)
Corporate Finance

Independent Legal Advisers to ZCI
Maitland International Webber Wentzel Bowens
Attorneys

Appendix VI

Salient Points from
The Barotseland Agreement 1964

1) **Citation and commencement**

   This agreement may be cited as the Barotseland Agreement 1964, and shall come into force on the day on which Northern Rhodesia, including Barotseland, becomes the Independent sovereign Republic of Zambia.

2) **The Constitution of the Republic of Zambia** shall include the provisions agreed upon for inclusion therein at the Constitutional Conference held in London in May 1964 relating to:-

   a) The protection of human rights and fundaments freedom of the individual;
   b) The Judiciary; and
   c) The public service and those provisions shall have full force and effect in Barotseland.

3) **Administration of Justice**

   1) Subject to the provisions of this Agreement the people of Barotseland shall be accorded the same rights of access to the High Court of the Republic of Zambia as are accorded to other citizens of the Republic under the laws for the time being in force in the Republic and a judge or judges of the High Court selected from among the judges who normally sit in Lusaka shall regularly proceed on circuit in Barotseland at such intervals as the due administration of justice may require.

   2) The people of Barotseland shall be accorded the same rights of appeal from decisions of the courts of the Republic of Zambia as are accorded to other citizens of the Republic under the laws for the time being in force in the Republic.

4) The Litunga and His Council

1) The Government of the Republic of Zambia will accord recognition as such to the person who is for the time being the Litunga of Barotseland under the customary law of Barotseland.

2) The Litunga of Barotseland acting after consultation with his Council as constituted for the time being under the customary law of Barotseland, shall be the principal local authority for the government and administration of Barotseland.

3) The Litunga of Barotseland, acting after consultation with his Council, shall be authorized and empowered to make laws for Barotseland in relation to the following matters, that is to say:-

   a) the Litungaship;

   b) the authority at present known as the Barotse Native Government (which shall hereafter be known as the Barotse Government):

   c) the authorities at present known as Barotse Native Authorities;

   d) the courts at present known as Barotse Native Courts;

   e) the status of members of the Litunga's council;

   f) matters relating to local government

   g) land

   h) forests

   i) traditional and customary matters relating to Barotseland alone

   j) fishing

   k) control of hunting

   l) game preservation

   m) control of bush fires

   n) the institution at present known as the Barotse Native Treasury

   o) the supply of beer

   p) reservation of trees for canoes

   q) local taxation and matters relating thereto; and

   r) Barotse local festivals.

5) Land

1) In relation to land in Barotseland the arrangement set out in the annex hereto shall have effect.

2) In particular, the Litunga of Barotseland and his council shall continue to have the powers hitherto enjoyed by them in respect of land matters under customary law and practice.

3) The courts at present known as the Barotse Native Courts shall have original jurisdiction (to the exclusion of any other court in the Republic of Zambia) in respect of matters concerning rights over or interests in land in Barotseland to the extent that those matters are governed by the

customary law of Barotseland. Provided that nothing in this paragraph shall be construed as limiting the jurisdiction and powers of the high Court of the Republic of Zambia in relation to writs for orders of the kind presently known as prerogative writs of orders.

4) Save with the leave of the court at present known as Saa-Sikalo Kuta, no appeal shall lie from any decision of the courts at present known as the Barotse Native Courts given in exercise of the jurisdiction referred to in paragraph 3 of this article to the High court of the Republic of Zambia.

6) Civil Servants

All public officers of the government of the Republic of Zambia who may from time to time be stationed in Barotseland shall be officers serving on permanent and pensionable terms.

7) Financial responsibility

The Government of the Republic of Zambia shall have the same general responsibility for providing financial support for the administration and economic development of Barotseland as it has for other parts of the Republic and shall ensure that, in discharge of this responsibility, Barotseland is treated fairly and equitably in relations to other part of the Republic.

8) Implementation

The government of the Republic of Zambia shall take such steps as may be necessary to ensure that the laws for the time being in force in the Republic are not inconsistent with the provisions of this Agreement.

9) Interpretation

Any question concerning the interpretation of this Agreement may be referred by the Government of the Republic of Zambia to the High Court of the Republic for consideration (in which case the opinion thereon of the Courts shall be communicated to that Government and to the Litunga of Barotseland and his Council) and any such question shall be so referred if the Litunga, acting after consultation with his Council, so requests.

Signed: K. D. Kaunda, Prime Minister of Northern Rhodesia
Witnessed: E. D. Hone, Governor of Northern Rhodesia

Signed: Mwanawina Lewanika III KBE
Witnessed: Imenda Sibandi, Ngambela of Barotseland

Signed: Duncan Sandys, Her Majesty's Principal Secretary of State for Commonwealth Relations and the Colonies

Witnessed: Richard Hornby, Parliamentary Undersecretary of State for Commonwealth Relations and the Colonies.

Annex to the Agreement

Clause 4: The Litunga and National Council of Barotseland have always worked in close cooperation with the Central Government over land matters, in the past have agreed that the Central Government should use land required for public purposes and have adopted the same procedures as apply to leases and rights of occupancy in the Reserves and Trust Land areas, where applicable. At the same time the administration of land rights in Barotseland under customary law and practice have been under the control of the Litunga and National Council in much the same way as customary land rights are dealt with in the Reserves and Trust Land Areas.

Clause 5: In these circumstances it is agreed that the Litunga should continue to have the greatest measure of responsibility for administering land matters in Barotseland. It is, however, necessary to examine the position of land matters in Barotseland against the background of the Northern Rhodesia Government's overall responsibility for the territory.

Clause 6: The Barotse memorandum has indicated that Barotseland should become an integral part of Northern Rhodesia. In these circumstances the Northern Rhodesia Government will assume certain responsibilities and to carry these out will have to have certain powers, so far as land is concerned, the Litunga part from confirmation of wide powers the Litunga over customary matters the position is as follows:-

1) The Northern Rhodesia Government does not wish to derogate from any of the powers exercised by the Litunga and Council in respect of land matters under customary law and practice.

2) The Northern Rhodesia Government would like to ensure that the provision of public services and the responsibility for economic development in Barotseland are not hampered by special formalities.

3) The Northern Rhodesia Government recognises and agrees that full consultation should take place with the Litunga and Council before any land in Barotseland is used for public purposes or in the general interest of economic development.

4) The position regarding land in Barotseland in an independent Northern Rhodesia should therefore be as follows:-

    a) There should be the same system for land administration for the whole of Northern Rhodesia including Barotseland, that is the Government Lands Department should be responsible for professional advice and services with regard to land alienation in all parts of Northern Rhodesia and that the same form of documents should be used for grants of land (i) for Government purposes and

(ii) for non-Government and non-customary purposes. The necessary preparation should be done by the Government Lands Department.

b) The Litunga and National Council of Barotseland will be charged with the responsibility for administering Barotse customary law within Barotseland.

Appendix VII

Glencore Comments on Mopani Tax Payments
Baar, Switzerland, 2 June 2011

Glencore welcomes the investigation by the European Investment Bank (EIB) into matters raised in relation to the amount of tax payable by Mopani Copper Mines plc (Mopani) (73.1 per cent owned by Glencore) in a draft provisional report prepared by advisers for the Zambian Revenue Authority.

This draft provisional report, which the Zambian Revenue Authority has described as "confidential, preliminary and an incomplete draft," was unofficially circulated in Zambia in February. The draft provisional report contains fundamental factual errors and both Mopani and Glencore have publicly refuted its 'conclusions' on numerous occasions. In particular the authors, in their findings, did not take into account that almost half of Mopani's copper output is third party ore processed in return for a small tolling fee. As they assumed Mopani had exposure to the copper price and revenue for 100 per cent of its production, they were unable to make sense of the company's numbers. In addition other errors are detailed below.

Mopani is confident that the amount of tax that it has paid has been correctly calculated and discussions continue with the Zambian Revenue Authority and all other interested parties, including the EIB, to clarify and resolve these matters.

Mopani is audited each year by Deloitte. In response to a request from Glencore to review the draft provisional report, Deloitte described "fundamental flaws in terms of methodology and approach applied" and reiterated that "for each of the years subject to audit, Mopani's statutory financial statements were audited by Deloitte Zambia and unqualified audit opinions were issued." The EIB signed a Finance Contract with Mopani in 2005 for an amount of USD 50 million out of a total investment of USD 2 billion in Mopani so far since privatization. Although this is the only loan any Glencore project has applied for from the EIB, Glencore has enjoyed the supportive relationship and assistance of the EIB in modernizing the long-standing assets acquired at Mopani in the 2000 privatization and improving their environmental performance in line with agreements with the Zambian government. Glencore will work diligently with the EIB to resolve these issues.

Further information on the fundamental errors in the draft provisional report, as previously publicly disclosed by Mopani on 20th April 2011.

'Finding': *Sales volumes are lower than expected*
Fact:

- The leaked document failed to properly account for the fact that about half of the copper metal produced by Mopani is derived from third party concentrates.
- Mopani receives a small, annually-fixed tolling fee per tonne (metric ton) for producing metal from third party concentrates.
- Mopani has been audited every year by a major international audit firm. One of the main audit procedures is the verification of sales. The annual audit has always been unqualified.
- Mopani is regularly audited by the Zambian Revenue Authority. Likewise no major discrepancies have ever been noted.

'Finding': *Mopani manipulated copper prices to engage in transfer pricing to favour Glencore*
Fact:

- This is untrue. All copper is sold at arms-length terms basis prevailing London Metal Exchange prices.
- Again the failure to take third party feed into account properly has led to an erroneous conclusion in this regard.

'Finding': *Gold and Silver hedges were improperly recorded and used to impact taxable income*
Fact:

- Mopani does not produce any of its own gold and very little silver
- Gold and silver largely stems from third party purchased materials
- Any hedges recorded were entered into to offset physical price exposure
- The net financial impact on Mopani's taxable income is zero
- Again a failure to properly understand the business processes of Mopani lead to this erroneous conclusion.

'Finding': *Operating costs rose for unexplained reasons*
Fact:

- The authors of the draft report used general inflation rates and compared these to Mopani increases. It is however a well-documented fact that worldwide mining cost inflation has been running at well above general inflation rates. As examples: At Mopani specifically, unions have successfully negotiated significant pay rises for workers, whose numbers have increased by 50% since privatization. Fuel prices have been increased by between 53% and 63%, electricity by similar margins.

- Again costs are audited annually by our external auditors and regularly reviewed by the Zambian Revenue Authority and to date no evidence of wrong doing has been brought to light.

In general the document goes wider and questions:

- Mopani's recovery rates on cobalt (which in fact are at design level for this process and in line with historical recoveries achieved at Nkana).
- The lack of record keeping on commissions paid to Glencore when in fact none were ever paid.
- Mopani's lack of co-operation when in fact on site facilities and tours of the operations were on offer and the Zambian Revenue Authority thanked Mopani in writing for its cooperation.

Glossary

AAC	Anglo American Corporation
AFRONET	Inter-Africa Network for Human Rights
AGOA	African Growth and Opportunity Act
AMAX	American Metal Climax
ANC	African National Congress
APP	Africa Progress Panel
AU	African Union
AVMIN	Anglovaal Minerals
BASMO	Barotseland Anti-Secession Movement
BK Conspiracy	Betti Katoto Conspiracy
BOSS	Bureau of Public Security of South Africa
BSAC	British South Africa Company
BSRG	Bein Stein Resources Group
CBU	Copperbelt University
CEE	Citizens Economic Empowerment
CNMC	China Non-Ferrous Metals Corporation
COMESA	Common Market of Eastern and Southern Africa
DBZ	Development Bank of Zambia
DFID	Department for International Development
DRC	Democratic Republic of the Congo
ECA	Economic Commission for Africa
EEC	Economic Empowerment Commission
ENRC	Eurasian Natural Resources Corporation
EPA	Economic Partnership Agreements
EXIM Bank	Export import Bank of the United States
FAO	Food and Agricultural Organisation
FDI	Foreign Direct Investment
FQM	First Quantum Mining
FRA	Food Reserve Agency
FRELIMO	Front for the Liberation of Mozambique
GBP	British Sterling

GFI	Global Financial Integrity
GRZ	Government of the Republic of Zambia
GRZ/ZCCM PNT	Mines Privatisation Negotiating Team
HIPC	Heavily Indebted Poor Countries
ICT	Information and Communication Technology
IG	Inspector General of the Police
ILO	International Labour Organisation
IMF	International Monetary Fund
IMR	International Mineral Resources
INDECO	Industrial Development Corporation
Induna	Barotseland Area Chief
JICA	Japan International Cooperation Agency
KCM	Konkola Copper Mines
KK	Kenneth Kaunda
LAZ	Law Association of Zambia
LIUTEBM	Livingstone International University for Tourism Excellence and Business Management
LONRHO	London Rhodesia Mining Company
Marketeer	A person who has a stall in a market
MINDECO	Mining Development Corporation
MMD	Movement for Multiparty Democracy
MOF	Ministry of Finance
MP	Member of Parliament
MUZ	Mineworkers Union of Zambia
NAMBOARD	National Agricultural Marketing Board
NAPSA	National Pensions Scheme Authority
NCCM	Nchanga Consolidated Copper Mines
NCZ	Nitrogen Chemicals Zambia
NGO	Non-Governmental Organisation
NRG	Northern Rhodesia Government
OAU	Organisation of African Union
Parastatal	Government Owned Enterprise
PRA	Privatisation Revenue Account
PWA	Portuguese West Africa
RAID	Rights and Accountability in Development
RAMCOZ	Roan Antelope Mining Corporation
RCM	Roan Consolidated Mines
RMB	Rural Marketing Board
RST	Roan Selection Trust
SACMEG	Southern and Eastern Africa Consortium for Monitoring

	Education Quality
SADC	Southern Africa Development Community
SME	Small and Medium Enterprises
SOE	State Owned Enterprises
TAZAMA	Tanzania Zambia Pipeline
TAZARA	Tanzania Zambia Railways
TIKA	Tito Kaunda Iron and Steel Project
UDI	Unilateral Declaration of Independence
UFP	United Federal Party
UN	United Nations
UNIP	United National Independence Party
UNZA	University of Zambia
UPND	United Party for National Development
UPP	United Progressive Party
VAT	Value Added Tax
ZAMTEL	Zambia Telecommunications Corporation
Zamtrop	ZSIS Account with ZANACO London
ZANACO	Zambia National Commercial Bank
ZANC	Zambian African National Congress
ZANU	Zimbabwe African National Union
ZAPU	Zimbabwe African People's Union
ZCCM	Zambia Consolidated Copper Mines
ZCCM-IH	ZCCM Investment Holdings
ZCI	Zambia Copper Investments
ZCTU	Zambia Congress of Trade Unions
ZEMA	Zambia Environmental Management Agency
ZEMU	Zambia European Mineworkers Union
ZIMCO	Zambia Industrial and Mining Corporation
ZPA	Zambia Development Agency
ZRA	Zambia Revenue Authority
ZSIS	Zambia State Intelligence Services or *ShuShuShu* in urban slang
ZTRS	Zambia Tanzania Road Services

Select Bibliography

Brelsford, W. V., *The Tribes of Northern Rhodesia* (The Government Printer, Lusaka, 1956)

Bull, Mutumba Mainga, *Bulozi under the Luyana Kings, Political Evolution and State Formation in Pre-Colonial Zambia* (Bookworld Publishers, Zambia, 2010)

Caplan, Gerald L., 'The secessionist challenge to Zambia', *Journal of Modern African Studies*, 6/3 (1968), pp. 343–60

Carrington, Lord, *Reflect on Things Past, The Memoirs of Lord Carrington* (William Collins, London, 1988)

Gewald, Jan-Bart, Hinfelaar, Marja, Macola, Giacomo (eds), *One Zambia, Many Histories: Towards a History of Post-colonial Zambia* (Lembani Trust, Lusaka, 2009)

Good, Robert C., *U.D.I., The International Politics of The Rhodesian Rebellion* (Faber & Faber, London, 1973)

Hill, Catharine B. and McPherson, Malcolm E. (ed.), *Promoting and Sustaining Economic Reform in Zambia* (John F. Kennedy School of Government, Harvard University, Cambridge, Massachusetts, 2004)

Kaunda, Francis, *Selling the Family Silver: The Zambian Copper Mines Story* (Self-published, Lusaka, 2002)

Kelly, M. J. (devised and prepared), *The Origins and Development of Education in Zambia, From Pre-Colonial Times to 1996* (Image Publishers Ltd, Lusaka, 2010)

Larmer, Miles (ed.), *The Musakanya Papers, the Autobiographical writings of Valentine Musakanya* (Lembani Trust, Lusaka, 2010)

Macmillan, Hugh, '"The Devil you Know": The impact of the Mulungushi reforms on the retail trade in rural Zambia, with special reference to Susman Brothers and Wulfsohn, 1968–80', in *One Zambia, Many Histories*, ed. Gewald *et al.* (Koninklijke Brill NV Leiden, the Netherlands 2008, reprinted by the Lembani Trust, Zambia, 2009)

Martin, Antony, *Minding Their Own Business, Zambia's Struggle against Western Control* (Hutchinson & Co Ltd, London, 1972)

Martin, David and Johnson, Phyllis, *The Struggle for Zimbabwe* (Faber & Faber Ltd, London and Boston, 1981)

Mumba, Goodwin Yoram, *The 1980 Coup: Tribulations of the One-Party State in Zambia* (UNZA Press, 2012)

Mwanakatwe, John, *John Mwanakatwe Teacher, Politician, Lawyer, My Autobiography* (Bookworld Publishers, Lusaka, 2003)

Mwondela, William, *Know the Peoples of Zambia Series 1* (Ministry of Local Government and Housing, Government Printer, Lusaka, *c.*1965)

Rotberg, Robert, I. *The Rise of Nationalism in Central Africa, The Making of Malawi and Zambia 1873–1964* (Harvard University Press, Cambridge, Massachusetts, 1967)

Sardanis, Andrew, *Africa, Another Side of The Coin, Northern Rhodesia's Final Years and Zambia's Nationhood* (I.B.Tauris & Co Ltd, London, 2003)

Sardanis, Andrew, *A Venture in Africa, The Challenges of African Business* (I.B.Tauris & Co Ltd, London, 2007)

Snelson, Peter, *Educational Development in Northern Rhodesia, 1883–1945* (National Educational Company of Zambia, 1974)

Williams, Susan, *Colour Bar, The Triumph of Seretse Khama and his Nation* (Penguin Books, 2007)

Zukas, Simon, *Into Exile and Back* (Bookworld Publishers, Lusaka, 2002)

INDEX